VW BEETLE

Gold Portfolio

1968~1991

Compiled by
R.M. Clarke

ISBN 185220 1933

Booklands Books Ltd.
PO Box 146, Cobham, KT11 1LG
Surrey, England
Printed in Hong Kong

BROOKLANDS BOOKS

BROOKLANDS ROAD TEST SERIES

AC Ace & Aceca 1953-1983
Alfa Romeo Alfasud 1972-1984
Alfa Romeo Alfetta Coupés GT. GTV. GTV6 1974-1987
Alfa Romeo Giulia Berlinas 1962-1976
Alfa Romeo Giulia Coupés Gold Portfolio 1963-1976
Alfa Romeo Giulia Coupés 1963-1976
Alfa Romeo Giulietta Gold Portfolio 1954-1965
Alfa Romeo Spider Gold Portfolio 1966-1991
Alfa Romeo Spider 1966-1991
Allard Gold Portfolio 1937-1959
Alvis Gold Portfolio 1919-1967
American Motors Muscle Cars 1966-1970
Armstrong Siddeley Gold Portfolio 1945-1960
Aston Martin Gold Portfolio 1972-1985
Austin Seven 1922-1982
Austin A30 & A35 1951-1962
Austin Healey 100 & 100/6 Gold Portfolio 1952-1959
Austin Healey 3000 Gold Portfolio 1959-1967
Austin Healey Sprite 1958-1971
BMW Six Cyl. Coupés 1969-1975
BMW 1600 Collection No.1 1966-1981
BMW 2002 1968-1976
BMW 316, 318, 320 (4 cyl.) Gold Portfolio 1975-1990
BMW 320, 323, 325 (6 cyl.) Gold Portfolio 1977-1990
BMW 5 Series Gold Portfolio1981-1987
Bristol Cars Gold Portfolio 1946-1992
Buick Automobiles 1947-1960
Buick Muscle Cars 1965-1970
Buick Riviera 1963-1978
Cadillac Automobiles 1949-1959
Cadillac Automobiles 1960-1969
Cadillac Eldorado 1967-1978
Chevrolet Camaro Z28 & SS 1966-1973
Chevrolet Camaro & Z28 1973-1981
High Performance Camaros 1982-1988
Camaro Muscle Portfolio 1967-1973
Chevrolet 1955-1957
Chevrolet Corvair 1959-1969
Chevrolet Impala & SS 1958-1971
Chevrolet Muscle Cars 1966-1971
Chevelle & SS 1964-1972
Chevelle & SS Muscle Portfolio 1964-1972
Chevy Blazer 1969-1981
Chevy El Camino & SS 1959-1987
Chevy II Nova & SS 1962-1973
Chevrolet Corvette Gold Portfolio 1953-1962
Chevrolet Corvette Gold Portfolio 1968-1977
Chevrolet Corvette Sting Ray Gold Portfolio 1963-1967
High Performance Corvettes 1983-1989
Chrysler 300 Gold Portfolio 1955-1970
Chrysler Valiant 1960-1962
Citroen Traction Avant Gold Portfolio 1934-1957
Citroen 2CV 1948-1988
Citroen DS & ID 1955-1975
Citroen SM 1070-1975
Cobas & Replicas
Shelby Cobra Gold Portfolio 1962-1969
Cobras & Cobra Replicas Gold Portfolio 1962-1989
Daimler SP250 Sports & V-8 250 Saloon Gold Portfolio 1959-1969
Datsun 240Z 1970-1973
Datsun 280Z & ZX 1975-1983
De Tomaso Collection No. 1 1962-1981
Dodge Charger 1966-1974
Dodge Muscle Cars 1967-1970
Excalibur Collection No. 1 1952-1981
Facel Vega 1954-1964
Ferrari Cars 1946-1956
Ferrari Dino 1965-1974
Ferrari Dino 308 1974-1979
Ferrari 308 & Mondial 1980-1984
Ferrari Collection No. 1 1960-1970
Motor & T&CC Ferrari 1966-1976
Motor & T&CC Ferrari 1976-1984
Fiat-Bertone X1/9 1973-1988
Fiat Pininfarina 124 & 2000 Spider 1968-1985
Ford Consul, Zephyr, Zodiac Mk.I & II 1950-1962
Ford Zephyr Zodiac Executive Mk.III & Mk.IV 1962-1971
Ford Cortina 1600E & GT 1967-1970
High Performance Capris Gold Portfolio 1969-1987
High Performance Fiestas 1979-1991
High Performance Escorts Mk.I 1968-1974
High Performance Escorts Mk.II 1975-1980
High Performance Escorts 1980-1985
High Performance Escorts 1985-1990
High Performance Sierras & Merkurs Gold Portfolio 1983-1990
Ford Automobiles 1949-1959
Ford Fairlane 1955-1970
Ford Ranchero 1957-1959
Thunderbird 1955-1957
Thunderbird 1958-1963
Thunderbird 1964-1976
Ford Falcon 1960-1970
Ford GT40 Gold Portfolio 1964-1987
Ford Bronco 1966-1977
Ford Bronco 1978-1988
Holden 1948-1962
Honda CRX 1983-1987
Hudson & Railton 1936-1940
Jaguar and SS Gold Portfolio 1931-1951
Jaguar XK120, XK140, XK150 Gold Portfolio 1948-1960
Jaguar Mk.VII, VIII, IX, X, 420 Gold Portfolio 1950-1970
Jaguar Mk.2 1959-1969
Jaguar Cars 1961-1964
Jaguar E-Type Gold Portfolio 1961-1971
Jaguar E-Type 1966-1971
Jaguar E-Type V-12 1971-1975
Jaguar XJ12, XJ5.3, V12 Gold Portfolio 1972-1990
Jaguar XJ6 Series II 1973-1979
Jaguar XJ6 Series III 1979-1986
Jaguar XJS Gold Portfolio 1975-1990
Jeep CJ5 & CJ6 1960-1976
Jeep CJ5 & CJ7 1976-1986
Jensen Cars 1946-1967
Jensen Cars 1967-1979
Jensen Interceptor Gold Portfolio 1966-1986
Jensen Healey 1972-1976
Lagonda Gold Portfolio 1919-1964
Lamborghini Cars 1964-1970
Lamborghini Countach & Urraco 1974-1980
Lamborghini Countach & Jalpa 1980-1985
Lancia Fulvia Gold Portfolio 1963-1976
Lancia Stratos 1972-1985
Land Rover Series I 1948-1958
Land Rover Series II & IIa 1958-1971
Land Rover Series III 1971-1985
Land Rover 90 & 110 1983-1989
Lincoln Gold Portfolio 1949-1960
Lincoln Continental 1961-1969
Lincoln Continental 1969-1976
Lotus & Caterham Seven Gold Portfolio 1957-1989
Lotus Elite 1957-1964
Lotus Elite & Eclat 1974-1982
Lotus Elan Gold Portfolio 1962-1974
Lotus Elan Collection No. 2 1963-1972
Lotus Cortina Gold Portfolio 1963-1970
Lotus Europa Gold Portfolio 1966-1975
Lotus Turbo Esprit 1980-1986
Motor & T&CC on Lotus 1979-1983
Marcos Cars 1960-1988
Maserati 1965-1970
Maserati 1970-1975
Mazda RX-7 Collection No. 1 1978-1981
Mercedes Benz Cars 1949-1954
Mercedes Benz Competition Cars 1950-1957
Mercedes Benz Cars 1954-1957
Mercedes Benz Cars 1957-1961
Mercedes 190 & 300 SL 1954-1963
Mercedes 230/250/280SL 1963-1971
Mercedes Benz SLs & SLCs Gold Portfolio 1971-1989
Mercedes S and 600 1965-1972
Mercedes S Class 1972-1979
Mercury Muscle Cars 1966-1971
Metropolitan 1954-1962
MG Gold Portfolio 1929-1939
MG TC 1945-1949
MG TD 1949-1953
MG TF 1953-1955
MG Cars 1959-1962
MGA & Twin Cam Gold Portfolio 1955-1962
MG Midget 1961-1980
MGB Roadsters 1962-1980
MGB MGC & V8 Gold Portfolio 1962-1980
MGB GT 1965-1980
Mini Cooper Gold Portfolio 1961-1971
Mini Muscle Cars 1961-1979
Mini Moke 1964-1989
Mopar Muscle Cars 1964-1967
Morgan Three-Wheeler Gold Portfolio 1910-1952
Morgan Plus 4 & Four 4 Gold Portfolio 1936-1967
Morgan Cars 1960-1970
Morgan Cars Gold Portfolio 1968-1989
Morris Minor Collection No. 1 1948-1980
Shelby Mustang Muscle 1965-1970
Shelby Mustang Muscle Portfolio 1965-1970
Mustang Muscle Cars 1967-1971
High Performance Mustangs 1982-1988
Oldsmobile Automobiles 1955-1963
Oldsmobile Cutlass & 4-4-2 1964-1972
Oldsmobile Muscle Cars 1964-1971
Oldsmobile Toronado 1966-1978
Opel GT 1968-1973
Packard Gold Portfolio 1946-1958
Pantera Gold Portfolio 1970-1989
Panther Gold Portfolio 1972-1990
Plymouth Barracuda 1964-1974
Plymouth Muscle Cars 1966-1971
Pontiac Tempest & GTO 1961-1965
Pontiac Muscle Cars 1966-1972
Pontiac Firebird & Trans-Am 1973-1981
High Performance Firebirds 1982-1988
Pontiac Fiero 1984-1988
Porsche 356 1952-1965
Porsche Cars in the 60's
Porsche Cars 1960-1964
Porsche Cars 1964-1968
Porsche Cars 1968-1972
Porsche Cars 1972-1975
Porsche 911 1965-1969
Porsche 911 1970-1972
Porsche 911 1973-1977
Porsche 911 Carrera 1973-1977
Porsche 911 Turbo 1975-1984
Porsche 911 SC 1978-1983
Porsche 914 Collection No. 1 1969-1983
Porsche 914 Gold Portfolio 1969-1976
Porsche 924 Gold Portfolio 1975-1988
Porsche 928 1977-1989
Porsche 944 1981-1985
Range Rover Gold Portfolio 1970-1992
Reliant Scimitar 1964-1986
Riley 1.5 & 2.5 Litre Gold Portfolio 1945-1955
Rolls Royce Silver Cloud 1955-1965
Rolls Royce Silver Cloud & Bentley 'S' Series Gold Portfolio 1955-1965
Rolls Royce Silver Shadow 1965-1981
Rover P4 1949-1959
Rover P4 1955-1964
Rover 3 & 3.5 Litre Gold Portfolio 1958-1973
Rover 2000 & 2200 1963-1977
Rover 3500 1968-1977
Rover 3500 & Vitesse 1976-1986
Saab Sonett Collection No.1 1966-1974
Saab Turbo 1976-1983
Studebaker Gold Portfolio 1947-1966
Studebaker Hawks & Larks 1956-63
Avanti 1962-1990
Sunbeam Tiger & Alpine Gold Portfolio 1959-1967
Toyota MR2 1984-1988
Toyota Land Cruiser 1956-1984
Triumph TR2 & TR3 1952-1960
Triumph TR4, TR5, TR250 1961-1968
Triumph TR6 Gold Portfolio 1969-1976
Triumph TR7 & TR8 1975-1982
Triumph Herald 1959-1971
Triumph Vitesse 1962-1971
Triumph Spitfire Gold Portfolio 1962-1980
Triumph 2000, 2.5, 2500 1963-1977
Triumph GT6 1966-1974
Triumph Stag 1970-1980
TVR Gold Portfolio 1959-1990
VW Beetle Gold Portfolio1935-1967
VW Beetle Gold Portfolio1968-1991
VW Kubelwagen 1940-1975
VW Karmann Ghia 1955-1982
VW Bus, Camper, Van 1954-1967
VW Bus, Camper, Van 1968-1979
VW Bus, Camper, Van 1979-1989
VW Beetle Collection No.1 1970-1982
VW Scirocco 1974-1981
VW Golf GTI 1976-1986
Volvo PV444 & PV544 1945-1965
Volvo Amazon-120 Gold Portfolio 1956-1970
Volvo 1800 Gold Portfolio 1960-1973

BROOKLANDS ROAD & TRACK SERIES

Road & Track on Alfa Romeo 1949-1963
Road & Track on Alfa Romeo 1964-1970
Road & Track on Alfa Romeo 1971-1976
Road & Track on Alfa Romeo 1977-1989
Road & Track on Aston Martin 1962-1990
Road & Track on Auburn Cord and Duesenburg 1952-1984
Road & Track on Audi & Auto Union 1952-1980
Road & Track on Audi & Auto Union 1980-1986
Road & Track on Austin Healey 1953-1970
Road & Track on BMW Cars 1966-1974
Road & Track on BMW Cars 1975-1978
Road & Track on BMW Cars 1979-1983
Road & Track on Cobra, Shelby & Ford GT40 1962-1992
Road & Track on Corvette 1953-1967
Road & Track on Corvette 1968-1982
Road & Track on Corvette 1982-1986
Road & Track on Corvette 1986-1990
Road & Track on Datsun Z 1970-1983
Road & Track on Ferrari 1950-1968
Road & Track on Ferrari 1968-1974
Road & Track on Ferrari 1975-1981
Road & Track on Ferrari 1981-1984
Road & Track on Ferrari 1984-1988
Road & Track on Fiat Sports Cars 1968-1987
Road & Track on Jaguar 1950-1960
Road & Track on Jaguar 1961-1968
Road & Track on Jaguar 1968-1974
Road & Track on Jaguar 1974-1982
Road & Track on Jaguar 1983-1989
Road & Track on Lamborghini 1964-1985
Road & Track on Lotus 1972-1981
Road & Track on Maserati 1952-1974
Road & Track on Maserati 1975-1983
Road & Track on Mazda RX7 1978-1986
Road & Track on Mazda RX7 & MX5 Miata 1986-1991
Road & Track on Mercedes 1952-1962
Road & Track on Mercedes 1963-1970
Road & Track on Mercedes 1971-1979
Road & Track on Mercedes 1980-1987
Road & Track on MG Sports Cars 1949-1961
Road & Track on MG Sports Cars 1962-1980
Road & Track on Mustang 1964-1977
Road & Track on Nissan 300-ZX & Turbo 1984-1989
Road & Track on Peugeot 1955-1986
Road & Track on Pontiac 1960-1983
Road & Track on Porsche 1951-1967
Road & Track on Porsche 1968-1971
Road & Track on Porsche 1972-1975
Road & Track on Porsche 1975-1978
Road & Track on Porsche 1979-1982
Road & Track on Porsche 1982-1985
Road & Track on Porsche 1985-1988
Road & Track on Rolls Royce & Bentley 1950-1965
Road & Track on Rolls Royce & Bentley 1966-1984
Road & Track on Saab 1972-1992
Road & Track on Toyota Sports & GT Cars 1966-1984
Road & Track on Triumph Sports Cars 1953-1967
Road & Track on Triumph Sports Cars 1967-1974
Road & Track on Triumph Sports Cars 1974-1982
Road & Track on Volkswagen 1951-1968
Road & Track on Volkswagen 1968-1978
Road & Track on Volkswagen 1978-1985
Road & Track on Volvo 1957-1974
Road & Track on Volvo 1975-1985
Road & Track - Henry Manney at Large and Abroad

BROOKLANDS CAR AND DRIVER SERIES

Car and Driver BMW 1955-1977
Car and Driver BMW 1977-1985
Car and Driver on Cobra, Shelby & Ford GT40 1963-1984
Car and Driver on Corvette 1956-1967
Car and Driver on Corvette 1968-1977
Car and Driver on Corvette 1978-1982
Car and Driver on Corvette 1983-1988
Car and Driver on Datsun Z 1600 & 2000 1966-1984
Car and Driver on Ferrari 1955-1962
Car and Driver on Ferrari 1963-1975
Car and Driver on Ferrari 1976-1983
Car and Driver on Mopar 1956-1967
Car and Driver on Mopar 1968-1975
Car and Driver on Mustang 1964-1972
Car and Driver on Pontiac 1961-1975
Car and Driver on Porsche 1955-1962
Car and Driver on Porsche 1963-1970
Car and Driver on Porsche 1970-1976
Car and Driver on Porsche 1977-1981
Car and Driver on Porsche 1982-1986
Car and Driver on Saab 1956-1985
Car and Driver on Volvo 1955-1986

BROOKLANDS PRACTICAL CLASSICS SERIES

PC on Austin A40 Restoration
PC on Land Rover Restoration
PC on Metalworking in Restoration
PC on Midget/Sprite Restoration
PC on Mini Cooper Restoration
PC on MGB Restoration
PC on Morris Minor Restoration
PC on Sunbeam Rapier Restoration
PC on Triumph Herald/Vitesse
PC on Spitfire Restoration
PC on Beetle Restoration
PC on 1930s Car Restoration

BROOKLANDS HOT ROD 'MUSCLECAR & HI-PO ENGINES' SERIES

Chevy 265 & 283
Chevy 302 & 327
Chevy 348 & 409
Chevy 350 & 400
Chevy 396 & 427
Chevy 454 thru 512
Chrysler Hemi
Chrysler 273, 318, 340 & 360
Chrysler 361, 383, 400, 413, 426, 440
Ford 289, 302, Boss 302 & 351W
Ford 351C & Boss 351
Ford Big Block

BROOKLANDS RESTORATION SERIES

Auto Restoration Tips & Techniques
Basic Bodywork Tips & Techniques
Basic Painting Tips & Techniques
Camaro Restoration Tips & Techniques
Chevrolet High Performance Tips & Techniques
Chevy Engine Swapping Tips & Techniques
Chevy-GMC Pickup Repair
Chrysler Engine Swapping Tips & Techniques
Custom Painting Tips & Techniques
Engine Swapping Tips & Techniques
Ford Pickup Repair
How to Build a Street Rod
Land Rover Restoration Tips & Techniques
Mustang Restoration Tips & Techniques
Performance Tuning - Chevrolets of the '60s
Performance Tuning - Pontiacs of the '60s

BROOKLANDS MILITARY VEHICLES SERIES

Allied Military Vehicles No.1 1942-1945
Allied Military Vehicles No.2 1941-1946
Off Road Jeeps: Civ. & Mil. 1944-1971
US Military Vehicles 1941-1945
Complete WW2 Military Jeep Manual
US Army Military Vehicles WW2-TM9-2800

16112

BROOKLANDS BOOKS

CONTENTS

5	Volkswagen 1500 - Semi Automatic Road Test	*Autocar*	Feb.	22	1968
9	VW Automatic Stick Shift Road Test	*Foreign Car Guide*	Apr.		1968
12	Two-Pedal Beetle Road Test	*Modern Motor*	Apr.		1968
16	We Drive the New VW Automatic	*Popular Imported Cars*	July		1968
19	Volkswagen 1300, Ford Escort 1100, Vauxhall Viva, NSU 1000C,	*Motor*	June	22	1968
	Triumph Herald 1200, and Austin 1100 Mk2 Comparison Test.				
25	VW - On the Road	*Motor Sport*	Apr.		1968
26	VW vs Corolla Comparison Test	*Road Test*	July		1968
33	EMPI GTV: Southern California's Muscle Beetle	*Car and Driver*	July		1968
36	Volkswagen's 1500 - Best Beetle Yet Road Test	*Wheels*	Aug		1968
40	Volkswagen 1200 36,000 Mile Report	*Motor*	Aug.	31	1968
44	VW 1500 Automatic Road Test	*Car and Driver*	Sept.		1968
48	The Beetles Burrow Factory Visit	*Foreign Car Guide*	Dec.		1968
52	VW, Torana, Mini, Datsun, Fiat 850, Corolla	*Motor Manual*	Apr.		1969
	Comparison Test				
56	Beetle Power	*Autocar*	May	1	1969
58	Have You Ever Asked Yourself....	*Sports Car Graphic*	Sept.		1969
	Why Would Anyone Want to Buy a VW?				
63	Bug Becomes Cool Beetle	*Road Test*	Nov.		1969
68	1970 VW Sedan...Stock Long Legs at Last! Road Test	*World Car Guide*	Jan.		1970
72	Volkswagen Beetle 1600 Road Test	*Car South Africa*	Feb.		1970
76	Beetles Forever	*Motor*	Apr.	11	1970
78	Volkswagen 1300/1500 Beetle	*Motor*	Apr.	18	1970
80	1970 VW Semi-Automatic Sedan Road Test	*World Car Guide*	Apr.		1970
84	Volkswagen A.S.S.	*Car and Driver*	June		1970
88	Volkswagen Super Beetle 1600 Road Test	*Autocar*	Dec.		1970
92	A 2-Litre VW Beetle? - Coming Up Right Away, Sir!"	*Motor Sport*	Dec.		1970
94	VW Super Beetle Road Test	*Road & Track*	Mar.		1971
96	Volkswagen 1300 Beetle Road Test	*Car South Africa*	Mar.		1971
100	Volkswagen '71	*Popular Imported Cars*	Mar.		1971
104	Superbug - Ultimate Beetle	*Wheels*	July		1972
109	The Baja Beetle	*Road Test*	Nov.		1972
112	VW 1500 Beetle Owner Report	*Car South Africa*	Apr.		1973
116	Superbug - Supercool? Road Test	*Modern Motor*	June		1973
122	The Beetle 1200, 1974 Style. Is it The Real Long Life Porsche?	*Wheels*	Oct.		1974
124	Beetle 1300 and Mini De Luxe Comparison Test	*Car South Africa*	Aug.		1977
129	Volkswagen 1600 'Fun Bug' Model	*Car South Africa*	Oct.		1974
132	Volkswagen Beetle Road Test	*Road Test*	May		1977
136	Volkswagen Beetle Convertible Road Test	*Road & Track*	Nov.		1977
139	Beetle, 1970 Onwards	*Car South Africa*	Nov.		1977
142	The Beetle That Tips its Hat	*Motor Trend*	Aug.		1978
144	Second Time Around	*Autocar*	June	6	1981
147	La Cucaracha Driving Impression	*Motor Trend*	Aug.		1983
148	Sun Country VW Beetle	*Road & Track*	Oct.		1983
149	Golden Beetle Road Test	*Car and Driver*	Mar.		1988
153	Bug Plug	*Thoroughbred & Classic Cars*	Apr.		1988
157	Beetle Service	*Car Mechanics*	Apr.		1982
160	Reach for the Sky - A Topless Summer	*Wheels*	Jan.		1987
164	Buying a VW Beetle	*Practical Classics*	Dec.		1986
170	Beetle-Mania the Mexican Way	*Autocar & Motor*	Jan.	9	1991

ACKNOWLEDGEMENTS

This is the second of our Gold Portfolios which cover the Beetle saloons: the first one covers the period up to 1967. The two volumes join our other 'road test' books on the Karman Ghia models, the buses, campers, vans and kublewagens.

We are delighted to record our thanks to those who have made this book possible. Our greatest debt of course is to the management of Autocar, Autocar and Motor, Car and Driver, Car Mechanics, Car South Africa, Foreign Car Guide, Modern Motor, Motor, Motor Manual, Motor Sport, Motor Trend, Popular Imported Cars, Practical Classics, Road & Track, Road Test, Sports Car Graphic, Thoroughbred and Classic Cars, Wheels and The World Car Guide. And once again, motoring writer James Taylor has kindly agreed to pen the few words of introduction which follow.

R M Clarke

Beetle fans recognise 1968 - the starting-point for this book - as the year when the 1500 engine became available, 12-volt electric's replaced the 6-volt system (yes, it lasted *that* long), and vertical lamps replaced the original sloping type. In the ensuing years, engines continued to get larger and more powerful, some models took on MacPherson strut front suspension in place of the original torsion-bar type, and there were several cosmetic changes.

By the early 1970's Volkswagen knew that the Beetle could not carry on indefinitely, and started work on a replacement model (which proved to be every bit as revolutionary as the Beetle itself had been). Yet when the replacement came on-stream and Beetle production at Volkswagen's Wolfsburg factory stopped, the car itself refused to die. The Emden plant in Germany continued to make Beetles until 1978, and several overseas subsidiary factories carried on turning the car out in large quantities. Indeed, the VW factory in Brazil is still doing so as this book goes to press in the first months of 1993!

The end, then, is still not in sight; and the number of enthusiastic owners which Beetles of all ages continue to attract suggests that the car will be with us for a great many more years yet. The articles in this book go a long way towards explaining what is so special about the Beetle, and should make more than a few converts to the cause!

James Taylor

VOLKSWAGEN 1500 SEMI-AUTOMATIC 1,493 c.c.

AT A GLANCE: Volkswagen 1500 Beetle with three-speed semi-automatic transmission and trailing arm rear suspension. Less than average performance and poor fuel consumption for its class. Much improved cornering. Initially dead feel to near fade-free brakes. Ride sensitive to small irregularities. Transmission makes this VW easy to drive and relaxing in traffic. Excellent finish.

MANUFACTURER:
Volkswagenwerk AG, Wolfsburg, West Germany.

BRITISH CONCESSIONNAIRES: Volkswagen Motors Ltd., Volkswagen House, Cargreen Road, South Norwood, London, S.E.25.

PRICES

Basic	£683	0s	0d
Purchase Tax	£158	4s	10d
Seat belts (approx.)	£10	0s	0d
Total (in G.B.)	£851	4s	10d

PERFORMANCE SUMMARY

Mean maximum speed	74 mph
Standing start ¼-mile	22.8 sec
0-60 mph	26.8 sec
Typical fuel consumption	28 mpg
Miles per tankful	246

AT the Frankfurt Show last September, Volkswagen announced extensive changes to the 1500 Beetle, in order to comply with the American Federal safety requirements. Optional selective automatic transmission was offered for the first time. A standard synchromesh gearbox is used with first gear removed, coupled to a torque converter and a servo-operated clutch, energized by a switch in the base of the gear lever. The tourqe converter housing is about an inch longer than the equivalent clutch housing, so to keep the engine in the same place, the drive shafts are inclined slightly in plan view. This means that an additional universal joint has had to be added at the outboard ends of the shafts, giving the semi-automatic Beetle only non-swing axle rear suspension for the first time.

Before the best can be got out of it, the transmission requires knowing. There is no clutch pedal, the clutch being freed immediately pressure is applied to the gear lever in the direction of the gear required. As soon as the lever is released the clutch re-engages and the torque convertor takes up the drive like any normal automatic. For traffic driving one simply puts it into bottom or second—keeping the brakes on to prevent creep—and forgets the gear lever completely. First gear (which is really second in the original manual box) runs up to 48 mph and second to 70 mph; on a 1-in-3 the car will pull away from rest in second, so it is only for extra acceleration that one ever needs bottom. If there are no steep hills, and one isn't in a mood for brisk getaways, it will perform equally happily in top. First gear becomes an emergency low for mountaineering with a heavy load, climbing long steep hills, or of course towing a caravan—when the torque convertor, slipping in too high a gear, might overheat.

In such conditions one drives as if with a normal three-speed gearbox—and one tends also to do so on the open road in order to get the best of the car's performance. It is here that a bit of practice helps to synchronize engine and road speeds and make smooth downward changes. We found it was best to speed up the engine immediately before letting-go the lever. So sensitive is the switch that operates the clutch that there must be no absent-mindedly grasping the lever preparatory to making a gear change—nor hanging on to it afterwards—for in either case the engine, freed of the load, quickly speeds up and damage can occur if the clutch is suddenly re-engaged at high revs. The driver's left knee, too, can be guilty of declutching—particularly if he is a big driver, whose knees have to be splayed out to clear the steering wheel.

Not surprisingly, one pays in terms of performance and fuel economy for the novelty of not having a pedal-operated clutch and the convenience of a torque convertor. The manual 1500 Beetle tested in November 1966 gave an overall fuel consumption of 27.4 mpg, while this version, at 25.6 mpg is only 2 mpg down, so the penalty is not great. This figure is surprisingly consistent, whether the car is being driven in city traffic or on the open road, though with an eye to economy—and further experience of the transmission—figures approaching 30 mpg should be attainable.

So far as acceleration is concerned, the semi-automatic version of the perennial Beetle compares rather less favourably with the manual. Though the actual gear change takes roughly the same time on both cars, since on both you have to shift a lever, the acceleration on the semi-automatic is reduced slightly by the churning of the torque convertor, but mostly by the loss of bottom gear for getting away quickly. From a standing start to 60 mph, for example, the semi-automatic takes 27.4 sec to the other

VW 1500 Semi-Automatic, Rear Engine, Rear Wheel Drive

PERFORMANCE

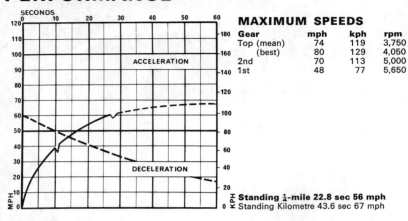

MAXIMUM SPEEDS

Gear	mph	kph	rpm
Top (mean)	74	119	3,750
(best)	80	129	4,050
2nd	70	113	5,000
1st	48	77	5,650

Standing ¼-mile 22.8 sec 56 mph
Standing Kilometre 43.6 sec 67 mph

TIME IN SECONDS

	0	6.2	10.6	17.1	26.8	
TRUE SPEED MPH		30	40	50	60	70	80
INDICATED SPEED		33	44	55	64	75	85

Mileage recorder 1.4 per cent over-reading.

SPEED RANGE, GEAR RATIOS AND TIME IN SECONDS

mph	Top (3.89-8.18)	2nd (5.52-11.58)	1st (9.02-18.93)
0-20	6.0	4.5	3.5
10-30	7.3	5.8	4.7
20-40	10.2	7.9	4.0
30-50	14.3	10.6	—
40-60	22.1	15.6	—

CONSUMPTION

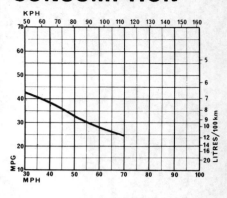

FUEL

(At constant speeds—mpg)

30 mph	42.5
40	38.1
50	33.1
60	27.8
70	24.7

Typical mpg	**28 (10.1 litres/100km)**
Calculated (DIN) mpg	27.5 (10.3 litres—100km)
Overall mpg	25.1 (11.3 litres/100km)
Grade of fuel	Mixture, 3-star, min 94 RM

OIL

SAE 30 . . . . negligible

HOW THE CAR COMPARES

Maximum Speed (mean) mph

50 60 70 80 90

- Volkswagen 1500 Auto
- Austin A60 Auto
- Ford Cortina 1500 2-door Auto
- Simca 1000 GLS Auto
- Vauxhall Viva SL Auto

0-60 (sec.)

30 20

- Volkswagen 1500 Auto
- Austin A60 Auto
- Ford Cortina 1500 2-door Auto
- Simca 1000 GLS Auto
- Vauxhall Viva SL Auto

Standing Start ¼-mile (sec.)

30 20

- Volkswagen 1500 Auto
- Austin A60 Auto
- Ford Cortina 1500 2-door Auto
- Simca 1000 GLS Auto
- Vauxhall Viva SL Auto

MPG Overall

20 30

- Volkswagen 1500 Auto
- Austin A60 Auto
- Ford Cortina 1500 2-door Auto
- Simca 1000 GLS Auto
- Vauxhall Viva SL Auto

PRICES

Volkswagen 1500 Auto.	£841
Austin A.60 Auto.	£852
Ford Cortina 1500 2-door Auto.*	£851
Simca 1000GLS Auto.	£800
Vauxhall Viva SL Auto.	£774

* Current 1600 price—1500 superseded

TEST CONDITIONS Weather: Dull, gusty, dry. Wind: 20-30 mph. Temperature: 10 deg C (50 deg F). Barometer: 29.5 in. Hg. Humidity: 70 per cent. Surfaces: Dry concrete and asphalt.

WEIGHT Kerb weight 16.5cwt (1,845lb-838kg) (with oil, water and half-full fuel tank). Distribution, per cent F, 38.9; R, 61.1. Laden as tested: 20.2cwt (2,265lb-1,027kg).

TURNING CIRCLES
Between kerbs L, 36ft 7in.; R, 33ft 1in.
Between walls L, 37ft 11in.; R, 34ft 5in.
Steering wheel turns, lock to lock 2.8

Test distance 944 miles. Figures taken at 3,500 miles by our own staff at the Motor Industry Research Association proving ground at Nuneaton.

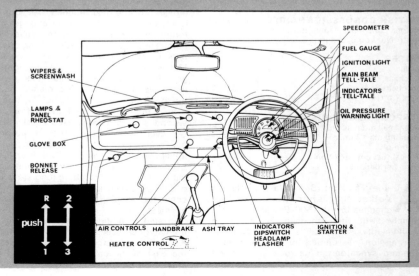

BRAKES

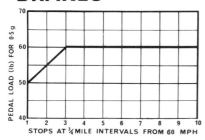

STOPS AT ¾ MILE INTERVALS FROM 60 MPH

(from 30 mph in neutral)

Load	g	Distance
20lb	0.10	300ft
40lb	0.30	100ft
60lb	0.52	58ft
80lb	0.66	46ft
100lb	0.96	31.4ft
Handbrake	0.46	65ft

Max. gradient 1 in 3

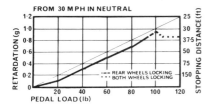

FROM 30 MPH IN NEUTRAL

SPECIFICATION

REAR ENGINE, REAR-WHEEL DRIVE

ENGINE
Cylinders . .	4, horizontally opposed
Cooling system .	Air: ducted fan
Bore. . .	83mm (3.27in.)
Stroke . .	69mm (2.72in.)
Displacement .	1,493c.c. (91.1 cu.in.)
Valve gear .	Overhead, pushrods and rockers
Compression ratio	7.5-to-1 : Min. octane rating : 91RM
Carburettor . .	One Solex downdraught 30 TICT-1
Fuel pump . .	Mechanical
Oil filter . .	Gauze strainer in sump
Max. power . .	44 bhp (net) at 4,000 rpm
Max. torque. .	74 lb.ft. (net) at 2,000 rpm

TRANSMISSION
Gearbox. . .	Three-speed all-synchromesh with torque converter and servo-operated single dry plate clutch 7.8in dia.
Gear ratios . .	Top 0.89-1.87 Second 1.26-2.65 First 2.06-4.33 Reverse 3.07-6.45
Final drive . .	Spiral bevel, 4.38-to-1

CHASSIS and BODY
Construction .	Separate platform chassis, steel body

SUSPENSION
Front . . .	Independent, torsion bars, trailing arms, telescopic dampers, anti-roll bar
Rear. . . .	Independent, torsion bars, trailing arms, fixed length drive shafts, telescopic dampers

STEERING
Type . . .	Worm and roller
Wheel dia. . .	15.75in

BRAKES
Make and type .	ATE Lockheed disc front, drum rear, no servo
Dimensions . .	F. 11.5in. dia.; R. 9in. dia. 1.57in. wide shoes
Swept area . .	F. 173.6 sq.in.; R. 88.7 sq.in. Total 262.3 sq.in. (259.3 sq.in./ton laden)

WHEELS
Type . . .	Pressed steel disc, 4-stud fixing, 4in. wide rim
Tyres—make .	Michelin
—type .	4PR cross-ply tubeless
—size . .	5.60-15in.

EQUIPMENT
Battery . . .	12 volt 66 Ah
Generator . .	Bosch 38-amp d.c.
Headlamps . .	Bosch or Hella 90/80-watt (total)
Reversing lamp .	Extra
Electric fuses .	10
Screen wipers .	Two-speed, self-parking
Screen washer .	Standard, pressurized
Interior heater .	Standard, bled cooling air
Heated backlight .	Extra
Safety belts . .	Extra, anchorages built in
Interior trim . .	Leatherette seats, pvc headlining
Floor covering .	Rubber moulding
Starting handle .	No provision
Jack. . . .	Friction pillar
Jacking points .	Two each side, under sills
Windscreen . .	Toughened
Underbody protection .	Wax coated underside

MAINTENANCE
Fuel tank . .	8.8 Imp. gallons (no reserve) (40 litres)
Engine sump .	4.4 pints (2.5 litres) SAE 30. Change oil every 3,000 miles. Clean oil strainer every 3,000 miles
Gearbox and final drive . . .	5.3 pints SAE 90. Change oil every 30,000 miles
Torque converter	6.3 pints ATF type A. No oil change needed
Grease . . .	4 points every 6,000 miles
Tyre pressures .	F. 16; R. 24 p.s.i. (normal driving) F. 19; R. 27 p.s.i. (fast driving) F. 17; R. 26 p.s.i. (full load)
Maximum load .	836lb (379kg)

PERFORMANCE DATA
Top gear mph per 1,000 rpm	19.7
Mean piston speed at max power	1,813 ft./min.
Bhp per ton laden	43.6

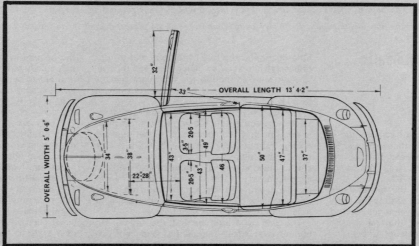

STANDARD GARAGE 16ft. x 8ft 6in.

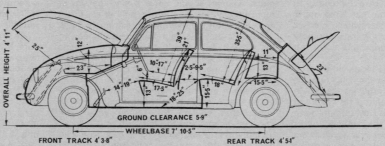

SCALE:
0.3IN. TO 1FT.
CUSHIONS UNCOMPRESSED

(*Left*) Though the shape may be unfashionable it is undeniably functional and practical, still retaining rubber-covered running boards

(*Right*) Safety improvements inside include recessed door releases, flat rubber-knobbed switches and a collapsible steering column

(*Left*) Note how little camber change of the rear wheels occurs during hard cornering with the new suspension—the inside front wheel is just clear of the ground

(*Right*) The motif on the "bonnet" is the only identification. Big heavy-gauge bumpers really do protect the tail, being sensibly mounted well clear

Volkswagen 1500 Automatic . . .

car's 21.9. Overall, this level of acceleration—for both cars—is well below that expected in the 1½-litre class. Engine power tails off so much above 60 mph that up-wind on a very gusty day we could not reach 70.

With the modifications to the swing-axles come trailing-arm links which reduce the considerable rear-wheel camber-changes during cornering. On the old layout, the rear wheels usually maintain negative camber under acceleration on corners—but when the driver lifted-off suddenly, and particularly if he brakes (when alarmed, for example, by a tightening-up of the bend), the back of the car lifted under weight transfer and the rear-wheel camber decreased abruptly—with a correspondingly abrupt reduction of tyre grip and cornering power.

With the new layout there is none of this. The car starts off as an understeerer, and remains that way at normal, touring cornering speeds. In fact, if you go into a corner too fast you can "scrub off" the excess speed by turning more acutely into the corner. In extreme conditions the inside front wheel lifts (which the driver feels as a lurch) and the car stays on its rightful side of the road without swinging wide. If you lift-off suddenly in a corner there is very

little change in the feel of the car, and it continues safely on course. On a wet road though, it often feels as though the tail might get the upper hand and greasy corners need a lot of respect.

The Beetle is still very susceptible to side-winds, corrective action being slow since there is too much free movement in the steering linkage (about 1.5 in. at the wheel rim). Like some other understeering cars, one can make small steering wheel movements without altering course. The brakes, without servo assistance and with discs at the front, are rather dead initially, but they showed few signs of deterioration during our fade tests.

The ride is a little behind the times—too bumpy over small irregularities and sensitive to cats' eyes; there is also a fair amount of road noise inside the car. Sound deadening has much reduced engine noise, which remains at a reasonably low level when pulling at almost any speed; on the overrun it is extremely quiet.

There is only a single dial directly ahead of the driver; it is clearly marked with speeds (still with the gear-change points for the normal four-speed gearbox) with inset fuel gauge and warning lamps for oil pressure, dynamo, main beam and turn indicators. In the centre of the metal facia are four flat, flexible rubber knobs that operate the screen wiper and washers, lamps, and the left and right cold air outlets from the scuttle to the screen. The grab handle and the glove locker lid release in front of the passenger are also rubber, and the steering wheel is well dished. Despite adjustments to

the heating system, it is a bit all-or-nothing—particularly at high engine speeds, since hot air is supplied by the engine's cooling fan through two exhaust heat exchangers. The system is very powerful though, and quickly warms up the car even after a frosty night in the open. The only exception to this is when one has to drive out into a traffic jam and is unable to get the engine working hard.

Another change in the Beetle is that the headlamp lenses are now vertical, and no longer follow the contours of the front wings. This does not seem to have had any appreciable effect on the lighting, which has a typical Continental cut-off on dipped beam. In the usual German manner, the dipswitch consists of a stalk to the left of the steering column which, when lifted with the fingers, dips the beams and leaves them dipped, requiring a second movement to return to main beam. This stalk also works the headlamp flasher—a sensible marriage of two controls.

We are obliged, after experience with a large number of modern cars, to judge—and criticize—the VW in the light of present-day standards. Despite its antiquity though it is very strong, well proven and immensely long-lasting. Particularly, it has the backing of first-class service throughout the world. Oil consumption is negligible and there are only four grease points. Sales figures show clearly that the Beetle still has an enthusiastic following—this new version will give an additional boost, despite its high extra price and performance handicap.

VW AUTOMATIC STICK SHIFT

By SLONIGER

▶ Who would have thought it? A VW with status extras! Let's face it, the original beetle had a sort of reverse status symbol in America and apparently still has with its continued record breaking sales and now they are throwing us a slider, too. A line of script across the motor lid of an otherwise '68 VW 1500 which says "automatic."

Strictly speaking the line of type is only half true. In the case of the VW 1500 at any rate (the 1600 is another breed of cat) it should say semi-automatic or perhaps selective-automatic. Apart from requiring too many chrome letters it would not be as impressive. Yet that automatic stickshift, two-pedal option could well be the best bargain from beetle-burg, dollar for dollar and trip for trip.

I wouldn't want to be dogmatic and claim it is the sole or even best-of-all-possible world's bargain, but it ranks high. Partly for the very reason that it is not a "conventional" automatic and partly because it only adds about 9% to the car's delivered price in Germany. The word automatic is worth $135 in the U.S. Measured against the already rather high cost of a 1500 it is worth every penny. Besides you get that new back axle for the same hundred odd bucks.

I am really reporting here on an automatic VW 1500, but there are basic changes for 1968 that have some bearing on the test, or at least on my time in the car, so I'll mention them briefly.

We can skip the basic package, familiar to one and all. Let's face it—the VW 1500 is really a 1933 engine in a 1938 body and all the outstanding craftsmanship, dealer service network and flat knobs can't change the fact.

Outwardly, new bumpers are the most noticeable feature. VW complied manfully with congressional demands, even if the bumpers look

like somebody stuck them in the wrong place. It proves again that law makers should stick to "the war on poverty" and leave car building to a going concern. After all most nose-tail crunches come with at least one car nose down so that mated-height bumpers do no good anyway.

Five minutes in a new VW prove that whatever whiplash safety you may gain with headrests, you lose twice as much to the danger of not being able to see the rear quarters. Two wing mirrors are an absolute must with these new seats, and I would be very tempted to bill my elected representative for them. Granted, if you have to have such

ABOVE: New rear suspension included with Automatic Stick Shift makes for surer footing in cornering or emergency evasive maneuvers. Inner wheel on turn maintains camber and does not tend to tuck under like normal suspension.

(Continued on Page 11)

ABOVE: A bonus feature of both the Beetle and 1600 models with optional transmission is the improved cornering ability of the new trailing arm independent rear suspension that is included in the cost of new transmissions.

RIGHT: With clutch pedal eliminated the brake pedal has been widened.

BELOW: Shift pattern is like a standard three speed box. In normal driving drive 1 and 2 are all that are required. Grasping shift knob disengages clutch to permit gear range selection. Torque converter broadens power range or torque of individual gears.

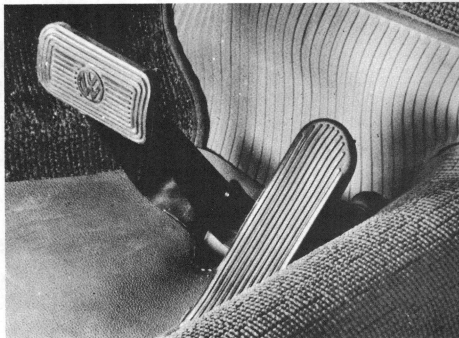

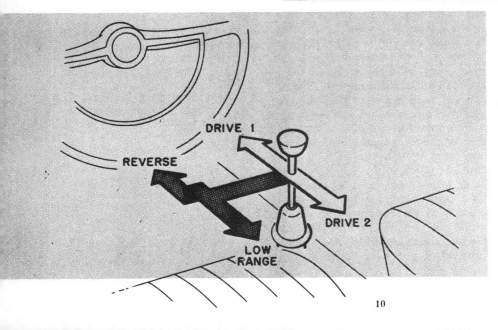

New 1500 beetles have many improvements and different bumpers. Even front hood catch is improved though it is now used less frequently.

VW AUTOMATIC

(*Continued from Page 9*)

retrograde items by law, Wolfsburg did better than some who added them later, still ... Washington says all 1969 models must have these vision blocking headrests.

I might note too that they are quietly offering the '68s without such vision blockers, in Germany at least, a delete option no less.

I was more impressed with things like the outside fuel filler that eliminates the need of opening the trunk lid. Similarly the new safety second catch for the trunk lid is an improvement, and the solid feel of the door handles is a good touch.

Even the flat knobs look safer and doubtless are though they are hell to use with gloves on. The ones you rotate are fine, but the light switch is not too easy to pull with a gloved hand. Four-way flashers (now, that is positively safety) and two-speed wipers must be welcomed by all.

Then there was the heated rear window option on our test car. The only reason I don't claim flatly that the two-pedal system is their finest bargain is the $12.50 German price for this advanced bit of very real safety. Flick a switch (hidden under the dash) and you have rear vision again, whether the problem is inside mist or outside frost. Absolutely no car should be without one, and more power to VW for pricing it so reasonably. Several continental cars are now offering the heated window option, and it is too bad it is not yet offered in the U.S. on VWs.

Moving the shift lever back was a nice step, and while a left foot rest might be pleasant for long hauls in the automatic, they get top marks for that big wide brake pedal. Left foot braking is an acquired art in Germany, but generations of Americans used to two pedals and perhaps buying the VW as a second car, will welcome the chance to use two feet on two pedals if they want. Also you can use the left foot to hold the car at traffic lights, as the automatic does creep.

Which brings us to the core of the matter—the obvious fact that some Volkswagens today reach the roads with a pedal missing. Strictly speaking the 1500 now has three normal forward gears. Reverse is now where low used to be but is protected by

a shift lockout. Thanks to the torque converter, taking up slack from a standstill, they could blank off first.

There is no automatic upshift nor is there kickdown. If you want a higher or lower gear you have to move the fairly normal looking floor lever to a different slot. The car declutches itself when you grasp the knob on top of the floor lever, thanks to microswitched messages. While you can't make any progress if you habitually drive with one hand on the lever (it's not good for a manual box either) the shift has pretty reasonable sensitivity.

The box always disconnected itself without pause during our test, but didn't react to a casual brush from hand or leg.

With practice you can actually shift faster than is possible with the manual box, a gain just about balanced by a very slight hesitation in pick-up through the convertor. And double-clutched downshifts to impress the sporting crowd are just as easy using right hand and right foot rather than two feet.

However—and here lies the appeal of the box for traffic jams and wives on errands around town—you can also put the box in any one gear and forget it. Thanks to the 2.1 torque multiplication the VW 1500 starts from rest in any gear and can be wound up to the point of valve bounce. The three ranges are: I—0/40 mps; II—0/65 mph and III—0/77 mph or so. The lower gear maxima equate to 5000 rpm which would give 90 in top—but don't bother looking for that.

In fact our test vehicle was too new for peak action, but you can figure on 75 with proper run-in. For purposes of quick comparison an automatic 1500 has about the same performance as a manual 1300 in good tune.

This applies to acceleration as well. The automatic does steal some dig, which, of course, is obvious. Taking 21.5 seconds as the norm for a manual 1500 beetle we find the automatic about 6 seconds slower for the same 0-60 run when you use the shift lever as in a normal car. Put in top gear the car takes 34.5 seconds to 60. Of course, the point is that you can put it in top and forget about shifting. In fact there is very little if any gain in using all three gears for drag racing.

Second and third will get you to 75 just as fast as all three. Incidentally, the final drive is lower at 4.375.

Near as I could figure, the power penalty for ease of driving is about 10%, but, of course, with only 44 DIN hp to start with, you can't be giving away too many slices. Fuel consumption is worse by about 5% too, but only if you drive the car hard to keep up with a sister manual 1.5. Used comfortably to get the real advantage out of its box I doubt if you'd notice much difference.

On the go second is your universal gear. It will move a 1500 off with normal European traffic from a light or a little better. Leaping onto freeways you might want first briefly, although the time lost shifting across the gate largely steals the slight gain in initial dig. Around town the 0-65 range of second with decent if hardly blazing acceleration is enough to make it a one-gear errand car.

The fact that you don't have little men shifting up or down a step just when you want to make revs steady actually makes it easier for beginners to drive. With smaller European engines "normal" automatics tend to hunt more than icy mountain roads really require.

For handy transport and/or second car duties the VW 1500 automatic amounts to a one gear automobile with emergency low and an overdrive like top.

And—I saved the best for last. The new back axle system, currently available only in automatic VWs is worth the extra money alone—except that it should have been put on the package ten years ago anyway. There is no particular engineering reason why it can't be added to manual beetles one day. This would give them another yearly major change—only this one really is monumental.

It is engineered quite like the Porsche 911 with angled trailing arms and two joints for the driveshafts replacing simple swing axles. The obvious and immediate gain comes when you hang the tail out— or try to. That trick is considerably harder now—or, if you want to put it in safety terms—the dreaded oversteer is far less likely to crop up without warning. In short the inside rear wheel tuck-under which made VWs so twitchy (or so much fun on gravel, depending on viewpoint) is greatly reduced.

In practice there doesn't seem to be a big, fat time gain around a measured circle over the old car, but any average driver can travel around a given radius bend faster, because he feels the gradually approaching limits that much better.

The name of the game, of course, is still automatic—the axle setup is a bonus. I hear from the grapevine that all VW 1500s will come forth in pure automatic form before long, leaving manuals to the 1200 and 1300 continental models. ●

TWO-PEDAL BEETLE

WHEN the VW "beetle" boom went bust a couple of years ago, the general opinion among observers was that Volkswagen would hustle out a brilliant new model to retrieve the situation.

VW didn't hustle out anything, because they didn't have anything brilliant — or new — to offer.

Only now, about two years later, are they in a position to offer something even halfway new — and that could easily be mistaken at first glance for the car Australia has known for the past decade.

The new model is an automatic beetle with 1500 cc. engine—and a host of other changes. The hopes, dreams and future of VW Australia ride very much on this car.

They ride, we think, pretty well. For, though this beetle looks at a passing glance much like the old one, it is dramatically different under the skin. In a hard day's testing around some of Victoria's trickiest roads, the 1500 cc. beetle really impressed us with its new sure handling at any speed and on any surface. The car of the thirties has at last been brought right up to the best of modern standards.

Just about the only thing remaining of the original People's Car is the philosophy behind it—and that, at least, has always been sound.

Although it looks much the same, the new car does not share even one panel with the VW 1300.

Let's look at the obvious changes first. Windows are bigger all round — 15 per cent, VW tell us — and this goes part way towards relieving the slit-eyed look of the old car.

Bumper bars are completely different—made of tougher steel and raised slightly higher from the ground.

Ventilated wheels with flat hubcaps improve the car's looks considerably.

There's an outside fuel filler, headlights are vertical, tail-lights bigger, door handles and boot catch improved.

Etcetera, etcetera, etcetera.

Standard of finish is right up to VW's usual teutonic impeccability.

Technicalities

The new motor is basically the same unit that's been fitted to "full-size" 1500 VWs since their introduction.

It's an air-cooled flat four — of course — with bore of 83 mm. and stroke of 69 mm.

All this is old-hat to VW enthusiasts.

LEFT: No clutch pedal on this Beetle. BELOW: Old and new bodies. Differences at rear include flatter, higher bumper, bigger tail-lights, rear window; at front, vertical headlights. BOTTOM: VW automatic in action. Suspension changes transform handling.

Torque converter transmission, 1500cc engine make this the handiest Beetle yet. Transformed handling makes it the best . . .

What is new is the "automatic stick shift" transmission, which at this stage is the only transmission offered on 1500 cc. beetles in Australia.

Later, manual 1500s will go on sale.

The three-speed transmission offers drivers the convenience of selecting one of three speed ranges, depending on circumstances, and then forgetting about it.

A torque converter multiplies engine torque and also permits the car to stand still with the engine running in any gear range without moving the shift lever.

A vaccum-actuated single dry plate clutch is operated automatically when the shift lever is touched — and this is a system which has its drawbacks.

Although the transmission has three ranges, the ratios most used are called "One" and "Two". In addition to these there is a low range suitable for towing caravans and climbing cliffs.

Ratio 1 is primarily designed for use around towns and in traffic, where a lot of lugging and low-speed work is necessary.

Once out on the highway, ratio 2, which is an overdrive (0.89), gives the beetle comfortably long legs, and reasonable economy.

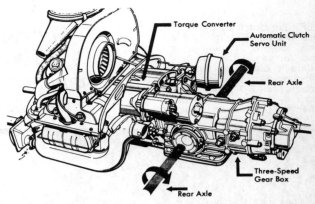

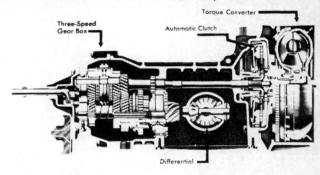

DIAGRAMS show details of the automatic transmission, with torque converter and automatically operated clutch. LEFT: Neat interior has the usual impeccable VW finish.

TWO-PEDAL BEETLE

Drive 1 is capable of winding out to 55 mph, according to VW, although we managed to get an indicated 72 mph. This sort of treatment overheats the transmission fluid, we're told.

Drive 2 can be used for starting, although progress is notably slow, and it will wind out to about 80 mph indicated.

To achieve a respectable rate of acceleration, drive 1 is used up to 30 mph or thereabouts, and drive 2 selected above that.

When we did our performance figures we used low as well, and by leaving our left hand on the gearstick, and winding the motor up, we were able to make very respectable clutch-type starts.

The transmission uses a conventional H-pattern, with reverse gear at the upper left and low range at the bottom left.

First and second ranges — the ones most used—are conveniently located opposite one another at top right and bottom right on the gate.

As we said, this transmission has some drawbacks. The most obvious concerns the automatic clutch and the fact that it disengages as soon as the shift lever is touched. If the lever is accidentally knocked by a knee, the clutch disengages. If the hand is inadvertently rested on the knob the clutch disengages. Incidents like this can cause embarrassment in some situations.

Apart from that, the transmission doesn't have a kickdown override such as is offered on most other automatics.

If you want rapid overtaking, it is still necessary to change gears, just like a manual.

The other major weakness is the fact that there is no "Park" position. Like BMC's Mini and 1100 automatic you rely on the handbrake to hold the car on hills. The handbrake is powerful enough to do this, but the park position is a comforting added safeguard.

Incidentally, this car incorporates almost all the U.S. Government's safety regulations, including collapsing steering, dual-circuit brakes, breakaway rear view mirror, impact-absorbing controls, etc.

Suspension, brakes

In these two departments, VW engineers have wrought some wondrous changes.

The suspension set-up is basically similar to that of VWs of old, but it has been subtly modified with the result that roadholding and handling are transformed.

Front and rear tracks have been increased, and the rear wheels have been de-cambered so that they now stand perfectly upright when the car is unladen.

The rear swing axles now use two universal joints each and this helps stabilise the car and minimise swing axle "tuck-under". Torsion bar settings have also been modified.

At the front, king-pins have been replaced by service-free ball joints. The entire front-end assembly has only four greasing points.

Brakes are now disc front (10.7in.), drum rear, without servo assistance. They provide extremely good stopping. Pedal action is progressive, and

the car's behaviour under brakes is very stable, without wheel locking or change of direction.

They came through our fade test with flying colors, and at the end of our 10 stops from 60 mph were providing stopping just as sure and trouble-free as ever.

On the road

The 1968 beetle is completely transformed. Gone is the heart-stopping twitchiness that characterised early beetles at any speed, and the later models when driven hard.

The automatic is as vice-free as any popular sedan we've driven. It is extremely difficult to hang out the tail, even on loose surfaces, the car wanting to understeer in all but the most extreme circumstances.

In an all-too-brief 110-mile pre-release test, which took us into the Melbourne hills out of Dandenong, we managed only two or three very mild tail-end slides.

For the rest of the trip it was simply a case of point it and push the throttle.

Another pleasing aspect of the automatic on the road is its new-found reluctance to wander, even in very strong cross-winds.

This has been a failure of all rear-engined cars, VWs included. Now it is one of the best in this department.

Performance was not brilliant, but the test car had done only 500 miles when we first picked it up, so it's hardly fair to expect it to go as well as a fully run-in unit—although VW have always claimed that their cars don't need to be run in.

Top speed was 74 mph, whereas the

(Continued on page 18)

DATA SHEET— VW AUTOMATIC

Manufacturer: Volkswagen A.G. Wolfsburg, Germany.
Test car supplied by Volkswagen (Aust.) Pty. Ltd., Clayton, Vic.
Price as tested: $2128.

SPECIFICATIONS

ENGINE

Air cooled, 4 cylinders, horizontally opposed.
Cast iron/alloy block, three main bearings.

Bore x stroke	83 x 69 mm.
Capacity	1493 cc.; 91.10 cu. in.
Compression	7.5 to 1
Carburettor	Single Solex d'draught
Fuel pump	Mechanical
Fuel tank	8.8 gallons
Fuel recommended	Super
Valve gear	P'rod ohv
Max. power (gross)	53 bhp at 4200 rpm
Max. torque	78 lb. ft. at 2600 rpm
Specific power output	35.5 bhp/litre
Electrical system	12v., 36 amp. hr. battery, 30 amp. generator

TRANSMISSION

Three speed torque converter automatic with single dry plate vacuum operated clutch.

Gear	Ratio	Max. mph
Rev.	3.07	—
Low	2.06	48
Drive 1	1.26	68
Drive 2	0.89	74
Final drive ratio	4.375 to 1	

CHASSIS

Wheelbase	7ft. 10in.
Track front	4ft. 3.8in.
Track rear	4ft. 5.1in.
Length	13ft. 2in.
Width	5ft. 1in.
Height	4ft. 11in.
Clearance	6in.
Kerb weight	15 cwt. 60 lbs.
Weight distribution front/rear	43/57%
lb/bhp	33.3 lbs.

SUSPENSION

Front: Independent longitudinal trailing arms, with torsion bar, stabiliser bar.
Rear: Independent with swing axles, torsion bars, and equaliser spring. Telescopic shock absorbers all round.

Brakes: Disc 10.9in disc/drum.	
Steering	Roller
Turns, lock to lock	2⅔
Turning circle	36ft.

Wheels: Steel disc with 5.60 by 15 tubeless cross ply tyres.

PERFORMANCE

Top speed	74.1 mph
Average (both ways)	73.7 mph
Standing quarter mile	22.8 sec.

Acceleration

Zero to	seconds
30 mph	6.5
40 mph	9.9
50 mph	16.1
60 mph	22.8
70 mph	40.9

	Low	Drive 1	Drive 2
20-40 mph	6.6	7.9	10.4
30-50 mph	—	9.0	12.2
40-60 mph	—	10.8	15.1
50-70 mph	—	—	20.5

Braking: Ten crash stops from 60 mph.

Stop	percent G	pedal pressure
1	.75	85
2	.80	85
3	.85	95
4	.85	95
5	.85	90
6	.85	85
7	.85	90
8	.87	90
9	.85	90
10	.87	90

Consumption: 24.4 mpg over 110 miles, including all tests; 30-32 mpg in normal country and suburban use.

Speedo error:

Indicated mph	30	40	50	60
Actual mph	30	39.4	49.0	58.4

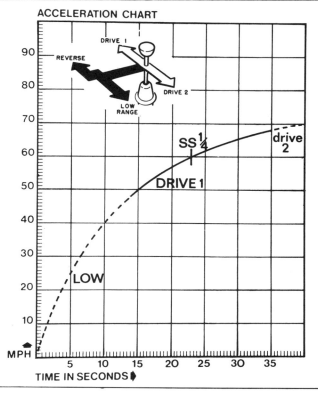

ACCELERATION CHART

DRIVE 1 · REVERSE · DRIVE 2 · LOW RANGE

SS ¼ · drive 2 · DRIVE 1 · LOW

MPH · TIME IN SECONDS

HOW VW AUTOMATIC COMPARES

MAXIMUM SPEED (mean) M.P.H.

60 · 70 · 80 · 90 · 100

- VW 1500 Auto. ($2128)
- Morris Mini Auto. ($1919)
- Morris 1100 Auto. ($2259)
- Toyota Corolla Auto. ($1948)

0-60 M.P.H. SECONDS

5 · 15 · 25

- VW 1500 Auto.
- Morris Mini Auto.
- Morris 1100 Auto.
- Toyota Corolla Auto.

M.P.G. Overall

20 · 30 · 40

- VW 1500 Auto.
- Morris Mini Auto.
- Morris 1100 Auto.
- Toyota Corolla Auto.

STANDING-START ¼-MILE (secs.)

30 · 20 · 10

- VW 1500 Auto.
- Morris Mini Auto.
- Morris 1100 Auto.
- Toyota Corolla Auto.

The New Selector Automatic adds $135 to the cost of a new VW.
The latest in rearends is also included for the added cost.

WE DRIVE THE NEW VW

THERE'S A PEDAL MISSING IN THE FAMILIAR BEETLE NOW. RESULT? LOTS OF NEW BUYERS

By THE EDITOR ■ Those of us who obtained vehicle operator's licenses so many years ago that we are reluctant to talk about it sometimes forget how many people there are in the United States who have been exposed to automatic transmissions to the exclusion of all else. We remember a time when driver's licenses were stamped "Conditional" and restricted the recipient to the use of automobiles with clutchless automatics. These drivers faced the severe penalty of having their license suspended it they attempted to drive a manual shift car. The new era of sporty cars with "four-on-the-floor" has been geared to the sale of automobiles a man could shift if he simply had to while his wife could drive all day without ever knowing what a clutch was. It seems inevitable, therefore, that with the phenominal success of the Volkswagen here some sort of an automatic transmission was mandatory.

Few Americans know that, for years, in the fine print of Volkswagen literature there lurked an optional semi-automatic transmission which could be obtained if one bothered enough dealers in an area until one broke down and placed the order. The

The only way to tell the Standard sedan from the automatic on the outside is the chrome lettering on the back. Inside, wider brake pedal; no clutch shows.

AUTOMATIC

WHO NEVER LEARNED TO SHIFT FOR THEMSELVES!

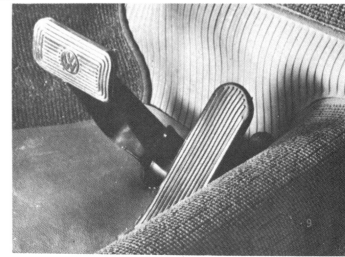

VW AUTOMATIC

(Continued from page 17)

Company proudly offers this new "Selector Automatic" just introduced and after driving it we're convinced that the one thing it will do for the people at the factory in Wolfsburg is increase the sales of their beetles here in the country!

We covered the technical aspects of VW's transmission which we've come to know as their "Automatic Stickshift" in our last issue pretty thoroughly. Driving it revealed a few things about it which we will mention right here before we go on to award it any kudos. First of all, like many, many transmissions with which American cars are equipped, it tends to creep at stop lights unless you hold it firmly with the foot brake. However, unlike many of the automatics from overseas, from zero to fifty is one smooth transition, without any clunks or hesitancy along the line. We thought we'd like the idea of shifting the car as if it were a three speed manual but found, over the long haul, that it was much simpler to push the lever into "drive 1 and leave it there, particularly around town.

Acceleration from a standing start is a little slower than the manual VWs we've driven so frequently over the past year but it is such a little difference that only the extremely critical will complain. If this is the first automatic one has driven he sould be careful not to reach out for that non-existent clutch pedal in a sudden stop. The brake pedal has been elongated and there is a very real possibility of applying it with a resultant bump of one's head on the windshield. People who are used to automatics will probably brake with the left foot, something this writer has never learned to do.

The new automatic is accompanied with a change in the rear suspension. This we discussed from the technical aspect in the previous issue. The effect of winds seemed to be reduced on the car we drove but we were so concerned with the new automatic transmission, we don't recall any spectacular improvement in the new Beetle's cornering capabilities. Overall performance, however, is strictly Volkswagen and, from where we sit, that is still a compliment. There are faster imports in this class nowadays; there are many quieter ones, too. Somehow, though, the mystique of the Beetle Volkswagen just goes on and on and on. If anyone offers as his sole reason for not buying a VW the fact that he never learned to shift his excuse went out of the window with the advent of this new introduction. We think there are many people here in the United States who have been eyeing the beetle longingly. This new automatic stickshift will certainly put them behind the wheel.

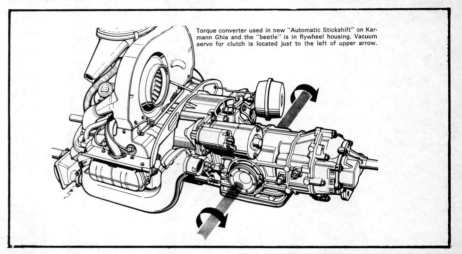

Torque converter used in new "Automatic Stickshift" on Karmann Ghia and the "beetle" is in flywheel housing. Vacuum servo for clutch is located just to the left of upper arrow.

BEETLE

(Continued from page 14)

factory claims 77.7 mph. One of VWA's engineers claimed he had the same car up over the 80 mark, and some of our colleagues achieved 79 in another automatic beetle.

The standing quarter-mile took 22.7 sec. (fastest) and averaged 22.8 sec. Using only ranges 1 and 2 and starting without the clutch makes acceleration distinctly slow. However, by holding the gearshift knob, building up revs, then releasing the knob, we were able to make quite respectable getaways.

Acceleration **isn't** brilliant, but people who buy an automatic aren't usually looking for sporty performance.

The beetle automatic is essentially a compromise, and like all compromises it won't please everybody. Dyed-in-the-wool VW-philes will welcome it as a fresh breath of wind from Wolfsburg. Older VW drivers looking for something a little lazier will probably go for it, too.

Fortunately, VW have been able to price it right. At $2128 tax paid, it falls right in the middle of the small automatic class.

For us, its real interest lies in truly excellent roadability. In the departments of braking, handling and roadholding, the 1500 automatic is a tremendous advance over any Volkswagen we've ever driven. It should help improve VWA fortunes in 1968. •

GROUP TEST

'Motor's' test team go driving in convoy to try groups of competitive cars under identical conditions

No. 6: Small family saloons

- **Ford Escort 1100**
- **Vauxhall Viva**
- **Triumph Herald 1200**
- **Volkswagen 1300**
- **NSU 1000C**
- **Austin 1100 Mk. 2**

This is the last in our present series of comparative road tests and it deals with six cars in the small family saloon class. The routine was on the same lines as in previous group tests, with the six cars and drivers setting off on a varied route to and around Wales over a period of two days. Each driver handled each car for about 50 miles at a time, the continuity of experience giving opportunities to form opinions on every aspect of the six cars with a degree of accuracy impossible with individual road tests spread over several months.

Unlike the baby saloons, of which a substantial proportion are sold as second cars to families who regard very small size as a virtue rather than a vice, this group is aimed almost exclusively at the one-car family who, mindful of economy, seek to pack in as much of the quart as will go into the pint pot. Thus it is not surprising that in the most popular of these cars we have found perhaps the best combination of performance, space and economy in any of the models tested so far. We imposed a nominal price of around £700 although this was exceeded slightly by the Viva, of which a more austere version is available, and by the Volkswagen 1300 for which there is compensation in its legendary durability and high resale value (as well as the option of the much cheaper 1200 model). Until recently NSUs were a little outclassed in price but recent substantial reductions throughout the range have brought the 1000C Super below £700 and added a further degree of unorthodoxy to a group of varied designs.

Performance

The basic design in this group is more consistent than some in that three out of six had orthodox front engine, rear drive layouts and all had four cylinders. But in the layout of the other three and in more detailed aspects of design there is greater diversity than in any group tested so far. The NSU and Volkswagen

Continued on the next page

The cars

Ford Escort 1100 de luxe 1,098 c.c. £691. Only completely new car in the group with the smallest of the BIP cross-flow engines. Lively performance and exceptional handling. Two doors, front engine rear wheel drive. Test car fitted with radial tyres and disc front brakes with servo costing £22 10s. extra.
Vauxhall Viva 1,159 c.c. £706. Smallest of the Vauxhalls with unmistakable GM lines. Good blend of performance, handling and roominess with boot to shame much bigger cars. Two doors, front engine rear wheel drive.
Triumph Herald 1200 1,147 c.c. £652. Now nearly 10 years old and still going strong thanks to minor modifications. One of very few small cars still retaining separate chassis construction and swing-axle rear suspension. Two doors, front engine rear wheel drive.
Volkswagen 1300 1,285 c.c. £747. Second largest in the ageless Beetle range. Solid and dependable

and much improved handling with softer springs and rear compensator bar. Two doors, horizontally opposed air-cooled rear engine, rear wheel drive.
Austin 1100 Super Mk. 2 1,098 c.c. £698. Basic and comparatively rare two-door model in the ADO16 range. Minor trim and embellishment changes in Mk. 2 version but virtually unchanged since introduction six years ago. Two doors, transverse front engine, front wheel drive. (At the time of the test only a Downton stage 1 modified model was available but all figures except fuel consumption for the trip are taken from our earlier road test of the standard car.)
NSU 1000C Super 996 c.c. £698. Smaller of the two four-cylinder NSU series just brought within price range by recent substantial cut. Greater emphasis on performance and handling than space. Two-doors, transverse, air-cooled overhead camshaft rear engine, rear wheel drive.

Group Test No. 6

continued

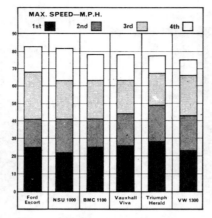

MAX. SPEED—M.P.H.

1st ■ 2nd ▨ 3rd ▨ 4th □

Ford Escort · NSU 1000 · BMC 1100 · Vauxhall Viva · Triumph Herald · VW 1300

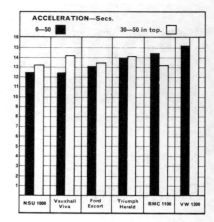

ACCELERATION—Secs.

0—50 ■   30—50 in top. □

NSU 1000 · Vauxhall Viva · Ford Escort · Triumph Herald · BMC 1100 · VW 1300

engines are air-cooled and, partly to ease the weight distribution problems associated with rear mounting, are made mainly of light alloys; the other four are iron throughout. The NSU and Escort have five main bearings, the others three; and independent rear ends outnumber live axles by four to two, only the Escort and Viva retaining this feature. Bore:stroke ratios range from the extremely over-square 1.53:1 of the Escort and the more orthodox modern 1.26:1 of the Viva to the well undersquare 0.77:1 of the 1100 with the VW, NSU and Herald distributed slightly above and below the square mark.

All the engines will rev quite happily to the limit of their breathing, but though bore/stroke ratio is sometimes supposed to influence flexibility and the BMC 1100 felt the most flexible and the Escort the least, this is not confirmed by the 30-50 m.p.h. acceleration times. These show very little difference between the Escort, NSU and 1100 and the VW is conspicuously slowest, mainly on account of its much higher gearing.

Not Welsh Nationalists planning another dam incident but "Motor's" testers paused on the brink above the Clywedog, Wales' newest, biggest and best. From left to right the cars are Herald, BMC 1100, VW, Viva, NSU and Escort.

Although they have the biggest engines, the Herald and VW produce the least power and have the lowest maximum speeds—by a comparatively small margin since only the NSU and Escort will top 80 m.p.h. A spread of nearly three seconds covers the 0-50 m.p.h. times, with the NSU and Viva the fastest at 12.5 s. and the VW slowest at 15.2 s. All six engines run reasonably smoothly throughout their ranges but there is some vibration towards the top end in the Herald and some people may object to the characteristic flat-four beat of the VW. The Escort and Viva are the quietest, the NSU the most raucous but this busy little

engine is probably more pleasant to listen to than that of the VW with its less purposeful clatter, the breathless high-speed rattle of the Herald, or the persistent gear whine of the 1100. Unlike the others, which get progressively noisier as they go faster, the NSU has a resonant period near 70 m.p.h. which tends to mar its motorway cruising ability since at this speed it is probably more obtrusive than the wind noise of the Viva or the transmission noise of the BMC 1100. The other three are comparatively restful near the legal limit, particularly the VW with its autobahn gearing.

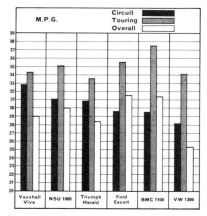

M.P.G.

Circuit
Touring
Overall

Cars: Vauxhall Viva, NSU 1000, Triumph Herald, Ford Escort, BMC 1100, VW 1300

Economy

Our 650-mile trip to Wales and back involved slightly higher speeds and rather more gear work than most owners will expect to indulge in. On the other hand none of the cars carried more than a driver and his overnight bag at any time while many owners would have families and luggage to consider. All the figures for the trip are on the heavy side of our road test touring consumption though the Viva's 32.9 m.p.g. trip consumption got fairly close to its 34.3 touring. The trip consumption of the BMC 1100 which rated very high on road test, is not really comparable as the group

test car was Downton modified and had to pay for its extra performance. Even so, its trip figure was better than that of the VW and about equal to the Escort's. To the satisfaction of PROs who thought we were too hard on their test cars, the Viva, Herald, VW, and NSU improved on previous road test figures but the Escort was rather worse. In monetary terms the consumption of the VW is better than it seems by nearly 3% as it tolerates 2-star petrol against the 4-star diet of the others, which brings it almost level with the Escort's 29.6 m.p.g. and means a spread of only 2 m.p.g. over the trip for all cars except the Viva, a variation unlikely to be significant in making a choice.

Transmission

Asked to comment on gear ratios, our assembled testers remained poignantly silent. And not without reason as, apart from the VW, the spacing of the ratios in each model is so nearly the same that they might have come from the same manufacturer. Two of the cars, the NSU and the VW, have all-indirect gearboxes but correcting these to the equivalent of a direct top gear shows that the BMC 1100, Herald, Escort and NSU have virtually identical spacing of top and third (1.41) with the VW and Viva slightly wider (1.48). In practice this shows up more prominently on the VW due to its reluctance to rev freely and this was the only car which ever seemed to be caught between two gears. The gap between top and second is

even more consistent, five cars falling inside the narrow band between 2.16:1 and 2.21:1 and the VW a little outside at 2.32:1. But the VW's exceptionally high overall gearing effectively makes up for its wider spacing when it comes to speed in the intermediate gears and it will easily match the others, which reach about 65 m.p.h. in third and just over 40 m.p.h. in second. Some drivers mentioned the rather low first gear of the NSU which helps it to get away from rest quickly but made it fussy on the really steep parts of the Welsh circuit.

Perhaps more important than ratios with this class of car, in view of the relative lack of power, is a really fast and easy gearchange, and all six are reasonably well equipped in this respect. A few years ago the VW shift was considered the last word in precision but it now shows up to be a little slow and long in travel beside the hot-knife-through-butter Escort, which everybody voted best. Even so, it was not quite as good as that on our road test Escort and would sometimes stick on engaging first from rest. The Viva change is also very good though the very short lever needs a long stretch and the gate is fairly wide. If it had shorter travel and a more substantial feel, the NSU change would be just as good while by comparison with these four the BMC 1100 is rather deliberate and heavy and, like the Herald, it lacks synchromesh on bottom gear. The Herald shift also has a very wide gate and lacks some of the precision of the others, an

Continued on the next page

The BMC 1100 was normally very neutral for its type but there were exceptional moments.

Whee! Fun and games with the Herald.

Group Test No. 6

continued

impression which some felt was made worse by the lack of symmetry in the fore-and-aft planes. Where fitted, synchromesh was adequate on all the cars, but none felt quite as unbeatable as the VW.

There is a little fan noise on both the air-cooled cars but their transmissions were completely silent, unlike the four British cars, all of which had a moan somewhere. On the Escort it was the rear axle, which may not be typical; we have commented before on the intermediate gear whine on both the Viva and Herald and the noisy idler gears prevalent throughout the BMC transverse range. Only the clutches on the Escort and NSU provoked comment, the Escort's because it was too light and sudden and the NSUs because the pedal came rather too far back from the floor and had that over-centre feeling which may be all right for a motorcycle handlebar lever but not for a pedal.

Handling and roadholding

Perhaps a lone test driver is likely to place greater emphasis on the subjects in this section than would the family motorist with his full load of dependants, luggage and livestock. But besides being more fun to drive, a good roadholding car will be safer and also faster if it has to waste less time recovering from a low cornering speed. With the exception of the Herald, which we will come to later, and some reservations on the VW's wet-road behaviour which we had no chance to examine on this occasion, all the cars impressed with their roadholding. Because these are fairly inexpensive cars and an inexpensive independent rear end seldom offers better roadholding than a well located live axle we weren't surprised when the Escort got full marks from most people.

The VW and Herald have swing-axle rear suspension, the VW with a rear compensator bar to retain the same vertical suspension stiffness with a lower roll stiffness. But none could match the Escort which can be thrown into a corner at almost any speed you choose and it just goes round on a safe and consistent line with very little roll and scarcely any response

if you lift off. The Viva is almost as good on smooth surfaces but more prone to hop on bumps, which greatly reduces cornering power on country roads. They both share light and accurate steering which enhances the pleasure of their handling although one of our drivers remarked on the lack of feel, saying that he would prefer rather more contact with the road before pressing either to the limit.

Both the NSU and BMC 1100 were highly praised for their roadholding, basically a straightforward measure of adhesion and handling though each reacted very differently. With semi-trailing i.r.s. and a very light engine over the wheels, instead of behind them, the NSU hardly behaves like a rear-engined car and, up to a point, can be thrown around with the same abandon as the Escort. Only on very bad surfaces, when severe pitching can be induced in the stiffly sprung suspension, does it display a tendency to sail straight on when entering a bend under power or to side step on the way out should the driver lift off.

The behaviour of the 1100 left us convinced that the degree of tuck-in or tail-out (whichever way you look at it), with BMC 1100s varies from car to car. On the Riley Kestrel, in an earlier group, which must have about the same power as this Downton car, it was fairly strong and care had to be exercised to judge the approach speed correctly to avoid the possibility of having to lift off too sharply in the turn. On this car the effect was less marked and though our steelier-nerved f.w.d. exponents regretted the lost ability to corner on opposite lock, ordinary drivers should find the handling of this car more reassuring in consequence. It would still understeer to a considerable extent under power, exaggerating the low geared steering but lifting off did little more than neutralize the situation, ready for another bite; nobody found it necessary to unwind frantically to keep the nose away from the inside hedge.

Both the VW and the Herald tended to lag behind the convoy on the rush round Wales mainly because they lack the roadholding of the other four. On the VW this manifests itself in the usual and predictable oversteer which is now less marked than it used to be and is easily controlled with the exceptionally precise and accurate steering. But everybody emerged somewhat shaken from the Herald; at anything above touring speeds the rear end jacks itself up into precipitous oversteer with the outside wheel tucked under on to the sidewall of the

tyre and the inside one scrabbling impotently at the surface to the accompaniment of a hefty thumping from the depths of the chassis. Some drivers may own one for years without reaching this point but there is always the chance of the unexpected. It has a redeeming feature in the steering which, like that of most in this group, is very quick and responsive but it was the only one which evoked complaints of kick-back.

Response to side winds varied very much with layout. The BMC is easily the best, the VW and NSU the worst in that order.

That it is possible to achieve a very comparable quality of ride with widely differing suspension was proven by the difficulty our testers had in choosing between the BMC 1100, VW and Escort. The VW seems best able to cope with the greatest variety of surfaces while the 1100, unmoved by sharp rutted tracks, could be provoked to considerable up and down movement on certain washboard surfaces. The Escort is generally very fair, much better than the stiffly sprung Viva which put several peoples' heads against the roof on the rough stuff. Neither the Herald nor NSU is very comfortable on bad surfaces, the Herald because a lot of road shock gets through to the occupants and the NSU because it seems to have too great a difference in suspension rates front and rear. Coupled with insufficient travel this means that the body is always on the move and fairly small irregularities can induce quite severe pitching.

Only the Escort was on radial tyres (an optional extra) and there was little evidence of the low speed road noise which often occurs with radials and they seem ideal wear for this car. There was a little light buzzing from the Viva and NSU, probably tyre induced, but this was nothing like as annoying as the thumping experienced in both the BMC 1100 and Herald and more directly related to suspension mounting. The Herald was particularly bad and the body responded with several sympathetic shakes and rattles of its own. The VW was voted as good or slightly better than the Escort for road noise.

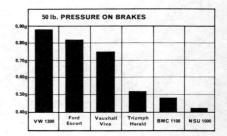

50 lb. PRESSURE ON BRAKES

Brakes

Disc front brakes are standard on the VW and BMC 1100 and an option on the others. We all felt quite happy about the brakes on all these cars and no trace of fade was reported. The Escort was fitted with optional front discs and had a servo which some people said made them too light though our road test figures show that a pressure of 50 lb. has slightly more effect on the VW. The NSU pedal is the heaviest, but not noticeably so, and since this and the VW are two more German cars in which it is impossible to heel-and-toe we concluded that motorists there do not bother with this practice. It was easiest to heel-and-toe in the Herald, quite practical in the Viva and possible in the BMC 1100 and Escort though both have rather small pedals very close together, and one of our drivers sometimes got his size 12 plates crossed up.

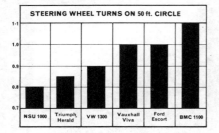

STEERING WHEEL TURNS ON 50 ft. CIRCLE

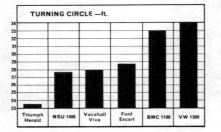

TURNING CIRCLE —ft.

Accommodation

With less than a 6-in. spread in wheelbase, there is not much difference in interior space and all six will just take four adults and very little more. They all had two doors but there is the option of four on the BMC 1100. Luggage room is very important in this class and here the Viva runs away with it, swallowing nearly 11 cu.ft. of our test boxes. Next come the Escort and Herald, 8 cu.ft. and the VW takes only slightly less if you fill both the front boot and the less accessible space behind the rear seat. The BMC 1100 achieves its great interior space at the expense of a rather small boot while the tiny compartment in the front of the NSU is of very little use for touring. The rear seats on both the VW and NSU will fold flat greatly to increase stowage with only two up.

There was unanimous approval of the Escort's driving position and its seats would be excellent if they were not quite so upright. The VW and BMC 1100 also have comfortable seats and on the VW and NSU, they recline. NSU seats are less conical than they used to be and much improved but there is still not enough support round the sides, a failing shared with the Viva which also lacks lumber support. After the Escort, the VW and Viva have the best driving positions, though the latter has insufficient fore-and-aft adjustment for a tall driver and the steering wheel is set rather high as it is on the NSU. A wheel set too low is but one shortcoming of the Herald, the only car from which several people climbed out complaining of aches and pains. You cannot sit straight because the pedals are so far offset, one shoulder presses against the door and the steering wheel against the left thigh. Since the main strength of the body is below the waist line, the seat belts have a low upper mounting and, like those in the NSU are prone to slip off the shoulder. The Viva is quite the opposite with a mounting just below the roof cantrail which gives a belt run rather too close to the neck for our liking. The belts in the other cars were quite comfortable.

All-round visibility is very important in cars used extensively in city traffic. The Escort, Viva and NSU are probably best and easiest to park and the Herald has a low waist and plenty of glass but rather thick and prominently sited screen pillars. The BMC 1100 has a high-set seat so the roof line limits forward visibility, a point which becomes much worse in bad weather, as the wipers leave large areas unswept. Despite numerous facelifts which have progressively increased the glass area the VW still has an old-fashioned high-waisted body, thick pillars and a flat windscreen so the area of visibility is much worse than from the others.

All our drivers, who on this session ranged in size from 5ft. 9in. to 6ft. 2in., preferred to drive all the cars with the seat right back and since this cut rear knee-room to less than 5 in. on the VW, Escort and Herald some compromise would have to be reached with rear passengers unless they were small children.

Continued on the next page

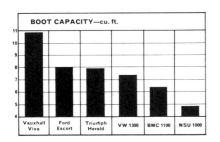

Vital statistics

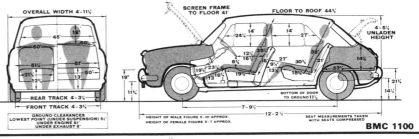

BMC 1100

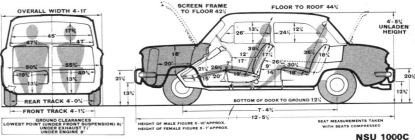

NSU 1000C

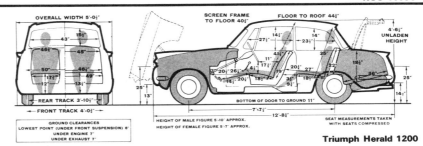

Triumph Herald 1200

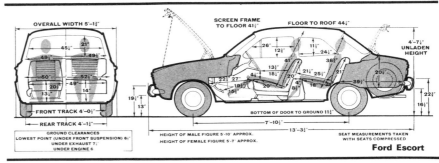

Ford Escort

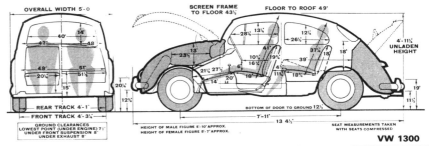

VW 1300

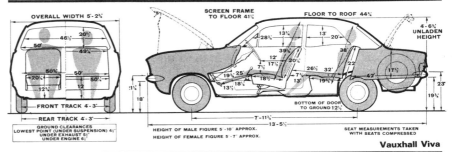

Vauxhall Viva

Specifications	Ford Escort	Vauxhall Viva	Triumph Herald	VW 1300	NSU 1000C	BMC 1100
Cylinders	4	4	4	4	4	4
Capacity	1,098	1,159	1,147	1,285	1,996	1,098
Brakes	drum (front disc optional)	drum (front disc optional)	drum (front disc optional)	disc/drum	drum (front disc optional)	disc/drum
Chassis lubrication	None	Every 30,000 miles to 4 points. (oil)	Every 12,000 miles to 4 points.	Every 6,000 miles to 4 points.	Every 4,500 miles to 2 points.	Every 3,000 miles to 4 points.
Fuel grade	4-star	4-star	4-star	2-star	4-star	4-star
Insurance rating	Group 2	Group 2	Group 2	Group 2	Group 1	Group 1
Service intervals	5,000 mls.	6,000 mls.	6,000 mls.	3,000 mls.	4,500 mls.	3,000 mls.
Tyre size	155 X 12	5.50 X 12	5.20 X 3	5.60 X 15	5.50 X 12	5.20 X 12
Weight	15.1 cwt.	15.3 cwt.	16.3 cwt.	14.9 cwt.	12.4 cwt.	15.8 cwt.
m.p.h. per 1,000 r.p.m. in top gear	14.8	16.0	15.7	18.5	14.8	14.9

Group Test No. 6
continued

Headroom is adequate in all of them.

Stowage for oddments varies: the Herald has a glove locker only, the VW and NSU have glove lockers and door pockets, the Viva a glove compartment and half width parcel shelf, the Escort only a small parcel shelf and the BMC 1100 a good-sized shelf and trays built into the doors.

Instruments and switches

Perhaps we are conservative. No matter how hard manufacturers strive to veer from the orthodox, we always finish up preferring a facia with neat, round, separate dials, or so it would seem from this group as everyone favoured the Escort and NSU. You get the same thing on the Herald and VW, of course, but the Herald's speedometer needle gets all mixed up with the mass of mile and kilometre calibrations while on the VW you must split 5 m.p.h. divisions. The strip speedo on the BMC 1100 is clear but nobody liked the rectangular instrument on the Viva owing to the distortion of linear calibrations behind an angular needle. Apart from the fuel gauge, most other information is left to warning lights but the BMC 1100, Viva and Escort have temperature gauges and the NSU a clock. On all six the instruments are grouped immediately in front of the driver.

The VW is an object lesson in simple switch-gear, combining nearly all you want into two flat, rubber knobs and a single column stalk. The NSU has a neat piano key switch panel and two stalks, the flasher on the right sometimes being mistaken for the indicators on the right—

the latter are not self-cancelling. The BMC 1100's tumbler switches are easy to use but unlabelled and the Escort's labelled keys would be better if grouped closer together. Nobody was very keen on the vague symbolism of the Herald's bunch of random knobs but the Viva was voted worst because, though the switches are sensibly symboled and arranged on a panel, it is tucked away below the steering column and invisible at night.

Heating and ventilation

Assuming that Vauxhall door seals bow out to release used air as well as Ford's positive extraction slots, the Viva has the best heating and ventilating system. A flap and an adjustable grille at each end of the facia ensure a reasonable fresh air flow without a concentrated blast and the heater is powerful and easy to use. The Escort arrangement is almost as good but, with the same vents for face level air and demisting, it is not quite so versatile. Both the VW and NSU have fresh air vents, but their through-put is neglible. Triumph and BMC don't even try. Fed by the exhaust, the VW and NSU heating systems are good of their type but you can't get such close control as with a water valve; the effect depends entirely on engine speed and at full chat the roar from the NSU's was like a 707 taking off. The push-pull temperature and distribution controls on the Herald are coarse and rather out of date.

Noise

In general terms the Viva was perhaps the quietest throughout its range and this example was not so spoiled by wind noise as some others that have passed through our hands. The Escort is certainly Ford's best effort so far for wind noise and the engine is reasonably subdued but for a remote tinkling which seems to come from the valve gear. The VW was also praised for low wind noise, certainly less than that of the BMC 1100 or the NSU, but the sewing machine sound of the engine may be more annoying than the 1100's various whines and whistles and possibly as obtrusive as the general thrash of the NSU, depending on how your ear is attuned. The Herald came off worst for its road noise and engine noise at high revs, while above 70 m.p.h. a steadily rising level of wind noise broke into a pulsating roar as pressure on the driver's window made it vibrate against the seal. **M**

● ● ● ● ● ● ● ● ● ● ● ● ● ● ● ● ●

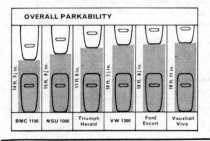

OVERALL PARKABILITY

BMC 1100	NSU 1000	Triumph Herald	VW 1300	Ford Escort	Vauxhall Viva
14 ft. 3 in.	15 ft. 9½ in.	17 ft. 6 in.	18 ft. 7½ in.	18 ft. 8½ in.	18 ft. 11 in.

'Motor' road tests of the cars in this group were published as below:

Ford Escort 1100 Super	17 February 1968
Vauxhall Viva	10 December 1966
Austin 1100	1 January 1966
Volkswagen 1300	16 July 1966
NSU 1000 LS (now 1000C)	13 November 1965
Triumph Herald 1200	28 November 1964

On the Road

This new feature, which will not necessarily appear every month, is intended to provide for coverage of those cars which are not entirely new models or are not sufficiently interesting to warrant a full road-test report or "road impressions" treatment and also to cover asides and items about motoring gleaned mainly while driving about the country, cars being for driving, not for parking or picnicking in or washing at the kerbside on Sunday mornings. . . . It takes the same title as the feature which Owen John, whose real name was O. J. Llewellyn, wrote every week for *The Autocar* from 1905 to 1930. He was a private owner who bought an already outdated Brush automobile in 1903 out of curiosity, using it on his travels as a Government official responsible for inspecting canal tunnels and bridges. He subsequently owned such vehicles as a 2-cylinder Clement-Talbot, a 19.6-h.p. Crossley, a Ner-a-Car motorcycle and a Poppe-designed 16/50 Rover saloon, of which he once wrote that it went like a dream " and gives me so little trouble that I can never find anything to write about it." At the same time he had a Rover "Nippy Nine" as a second car, used by his family, and later a 10–25-h.p. Rover. It is perhaps appropriate that at the time of commencing this feature I, too, am running a Rover; but then many motoring writers favour this make of car; for example, Edward Eves (until recently), John Eason-Gibson, Rab Cook, David Phipps, Michael Kemp, John Langley, Harold Dvoretsky, Dr. Keith Jollies and others.

Owen John drove big mileages on business, commenting on roads, hotels, scenery and the changing scene as he did so, and he was offered various cars and products to comment on, apart from using his own vehicles. So this feature, although it appears monthly instead of weekly, and is unlikely to run for a quarter of a century, will be following in the wheeltracks of this prolific writer whose outpourings spanned the veteran, Edwardian and vintage periods of motoring, with the proviso that I shall be less literary than O. J. but will include a bigger dosage of technicalities, as befits the changed face of motoring journalism.—Ed.

* * *

ONCE a confirmed Beetle fan, these days I find myself driving only occasionally one of the original-shaped Volkswagens. But my one-time fanaticism for them sticks, because I am sometimes still accused of flaunting them at the expense of British cars, although a dozen years have passed since I paid homage so avidly to Wolfsburg products.

Today I regard a Volkswagen as sound transportation, excellent value-for-outlay, rather as one regarded the Model-A Ford as the vintage years ebbed away. The original Beetle, as imported into Britain, was in many respects far ahead of contemporary cars from Birmingham, Coventry and Dagenham. The present VW is not to everyone's taste and other cars in like categories certainly compete with it and even out-flank it. Yet so cautious is human nature that when, in my opinion, it was the only car to buy at the price, its very unusualness turned many British families away from it; now, when I am only too willing to listen to reasons why a VW will not fill a particular person's requirements, more and more people are clamouring to purchase them.

Just look at the figures! Volkswagenwerk have been producing an average of 1.5-million vehicles a year in recent times, of which 460,000 were exported to America in 1967. They are now, by a narrow margin, second only to Fiat as the largest motor vehicle producers in Europe, with 585,000 cars sold between January and June last year and over 10½-million Beetles built between 1958 and 1967 (compared to Ford's 1.8-million Anglias) although their output is not augmented by baby cars at one end of the spectrum or heavy commercial vehicles at the other.

The VW I tried was the two-pedal, semi-automatic 1500 Beetle. That is to say, it had no clutch pedal and the gear-change was effected by a normal lever operating a micro switch at its base. I met a somewhat similar but less smooth system on small Renaults and other cars many years ago, and didn't much like it. But since then automation has grown in esteem among the World's car-using population and sales suffer if two-pedallers aren't available. So Volkswagen, ever a make to progress with current trends, had to get going with

Owen John with his 16/50 Rover.

automatic transmission. They now offer this as full automation on the 1600 and in this 3-speed stick-shift form on the 1500. The latter provides for starting easily from rest without touching the gear-lever even if it is in the 4.375-to-1 top-gear position. A boon to lady drivers, novices and the nervous. . . . It also enables a " normal " driver to select the two lower gears and change out of them as he (and some shes) desires. Apart from the fact that the changes are heavy and notchy, in contrast to the excellence of VW synchromesh, there are no snags, although those capable of coping only with automation may regard as such the absence of a hill-hold. Because the " electrikery-gremlins " are at the base of the gear-lever, not in its knob, resting a hand lightly on the lever does not throw out the clutch; but a straying knee will do this. (This is an improvement on those horrible semi-automatics in which a hand laid lightly on the gear-lever throws the car out of gear, as on Fiat, N.S.U. and even the £3,500 Porsche 911L, the 911L I tried recently also stalling in the most inconvenient situations.) There is enough creep to make starting easy and the flexibility of the 83 × 69-mm. flat-four engine, aided by the torque converter, is extraordinary. One tester wrote that he had driven across London in top gear. I wasn't quite as automated as that, but I discovered that corners could be taken at a crawl without changing down, entirely without protest, and pick-up out of them wasn't all that sluggish. Clearly, this semi-automatic VW is the beginner's delight.

The disadvantages are a good deal of noise, and a fuel consumption of 27 m.p.g.—but of the least-expensive 91-octane petrol. (Absolute range = 241 miles.) The advantage is that the adoption of semi- and fully-automatic transmission has forced VW to abandon swing-axle i.r.s. on these models for an ingenious trailing-link i.r.s., with a transverse torsion bar. This has further improved Beetle cornering, until it is now perfectly normal. So driving the car presents no oddities.

CONTINUED ON PAGE 172

The shape of the Beetle hasn't really changed since its introduction as a private car just before the war. This is the semi-automatic transmission 1500. The sign by which it was photographed suggests the New Forest or even Scotland. In fact, it was taken within 50 miles of London.

COROLLA vs VOLKSWAGEN

There still exists a segment of the car buying public who wouldn't have a small economy car as a gift. These are the insecure who need a behemoth vehicle as an ego prop. There are also those with profound prejudices who view all imported cars as a threat to the very foundations of 'Americanism, Home and Motherhood' and infiltration by a 'Godless, Atheistic, Foreign Conspiracy.'

There are others who would love to have one but for budgetary considerations are limited to one vehicle which must be large enough to haul the entire family and its goods.

A much larger, and growing percentage of the U.S. population is looking with increasing jaundice at the cost spiral of the Detroit product, its fast waning fuel economy and deteriorating quality of manufacture. With nowhere else to go these people are looking with more and more favor on the economy imports.

The reasons, of course, are low initial cost, good fuel economy and small expenditures for maintenance.

Not to be overlooked is the youth element. These are the students and young marrieds who have no need for large cars and to whom economy is an overriding consideration.

For many years the VW enjoyed the position of being a 'reverse status symbol.' The very antiquity of its uncompromisingly ugly shape gave it an appeal not dissimilar from that accorded an underdog or runt of the litter. That this view is changing is evident on any large college campus. Where the 'Beetle' was once the male collegian's vehicle of choice, it now is relegated to the role of 'a girl's car.' The very fact of there being millions of bugs on the road has bred the contempt of too much familiarity.

The success of the sparkling performer, the 90 hp Toyota Corona sedan, offered with either manual or

On the drag strip, Corolla, with smaller and more economical engine outperforms the VW.

automatic transmission, has proved that the economy car buyer enjoys the benefits of good fuel economy coupled with agreeable styling and a host of comfort and convenience features.

The P.O.E. price of $1870 put the Corona at a slight price disadvantage with its obvious competitor, the VW beetle with a West Coast P.O.E. of $1777. However, comparison of these two cars on price alone does not give a true picture as the Toyota offers more power, four doors, plus a

Battle for VW dollar is joined

number of other desirable features and will run rings around the VW in just about every category.

Now Toyota has unleashed a new and potent weapon in the battle for the economy car buyer's dollar. The newcomer in the low price field is the Corolla and its target is the heart of the VW price bracket with a P.O.E. of $1575 and full list of $1714.

ROAD TEST feels that a close comparison of what these cars have to offer should shed some light on the question as to whether the VW can reign supreme forever or whether obsolescence of design in virtually every category except engine will have finally caught up with the Wolfsburg insect.

Styling

The new entry from Toyota, the Corolla, reflects the clean exterior styling of its big brother the Corona but has its own distinctive appeal. Viewed from any angle it is a classic example of a good blend of style and function. Its size is deceptive, being smaller than the VW in exterior dimensions but offering greater use of interior space.

In the fastback, two plus two configuration, the Corolla should have quite enough of the sports car look to make it an instant smash with the younger set. Economy they will get but with the added bonus of pizzazz.

While the VW has had minor face lifting touches through the years it still retains the basic shape of the first beetles brought to this country. There are those who call it functional but few find it really attractive.

Simplicity is the key in all the lower priced cars and in this vein the Corolla has the usual single pair of headlights. Turn indicator lights are mounted below the bumpers. The bumpers not only protect the lights but offer good wrap around protection. There are overriders on the bumpers for added protection of the vertically louvered grille. There should be good protection of the Corolla from those who 'park by ear.'

In contrast, the VW bumpers while appearing very sturdy, are really of quite light metal and overrides are only available at extra cost. Wrap around protection is minimal.

Along the flanks the Corolla has a decorative chrome strip at door latch level. ROAD TEST believes this would have been more practical at the widest point on the side as armor against the hammer handed in parking lots. But then, the VW has no side strip at all.

Visibility from the Corolla is ex-

Bumper overrides are standard equipment on the Corolla, an extra cost option on VW. Toyota is actually smaller on the outside, bigger on the inside than VW.

Corolla has an edge over the VW in turning radius. 15 ft. against 18½ ft. This is a decided advantage during parking maneuvers.

Body lean is not alarming when viewed from the inside. Corolla is under full control in a hard corner.

cellent. The slim pillars front and rear afford maximum vision at eye level with almost 90% of the area being glass. Over the sloping hood, even short drivers have a good view. While the same is true in the VW, the beetle's driving position feels excessively high and lacks the secure feeling of sitting *in* the car.

Rear vision in the Corolla is also good in sharp contrast to the VW which was never good and now is further complicated by the head rests built into the front seats which obstruct snap views over the shoulder.

Handling & Roadability Brakes & Safety

Reams have been written about the handling characteristics of the VW. Almost nowhere has it been praised. There is little point here in reflogging that dead horse.

Performance is, and always has been, one of Toyota's strong selling points. The Corolla continues in this fine tradition. The car handles like a sports car and it is difficult to remember that it is basically a transportation type vehicle. Its handling on sharp corners gives the driver perfect

Trunk space in the Corolla is more than adequate for an extended journey. The one large bag fits in VW trunk only because it has soft edges.

control and there is plenty of warning before the rear end starts to break away. A quick flick of the wheel and the car is under control. Body lean from the driver's seat is quite moderate. With three passengers on board on a winding mountain road, the car's handling can not be faulted and it is always surprising to look at the speedometer on some of the bends and see just how high it reads. The car is rock steady on the road and is certainly not twitchy as is the VW in either a crosswind or when meeting large trucks.

The four speed all synchromesh transmission is extremely smooth in operation and the synchromesh is such that speed shifting can be done with minimum effort. The action of the lever is a little 'whippy' but is quickly mastered. The lever 'falls readily to hand' being no more than a hand span away from the wheel.

The shift pattern is etched on the knob and there is no tricky work required to find reverse. While VW has a decal describing the shift pattern, reverse on the manual is still the tiresome 'push down then back' that is most difficult to diagram. Even on the VW automatic reverse is a chore.

Steering wheel diameter on the Corolla is 15¼ in. and positioning is just right for 'arms out' driving. Turning radius gives a decided edge to the Corolla at 15 ft. against 18½ ft. for the VW.

On the drag strip the Corolla outperforms the VW despite giving away 400 cc of engine displacement. The Toyota's et. with a tight new engine is

20.38 as against the VW's 20.46. Top speed through the traps is 66.96 mph for the Corolla compared with 61.81 for the VW.

The Volkswagen has been criticized for years for its erratic braking. For 1968 there have been no apparent changes. Stopping distance for the Corolla is about the same, approximately 145 ft. from 60 mph. The Toyota, however, does it more smoothly without the judder common to the VW on hard deceleration.

Power & Performance

The VW engine is now a classic design. It continues as a horizontally opposed, four cylinder, four stroke, overhead valve, air cooled, definitely oversquare (bore 3.26 in., stroke 2.72 in.) powerplant. Displacement is now 1493 cc (91.10 cu. in.) and it delivers 53 HP at 4200 rpm. With the weight of the beetle at 1825 lb., each of the VW horses has 34.43 lb. to push.

Since the beetle is engineered for continuous flat-out operation in fourth gear, ratios in the standard all synchro four-speed gear box are relatively low. In top gear, the VW pulls an overdrive ratio of 0.89:1.

The Corolla engine, tilted 20° to the left, is liquid cooled and is a straight 4 cylinder O.H.V. unit with a *five* main bearing crankshaft. The engine is oversquare (bore 2.95 in., stroke 2.40 in.) with a displacement of 1100 cc, (65.8 cu. in.) and delivers 60 HP at 6000 rpm. The maximum torque is 61.5 ft./lb. at 3800 rpm. A single downdraft two barrel carburetor is fitted. With the weight of the Corolla at 1640 lbs. with full fuel (900 lbs. front, 720 lbs. rear), each horse is going to pull 27.33 lbs. The weight to horsepower advantage of the Corolla is not the whole story. A good part of the difference lies in the final drive ratios; 1.00:1 on the Corolla against 0.89:1 for the VW.

It is on the highway rather than on the drag strip that performance is most meaningful. On a trip from Los Angeles to Las Vegas with three aboard including luggage the Corolla passed VWs with ease on uphill stretches.

Comfort & Convenience

Although overall measurements have changed, the VW passenger compartment dimensions are the same as before. Entry and exit to the front seat are rated 'fair' because there is still not enough foot maneuvering room between the seat and forward door post. Once inside, leg room is adequate in front. Getting into the back seat is a chore for all but kids and leg room for an adult is zilch.

Interior room in the VW is hard to describe, the windshield and dashboard are awfully close. Head room front and rear is good and the new vinyl seats are an improvement. They are also more comfortable in all respects and the front seats have a four position back adjustment as well as the incorporated built-in head rest.

The Corolla is roomy in the extreme and all passengers can seat themselves comfortably. The seats themselves are just exactly right for rake and long arm driving style is a natural with this car. Leg room in the seat behind the driver is a little restricted if he is in the 6 ft. range but by allowing the knees to spread apart, the subsequent seating position is quite satisfactory. Head room front and rear is good. The bucket seats are well padded and give excellent lateral support. As the car can be thrown around quite a lot, the seats really come into their own on a corner, firmly holding the driver in place.

The VW has all its instruments grouped in a single housing whereas the Corolla uses two circular dials. The one on the right is the speedometer which incorporates a trip odometer, and is a most legible instrument to read at a glance. The numbers are clearly spaced in 20 mph increments and the odd numbers are omitted and marked simply by a single line. The other dial, which contains the warning lights, fuel gauge, temperature and hi-beam warning lights is also easily read in a hurry. Both dials are recessed enough that there is no glare on the windshield for night driving. The turn signal indicators are separate and mounted between the two dials. The other switches are for

lights, wipers and cigarette lighter. All knobs are of the new safety rubber type.

The Corolla has a most effective heater system which comes on with all the power of a Bessemer steel furnace. It can warm the interior to sweltering standards in the space of a couple of blocks. The Corolla does not have the flow-thru ventilation system of the Corona but as the rear windows open outwards (extra on VW), the same effect can be produced with subtle use of the fresh air controls.

One of the standing complaints with VW has been the high noise level inside the car. In contrast the Corolla is one of the quietest sedans of its size on the road today. Normal conversation can be carried on between all passengers, front and rear, with the car cruising at 70 mph. With the comfortable seating, low noise level and good temperature control, this car must rate highly on these fatigue re-

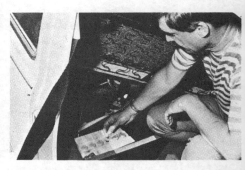

Battery location is up front and accessible in the Toyota Corolla. VW still hides the battery under the rear seat where replacing belts adds to the inconvenience.

ducing features.

Among the bonuses offered by the Corolla is a very useful, full width, under-the-dash package tray. The car also has a small non-lockable glove box and the whole instrument panel has a padded top to it. The radio recess is just above the heater controls.

The pedal position on the VW has long been a bone of contention with owners who have to adjust to the off center position due to intrusion of the

A thoughtful touch is Toyota's inclusion of cup recesses in the glove box door. Door is level when open.

front wheel arches and the small amount of space on the floor at that point.

The Corolla pedals are placed exactly right and the movement from the gas to the brake pedal is to all intents and purposes, horizontal. The handbrake is centrally mounted on the tunnel between the seats and can easily be operated for starts on steep hills. The turn signal switch is the normal stalk on the left of the column. The horn is part of the single spoke of the steering wheel. All instruments are easily seen through the wheel, nothing is hidden. Which brings to mind the hidden battery of the VW. It still lurks under the rear seat. On the Corolla it is up front in the engine room where it may get warm but it will surely get water.

The 9.5 gallon fuel tank is located midships between the rear seat and the trunk. The filler cap is on the driver's side and requires a key to open. With the car on the road, and the 500 lb. load to Las Vegas, the average fuel consumption was 32.2 mpg when cruising at 65-70 mph. Volks-

wagens get 23.5 mpg.

Luggage Capacity

The VW has certainly never shown any great capacity for stowing other than small items. The Corolla offers lots of space and good sized suitcases can be carried in the flat floored trunk. The spare tire is under the floor mat in the compartment.

Quality Control

For years the VW has been the yardstick whereby both imports and domestics have been assessed for quality for money spent. It has undoubtedly been well earned and the general appearance of the car and the durability of the interior can be ascer-

tained by glancing inside any of the older models still around.

The Toyota Corolla is a newcomer on the market and the wear factor over the years cannot be commented upon at this time. However, it is evident that Toyota expects its cars to last and the quality can be seen on the cars at first glance.

It is impossible to find fault with the paint, trim, chrome, fit or detailing on any Toyota product. In this low priced machine, to find the same meticulous attention to detail speaks well of their inspection department. Superb construction techniques and quality engineering make this low priced car an exceptional buy and ensures the buyer excellent value.

Key to the Toyota trunk is no cause for fumbling. Both sides are the same, there is no upside down.

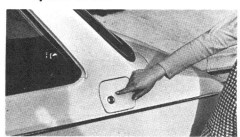

Lockable gas filler indicates midships position of fuel tank.

In addition to full width parcel shelf there is room on the cowl for parking sun glasses. VW boasts neither convenience.

The new Corolla Fastback is aimed at the youth market. This newest entry is a 2+2 with zesty performance to go with its styling.
Model to be imported will have left-hand drive, different outside mirror location.

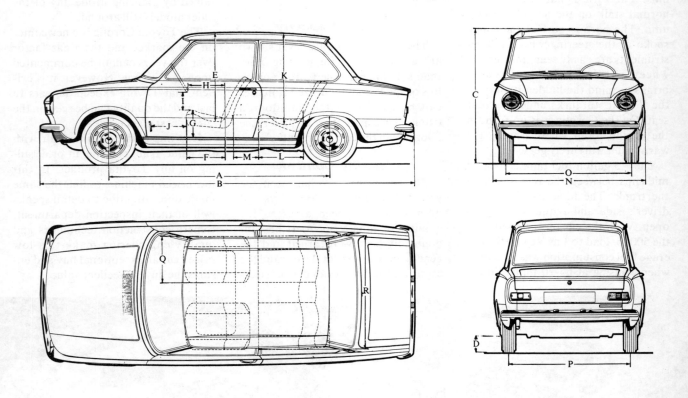

	A	B	C	D	E	F	G	H	I	J	K	L	M	N	O	P	Q	R	NOT ILLUSTRATED	
ALL MEASUREMENTS IN INCHES	WHEEL BASE	OVERALL LENGTH	OVERALL HEIGHT	GROUND CLEARANCE	FRONT SEAT TO HEADLINER	FRONT SEAT DEPTH	SEAT CUSHION TO FLOOR	FRONT SEAT BACK TO STEERING WHEEL, MIN./MAX.	STEERING WHEEL TO SEAT CUSHION TOP	PEDAL TO FRONT SEAT MIN./MAX.	REAR SEAT TO HEADLINER	REAR SEAT DEPTH	REAR SEAT TO FRONT SEAT BACK, MIN./MAX.	OVERALL WIDTH	TREAD WIDTH FRONT	TREAD WIDTH REAR	FRONT SEAT WIDTH	REAR SEAT WIDTH	FRONT DOOR WIDTH	TRUNK CAPACITY, CU. FT.
VOLKSWAGEN	94.5	158.7	59.0	7.2	35.0	18.5	13.0	13.0 17.5	5.7	17.2 22.5	32.0	17.7	4.5 14.5	61.0	51.6	53.1	43.7	52.0	34.0	5.0
TOYOTA COROLLA	90.0	151.4	54.3	6.7	34.5	11.0	14 19	15.0 18.8	6.0	14.5 19.0	34.0	18.8	6.5 11.0	58.5	48.4	48.0	43.0	49.4	40.5	8.6

Quart in a pint pot

As we said in the introductory remarks, the size of the Corolla is most deceptive and until the reader actually sits down and compares figures, the results will certainly be impressive as to just how the Toyota people have achieved their roomy interior in a car that is 7 ½ ins. shorter overall and 4 ½ ins. shorter in wheelbase.

The sum of 'J, F, M, & L' gives an indication 'to the amount of space available for passengers, 58.7 ins. in the Corolla, as opposed to 57.9 ins. in the VW. Seat widths front and rear are almost the same with a slight edge to the VW in the rear. However, the arm rest built into the wall in the Corolla increases the seating area in effect and equalizes the 2 ins. discrepancy.

Rear seat headroom in the Corolla is 2 ins. more than the VW and is accounted for by the body shape.

What is noticeable in these small cars, is the clever attention to detail that must be adhered to to ensure that literally every inch of available space is used to the maximum. When the engineer is working inside such small tolerances, a matter of an inch or two can make all the difference between comfort and agony for a driver on a long trip. The figures for the Corolla speak for themselves and represent a logical development commensurate with a more modern design; having started with a clean sheet of paper. It's that simple. ♠

EMPI GTV: Southern California's Muscle Beetle

BY PATRICK J. BEDARD

Anything can happen in Southern California— even $2800 VW beetles with candyapple paint jobs, reversed wheels, meticulous pinstriping, chromed exhaust systems and flash and filigree throughout the engine compartment. The extent to which things have already happened in Greater Disneyland is pointed out by the fact that Volkswagen is outselling Mustang in the Los Angeles area.

PHOTOGRAPHY: JULIAN VEOVICH

Anything can happen in Southern California: flood, fire, pestilence; instant stardom, enormous fortune, Ronald Reagan. Even the EMPI VW. Everything else is commonplace, the EMPI demands geographic conditioning.

After all, a $2820 Volkswagen beetle registers on the rational mind more as a typographical error rather than a genuine device. An econo car for that kind of bread would be an anomaly north of Oxnard—but not in *Southern* California.

First off, you have to understand that the VW is something entirely apart from an economy car: it's an American fixture by way of Wolfsburg, a steel and plastic turtleneck sweater—an enduring institution. Something about cross-pollination. You aren't judged by the year of your VW —VW's ad agency has seen to that ("Your '68 VW looks almost exactly like the one you forgot to buy in 1948"). The whole thing is whether you have one or not. The magic about VWs, at least from the Wolfsburg point of view, is that its American buyer is apt to be almost anybody. Sweet young working girls who can't afford the payments on a 6-cylinder Mustang (and many who can) buy VWs just because they're cute. And besides, they somehow know the beetle is as reliable and as easily serviced as a wooden pencil, or an apron,

or a glass of Alhambra's pure spring water.

None of this is very attention arresting information because you've seen it happen in your own community. On the other hand, did you know that the drive-in set in Southern California—that should be making the scene in '55 Chevys with many-carbureted 327s—is now seeking their pleasures in Volkswagens with outrageously reversed wheels and snaky exhaust pipes? Talk about your inverse social phenomena. Southern California oracles explain that it's a whole lot easier to convince parents that you need a VW than a bored-out Chevy or a GTO. Everybody knows that VWs don't cost much and the insurance rates are low and the kids won't be able to get them going fast enough to hurt themselves and, besides, there's that curious trans-Atlantic enchantment.

I'm not buying that, or at least, not as the only reasons. The kids are too smart. They wouldn't touch a VW with a dinged surfboard just because it was good for them—no sir. They have to have the *in* car, and today that's the Volkswagen—so much so that it's currently outselling Mustang in the Los Angeles area.

If you can overlook the obvious difference in size and power between the '55-'57 Chevys and the VWs there are certain similarities and a pretty logical reason why

they should become so popular with the now generation. The young want cars that are more than just transportation—they want cars that say something about the people who drive them. Each micro-citizen seeks to have a car different from each other micro-citizen but most of all from his elders. Still his car must fit within the frame of reference of his peers so he can be quickly judged and admired. To do that you need a car that is well-known—a Chevy or a VW. Once you have the car you individualize it by substituting a few special parts for original ones through the magic of mag wheels or engine bolt-ons and this is no problem because a number of West Coast entrepreneurs are manufacturing trick VW pieces. Isn't it obvious? Those poor VWs are so damn stark and undernourished they're just crying for some enthusiastic type to help them. They're perfect. Expressing yourself with a VW is as easy as writing your name in chalk on the sidewalk.

All this wouldn't be true if it weren't for the specialty parts people, so a good bit of the credit (or blame, depending on how you want to look at it) for Volkswagen's booming popularity should go to EMPI. EMPI lives in the budding desert oasis of Riverside, California, and has a wider variety of trick VW parts and surprises than could ever be discovered in one day's skulking around the works. To understand EMPI you have to know its major domo, Joe Vittone—and a short conversation with Vittone makes it easy to understand EMPI's success. Vittone looks like a precision part himself—his hair goes just in the direction he wants it to, the trousers of his shiny business suit have perfect creases and he talks in the manner of a man who declines to understand the meaning of the word "no." "Maybe" is only a few weeks work away from "yes." He likes intricate mechanisms and he likes money—maybe not in that order, but it doesn't really matter.

Vittone established a VW dealership in Riverside during the mid-Fifties, but because he really liked parts best he spent most of his time in the service department. In those days VW valve guide life-expectancy fell somewhere between that of an oil filter and a fan belt, and when the guides were gone you bought new heads. To Vittone's eye for business here was an opportunity, and it wasn't long before EMPI was established to build replaceable valve guides. Right off, it would make sense that a company making only one product is on shaky ground, so Joe was casting around for more ways to solve VW owners' dilemmas and at the same time keep EMPI healthy. About then it occurred to him that his body shop was being kept pretty busy repairing the VWs that his customers were tipping over with a sort of Teutonic regularity. There was opportunity striking again and the result was the camber compensator which is now universally accepted as God's Answer to pigeon-toed VWs, and EMPI's most famous product. All this is just background information to show that there is a reason for everything that happens at EMPI.

One more piece of background information—an important part of the profit picture in selling new cars is in the accessories. Volkswagen wasn't all unknowing, but its list of recommended accessories (including those curious mud flaps) was completely uncool in Vittone's mind. In fact, even the word "accessory" shuts him off. Who in the hell wants accessories? It even sounds dumb. "Options" is a much better way of saying it and he has instructed all of his salesmen that "options" it will be forevermore. Besides, he reasons, how many Impalas and Caprices would Chevrolet sell if all that was offered was the basic Biscayne and it was up to the customer to make his Chevy sexier by tacking on options? It would never work but that's what Volkswagen was trying to do. From that thought was born the EMPI GTV in four denominations: Mk I through Mk IV, with list prices up to about $2820 for the Mk IV, depending on which tires it wears. As I said before, that's a lot of

bread for a VW and it's disturbing when you find out the radio isn't standard equipment on a GTV. Only a guy with a lot of crust would try to sell VWs at that price. Vittone has a lot of crust and he's doing it.

In the past, *C/D* has dared to suggest that the VW's handling was on the scary side, the engines were powerless, and the cars were uncomfortable to ride in for any distance. In general—we had a tendency to say—the VW fell short of perfection; although not in the quality area. And what happened? The office filled up to ear lobe level with poison pen letters every time.

After nearly bleeding to death from paper cuts it's been made fairly clear that the world doesn't care that the VW is not a great car. The VW is loved as an institution and not as a car at all. So for that reason and the profound hope that the activists among you will not be provoked, I've chosen not to measure the GTV in terms of automotive perfection but rather whether or not it's a good VW.

You'll be pleased to know that as a VW, it's terrific.

Your GTV Mk IV option money buys a list a full 47 separate items long, which are either in addition to, or a replacement of, standard pieces on the beetle. Many of them are of the dress-up variety: totally unrestrained paint striping, chrome door handle guards, chrome fender guards, chrome door edge guards (do you get the idea EMPI is big on guards?), chrome fan belt guard, and a simulated walnut dash—but some of them are really well-engineered parts which vastly improve the performance and handling of the car. The package includes heavy duty shock absorbers, a front anti-sway bar and a rear camber compensator, as well as a set of 5.5-inch-wide Porsche-style chrome steel wheels. The standard VW wheels are a skinny 4 inches wide. Even the Porsche 911 didn't have 5.5-inch wheels until '68, so you can see that the GTV is right up with the times.

The Porsche influence can be seen in the steering wheel too. The GTV had one of EMPI's beautiful flat-black 4-spoke wheels with the leather covered rim that was downright elegant. The floor wasn't overlooked in EMPI's add-on elegance campaign either. It gets a kind of wall-to-wall carpeting in the form of a cocoa mat which, according to one of the EMPI spokesmen, stops a good bit of the road noise that normally comes through VW floors.

Without a doubt the most conspicuous add-on of all is the GTV emblem which gets affixed to the beetle's epidermis in three select locations. Obviously, subtlety is not part of the package.

No one who cares about innards (Vittone for example) would ever be satisfied with the standard VW instrumentation. The GTV is a meter-reader's paradise with its

precision-looking tach, ammeter, and oil pressure and temperature gauges—all good stuff that VW has given every reason to believe it would never supply in a million years. Of course, the beetle panel wasn't made with those additions in mind so things are a little crowded. The instruments, by necessity, are on the small side, and sometimes you have to peer around the steering wheel spokes to find out what's going on, but it's a whale of a lot better than the dark-side-of-the-moon approach Wolfsburg offers.

About this time you've got the idea that no part of the venerable beetle is sacred to EMPI. You don't know the half of it. When Dean Lowry (the Inch Pincher man) and J.C. Vittone (the motorcycle drag racer who survived) put their lusty Southern California hot rodder prefrontal lobes together, a poor VW's 1500cc windmill loses its virginity. EMPI makes so many high-performance VW engine parts that nobody but Vittone and Lowry know what's what. The GTV Mk IV gets a few of the tamer pieces like the 2-bbl. Solex carburetor on a little-boy-blue-enameled tubing intake manifold and the extractor exhaust system complete with sausage shaped muffler and a chrome outlet. A special air cleaner and a distributor with a revised advance curve round out the standard Mk IV package. All pretty tame stuff—so Lowry walked a little farther back into the parts room before he put this engine together. One of EMPI's more recent triumphs is its big bore cylinder barrel and piston kit which will increase the displacement of any 1300, 1500, or 1600cc VW to 1688cc—and my red lady-bug had those very pieces. To complete the engine picture, EMPI's sport camshaft was substituted for the VW cam even though standard valve springs were used. While EMPI was substituting, in went the absolutely bullet-proof competition clutch. It may be just a coincidence, but I wonder if they found out that occasionally I seek a moment of truth on the drag strip. To set the record straight, the barrel and piston kit, sport camshaft and heavy duty clutch aren't part of the GTV package so the cost of this car would slip over the three grand mark, but keep in mind it's all in the spirit of building a better VW.

At this point in time my foremost objective was to get this big-muscled beetle out of sight of its protective owner's eyes so that I could find out for myself what it was all about. Of course EMPI has a dynamometer and Vittone volunteered that this combination was worth 75 to 80 hp depending on how carefully the engine was put together. But horsepower numbers don't produce the same sensation as a gas pedal to the wood. "I'll be good to it," I promised, but they shook their heads sadly. They knew better they were trying to say, but manners precluded their saying it. "Don't take it much over five grand because the valves like to bump into the pistons with the standard springs," cautioned one of the mechanics. I hooked up the seat

CONTINUED ON PAGE 47

"VW makes changes and the changes make sense" comes under the heading of· hoary sayings by now, and most people are quite used to meeting a new model Volkswagen and being unable to detect any of the 173 changes made since the year before. All too often the unbending Wolfsburg firm was inclined to claim a change in the angle of inclination of a door hinge retaining pin as a major contribution to road safety, the stability of the International monetary system and the easing of the cold war. So one can forgive some scepticism about every new beetle that appears.

However, one's view of this changeless shape had to be modified when Volkswagen Australasia announced earlier this year that it was going out of local manufacture back to a CKD assembly basis. The obvious advantages of this, despite economic losses in premature disposal of plant and tooling, were that the company could tune in on all the latest European changes which previously, for the sake of local content, were kept out of the Australian beetle. For instance, it is certain that if the beetle were still being made here we would not have seen the 1500-engined manual version released as we did in mid-May. And that would have been a great pity, for this is probably the best Volkswagen yet built.

One unfortunate turn, however, is

Volkswagen's 1500-engined manual is the . . .

BEST BEETLE YET!

Below: Needing a slight outward bulge in the lid to fit, the 1500 engine happily occupies most of the space in the tail. Noise is low.

that after it took VWA five years to "Australianise" the beetle we have suddenly gone all European again; by that we mean that the wiper pattern is now decidedly left-hand-drive, with the right corner of the screen unswept (and this is not a happy position, particularly with the thick screen pillars the design has always had) and the bonnet lock is back on the left hand side of the car. Small things, but they are the prices you pay for the International look.

The new car is the direct result of Volkswagen's extensive modification to adapt the beetle to the new American safety regulations. Thus the bumpers are higher and stronger to meet height and impact requirements, the headlights have been lifted to a vertical plane to meet lighting demands and the wheel rims have been modified for better blow-out retention. These are the exterior signs to pick the new beetle — plus a perceptibly larger area of glass (the company says 15 percent), a slight outward bulge in the rear lid to take the bigger engine, and a flap on the right hand

side, just in front of the door, which conceals the fuel filler cap. Most VW owners won't like this, for the old system of filling straight into the 8.8 gallon tank through a huge pipe under the front bonnet was probably faster and more thief-proof, but all we can report is that gas station attendants were delighted. Apparently more than one has creased his scalp on a VW bonnet before today.

In any case, these changes were all brought in with the automatic 1500 version several months ago. We tested the auto version then, and commented favorably on the improved handling — despite quite marked understeer, of all things — but this was the result of altered rear suspension geometry. Because the driveshafts couldn't come straight from the gearbox casing they angle back to the outboard assemblies, are jointed at both ends with sliding-ball universals, and are subject to location by trailing arms. This controls rear wheel camber change completely.

However, the manual version still has the swing-axle system, but with a new "equaliser spring" which is aimed at keeping the wheels more vertical. This works along the lines of the old Mercedes-Benz idea, which controlled the deflection movement of a low-pivot swing axle system by a transverse coil spring between lower suspension mounting and the differential housing.

The manual has the same altered ball-joint front end as the auto's, plus the steering damper (back again). The big discs are there on

Above: Handling is improved with extra poke; car oversteers much less. On dirt roads the ride and stability is top of the class.

Below: Safety-crammed interior also features good driving position, despite awkward pedals. Steering column shears upon impact.

TECHNICAL DETAILS

MAKE	VW	MODEL	1500
BODY TYPE	2-door sedan	PRICE	$1998
OPTIONS	nil	COLOR	buff
MILEAGE START	1771	FINISH	1887
WEIGHT			15.2 cwt

FUEL CONSUMPTION:
Overall .... 24 mpg
Cruising .... 27-29 mpg

TEST CONDITIONS:
Weather: fine, Surface: hot-mix bitumen. Load: two
persons. Fuel: premium grade.

PERFORMANCE

Piston speed at max bhp ....1900 ft/min
Top gear mph per 1000 rpm .... 19.8 mph
Engine rpm at max speed .... 4100 rpm
Engine rpm at cruising speed .... 3000 rpm
Lbs (laden) per gross bhp (power to weight) 32

MAXIMUM SPEEDS:
Fastest run .... 80.0 mph
Average of all runs .... 78.9 mph
Speedometer indication fastest run .... 83 mph
In gears: 1st 27 mph, 2nd 49 mph, 3rd 69 mph, 4th
78 mph.

ACCELERATION:
(through gears)
0-30 mph				6.2 sec
0-40 mph				9.0 sec
0-50 mph				14.1 sec
0-60 mph				20.5 sec
0-70 mph				27.0 sec

	3rd gear	4th gear
20-40 mph	8.7 sec	14.5 sec
30-50 mph	8.2 sec	12.7 sec
40-60 mph	8.7 sec	13.7 sec

STANDING QUARTER MILE:
Fastest run .... 21.2 sec
Average of all runs .... 21.4 sec

SPEEDOMETER ERROR:
Indicated mph:	30	40	50	60	70
Actual mph:	29	39	48	57	67

SPECIFICATIONS

ENGINE:
Cylinders .... four, horizontally opposed
Bore and stroke .. 83 mm (3.27 in.) by 69 mm (2.72 in.)
Cubic capacity .... 1493 cc (91.1 cu in.)
Compression ratio .... 7.5 to 1
Valves .... push rod overhead
Carburettors ... single downdraught, automatic choke
Fuel pump .... mechanical
Oil filter .... yes, plus oil cooler
Power at rpm .... 53 (SAE) at 4200
Torque at rpm .... 78 ft/lb at 2600

TRANSMISSION:
Type .... four-speed, all-syncromesh
Clutch .... single dry plate
Gear lever location .... central floor
Overall ratio:
1st	15.675
2nd	8.497
3rd	5.199
4th	3.671
Final drive	4.125 to 1

CHASSIS AND RUNNING GEAR:
Construction ...... tubular centre section, welded-on
platform
Suspension, front .... torsion bars, trailing arms
Suspension, rear ... torsion bars, trailing arms, swing
axles
Shock absorbers .... telescopic
Steering type .... worm and roller
Turns 1 to 1 .... 2.6
Turning circle .... 35 ft
Steering wheel diameter .... 15½ in.
Brakes, type .... disc front, drum rear
Dimensions .... NA
Friction area .... NA

DIMENSIONS:
Wheelbase	7 ft 10½ in.
Track front	4 ft 3¼ in.
Track, rear	4 ft 5½ in.
Length	13 ft 4 in.
Height	4 ft 11 in.
Width	5 ft 1 in.
Fuel tank capacity	8.8 gal

TYRES:
Size 5.60-15
Pressures 20-26
Make on test car .... Goodyear G8

GROUND CLEARANCE:
Registered .... 7 in.

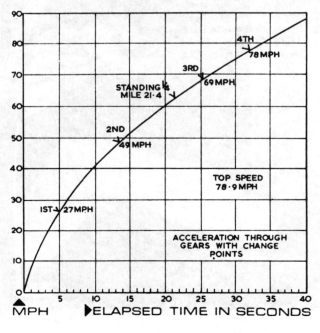

Acceleration graph — ACCELERATION THROUGH GEARS WITH CHANGE POINTS. 4TH 78 MPH, 3RD 69 MPH, STANDING ¼ MILE 21·4, 2ND 49 MPH, 1ST 27 MPH, TOP SPEED 78·9 MPH. MPH / ELAPSED TIME IN SECONDS.

the front, together with a dual braking system and a transparent fluid reservoir (everybody's catching up with the Japanese on these). Other effects of the American regulations include a collapsible steering column, pop-out rear vision mirror, squashy knobs on the dash and a very neat impact-resistant glovebox lock. You also get a 12-volt ignition system, electric fuel gauge, vacuum washers and locking seat backs.

All right, so VW made changes and this time the changes did make sense. But how good is the car? The price — $1998 including tax — seems spot on, particularly as nobody in his right mind could expect to sell a beetle for over $2000, and particularly now the Japanese cars have been restored to a sane price comparison. The standard of finish, with new mock-perforated seat trim, is a little better than it was on the locally-made cars and in any case is right up to the Volkswagen tradition of making all ends meet and having no rough spots anywhere. You can't fault the car on finish.

However, it still has the pitfalls that come as standard equipment with this old body design, and no amount of increased glass area or altered trim fabric can conceal them. First off, it is noticeably and annoyingly cramped inside. You just can't get away from the fact that the body shape does not allow four people to sit comfortably, when you compare it with a Morris 1100 or a Corona — both in the same price bracket — or even with a Mini, which has a much shorter wheelbase. The rear side windows don't open and the sloping back window tends to collect raindrops on the outside and fog on the inside, so it all starts to get a bit hopeless.

But by the same token the other advantages are still there. The ride, always good, is if anything better, and with its 15 in. wheels the beetle romps over rough stuff better than most cars of around this size and price. The engine is still relatively lowly-stressed and will take an enormous amount of punishment. The gearbox is still marvellous and the car's general durability — although no longer as legendary as VW would have you believe — is well above par for the course.

But it's surprising how our values change. The 1300 beetle went slightly better than the 1200, but the 1500 is not that markedly faster. The engine is typically deliberately under-breathed, with single carburettor and maximum torque developed at 2600 rpm, although the power peak is 4200 rpm. Fuel consumption is proportionally worse — we averaged between 26 and 29 mpg hard-driven, but we can't see the car returning anyone more than 33 mpg in the best conditions. A top speed of 78 mph is not marvellous these days, although you must allow for the VW's ability to cruise endlessly at full bore without harm and with very low piston speeds. But third gear overtaking demands good judgment, particularly around 60 mph when to go-or-no-go rests on a decision whether to use third or top.

However, there is a decided boost to mid-range torque that shows up markedly around town. Between 25 and 45 mph the little car really pulls hard, and even though you still must use the gears it has a good reserve of useful acceleration in second and third for picking those traffic gaps. The noise level seems lower than that of the 1300, but this must be a strictly subjective assessment. First gear is still too low, but second is nicely flexible. The car is now far more versatile in top gear, and can actually trickle along at 18-20 mph in top and then accelerate away reasonably smoothly, except for a mild flat spot in the test car.

The gearlever was shortened, straightened, and moved almost 3 ins. rearward to give a more positive feel than that of the old cranked lever. However, the end result is still that you have to stretch a little for first and third if you like to drive with the seat back any distance. But the gearbox is still delightfully smooth and fast, with less "clunk" than before. On the test car, which was still very new, we found second gear a little hard to engage at times.

The car stops very well without fade, hooking or pulling, but on a wet or loose surface the discs will lock the front wheels first, which indicates that the engineers still haven't been able to balance out the front/rear braking effort against the considerable rearward basis. By the same token the handbrake (also shortened) will lock the back wheels, which is most reassuring. The pedal is not assisted, and pressures aren't very high, but there is still some feedback to the pedal, which is not helped by the over-centre action. Otherwise the pedals are nicely placed, although the rubber pad kept slipping off the accelerator in the test car.

We liked the steering a lot. It is sensitive and quite accurate, very light to use and with only some reaction on rough roads. There is none of the feedback which older VWs develop through the rim. The handling is still VW in that it is generally neutral changing to oversteer, but the little car sticks far better than before. But when it finally slides it lets go a little suddenly. However, this happens — and we couldn't say this about earlier cars — at higher road speeds than most drivers will ever reach. For normal fast driving the car is quite stable and enjoyable, and is now a good handler in anyone's language. The headlights are incredibly good, with excellent spread and reach — far different to the old cars.

We liked the interior a lot. All the control knobs are flexible, and the windscreen washers shoot a thick jet of water on to the screen. The glovebox shuts with a combination twist-and-magnet system that ensures the lid won't fly open in a shunt. The quarter vents lock with cunning little round knobs that will defy any thief with a crooked bit of wire, because you can flip the catch but the knob must be pulled out to make the catch clear the lock. Door handles are little recessed hooks and the window winders are also flexible. Unfortunately the glass needs five turns to raise or lower — far too many. The interior mirror covers the entire rear window, but a real bonus is the exterior mirror — one of the wide rectangular type that scan an incredible amount of road behind. These are by far the best exterior mirrors in the business.

The seats have not changed in shape, but now have catches in the squabs to lock them when down. In the test car the front passenger seat and the rear seat jiggled and squeaked when empty. The German philosophy is that a firm seat is better than a soft seat, and after a hundred miles or so you find yourself agreeing with this. The seats are fairly wide and flat and don't seem to offer much sideways support but the VW can't generate the cornering forces that will upset the occupants. Entry to the rear seat is not easy, as the squabs won't fold very far forward before binding on the cushion, leaving the odd greasy mark, incidentally. A multi-sided cam allows the squab to be adjusted for rake — and you can get very comfortable at the wheel.

The floor is a mixture of rubber and very tough carpeting, and the interior is quite easy to clean. The outside of the car is, as always, easy to wash, with good quality brightwork and a deep paint finish that promises years of rust-free life. We also liked the headlight flasher incorporated with the dipswitch in the stalk on the left of the steering column, and the

CONTINUED ON PAGE 93

39

**staff car
36,000-mile
report**

by Arnold Clifford

Volkswagen 1200

*Many fine qualities, handling
good in dry, poor on wet roads,
no sign of rust or corrosion*

IF the pre-war craze for giving cars pet names persisted today, I would have no hesitation in naming this 1965 VW 1200 Jekyll and Hyde. Never have I known a car with such a dual personality, which makes it extremely difficult to write without bias about a car which, in many ways, is such a joy to possess but which, on the other hand, can sometimes be such misery to drive. In fact, it says much for the car that the usual 24,000-mile report was dropped in favour of a 36,000-mile assessment, because the VW's ruggedness and reliability were such that mere 12,000-mile stints provided very little to write about.

A driver's attitude to his car must, of course, be conditioned by his priorities in desirable characteristics. Top of my list of requirements are: lively acceleration, good brakes, roadholding, all-round visibility and driving comfort. Because of this, the Beetle is not my ideal car, but in all fairness I must say that after two years and 24,000 miles with VW ELR 571C I have acquired a considerable respect and admiration for its many fine qualities.

Handling

In the 3½ years since this car was made, VW have modified the suspension and running gear of the Beetle to good effect but in my estimation the greatest fault of this early car is its poor handling on wet roads. The back end will swing round on the slightest provocation although it is difficult to know how much to blame the car and how much the (original) tyres. If wind and rain are encountered at the same time, driving the VW becomes a positive misery. On dry roads, handling is good, the steering being light and precise and only when cornering fast is some oversteer noticeable. In snow, too, traction was found to be particularly good.

In his 12,000 mile report (*Motor,* w/e July 23, 1966) Anthony Curtis mentioned front-wheel locking when braking but very rarely have I experienced this: it was the back end that usually went first. He also suggested that the lack of wet-road adhesion was due to the type of Michelin tyres fitted as standard and that some improvement could be made by fitting radial-ply tyres at the rear and cross-ply at the front. VW service agents I have spoken to have suggested that radials all round would effect considerable improvement but I have had no opportunity of trying these as the original tyres are still on the car, still with some 2½-3½ mm. of tread left.

Visibility leaves much to be desired, because the screen wiper spindles are offset to the driver's side to give the best wipe pattern for left-hand drive. This leaves a large triangular unwiped area which, combined with the thick door pillar, seriously restricts the view on right-hand turns. This is something for which there can be no excuse. The makers have long had a good export market in right-hand drive countries and should by 1965 have arranged for a

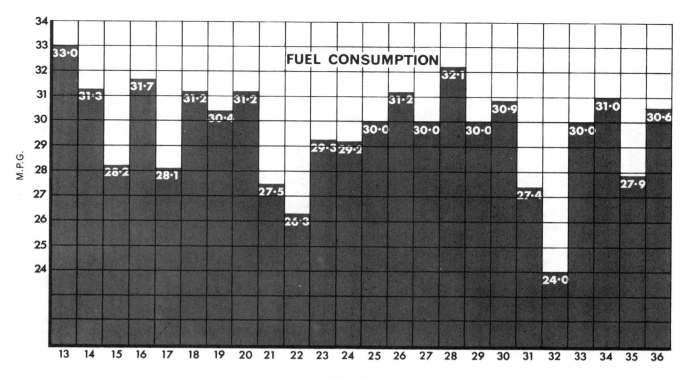

FUEL CONSUMPTION

M.P.G.

Miles x 1000

Petrol consumption, largely of 93 octane, has been fairly consistent at around 30 m.p.g. except during the initial period of the twin carburetter conversion at 21,000 miles and at around 32,000 miles during a bad spell of winter weather.

VW 36,000 mile report

suitable modification. Apart from this, the wipers work well, and strongly. The air-pressurized screen washer is also efficient, but it was soon found essential to check the water level in the bottle at frequent intervals and keep the air pressure up to 36 p.s.i.

Performance

Apart from the restrictions on acceleration imposed by wet weather conditions, ELR 571C is comparatively lively, especially so after a Speedwell twin Stromberg Sprint conversion set was fitted at 21,000 miles. (*Motor,* w/e May 20, 1967.) This has improved performance, except top gear acceleration, and also improved the maximum speed. (See comparative performance table.) This deterioration in top gear performance, however, is of little consequence as the VW demands the use of the revs and the gearbox—and the gearchange is a delight. The twin carburetters have made very little difference to fuel consumption, the average, up to the time of their fitting, being 30.6 m.p.g. and since then, 29.3 m.p.g. and it should be mentioned here that some 30% of the car's use has been in London's traffic.

Unfortunately, it has given rise to two problems, one major and one minor. Fitting it into the already overcrowded engine compartment has made it extremely difficult to get at the two forward sparking plugs. One garage took four hours to get them out and put them back. A manual choke replaces the automatic choke and first-time starting is not now quite so certain. In fact, in cold weather, it is desirable to pull out the choke just before switching off to ensure a quick start next morning. Although first-time starting in the coldest weather is almost 100% certain—it could be guaranteed with the original automatic choke—the engine takes some time to settle down to pull strongly, and the heater also takes about five minutes before it gives a reasonable flow of warm air. However, as air is bled from the engine cooling system it is not particularly fresh and it is not unusual for petrol fumes to be drawn in.

Durability and reliability

The interior of the VW may be somewhat austere, but the quality of the coachwork and trim is beyond praise. After 36,000 miles, the paintwork is near perfect, except for some chipping at the front caused by stones being thrown up by other vehicles and scuffing of the door pillars by shoes. The chrome, too, is still in excellent condition. There is no sign of rust or corrosion at the usual tell-tale spots, such as the bottom edges of the doors. None of those annoying little faults, like door handles falling off, or trim coming adrift, has been experienced. The quarter lights still open and close perfectly, the rubber flooring is almost unmarked, and not one light bulb has failed.

The car has been remarkably free from rattles and squeaks, the only noise, quite minor, coming from the doors and caused by flexural movement when traversing rough ground. Of course, as is to be expected with an air-cooled motor, there is some engine noise but this is more noticeable to people outside the car than to those inside and it gets left behind at speed. Rough road surfaces can be heard as a rumble as well as felt but I do not find this particularly distracting and it is compensated for by the firm feel of the ride.

For me, the driving seat is not comfortable, being too deep from front to back for one of my height—I am 5ft. 8in.—and the hard edge presses uncomfortably into the backs of my knees unless I use a cushion at the small of my back. The rake of the seat back is adjustable but even in its rearmost position it is still somewhat uncomfortably upright.

Of course, troubles have been experienced, but the overall impression is of rugged reliability—of a car that will always get you there and will go on for ever, uncomplaining. The car has, in fact, let me down on the road four times, but it cannot be blamed for two of them. The first time was just after the Speedwell kit had been fitted when, quite suddenly, the car refused to answer to the accelerator and remained at tick-over. Examination revealed that the throttle linkage had come adrift. Fortunately, the spindle was still lying on the engine undertray, and a locknut was found in the tin of bits and pieces I always carry.

Then at near the 27,000-mile mark, the electrics failed one morning on the way to the office and the car had to be left in the hands of a nearby garage. When I collected it later I learned that the cause was a fractured cable between the ignition switch and starter motor.

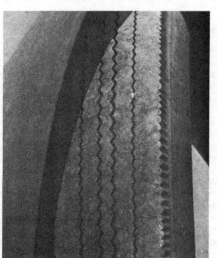

Above: get behind a lorry on a wet country road and the VW driver will soon find the vital 45° view to the right severely restricted, because the wiper spindles are mounted for left-hand drive.

Left: the Michelin tyres originally fitted as standard may not have good wet road adhesion properties but they last. This offside front tyre still had 3 mm. of tread after 36,000 miles.

Right: the badly worn clutch was replaced at 18,900 miles.

Below: after 36,000 miles there is still no sign of corrosion round the bottom of the doors or at the lower edges of the wings.

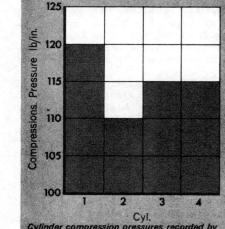

Cylinder compression pressures recorded by VW service agents, Hawksley Court Garage Ltd., of London N.16 at the 18,000-mile service.

VW 36,000 mile report

continued

A puncture in the nearside front tyre gave me cause to appreciate the easy operation of the jack. Then at around 34,500 miles, I began to experience sluggish starting culminating eventually in having to suffer the humiliation of a push start in traffic. A new battery cured that trouble.

Service history

Volkswagen 1200 ELR 571C was originally bought in April 1965 and I took it over in August 1966 with 12,200 miles on the clock. My first impressions were that the brakes were very fierce,

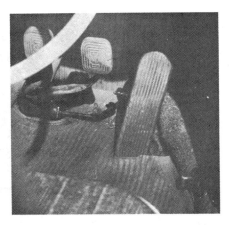

Constant scuffing by shoes has failed to make much impression on the rubber carpet.

Before and after the Speedwell Twin Stromberg conversion. The forward sparking plugs lie almost inaccessible in the depths below the carburetters.

particularly at low speeds, and that there was some clutch noise. However, as the miles built up there was some improvement, and I assumed that the fact that the car had been left in our car park for nearly a month before I took over, could account for some "rustiness".

By the time the 15,000 mile service became due, the clutch was behaving itself but the brakes were still fierce and noisy if applied when the front wheels were turned out of the straight-ahead position. Examination revealed a small hair crack in the leading shoe of the nearside front brake. Both front brakes were relined and the opportunity taken to clean out all brake drums as there was some accumulation of dust.

The clutch started to become noisy again and at 18,900 miles it was replaced. At the same time, the crankshaft and mainshaft oil seals were renewed. The total cost was just under £20. When the car had done nearly 21,000 miles, it was run into at the back denting the engine cover, twisting the bumper and pushing the tail pipes out of line. The repair bill came to £35. At 23,000 miles the silencer developed a leak and a replacement was fitted: the shunt in April had obviously weakened it. This cost just under £8. At 33,700, the horn and indicators became weak in operation, the fault being traced to a loose connection in the steering column head. Then at 34,000 miles, the horn, indicators and brake lights failed. A blown fuse was the cause.

Oil consumption has been consistently negligible. The engine oil has been changed every 6,000 miles, but apart from this the amount of oil necessary for topping up to level has been only $3\frac{1}{2}$ pints in nearly 25,000 miles.

The 36,000 mile service, which, because of holidays, was not carried out until 37,000 miles were on the clock, brought a report that the brakes were in need of relining all round.

And with the mention of holidays. I would conclude with a reference to the luggage carrying capacity of the Beetle. It really is deceptive. The front luggage compartment which looks so shallow will take a large expanding suitcase, so too will the space behind the rear seat, but it is not easy to get at. **M**

COMPARATIVE PERFORMANCE

	Road Test Car	ELR 571C Before Sprint Conversion	ELR 571C After Sprint Conversion
Maximum Speed			
Mean	71.0 m.p.h.	70.9	74.1
Best	74.0	74.3	80.0
Acceleration			
0-30 m.p.h.	7.5s	5.4	4.9
0-40	11.7	9.4	8.1
0-50	18.2	15.5	12.6
0-60	32.6	27.4	20.3
In top			
20-40 m.p.h.	13.2s	15.4	18.6
30-50	16.8	15.9	19.8
40-60	27.1	24.2	24.0

What VW Owners Say

We asked 10 VW owners for their opinions. Almost without exception they praised the reliability, ruggedness, general finish and low running costs.

Six criticised its handling in the wet and in cross winds and three who had changed to radial-ply tyres reported handling as much improved. Brakes were generally agreed to be good, acceleration fair, and cruising performance excellent. Three owners reported clutch replacement after 12,000 miles, one having to have the clutch replaced four times in 35,000 miles. The heat came in for some criticism, largely because the system does not provide for fresh air ventilation. The luggage space, too, was thought to be somewhat inadequate.

All but one reported fuel consumption in the region of 34-40 m.p.g. Of the nine who used their nearest VW dealer all but one reported excellent service.

Would they buy another of this model? Eight say yes, two say no.

VW 1500 Automatic

There is no stopping an idea once its time has come, as Ada Louise Huxtable was surely not the first to say (*C/D*, January; April; July). In fact, ideas may only be a matter of timing. Like Volkswagen's "Automatic Stick Shift," for example. Introduced 9 months ago, this $135 option is now ordered on approximately 40% of all the VW Beetles sold in the U.S.

Widely unheralded is the fact that Volkswagen went through all this before, six years ago. In '62, Volkswagen announced the "Saxomat" transmission, only to drop it again in '63. The world wasn't ready for a VW with an automatic clutch. Perhaps the VW drivers of the day were too virile to pay extra for a sissy transmission. After all, the VW had an unsynchronized "crashbox" up until 1952.

But times have changed. Not only is the world full of little old ladies in Spring-o-lators, but they're all driving Beetles and they're apparently ready for an automatic transmission with a sock-o name. You'll have to admit "Automatic Stick Shift" is a lot more sock-o, geriatrics-wise, than "Saxomat."

All the Automatic Stick Shift is is a regular VW's 4-speed manual transmission with first gear removed, a tighter final drive installed (4.38 v. 4.12), and a torque converter added (with a 2.1-to-one ratio at stall—which more than makes up for the missing first gear).

The clutch is retained, just to decouple everything during shifts or when idling around in neutral. It's connected to a vacuum cylinder which is triggered by a pressure-sensitive switch buried in the root of the shift lever, *ergo* no clutch pedal.

In other words, the A.S.S. (if Volkswagen will excuse the acronym) is exactly like the Porsche Sportomatic (*C/D*, March), except that it has three gears to the Porsche's four.

The VW's torque converter is made by Borg-Warner, and unlike the Sportomatic, has a fairly low stall speed (about 2000 rpm to the Sportomatic's 3000), so it feels more closely coupled to the engine's speed than the looser Porsche unit. Nevertheless, VWs have always felt very *mechanical*, and the A.S.S., while no gluepot-twirler like the old Chevy Powerglide, just doesn't feel as solid as you'd expect a VW to be.

In operation, the A.S.S. is a snap. First gear starts are recommended only for getaways with a heavy load, or on steep hills, or for "sports-type driving." So, thanks to the magic of hydrodynamics, you normally drive away in what was once third gear, and shift once, into what was fourth. The one-time second gear is now labeled "Lo," the ex-third is now "1st" and the old fourth is now "2nd."

Acceleration with the A.S.S., surprisingly, isn't adversely affected all that much. Quarter-mile figures for the various models look like this:

Model	1/4-mi. time & speed	
1200	22.8 sec.	56 mph
1300	25.7	59
1500	20.4	65
A.S.S.*	21.1	63
A.S.S.**	22.0	62
1600†	20.8	65

*Using "Lo" & "1st"; **Using "2nd" only;
†Fastback

Obviously, thrill-crazed, speed-hungry fun-seekers will not be able to satisfy their base urges with the A.S.S., no matter what they try. Except for the fact that the torque converter fluid could boil over, you may as well leave the car in high gear all the time. (A warning light goes on if the fluid overheats; it goes off when you shift into a lower gear.) You *can* whip it into "Lo" for the occasional Red Light GP, but you're going to lose anyway, so why bother?

The *real* issue is whether or not the A.S.S. is worth $135 extra. If it was the A.S.S. alone, the answer would probably be "no" (Chevy's shift-it-yourself "automatic" costs a mere $65). However, the issue is pleasantly complicated by the fact that you get an entirely new rear suspension layout when you order the A.S.S.

Gone is the pure, unadulterated swing-axle system of yore. In its stead: a modified swing-axle with double-jointed half-shafts and diagonally pivoted semi-trailing arms (like BMW, Triumph, Porsche, Datsun, and the new Mercedes—not to mention Volkswagen's own box-like vans, trucks, and mini-buses). The change to this universally accepted rear suspension system, says Volkswagen, is because the insertion of a torque converter forced the

(*Text continued on page* **47**; *Specifications overleaf*)

Although it might be heresy,
the Volkswagen Automatic Stick Shift,
with its Porsche-type transmission
and new rear suspension, should
be designated as a new model—
it very definitely is
a much more secure car than
the standard Beetle.

PHOTOGRAPHY: IRV TYBEL

ACCELERATION standing ¼ mile, seconds

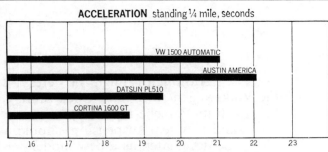

- VW 1500 AUTOMATIC
- AUSTIN AMERICA
- DATSUN PL510
- CORTINA 1600 GT

(scale: 16 17 18 19 20 21 22 23)

BRAKING 70-0 mph panic stop, feet

- VW 1500 AUTOMATIC
- AUSTIN AMERICA
- DATSUN PL510
- CORTINA 1600 GT

(scale: 160 170 180 190 200 210 220 230)

FUEL ECONOMY RANGE mpg

- VW 1500 AUTOMATIC
- AUSTIN AMERICA
- DATSUN PL510
- CORTINA 1600 GT

(scale: 6 10 14 18 22 26 30 34)

PRICE AS TESTED dollars x 1000

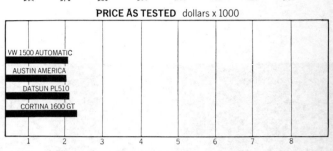

- VW 1500 AUTOMATIC
- AUSTIN AMERICA
- DATSUN PL510
- CORTINA 1600 GT

(scale: 1 2 3 4 5 6 7 8)

VOLKSWAGEN 1500

Importer: Volkswagen of America, Inc.
818 Sylvan Avenue
Englewood Cliffs, New Jersey
Vehicle type: Rear-engine, rear-wheel-drive, 4-passenger 2-door sedan
Price as tested: $2078.50
(Manufacturer's suggested retail price, including all options listed below, Federal excise tax, dealer preparation and delivery charges; does not include state and local taxes, license or freight charges)
Options on test car:
Basic sedan with sunroof ($1789.00), leatherette upholstery ($30.00), whitewall tires ($29.50), semi-automatic transmission ($135.00), Blaupunkt AM radio ($85.00), dealer preparation ($30.00).

ENGINE
Type: 4-cylinder opposed, air-cooled aluminum-magnesium block and heads, 4 main bearings
Bore x stroke . . . . 3.27 x 2.72 in, 83 x 69 mm
Displacement . . . . 91.1 cu in, 1493 cc
Compression ratio . . . . 7.5 to one
Carburetion . . . . 1 x 1-bbl Solex 30 PICT Z
Valve gear . . Pushrod-operated overhead valves
Power (SAE) . . . . 53 bhp @ 4200 rpm
Torque (SAE) . . . . 78 lbs/ft @ 2600 rpm
Specific power output . . . . 0.58 bhp/cu in, 35.5 bhp/liter

DRIVE TRAIN
Transmission . . . . 3-speed, all-synchro with automatic clutch and torque converter
Max. torque converter ratio . . . . 2.2 to one
Final drive ratio . . . . 4.38 to one

Gear	Ratio	Mph/1000 rpm	Max. test speed
I	2.06	9.1	40 mph (4400 rpm)
II	1.26	14.7	65 mph (4400 rpm)
III	.89	18.6	76 mph (4080 rpm)

DIMENSIONS AND CAPACITIES
Wheelbase . . . . 94.5 in
Track . . . . F: 51.6 in, R: 53.4 in
Length . . . . 158.7 in
Width . . . . 61.0 in
Height . . . . 59.0 in
Ground clearance . . . . 6.9 in
Curb weight . . . . 1920 lbs
Weight distribution, F/R 40.4/59.6%
Battery capacity . . . . 12 volts, 45 amp/hr
Generator capacity . . . . 360 watts
Fuel capacity . . . . 10.6 gal
Oil capacity . . . . 2.5 qts

SUSPENSION
F: Ind., trailing arms, torsion bars, anti-sway bar
R: Ind., double-jointed half shafts, torsion bars with trailing arms, diagonal links

STEERING
Type . . . . Worm and roller
Turns lock-to-lock 2.8
Turning circle curb to curb . . . . 35.3 ft

BRAKES
F: . . . . 9.0 x 1.57 cast iron drums
R: . . . . 9.0 x 1.57 cast iron drums

WHEELS AND TIRES
Wheel size . . . . 15 x 4.0-in
Wheel type . . . . Stamped steel, 4-bolt
Tire make and size . . . . Continental 5.60-15
Tire type . . . . Tubeless, 4 PR
Test inflation pressures . . F: 16 psi, R: 24 psi
Tire load rating . . . . . 785 lbs per tire @ 24 psi

PERFORMANCE
Zero to	Seconds
30 mph	4.6
40 mph	7.4
50 mph	12.3
60 mph	16.6
70 mph	29.0

Standing ¼-mile . . . . 21.1 sec @ 63.0 mph
Top speed . . . . 76 mph
80-0 mph . . . . 219 ft (.75 G)
Fuel mileage . . . . . . 22-26 mpg on regular fuel
Cruising range . . . . 233-275 mi

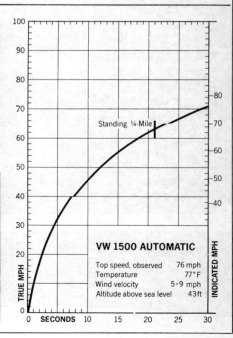

VW 1500 AUTOMATIC

Standing ¼-Mile

Top speed, observed	76 mph
Temperature	77°F
Wind velocity	5-9 mph
Altitude above sea level	43ft

TRUE MPH / INDICATED MPH / SECONDS

VW 1500 AUTOMATIC

(Continued from page 44)

transmission forward, so the differential no longer lines up with the rear wheels.

Bull.

The new rear suspension is to improve the Beetle's handling. Which needed it. Which the new suspension does.

The "tippy" feeling of the old *old* Beetle is virtually eliminated by the new set-up. In truth, only a vestige remains in the Beetles with standard suspension, now that Volkswagen has modified the weight distribution, the center of gravity, the roll couple, and pulled a few other tricks.

The A.S.S. Beetle still understeers initially and at low speeds, still oversteers finally and at high speeds. But it is more predictable and less scary than, say, a '55 Beetle.

Despite the improvements wrought by the new suspension, this car is still not one of the better-handling small cars, losing by an enormous margin to more modern designs like Alec Issigonis' Mini.

Handling and the semi-automatic transmission aside, our test car is the same old Bug we tested in January, 1967. This ubiquitous vehicle, tracing its lineage back to the mid-Thirties, now accounts for almost 5% of *all* cars sold in the U.S. Yet it continues to defy Mittelamerika with such arrogance and bossiness as evidenced by these blurbs from the owner's manual: "In front of you—the instrument panel," and, "A clean smart car looks better." Come to think of it, little old ladies talk like that, too.

We have a few minor gripes and a couple of big ones—those throne-like front seats. Their built-in headrests may be the safest thing since Ivory Snow, but they do nothing whatsoever to alleviate the claustrophobia that is inevitable in the cave-like interior of a Beetle.

On the whole, the VW's safety-padded controls are among the easiest to actually get a hold of and operate. Some automakers have recessed or softened their controls to the point where the cars are only barely drivable.

Minor beef: the brake pedal is extremely awkward to use with either foot. First, it's about six inches aft of the accelerator pedal. Second, it's pivoted from the floor, not—like most 20th century automobiles—from above, so it's difficult to get the right angle to proportion your braking effort. Lower the brake or raise the gorge.

The semi-trailing arm suspension is available only as part of the A.S.S. option "package," just as the electronic fuel injection is only available on the Fastback and Squareback models. Which points up the fact that a Volkswagen is no longer just a Volkswagen. There are almost as many models as any Detroit automaker

CONTINUED ON PAGE 121

EMPI GTV

(Continued from page 35)

belt. The brave little engine started with a quick twist of the key and I gave them my no-sweat-I-know-all-about-cars reassuring nod as I began the search for reverse. If you're a VW veteran you know that finding reverse is a good trick even for an expert, but the GTV (naturally) had EMPI's quick-shift mechanism which reduces the H-pattern to the size of a commemorative postage stamp. You guessed it. I made a couple false starts at the shop wall before I found the elusive gear. Made a mental note to order humble pie for lunch and headed for the freeway to L.A., wondering if the Sunset Strip bunch would accept me despite my thinning hair.

Right off I noticed that the extractor exhaust made that kind of defiant buzz that prompts Sprite and Spitfire drivers to downshift and air conditioned Buick drivers to shake their heads in disgust. As expected, it was torquey as hell, for a beetle that is, and all of those extra ccs made me feel pretty smug as I buzzed along the desert blacktop. Well, I never was big on restraint and it wasn't very likely that there would be a radar trap out in the middle of nowhere. Vittone would never know, so I just opened up that Solex and let it happen. "Not bad for a Volkswagen," I thought when it peaked out several needle widths past 90 even though the tach indicated only 4200 rpm. Obviously it would have gone faster with a shorter gear, but I consoled myself with the thought that even super beetles weren't meant for LSR assaults.

In the course of the following few days fun-seeking I ended up, true to form, at Orange County Raceway for a little banzai session. "All in the interest of obtaining accurate performance data," I told my bothersome conscience which had been kicking up quite a fuss about abusing Vittone's car, and forthwith I discovered that I was more right than my conscience. Laugh if you like, but muscle beetles are more fun than a lot of real cars on a drag strip. The terminal speed always came out in the 72.20s no matter what I did, but the ETs depended purely on how many Rs the tach said when I popped the clutch. After a particularly satisfying 17.91-second run with a 4000 rpm start that did the impossible—squeaked the rear tires—my conscience returned with unappeasable fury so I headed for the road course to wear out a different part of the car.

No one has ever put me in the A.J. Foyt category but I'm not afraid to push a *car* through a fast corner—a commitment that heretofore has not extended to VWs. Man, they're not to be trifled with. They feel so narrow and twitchy. Even Vittone admits to fixing a lot of crinkled roofs. So that's when the surprise came. The GTV is a whole new deal. The body roll is less than you'd expect, and, even though it's still a bit twitchy, it twitches when you want it to and not whenever it feels the mood. It still seems incredible, but I actually hung the tail out in a big slide without going straight over on my gourd. Doing that in a standard VW is like wearing a Don't Kick Me sign on Muscle Beach. I'd still be more careful of a GTV than most cars but for a VW it rates Magna Cum Laude.

Sorry to say the GTV didn't cause much of a stir on the Strip. The wheels weren't really offset far enough, and I later discovered that the pin striping wasn't sufficiently psychedelic to cause even a faint hallucination. Besides, I think they knew it wasn't my personality the muscle beetle was expressing anyway.

There was no reason to hurry back to Riverside so I took it easy, wallowing quietly in the thought that the GTV was a good 7 mph faster in the quarter than an ordinary 1500 and confident that it probably wouldn't tip over no matter what I did. When I pulled into EMPI that same mechanic started inspecting the car for oil leaks and other signs of distress and Vittone asked, "How do you like my car?"

"Terrific for a Volkswagen," I said—which was something of a cop-in. At that I was lucky. There was a moment somewhere between Vittone and the door when it looked like I'd have to confess the car really turned me on. ●

THE BEETLES BURROW

A Picture Tour of VW's Wolfsburg Plant
by Robert Marx

Once they put the roof back on some 20 years ago Volkswagen's Wolfsburg plant became and still is the world's largest. And in this relatively short period of time it has turned out well over 12 million Beetles all outwardly looking pretty much the same.

It is this surface sameness that also has permitted a degree of automation in the plant that may be matched by some of the most modern steel mills but not by any other automaker. Under the surface, of course, there is hardly a part today that could be interchanged with the original car. But the dimensions are about the same and this fact, in turn, allows the investment in gargantuan machines and fixtures that in some instances individually have cost more than all the equipment combined in more orthodox operations such as Porsche or Glas.

Take for example, the automatic body jig, measuring 200-feet long and 50-feet high, that gobbles the roof and front and rear body sections and welds them together in 303 places to create 240 complete bodies every hour. It is operated by a few technicians whose main job is to monitor the gauges and lights that flash warnings of a rare malfunction. If traditional assembly methods had been employed, it is estimated that 440 men and 100,000 square feet of manufacturing space would have been required instead of just about one-tenth of that occupied by the jig.

You can see now why VW's reluc-

tance to replace the Beetle is not entirely due to its continued popularity. Dozens of machines like this jig and miles of specialized conveyor systems would be obsoleted, not to mention the losses due to plant downtime and worker retraining.

Although almost all body stamping and assembly operations, including paint, are completely mechanized and you see few people about, the scene changes abruptly when you come into the well-lit trim and final assembly halls. Hundreds of assorted specialists swarm over

This is where the Beetle begins. Sheet steel is fed from one of many large rolls (center) into heavy body panel presses where the part is cut, formed and trimmed in one automated operation.

Supervisory technicians discuss adjustments in front of part of the body jig, a completely automatic unit which takes roof, front and rear body sections and welds them together.

As the welded body shells exit from the jig, a few human welders riding on trolleys are required to finish inaccessible joints with hand guns.

Photos by Robert Marx

Pretty girls in thought-provoking but practical attire almost outnumber the men on the trim lines. The lines move slowly, allowing this fraulein to relax while she installs a window regulator.

The "USA" sign on the tip of the front hood (left) tells the works that U. S. specification glass, lamps, speedometer and other special equipment must be installed.

Some idea of the immensity of the plant may be gained from this picture of rows of painted bodies on their way to the trim lines. Enameling is done in automated ovens where spray guns with electronic sensors follow the body contours much like a blind person reading braille.

BEETLE TOUR

six identical and parallel assembly lines to which overhead converyors bring the car bodies, by now enameled and shiny and with doors and hoods in place. Here everything from wiring and windows to lights, door panels, ash trays and assorted accessories are put in place. Most visitors are amazed at the large number of young people working there, including many attractive girls. Perhaps a majority are non-Germans brought in from as far away as Turkey and Algeria to alleviate the acute shortage of native workers.

At the end of these trim lines the completed bodies are lifted off and conveyed, again on overhead trolleys, to the final assembly lines where the chassis, with engine and transmission already in place, are mated to the bodies. After installation of tires, batteries and a bit of gas, the finished VW's are driven off to

This chassis is close to meeting its partner for life, unless it ultimately gets a second chance as a dune buggy. Man in foreground with paper is an inspector. There is one to every nine workmen and his word is law.

The ultimate in fuel economy—one-man pedal power? No, just a scene on the trim-assembly line where up to four people at a time converge on the slowly moving car bodies. Man working in the engine compartment is actually sitting on the conveyor belt while the girl walks.

The Beetle now has its shell and an omnipresent inspector, identifiable by the emblem on his coveralls, checks once more for scratches or dings that may have been picked up along the line.

This is the critical point in the assembly line where the body meets its chassis. Will it match? It undoubtedly will thanks to 20-years experience with the same methods and parts.

This wheel mounting machine is one of the few machines that Volkswagen adopted from U. S. assembly lines. It centers the wheel and tire and torques all the lugs in one swift operation. Within seconds this Beetle will be drivable and on its way to a customer.

various test stations and then to marshalling yards outside the plant. Engines, transmissions and axles are not made in Wolfsburg but are brought in from specialized VW factories in Hannover, Kassel and Brunswick.

I visited Wolfsburg on a snowy winter day and from some spots on the factory grounds, the bleak towers and barb wire that mark the mined border between East and West are forbiddingly visible. Winter is the best time to tour the plant because visitors are relatively few in number and the guides take you right down among the machinery and workers. In the summer thousands are herded through every day and the large groups are confined to overhead walkways.

My pictures, of course, can only give a glimpse of what goes on in the 384-acre plant, an area so vast that except in certain sections, its 48,000 workers seem to barely populate it.　●

GIANT COMPARISON

TAKE SIX SMALL CARS, ALL PRICED under $1900 and regarded as ideal women's cars, then compare. Which one represents the best buy for a woman? We take a long, hard look at six basic models of the VW, Corolla, Fiat 850, Mini, Torana and Datsun 1000 and come to the conclusion that the ladies have never had it so good.

The figures show an increasing number of Australian women taking to the nation's roads. The booming small car market, the toughest there is here, has plenty to offer. But the choice is not always easy for budget buyers, even if they are beyond the "you-put-petrol-in-this-end-I-think" stage.

Just what IS an ideal woman's car? Here we find some curious contradictions, but one fact emerges clearly: a car is not necessarily "right" for a woman just because it's small. Some small cars, obviously, are better left in the hands of enthusiasts. The Renault 10, in our book, falls into this class. It's one of the best in the small car business, but we are inclined to believe its virtues would be somewhat lost on the average woman driver.

So it boils down to which one to buy. On the following pages we make six suggestions which, we feel, represent the best small car motoring value for women.

How do we rate the aforementioned line-up after several thousand miles of road testing? Well, objectively, the Mini gets the nod, followed by the Torana, Vee Wee, Corolla, Fiat and Datsun. As to why we do, read the reports and summary of each car on pages 45, 46, 47.

To understand our choice it's first necessary to examine what women drivers expect from a car. Probably the thing they want most, apart from ease of driving and reliability, is traffic-ability — the important ability to manoeuvre in congested city traffic. Fancy body lines, sophisticated suspension systems and neck-snapping performance don't make a car any easier for women to park or slide through a narrow slot in traffic to pick up lost time for a hair-dressing appointment or junior's dental appointment.

For most women motorists, then, convenience in city driving is more important than handling on the open road. The average man appears to spend something like 80 per cent of his time driving in town. Women undoubtedly stick more to the suburbs, but the traffic obstacles there are fast becoming just as bad as in the cities.

Ease of driving is a major part of traffic-ability, and here the car's turning circle and lightness of control is another big consideration. The car must be easy to drive. Stiff gear changes, heavy steering, heavy brakes and other driver discomfort factors are not likely to win any friends among the high-heel set.

Roominess is almost as important. The car might be small but, boy, it often has to carry a frightening collection of bits and pieces, apart from the bassinet-shopping bit. Ask any husband about the handbag on wheels caper . . .

Economy of operation comes next. We may be living in affluent times, but second family hacks, no matter how modest, still chew up the brass. MPG, then, is likely to sway many potential female buyers. The single girl probably is just as conscious of a car's petrol-oil sipping rate as the married man.

The need for complete reliability is obvious. Women, more so than men, expect reliability in a car — e v e n though their contribution towards reliable motoring often ends with petrol, oil and an occasional lube job. A car with few servicing problems is therefore needed.

Bolt-on goodies may not impress the average male driver, but women seem to go for them. A well-positioned vanity mirror is more likely to influence a potential woman buyer than the best heater/demister system. Women go for spacious glove boxes, coat hooks, attractive interiors and other sales-geared creature comforts.

We all know safety doesn't sell cars, so it's hard to accurately gauge women driver reactions to safety aids. However, some backyard research on our part leads us to believe that women are more inclined to buckle on seat belts than men. It is therefore reasonable to assume that they're AWARE of the need, particularly if they drive with small children.

Comfort and functional efficiency are just as important to mum on her bi-weekly shopping forays as they are to the man who is behind the wheel two hours a day. This means instrument layout and driving controls must be within easy reach.

Performance, as we mentioned earlier, appears to be relatively unimportant. From our experience, women drivers seem content to get from A to B without the heartburn of the green light grand prix male mob. There are, of course, a few club-footed Cynthias around, but they're the exception rather than the rule.

However, women do like a car to be smooth and free from noise and clamor. For this reason, we ruled out a couple of small Japanese cars (no names, no pack drill and there are no prizes if you guess which ones we mean).

To start at the beginning — on the showroom floor — the Torana, in our view, wins the good looks stakes, followed by the Corolla, Fiat, Datsun, Mini and VW, in that order. The Torana, Corolla and Fiat all share crisp, uncluttered body lines, which should appeal strongly to women buyers. The Datsun's lines are soothingly modern, if a trifle boxy, and the Mini looks like . . . er . . . a Mini.

In the manoeuvrability stakes, t h e Mini killed all opposition with its Lilliputian 10ft. ½in. overall length, compared with the Corolla's 10ft. 7in., the Fiat's 11ft. 8in., the Datsun's 13ft. 1in., the Torana's 13ft. 5in., and the VW's 13ft. 10in. The sheer compactness of the Mini, coupled with its high degree of controllability, gave it the clear edge in both parking and in the city traffic squeeze.

On paper, however, turning circles and steering locks told a different story. The Datsun had the best lock: 26ft. and three turns. The Corolla, 29ft. and 3.2 turns, and the Fiat, 29ft. and 3½ turns, came next, followed by the Mini, 31ft. 7in. and 2 turns, the Torana, 31ft. and 3.4 turns, and the VW, 36ft. and 2½ turns.

In practice, all six were easy cars for women to drive and park. Through-the-gear performances varied, but all kept up well with the traffic. With the VW, however, its long-legged gearing meant keeping a close eye on city speed limits.

Little separated the cars in ease of driving, but the Mini, we felt, was the most fun car to drive. All boasted light controls ideally suited to women drivers.

In the gear-changing department, the Torana's stubby lever was sweetly smooth, while the Mini's lever allowed fast, precise changes with a minimum of fuss. Travel between ratios in the VW was a bit long, but no one would contest the fact that it's one of the best changes in the business. Gear ratios were nicely spaced in the four other cars. All test cars, except the Mini, had full synchromesh.

Clutch action was light in all the cars, allowing smooth, positive changes by women drivers. Driving response was particularly light and sensitive in the Mini, Torana and Corolla.

Braking was pretty much on a par. All shared hydraulics, but the VW and Torana had a divided system as an added safety margin. The Mini, VW, Torana and Fiat systems worked well, resisted locking on dry, stable surfaces and

6 *under $1900*

torana
vw
mini
datsun
fiat 850
corolla

GIANT COMPARISON

VW makes up for lack of boot space with fold-down rear backrest which provides capacious luggage area.

proved relatively fade free. The Corolla's brakes, although adequate, lacked feel. The Datsun's appeared initially spongy, but gave straight-line stops.

The pedals in all six cars were set fairly close together — in the Fiat they were offset to the left — and heel-and-toe changes presented no problems.

Controls and instruments were generally within easy reach of a safety-belted woman driver. Here once again we felt the Mini, with its flat steering wheel, long floor shift and binnacle-mounted instruments, made the best use of available space without affecting driver comfort. Instrumentation in all the cars was a bit on the spartan side — but it told a driver most things she needed to know.

Head and leg room was just about what you'd expect in cars this size— but here the Mini made better use of its usable interior space. Good planning leaves room for four adults and a bit of luggage. The five other cars also seat four in varying degrees of comfort. Leg room in the back in all of them is all and more than the buyer of a low-priced car expects. Apart from the Torana, usable boot space for family needs was nothing to get wildly excited about.

Of the six, the VW and the Fiat were the most flexible for a woman's driver's needs. In each car, the rear seat could be folded down to carry a bassinet or shopping.

Seating in all six test cars consisted of two front buckets and a back bench. Four adults were a comfortable passenger load, even though the back bench in the Torana and VW would squeeze three in at a pinch for short travel. The front seats of the VW, in true Volsky tradition, were firm, but well shaped, while the seats in the Datsun were a bit thin for our taste. All the others gave good back and thigh support.

The Mini emerged as the clear winner in the carry-all department. It had plenty of room for bits and pieces in its full width parcel tray and deep door pockets. The five other cars all had glove boxes of varying sizes and some room behind their back seats for parcels. The VW had leather door pockets for maps, sun glasses and other small paraphernalia.

Economy ranged from 34 mpg up to 42 mpg, with the Mini and the Fiat giving the most miles to each gallon of petrol. The Corolla returned 40 mpg, the Datsun 39 mpg, the Torana 35 mpg and the VW 34 mpg, hard driven over 200 miles. The Mini, with the smallest petrol tank of them all (5½ gallons) had a touring range of 220 miles. The Fiat's range was 284 miles, the Datsun 295 miles, the Torana 250 miles, the Corolla 320 miles and the VW 280 miles.

When we came to compare reliability, it resulted in a photo-finish between the VW and the Mini. Both are completely reliable little cars. The VW finally got the money — and the prize for being the toughest customer in the field. Relia-

bility of a less rugged kind was evident in the Mini — although we know which one will last the longest. Fiat has a good record of longevity, and the Toranas seem to be standing up to it OK. We've heard no serious complaints about the reliability of the two other test cars.

Servicing presents no major headaches with any of the cars. GM-H's nation-wide dealer facilities give the Torana an edge here, but BMC are not really that far behind. VW are quite good, and we've yet to hear of any real problems in servicing the Datsun, Corolla or Fiat.

Trim in the Mini, Torana, VW and Fiat was pretty much on a par — and very good considering the asking price. All six cars had rubber floor mats and seats covered with vinyl plastic that should be relatively easy to clean. The seat coverings in the VW and the Mini appeared to be the sturdiest. The Mini and Torana fought for second place behind the VW in quality of finish.

Performance is not likely to attract women buyers, nor is top speed. In this department the Corolla bolted in, while the Mini finished last. The Corolla, with a 0-50 mph time of 11.6 secs., led the Datsun, 12.1; the Torana, 12.4; the VW, 14.6; the Fiat, 15.2, and the Mini 15.3. The Corolla was the fastest overall, with a top speed of 88 mph. Best from the others was: Torana 85 mph, VW 76 mph, Fiat 78 mph, Datsun 76 mph and Mini 75 mph.

Even in its basic form the Datsun comes out way in front on equipment fitted. It has a heater/demister, two-speed electric wipers, reversing lights

Torana has divided brake system for extra safety in the event of brake line damage

and tinted windows. Heater/demister systems are standard on the Fiat and VW, but extra cost options on the three other cars. Although many of the bolt-on goodies of other Japanese cars are missing on the Corolla, there are other nice touches. For example, arm rests for back-seat passengers are cunningly let into the side panels to expand hip and shoulder room.

All six are powered by four cylinder engines — the Fiat and the VW housing theirs in the back, the Mini transversely in the front. All started readily from cold and pulled quite well immediately, the VW being the most enthusiastic and the Datsun the most reluctant.

The Mini's ride was surprisingly quiet and free from road noise, and good body damping kept road noises at an acceptable level in the Torana and Fiat. The Corolla was reasonably quiet, the Datsun let in a fair amount of wind noise at speed and the VW, while it was more muted than VW's of old, was not as quiet as the others.

The Torana seemed the safest. It had a dished steering wheel at the top of a collapsible steering column, a safety padded instrument panel and safety catches on the front seats. All six had safety rear vision mirrors and seat belts. The Mini, Torana, VW and Fiat all had well-padded sun visors. The Mini was fitted with safety glass all round.

On our next page you'll find our scrutineer's run-down on each car. Now would the ladies please adjust their gloves and step into the centre of the ring? . . .

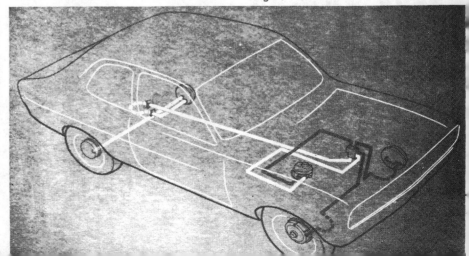

torana

PRICE: $1820, inc. tax.

ENGINE: Four cyl. of 1159 cc capacity, develops 56 bhp at 5400 rpm, on a comp. ratio of 8.5 : 1.

TRANSMISSION: Four speed, all synchromesh, floor shift.

SUSPENSION: Front by independent, long and short arms, coil springs, telescopic shock absorbers; back by coil springs, trailing arms and telescopic shock absorbers.

STEERING: Rack and pinion, 2 turns, 31ft. 7in. turning circle.

BRAKES: Hydraulic drums.

DIMENSIONS: Length 13ft. 5in., width 5ft. 3in., height 4ft. 6in., weight 15 cwt.

TOP SPEED: 85 mph.

FUEL BILL: 35 mpg.

HOW IT HANDLES: Excellent general stability.

THINGS WOMEN WILL LIKE: Light controls; after-sales service.

THINGS WE DIDN'T LIKE: Stubborn cold morning starts; angle of instrument cluster; poor positioning of door arm rests; head room for lanky back seat passengers.

SUMMED UP: A pretty-bodied car with lots of women's appeal.

vw

PRICE: $1789, inc. tax.

ENGINE: Four cyl., rear-mounted, of 1285 cc capacity, develops 50 bhp at 4600 rpm on a comp. ratio of 7.3 : 1.

TRANSMISSION: Four speed, all synchromesh, floor lever.

SUSPENSION: Front by independent trailing arms and torsion bars, anti-roll bar, back by independent swing axles and torsion bars.

STEERING: Worm and roller, 2½ turns lock to lock, and 36ft. turning circle.

BRAKES: Hydraulic drums; divided system.

DIMENSIONS: Length 13ft. 6in., width 5ft. 3.8in., height 4ft. 11in., weight 15½ cwt.

TOP SPEED: 76 mph.

FUEL BILL: 34 mpg.

HOW IT HANDLES: Good, once you get used to the oversteer and sensitivity to cross winds.

THINGS WOMEN WILL LIKE: Reliability; feeling of "unburstability"; economy; after-sales service.

THINGS WE DIDN'T LIKE: Noise levels; rear head and leg room; spartan instrument panel; body styling.

SUMMED UP: A go-anywhere, tough little car that deserves a second look.

mini

PRICE: $1669, inc. tax.

ENGINE: Four cyl. OHV, transversely mounted, of 988 cc capacity, develops 40 bhp at 5250 rpm on a comp. ratio of 8.3 : 1.

TRANSMISSION: Four speed, floor shift.

SUSPENSION: Fully independent with "Hydrolastic" displacers and auxiliary springs.

STEERING: Rack and pinion, 2 turns lock to lock, 31ft. 7in. turning circle.

BRAKES: Hydraulic drums.

DIMENSIONS: Length 10ft. 0½in., width 4ft. 7½in., height 4ft. 5in., weight 12½ cwt.

TOP SPEED: 75 mph.

FUEL BILL: 42 mpg.

HOW IT HANDLES: Sure-footed, due to better power to weight ratio; highly manoeuvreable.

THINGS WOMEN WILL LIKE: Park-anywhere qualities; economy; comfortable seating; lightness and layout of controls; after-sales service.

THINGS WE DIDN'T LIKE: Lack of boot space; head and leg room for lanky passengers; front tyre wear.

SUMMED UP: The Mini's far from being the complete car, but it's fun to drive, cheap to run, surprisingly tough and has loads of cheeky charm.

datsun

PRICE: $1738, inc. tax.

ENGINE: Four cyl., 988 cc capacity, develops 62 bhp at 6000 rpm on a comp. ratio of 8.5 : 1.

TRANSMISSION: Four speed, all synchromesh, floor shift.

SUSPENSION: Front by transverse leaf springs, wishbones and telescopic shock absorbers; back by semi-elliptic leaf springs.

STEERING: Re-circulating ball type, 3 turns lock to lock, 26ft. turning circle.

BRAKES: Hydraulic drums.

DIMENSIONS: Length 12ft. 6in., width 4ft. 9in., height 4ft. 5in., weight 13 cwt.

TOP SPEED: 76 mph.

FUEL BILL: 39 mpg.

HOW IT HANDLES: Good for a baby car.

THINGS WOMEN WILL LIKE: 26ft. turning circle; light clutch; rubber-faced bumper over-riders; indicators on the front body panels.

THINGS WE DIDN'T LIKE: Starting manners; high accelerator pedal; noisy heater fan; brakes.

SUMMED UP: Economical, fun motoring for four — and at the asking price has a lot going for it.

fiat 850

PRICE: $1698, inc. tax.

ENGINE: Four cyl., rear-mounted, of 843 cc capacity, develops 42 bhpm at 5300 rpm on a comp. ratio of 8.8 : 1.

TRANSMISSION: Four speed, all synchromesh, floor shift.

SUSPENSION: Front fully independent by transverse lead spring, twin stabilisers and tubular damper; back independent with coil springs.

STEERING: Worm and sector, 3½ turns lock to lock, 29ft. 3in. turning circle.

BRAKES: Hydraulic drums.

DIMENSIONS: Length 11ft. 8¾in., width 4ft. 8in., height 4ft. 6½in., weight 13¾ cwt.

TOP SPEED: 78 mph.

FUEL BILL: 42 mpg.

HOW IT HANDLES: Road-holding very good; little body sway on corners.

THINGS WOMEN WILL LIKE: Economy, light controls, fold-down rear seat.

THINGS WE DIDN'T LIKE: Joggy ride over bitumen; poor standard of roof lining.

SUMMED UP: Easy to drive, comfortable and worth checking out.

corolla

PRICE: $1798, inc. tax.

ENGINE: Four cyl. inclined 20 deg. right, alloy head, 1077 cc capacity, develops 60 bhp at 6000 rpm on a comp. ratio of 9:1.

TRANSMISSION: Four speed, all synchromesh, floor shift.

SUSPENSION: Front by Macpherson struts, telescopic shock absorbers, back by semi-elliptic leaf springs and live axle.

STEERING: Worm and roller, 3.2 turns lock to lock, turning circle 29ft.

BRAKES: Drums, front and back.

DIMENSIONS: Length 12ft. 7.4in., width 4ft. 10½in., height 4ft. 6in., weight 13¾ cwt.

TOP SPEED: 88 mph.

FUEL BILL: 40 mpg.

HOW IT HANDLES: Easily and predictably. Mechanicals commendably quiet.

THINGS WOMEN WILL LIKE: Comfortable seating for four; arm rests for those in the back; light controls; bright, spirited performance.

THINGS WE DIDN'T LIKE: Lack of feel in steering and brakes; spare wheel under floor.

SUMMED UP: With its pleasant shape, inside space and nippy performance, the Corolla is a must for women considering cars in this price bracket.

Beetle Power

A look back at the origins of the VW engine by Edward Eves

Born as a piece of political machinery the VW has been described as not so much a car as a way of life. It is powered by an unusual and expensive-to-make four-cylinder engine, air cooled with horizontally opposed cylinders. Capacity started at 985 c.c. and has been almost doubled in the latest 411 model. Ferdinand Porsche investigated some interesting power units before this configuration was decided on. It is now a legend.

IT is difficult but fascinating to try to unravel the very beginnings of the VW engine. It is easy to say that Karl Rabe and Xavier Reimspiess, under the direction of Ferdinand Porsche, designed a 985 c.c. horizontally opposed, four-cylinder, fan-cooled engine to power Hitler's KdF-Wagen—strength through joy car. But the events that led up to this choice of configuration are tantalizing and obscure.

Long before Hitler came to power, Porsche, who had designed outstanding four- and six-cylinder Austro-Daimler water-cooled aero engines and then went on to design a four-cylinder twisted-boxer air-cooled engine for the same company in 1912, had been taken with the idea of streamlining as a means of saving power. As early as 1924 his business manager, racing driver Adolf Rosenberg, had raced the rear engined Benz Tropfenwagen, which, in turn, had been inspired by the teardrop car built by Rumpler-Berlin in 1917.

Undoubtedly the Rumpler convinced Porsche about easy-to-propel streamlined cars, while his work on air-cooled aero engines which are essentially slow turning and reliable, with good torque at low revs, convinced him that this type of engine would be ideal to drive a low-drag car, given clear roads. The creation of the *autobahn* system fulfilled the latter requirement and the request from Hitler to design a People's Car gave him the chance to bring the low-drag, low-power car to fruition.

Very few designers produce a clear-cut design first go. Although Porsche had designed a 1500 c.c. horizontally opposed engine for NSU in 1933, a variety of engines was tried before the horizontally opposed four-cylinder configuration was chosen for the KdF-Wagen. Most mundane of the projects was a boxer-twin which was discarded on the grounds of lack of flexibility. The most interesting was a four-cylinder two-stroke in which two of the cylinders acted as pumps. It suffered from overheating, probably because there was no bulk of oil to carry heat away from the pistons. Most extraordinary was a twin-cylinder, single-sleeve-valve unit which had a habit of breaking the sleeve connecting rods, whereupon, as the ultimate triumph of hope over experience, Rabe tried to actuate the sleeves with cams and torsion bar springs.

Development of these engines was stopped in 1936 in favour of the now classic air-cooled four. Cylinder dimensions of the prototype were fixed at 70 x 64 mm giving a capacity of 985 c.c. but only a limited number of these units were built—by Daimler Benz—as propellants for publicity cars used by the Nazi Party heirarchy. The 75 x 64 mm engine was developed for the military Kübelwagen-command cars and the fascinating Schwimmkübel, which were the only vehicles to be made in the Wolfsburg plant

before peace broke out.

In the sparse post-war years the tooling for this engine was all that was available and was naturally used to produce the engines for early post-war Volkswagens.

Over the years the VW engine has changed only in detail. Short overall length and light weight were *and are* main design parameters because of the need to reduce the polar moment of the car in view of the overhung rear engine position. It therefore has a magnesium crankcase and light alloy cylinder heads. The opposed cylinder layout keeps length to a minimum and the weight in the right place, low down. Designed in 1936 when 30 bhp was considered plenty, the crankshaft was indeed short of bearing area if attempts were made to produce more power as some tuners found to

their cost. The major power increments in the VW coincide with the availability of high duty bearing material and in 1961 by an increase in the length of the crankshaft.

Rigidity was increased by extending the crankshaft, which is part of the main casting and does not have a separate cover, and supporting the nose in what is effectively a fourth main-bearing. The timing gears and the distributor skew gear are mounted on the section of shaft inside the chamber and the fan pulley externally on the end of it. The crankcase is split vertically, each half including half of the bearing-housings for the crankshaft and camshaft. The two halves are tied together with long studs passing horizontally through the bearing diaphragms and by nuts and bolts at the flanges. Although this construction pre-

A typical 1937 engine, the first to have an oil cooler, which differs very little from the one which is well known to millions of post-war VW owners

Component parts of the twin-cylinder engine which was tried and found wanting in terms of flexibility. In common with all VW prototype engines, it was air-cooled

Many engineers occupied themselves with sleeve valve engines before the war. Porsche tried this twin-cylinder model with cam-operated sleeves closed by torsion bars. The cam can be seen next to the left-hand crankshaft web. It was not a success because of excessive sleeve friction

BEETLE POWER...

cludes removing the sump, which is part of the casting, cleaning is no longer a problem with modern oils and the layout makes for a very rigid crankcase. An inspection plate is provided in the bottom of the sump through which some cleansing can take place.

Separate cast-iron cylinders are used with one-piece heads, the whole assembly being held down, motor cycle fashion, with long studs, eight per side, tapped into the crankcase. The unusual port layout, with vertical inlet tracts and with the exhaust ports coming out of the ends of the heads, is necessary to maintain exhaust pipe ground clearance and also allows the push-rods—the camshaft is located under the crankcase—an unobstructed passage to the valve gear. Oil return from the rocker covers is by way of the push-rod tubes which are inclined, to facilitate the process. Pressed steel rocker covers retained by wire clips seal the rocker chambers which are partly formed in the cylinder head castings.

With these slow-running engines long accelerating and decelerating ramps are not required on the cams, so the valve tuning appears less extreme than it really is.

The early 1,130 c.c. engines had inlet tuning of 2:37deg. and 37:2 for the exhaust. This was opened out to 6:35 (inlet) and 42:3 (exhaust) on the 34 bhp, 1,192 c.c. model. As a comparison the latest 411 engine has inlet and exhaust openings of 4:39 and 40:3deg. respectively.

Combustion chamber shape is exceptional these days in being a quite straightforward truncated pent-roof type with the valves parallel with the cylinder axis but offset slightly below it. Early engines had flat top pistons giving a compression ratio of 5.8 to 1 in deference to the low octane value of the fuel then available; the latest 1300 unit has pistons giving a ratio of 6.8 to 1.

Lubrication is by a gear type pump driven off the end of the camshaft. From the outset the VW has had an oil cooler mounted in the

Calculated to excite the technically-minded, this four-cylinder two-stroke with two cylinders pumping was discarded because of overheating. The object on the right is the combined starter and dynamo

Only a few of these engines were built to power Nazi Party show cars

cooling shroud. Porsche no doubt deduced from his experience with the two-stroke prototype, that an air-cooled engine mounted at the back of the car, out of the airstream, must dispose of some heat by way of the lubricating oil. This is born out by the Porsche racing cars which have oil-coolers almost as big as the coolant radiator of a liquid-cooled engine.

On all early engines, and on most of the latest ones, mixture is supplied by a single carburettor, of Solex manufacture, mounted on an exhaust heated manifold fabricated from steel tube. This manifold is so like a pair of sit-up-and-beg bicycle handlebars that one British engineer on seeing it remarked. that he

A rare cutaway drawing of the Type 60 VW which shows a twin-cylinder engine. Note the rear petrol tank and the forward-mounted battery.

supposed the sports model had a fully dropped manifold. Te eliminate icing and to evaporate loose fuel the manifold hot spot extends almost a third of the length of the horizontal section of the manifold and consists of a steel tube siamesed to the main tube by welding. An early attempt to make an exhaust heated jacket—it was fitted on early 1,192 c.c. cars—ended in failure. The exhaust gas burnt through the inlet manifold, thoroughly upsetting the carburation and many thousands of manifolds had to be replaced by the old type, which is still used.

At one time it was considered inadvisable to fit twin-carburettors to standard VW engines, probably because of the marginal bearing loadings. But the 1500, 1600 and 411 engines do not suffer from this shortcoming. The latest carburettor types for the 1600 and 411 are Solex 32 PDSIT and the Solex 34 PDSIT respectively. The 1300 and 1500 Beetles use the Solex H30 PIC and the Solex 30 PICT instruments.

Porsche experimented with cast-iron crankshafts in the prototype stage and they broke, since when all VWs have had forged crankshafts. The connecting rods are likewise steel forgings, split at right angles with fully floating gudgeon pins and diecast light alloy pistons.

Cooling air is circulated by a centrifugal fan supported by a cast bracket on the crankcase and working in a sheet metal housing on top of the engine. The amount of air passing through the fan is regulated by a thermostatically controlled annular throttle ring in the inlet trumpet. Vanes inside the duct share the air equally between the two cylinder banks. Flap valves in the exit duct below the cylinder allow part of the waste hot air to be channelled to jackets surrounding the exhaust pipes, where it is heated further and fed into the car heating system.

When Porsche showed his proposals for this power unit for the KdF-Wagen in 1936, established German manufacturers threw up their hands and said "this aircraft engine" could never be made for the price. Any production engineer would say the same today if he didn't know that VW production tooling had not only made the whole thing possible but had made it an extremely worthwhile proposition.   □

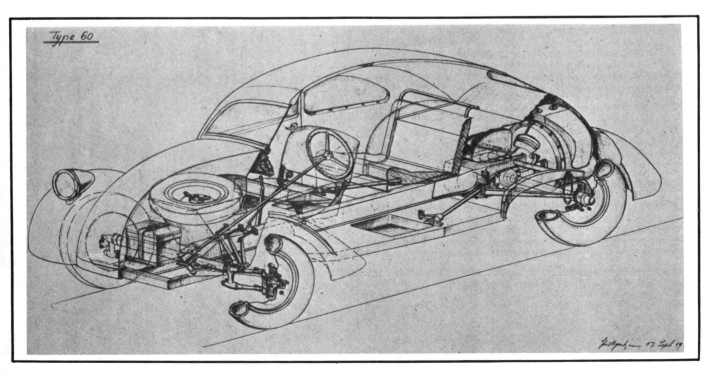

Type 60

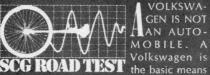

SCG ROAD TEST

A VOLKSWAGEN IS NOT AN AUTOMOBILE. A Volkswagen is the basic means of transportation for those people who don't need a car for its status, for its extension of their ego, or for the augmentation of their physical powers. As such, or as non-such, it really isn't logical to run a comparison test of it against an automobile. It would make as much sense to compare the telephone—a basic means of communication—to an automobile.

It is said that the happiest drivers in the world have Cadillacs and Volkswagens. That is, they are the owners who were rewarded far greater than their expectations. When you buy a Volkswagen, all you expect is an inexpensive and reliable vehicle for transporting yourself from point A to point B with a minimum of attention—either yours or your spectators'. Well, that's all it does, but it does that simple chore so straightforwardly that you begin to take it for granted that that is all a car is supposed to do.

The great majority of car owners, however, think differently. Since their car is their alter ego, it must also entertain, impress, coddle, carry five extra persons once or twice a year, run twice as fast as the legal limit, win every redlight-to-redlight drag race, haul more luggage than any ten people could rightfully need on a two-week trip, and most important, be the ubiquitous, silent yardstick of their success. That's the majority. Presently. But the world's auto manufacturers are worried, and justifiably, because every year the standard of the "water-class" of cars nibbles off just a little larger share of the market. *Every year*—for a decade. Perhaps this says something about society that all the sensationalistic journalism and public opinion polls and demonstrations don't. I sure as hell hope so. With all due apology to certain theological groups, perhaps this is the beginning of the Forth Reich, the right Reich, a *social* Reich.

Dr. Ferdinand Porsche was without a doubt one of the ten most brilliant automotive engineers in history. With the Volkswagen and Porsche to his credit, few persons are even aware of his most advanced design, the Cisitalia, a contemporary with today's Formula 1 cars that was never developed after his death due to political complications. But now we can all wonder at whether it was managerial genius or sheer chance that retained and refined his original VW design for over two decades. The Beetle is outdated now, but the general public doesn't know that, just as they don't know that its proper successor, the F.I. sedan, has already arrived.

Have you ever asked yourself...

BEETLE

PRICE

Base . . . . $1935 (POE West Coast)
As tested $2280
Options . . Radio, whitewalls, air conditioning

ENGINE

Type . . . . Flat 4, air-cooled, aluminum block,
aluminum head
Displacement . . . . .91.1 cu. in. (1493 cc)
Horsepower . . . . .53 hp at 4200 rpm
Torque . . . . .78 lbs.-ft. @ 2600 rpm
Bore & stroke . . . . .3.27 in. x 2.72 in.
(83.0 mm x 69.0 mm)
Compression ratio . . . . .7.5 to 1
Valve actuation . . . . . .Ohv, rocker actuated
Induction system . . . . .Solex 30 PICT-2
Exhaust system . . Cast iron headers, 4 into 2
Electrical system . . . .12-volt generator, point
distributor
Fuel . . . . .Regular
Recommended redline . . . . .4200 rpm

DRIVE TRAIN

Clutch . . . . .Dry disc, cable actuated

Transmission	Gear Ratio	Overall Ratio
1st Synchro	3.80	15.68
2nd Synchro	2.06	8.50
3rd Synchro	1.26	5.20
4th Synchro	0.89	3.67

Differential . . . . .Spiral bevel, 4.125

CHASSIS

Frame . . . . .Unit construction, rear engine,
rear drive
Front suspension . . . .Double trailing arms,
torsion bars, tube shocks, anti-roll bar
Rear suspension . . Single trailing arm, torsion bars, tube shocks
Steering . . . . .Worm and gear, 2.8 turns,
turning circle 36.0 feet
Brakes . . . . .Split hydraulic, all drum,
swept area 96.1 sq.in.
Wheels . . . .Steel disc, 15-in. dia.; 5-in. wide
Tires . . . . .Continental 5.60 x 15 bias ply,
pressures F/R: 16/24 (rec.), 22/30 (test)

BODY

Type . . . . . . .Unit steel, 2-door, 5-passenger
Seats . . . . .Front buckets, rear bench
Windows . . . . .2 manual, 2 vents
Luggage space . . Front & rear trunk, 8.6 cu.ft.
Instruments . . . . .90 mph speedo
Gauges: fuel
Lights: gen., oil

WEIGHT AND MEASURES

Weight . . . .1900 lbs. (curb), 2130 lbs. (test)
Distribution F/R 39.5%/60.5%
Wheelbase . . . . .94.5 in.
Track F/R . . . . .51.6 in./53.3 in.
Height . . . . .59.1 in.
Width . . . . .61.0 in.
Length . . . . .158.6 in.
Ground clearance . . . . .5.9 in.
Oil capacity . . . . .2.5 qt.
Fuel capacity . . . . .10.6 gal.

MISCELLANEOUS

Weight/power ratio (curb/advertised) . . .36.0
(test/dyno) 53.0
Advertised hp/cu.in. 0.58
Speed per 1000 rpm (top gear) . . . .19.8 mph
Warranty . . . . .24 mos./24,000 miles

AERODYNAMIC FORCES AT 100 MPH

150 lbs.   0 lbs.   370 lbs.

.70 g   CORNERING CONDITION

4.2°   CORNERING CONDITION

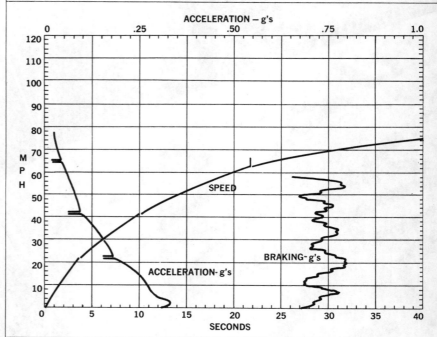

PERFORMANCE

Acceleration . . . . .0-30 (6.0 sec.) 0-60 (20.4 sec.)
0-quarter mile (21.5 sec., 63.0 mph)
Top speed . . . . .78 mph (claimed) at 3940 rpm (factory limited)
Braking . . . . .Distance from 60 mph: 164 ft. (0.73 g av.)
Number of stops to fade: Not attainable
Stability: Excellent
Maximum pitch angle: 0.5°
Handling . . . . .Max. lateral: 0.68 g right, 0.70 g left
Skidpad understeer: 4.8° right, 6.6° left
Maximum roll angle: 4.2°
Reaction to throttle, full: more understeer; off: less understeer
Dynamometer . . . . .Road horsepower: 40
Condition of tune: Carburetion slightly lean

Speedometer	30.0	40.0	50.0	60.0	70.0	80.0
Actual	28.0	37.5	45.5	55.5	65.5	77.0

Mileage . . . . .Average: N.A.
Miles on car: 9000 to 9600
Aerodynamic forces at 100 mph:
Drag . . . . .370 lbs. (includes tire drag)
Lift F/R . . . . .150 lbs./0 lbs.

TEST EXPLANATIONS

Fade test is successive max. g stops from 60 mph each minute until wheels cannot be
locked. Understeer is front minus rear tire slip angle at max. lateral on 200-ft. dia.
Digitek skidpad. Autoscan chassis dynamometer supplied by Humble Oil.

WHY WOULD ANYONE BUY A VW?
Continued

But enough of this chit-chat. If you weren't a VW enthusiast you wouldn't have read this far, and you probably know that there's been nothing new in these cars for almost a year now. However, with our new electronic test equipment and road test procedure, we are now able to tell you some things about these cars that you've never heard before.

Tell Me Doctor, Is It Safe?

You've all seen newspaper photos of a little compact import, impact-welded to the front end of an unharmed semi-truck cab. Pure sheedy sensationalism. The people in the car were no deader than the truck driver would have been if he had tried to relocate a freeway overpass abutment. It's all a matter of scale — relatively speaking. A minor furor was created when the Feds released a movie of a collision they staged between a Volkswagen and a full-size Ford. The VW definitely got the worst of it. So what. It's an accepted scientific fact that when two objects of similar construction collide, damage is going to be inversely proportional to their relative mass. This produced the obvious response from an unknown satirical wit, "That proves it. We've got to get rid of them. We won't be safe until we've banned all full-size Fords from the highways." But walls smash trucks that hit full-size sedans that bump pony cars that collide with compacts that cream crampacts — that run over dogs.

Great fleas have little fleas,
Upon their back to bite 'em,
And little fleas have lesser fleas,
And so ad infinitum.
— Anonymous paraphrase of Jonathan Swift,
On Poetry, A Rhapsody (1733)

Does this mean that we all must have the same size vehicles running the same speed in the same direction with no obstacles? Let's look a little deeper. From a theoretical standpoint (simplification to absurdity) a human can survive a complete stop from freeway speed in *5 feet* if properly "packaged." Volunteers have shown that 30-g decelerations can be tolerated for split seconds without permanent harm if the forces are distributed and there is no contact with solid objects. Therefore, if the impact can be controlled (the antithesis of "accident"), and the interior doesn't intrude, 5 feet of body crush-space would be adequate for a limp-away collision. In a VW sedan it is 5 feet from the front bumper to your knees. But don't try it! The engineers haven't quite reached the theoretical ultimate yet.

The other major approach to auto safety engineering is accident avoidance, and this is where Corvair was attacked. Chevrolet spent millions in proving that a rear-engined, swing-axle car — like the older VWs — was just as good as any other car in avoiding an uncontrollable condition, as long as you knew how to drive. But then both manufacturers recognized the

flaw in that reasoning, and revised the rear suspension to make it even harder to get bent out on a curve.

The problem with the original design was in its tendency toward "jacking." When a car with swing axles rises, the tire patches move inboard, making the tread narrower, or conversely, in a cornering condition the tire patches move inboard, causing the car to rise, causing more roll, etc. This is an unstable condition and eventually the car may simply rise up on tip-toes and fall over.

They can't do that anymore. No way. The revised rear suspension is so foolproof that we had no fear of any maneuver on the skidpad, including broadslides, "J" turns and power oversteer. The Squareback was able to lift an inside front wheel due to its higher center of gravity, but was nowhere near going over. The only way you'll ever get one of these cars on its top is to drive it off the road and/or hit something while going sideways.

While on the skidpad, some other points redemonstrated themselves. In the first place, all three cornered faster to the left, with the driver's weight on the inside of the turn. Secondly, the higher the center of gravity, the slower the corner: Karmann, 33.0 mph (0.71 g); Beetle, 32.5 mph (0.70 g); Squareback, 32.0 mph (0.68 g), though there obviously wasn't much difference and *all* the Volkswagens were better than most of the cars we have tested, except the Lotus Elan +2, which did over 0.80 g.

Thirdly — listen — they all showed steady-state *understeer*. That's right, on asphalt at those speeds we were not able to make the Karmann or Beetle oversteer with either full or zero throttle, though the Squareback did with some coaxing. For some reason, probably front alignment, the 1600 Squareback had almost neutral steer in a right turn and could therefore be induced to "hang it out" with full throttle. So have no fear, your VW is legally a controllable vehicle. OK, you uncaped crusader, Nader, let's see you start something *now*. Just try.

They're pretty good at braking, too, with discs on the front of the Karmann and Squareback that haul them down at 0.79 g and 0.77 g for as long and as quick as you want to repeat 60 mph stops. The Beetle was a little worse at 0.73 g, but still no fade, and all were very controllable — by regulating pedal pressure in relation to tire squeal.

Nothing much exciting happened in the drag race, except that we got a lot of wheelspin in the Beetle. It's pretty easy if you don't know how — just take your eyes off a gas pumper while he takes off with your gas cap. Under acceleration the fuel runs out, down the fender, over the running board and under the right rear tire, and when you look back the sun has evaporated it, causing great ?-?-? for a while. This also caused one very exciting left turn oversteer before the problem was discovered and corrected.

Still, without smoking right-rear tires the race was as you might expect, the 1600-cc Squareback winning with a 20.5-second

e.t., the low-drag Karmann second with 21.1 seconds and the Beetle last at 21.5 seconds. The last two only had the 1500-cc engine, of course, but they weigh about 300 pounds less, too.

Our aerodynamic testing has really gone over big. Everyone wants to know how bad their car lifts and how its air drag compares with other similar cars. To reiterate, the drag figure we give is taken at about 70 mph — and includes rolling resistance (tires) — and is then extrapolated to 100 mph just for a convenient reference. To be more accurate we might try to subtract out mechanical drag, but *total* drag is still what matters on the road.

Surprise! The Karmann had the lowest drag figure at 320 pounds. But the Squareback was second with 340 pounds and the Beetle a bad last with 370 pounds. Maybe Mr. Kamm had something there after all. According to aerodynamic theory, the rear of the "bug" slopes away too rapidly and the airstream probably separates just below the roof line. Well, anyway, it *looks* more aerodynamic.

The Beetle also has a bad front/rear aero lift ratio. At freeway speeds, the front picks up about 75 pounds, and the rear, zero. In a curve, this means understeer, but in a crosswind, oh woe — you guessed it — instability. The Karmann is middle ground: same at the front, more lift in the rear, and finally, the Squareback is balanced with equal lift front and rear. The Squareback has more rear lift than the Beetle? Say, maybe those long-tailed Porsches are on to something good?

Top speed, as long as it's over 70, is our "care-less" test. The factory says Beetle, 78; Karmann, 82; and Squareback, 84 mph. Who are we to argue? After 30 seconds of acceleration we got to 70, 71 and 74 mph, respectively, if not respectfully. Oddly, the "factory" speeds correspond roughly to rpms at which occur both peak horsepower and the nominal redline point. And that speed is also called "cruising speed." So don't write in and tell us that yours goes faster — until you've had your speedo calibrated — and *then* don't tell us either. Until they have a class for VWs at Bonneville, our interest in those figures is exceedingly minimal. But however fast you drive, be careful of the speedo. In the Beetle and Karmann it was way off (on the safe side) and had a tendency to get delayed, reading differently going up from going down.

Our gas mileage, of course, wasn't what the factory predicted: 26.7 mpg for Beetle and Karmann, 26.1 for the F.I. Squareback, but you can imagine how Sports Car Graphic staffers drive in L.A., and the Beetle disqualified itself by running off at the filler spout. Still, we ranged from 22.2 to 26.8 in the Karmann, and the F.I. showed about 22 mpg.

Well, so much for the facts and figures. Since you're still with us you must be a masochist, so stick around and we'll give you our opinions now.

The Beetle is dead, but no one realizes that fact until they've had a chance to drive the 1600 Squareback or Fastback. However, for $700 more, it seems that all you get is more space and 100 cc's. Driving the 1500s you get the feeling that the power is just "adequate," but in the 1600, the power is still just "adequate."

Shifting is a real nuisance, not only the amount required because of the low power and narrow range, but the clumsiness and washiness of the stick. Something deep down inside tells me their automatics are going to be very hot sellers. Another auto-trans promotional stunt is an over-weight clutch pedal that tempts you to shift into neutral at stop signs. All in all, you get the impression that you're doing something wrong when shifting, except that occasionally it goes right into the gear you intended it to.

Maverick made a big deal about having a smaller turning circle than VW, but it looks like that's not saying much. For a car with such a short wheelbase it's surprising to learn that even a Detroit pony car can turn more sharply, which brings up the pros and cons of big-diameter tires. The incongruity of 15-inch wheels on such a tiny car has become accepted on VW, but they obviously account for the limited front seat footroom and offset pedals caused by encroachment of the huge wheel wells. On similar-sized cars, the use of 14-, 13- and even 10-inch-diameter wheels permits more interior space and a tighter steering angle, but VW overweighs the advantages of more brake room, tire and fuel economy, and the off-road maneuverability and traction of larger diameter tires.

There weren't any complaints about the handling at freeway speeds in the Karmann and Beetle, but then we weren't able to arrange any crosswinds. On the other hand, the minimal understeer that was noticed in the Squareback on the skidpad resulted in a feeling of instability at speed. In other words, if you make a sudden maneuver, the car tries to overshoot as it rolls. Either more rear roll understeer or roll damping might be in order here. Still, no duress. As long as you drive sanely, you'll never get upset by its handling performance.

Sane driving is probably VW's biggest problem. We observed a terrible tendency to drive madly in these cars just because you could go flat-out most of the time without breaking any laws. You also get the impression that smallness can get you in anywhere — under semi-trailers, on sidewalks, in elevators. Something about these bugs brings out more "Mr. Hyde" than a street super-stock . . . probably the impression that you can get away with it, since VWs are as invisibly common as grass — the perfect spies' car. "More anonymous people drive Volkswagens than any other kind."

Returning to the inside, we find all manner of goods and bads. The first thing that grabs your eye in the Karmann is a genuine imitation wood-grain simulated paper-covered dash. That's the bad, the good is that it was so neatly folded inside the corners of the glovebox door that you hardly noticed. The one-hand seatbelt latch is the most convenient restraint of any car we've tested, and can be easily and safely buckled even while driving. And it's neat — it almost becomes a reflex action to flip it from the doorpost hanger to the anchor on the driveshaft tunnel. The bad: due to its anchor location, the diagonal shoulder harness is a real falling bra strap that tends to restrain only your left bicep. Visibility is average, good, very good as you proceed from Karmann to Squareback, but bad where the immovable rear view mirror can completely hide a car at 30 yards or a truck at 50 yards. If you are really concerned with what might be in that concealed zone, the easiest solution is to tilt the mirror to near vertical.

Ah, but what really concerns people is how much space you don't have on the inside — they say. Let's qualify that. The Karmann is roomy — it has as much interior space as' a Miura. The Squareback is cramped — it must have half the room of a Rolls Royce Silver Ghost. But the Beetle has much more interior volume than the Karmann, and in turn is half as big as the Squareback, which has the same seating arrangement plus luggage space. However, the Karmann is only a 2+2, while the Beetle is a 5+0, and the Squareback is a 5+. Therefore, how old is Charley's wife?

To be honestly objective, the front seat room in all three is quite adequate, but rear seat room in any is absurd. To get an average person in the jump seat of the Karmann means the driver has to slide forward until his knees join against the dash and his tie gets wound up in the steering wheel. The Squareback rear seaters at least have head room, though fat good that does their poor bent peds. But it does make a Great Experiment — after 22.3 miles, any 2 persons so subjected will have become either enemies or lovers.

Technical details of the cars aren't worth going into — there can't be anything duller than reading a description of the parts in a 20-year-old design (unless it's having to write it), but perhaps you'd be interested in one automotive engineer's opinion of that design. The passenger packaging is good for ordinary operation with an ordinary passenger load of two adults and occasional children, but there isn't enough sheet metal crush space for protection against unfair drivers who want to thrash you with a big 4-wheeled deadly weapon. And luggage space is sufficient for moderate trips, considering the miniaturization and disposability of clothing, plus it may be in the best location, considering front-end collision again, except that the SAE thinks the gas tank ought to be between the rear wheels for best protection. Suspension design was bloody bad until a few years ago when they modified the rear, so now it's only half bloody bad. The only redeeming feature up front is that it saves a little space, but the idea of leaning tires to the *outside* of a curve . . . well, suggest that to a bicycle rider. As for the driveline, *no hey mejores*, as our Southern neighbors say, meaning: "The horses are starving, officer." However, the location is perfect unless you think you are a battering ram, or unless you are a racer, in which case you might put the engine in *front* of the rear axle, and the rumor is out that VW/ Porsche is building such a production car.

Air-cooled engines? Great for low horsepower and simplicity. Opposed four-cylinder layout? Great for space-saving. Electronic fuel injection? *Pow!* They're not the first to use a "computer" in a production car, but if they can get wide customer approval of such a system, friend, we're on our way to automatic *everything*. Cry not, rugged individualists, you'll still have a go pedal, stop pedal and steering mechanism, but computer-controlled stability, emergency warning and evasion, performance optimizers, personal-comfort tailoring, etc., will give you added capabilities you cannot imagine. Technologically, they could all be incorporated today, except for cost, and cost depends on quantity, which depends on acceptance, and VW may be paving the way. Though apparently the real reason they did it was for better smog control, since there's no other discernible difference in performance from a carbureted engine.

Speaking of cost, don't let anyone tell you that any different feature on a VW is different because the parts are cheaper that way. By the time you amortize tooling and engineering over ten million identical units of *anything*, it doesn't matter how it was designed, the primary cost per unit can almost be based on pounds of raw material and labor in assembly. Cost of repair may be less, also, because of the lower parts inventory required, familiarity (to VW mechanics) of operations, and accessibility. The instrument panel assembly is brilliant in simplicity, just lay across the open front trunk snap out a piece of cardboard — and there the stuff is. I'd be willing to pay extra for such a feature on my Yankee machine.

O.K., let's wrap it up. These cars have drawbacks and deficiencies — a crank actually fell off one of our cars and a friend got one delivered with the rear alignment so bad that the tires were gone in 18,000 miles — but maybe it isn't fair to complain since you don't expect much in the first place. They don't have most of the faults we have found in other test cars — but then they don't have the virtues either. The purists may hate Bugs, and no one worse than a Porsche owner. But the fact remains, man, a Bug will get you across town just as fast, and probably cheaper, especially when you get pranged. Love 'em, hate 'em, or ignore 'em, but you've got to admire them, because the thing they are supposed to do — transport you — they do extraordinarily well.

BUG BECOMES COOL BEETLE

Air condition a Volkswagen?

There is a whole generation of drivers today to whom the Volkswagen Beetle is an integral part of the automotive picture, and to many fiercely loyal owners, the car is a way of life. There have been reams of material written on the phenomenal little car that changed the motoring habits of so many Americans. In fact it is the Volkswagen that has influenced Detroit to go into manufacture of sub-compacts with attendant advertising attempting to 'put down' the imports. Currently ROAD TEST Magazine thinks that the car is due for testing in the same manner as every other car. Therefore, we recently spent a couple of weeks with the latest standard Beetle in an effort to separate legend from logic and do a realistic test on the car today.

Styling on the Beetle has certainly entered the 'classic' realm. Physically the car resembles the original 1930 design very strongly, but over the years constant refinements have occurred. Some changes have been caused by various laws and restrictions imposed on all cars by the U.S. Mostly the change has been evolution of the concept. Overall the styling is antiquated, but it is purposeful. While we duck the figurative brickbats of Beetle lovers everywhere, we will state that part of the excellent resale value of the car is due to the total lack of drastic changes in styling. This makes it difficult for the ordinary guy to tell at a glance just how old or new a Volks might be. Since beauty is in the eye of the beholder the Beetle is attractive to many, but we doubt if it can be described as beautiful even by the most loyal owner.

The basic price on the Volkswagen with the standard four-speed transmission is $1877 POE Los Angeles. Our test unit had a few extras such as whitewall tires ($29.50), push-button radio ($65.95), and last, but far from least, a real air conditioning unit. The air conditioning can be ordered on the car as a dealer installed option. VW has tried several different types of cooling devices, and the unit on our test car was made by Meir-Line and manufactured in the City of Industry, California. There is some variation on the price — we were quoted anywhere from $350 to $395 for the unit installed. The labor charge is a good part of the price. The compressor is mounted on the left side of the engine in the rear compartment. It drives via its own notched belt from an extension on the fan pulley. The ducts are installed just under the radio in the center of the dash with a rheostat switch to control the fan blast. The ducts can be aimed in several directions by swiveling the knobs. With the switch on medium initially, then turned to low, the car is cooled instantly. The Meir-Line air conditioning remained completely effective even on a hot and smoggy July day in Southern California.

The price on the air seems a bit steep compared to the overall price of the car. However, for the person who does a lot of hot weather driving, it would be well worth the additional cost. Fuel economy dropped off slightly when the air conditioning was running all day — the difference with and without the air in operation came to just over one mile per gallon. One of the biggest plusses for this particular unit is the fact that there is

The Volks tosses up a sporting rooster tail on the El Mirage Dry Lake. Cornering is more positive these days since suspension changes have reduced the amount of oversteer.

no appreciable power loss on the car. Hillclimbing ability and normal acceleration speeds are relatively unaffected by the supposed drain on power of the air conditioning. Nor does the engine stall or stutter at idle when the unit is on. Once we cured some minor leaks in the hoses, thanks to super tape, the operation of the air conditioning was trouble free and super cool.

An outstanding feature of the Volkswagen is the high level of quality control. This is unusual for a mass-produced car, particularly for such a low priced model. The paint and the upholstery are really well done, and absolutely everything fits exactly where it should. The weather sealing is so tight that it is hard to close the doors with all the windows rolled up. Despite rather hard use as one of the few air-conditioned Beetles in VW's West Coast press fleet, our test Volks was delightfully tight and rattle free on the road. All the knobs and handles were still in place and functioning properly too. This is admirable and directly relates to good care in assembly and final inspection.

Power train

The Volkswagen air-cooled engine scarcely needs an introduction to the American public. The horizontally opposed, four-cylinder engine is justly famous for myriad applications. The 1500 engine is actually 1493 cubic centimeters or 91.1 cubic inches. It is an outgrowth of the basic 1300 used in the early sixties. The increased capacity came with a larger bore to 83 millimeters while the stroke remained the same at 60. The power output is 53 SAE horsepower at 4200 rpm, a figure that is quite believable. With a 7.5 to 1 compression ratio the engine is very happy burning regular grade gasoline. One single throat Solex carburetor supplies the fuel through a mechanical fuel pump. The Volks has an automatic choke that provides instant starting in any climate. The air-cooled engine warms up quickly and the choke drops off in a very short time.

The lightweight VW engine has a tremendous reputation for reliability. Despite pushing the engine past the indicated rev limits, and hard driving on the top of the revs, there was never a protest from the engine nor was the function disturbed one bit. The VW engine is a noisy unit and a good deal of the noise intrudes into the passenger space. Volks lovers learn to live with the racket, or perhaps they just turn the radio up a notch.

Access to the working parts of the engine is reasonable, but the would-be-mechanic soon develops a crick in his back from leaning into the back deck. The extra plumbing on our air conditioned test car did make the engine bay appear really overstuffed, and knuckle scraping could be expected during the first stab at changing a spark plug on the left side.

The four-speed, all synchromesh gearbox is smooth to use and the synchromesh is effectively unbeatable. The floor mounted gear stick is of medium length and the throws are fairly long. In fact the shorter driver needs to stretch to reach third gear if he is driving with the full safety harness restraining his body. The shift linkage has a good deal of free play which is both traditional and understandable on a rear-engined car, but it is not entirely necessary. Gear spacing is well mated to the engine performance. The final drive ratio of 4.12 to 1 is a good compromise for traffic acceleration and highway cruise. Third gear is fine for puttering around town at any traffic speed above 20 miles per hour. Reverse gear has a lockout for safety and one must push the gear lever into the floor to get past the lockout loading and into reverse. The gear pattern is marked on the face of the ashtray for the uninitiated.

Roadability and handling

There has been a great deal of controversy in recent years about the inherent poor handling qualities of rear-engined cars. The VW came in for its share of criticism during the witch hunt that contributed to the demise of the Corvair. However, the Volks survived all the adverse comments and is selling better than ever. Overall handling is a far

64

The speedometer contains the fuel gauge and warning lights and is surrounded by the radio speaker. All the knobs are within easy reach of the belted in driver. The air conditioning controls below radio are simple to operate.

The unique body shape of the Beetle has survived many eras of styling since it was conceived way back in the '30s by the celebrated Dr. Ferdinand Porsche. It is a perfect example of the theory of form following function for practicality.

cry from the sports car criteria, but the Volks is a sedan, literally the 'peoples car.' The original design and subsequent modifications never intended the Beetle for performance work, but rather for good, reliable transportation. Viewed in this light the overall handling is agreeable. With a rear weight bias of 60 percent, the tail will often wag the dog if the driver gets over enthusiastic. All models now have subtle suspension changes that reduce the oversteer characteristics in hard cornering. The new rear suspension utilizes a combination of trailing and semi-trailing arms combined with the double-jointed half shafts that really lessens the oversteer and the need for a camber compensator. In spite of the large, by today's standards, fifteen inch wheels the steering effort is fairly light and not at all tiring.

So the modern Bug has good manners without any unusual feel at boulevard speeds. It is only when pressed into a hard corner that the oversteer comes on. Wet roads, too bring out an uncertain feeling in the steering wheel, but regular Volks drivers soon learn the limits of the Bug. In normal driving the handling presents no problem. Of course there is an endless supply of performance and handling goodies on the market for the Bug. Several big companies owe a great deal of their success to the huge market for VW performance and dress-up accessories.

The VW is quite unstable in cross winds and the driver really needs to concentrate to stay in his lane in high winds. Wind wander is common to rear-engined cars, but the Beetle body has always seemed overly sensitive to winds or even the draw from a big truck.

Power and performance

Straight line performance is hardly exhilarating. Still the Volks was not meant to be thrashed about on drag strips. We recorded a creditable quarter mile time of 20.79 seconds with a speed of 61.98 mph in the lights. 0 to 60 fell right in the 20 second bracket. Passing time from 40 to 60 mph averaged out to 11 seconds in third gear. Top speed recorded matched the factory figure of 78 mph. In fact all performance figures matched those in the owner's manual, which is a refreshing change from the normally optimistic numbers quoted on performance. One interesting feature that is traditional on Volkswagens is the fact that top speed and cruising speed are the same. In other words you can drive the turnpike all day at 75 mph with the engine turning over at about 4,000 rpm. Shift points are marked on the speedometer, and these will do for ordinary driving. We exceeded the marked points in order to get maximum performance at the drag strip. We don't recommend this practice for constant use, but it did increase the performance

figures by a bunch, and it didn't do any apparent damage.

Fuel economy is down from the smaller engined models. We averaged close to 25 miles per gallon in everyday use which included high speed freeway driving and a good portion of stop and go commuter traffic. A straight run on the Interstate would undoubtedly yield an average near 27 mpg. We ran through one tank of gas with the air conditioning on all the time, and with varied driving conditions we recorded 23.9 mpg.

Brakes and safety

The excellent and often superfluous braking systems utilizing disc units found on most European cars are not offered on the Beetle. Front disc braked Bugs are available in other parts of the world, but in America all Beetles have drum brakes all around. The drums are adequate for the lightweight car and they provide positive action on repeated stops from 60 mph. But the distance required to stop is longer than average for the size and weight class. There was some fade encountered during the brake test, but it was evenly distributed and the Bug always stopped fairly straight. The hand brake is really effective. With the test car we tried to drive away with the parking brake engaged, and the car just wouldn't move and the engine would stall. Most parking brakes are mere decor and it is a pleasure to find one that can be trusted.

Overall the brakes would receive a good rating, but they are not as effective as brakes on some of the competition.

The required safety equipment has been installed in the Beetle without really changing the overall appearance. The exception to that is the new seats that have the headrest as an integral part of the seat. These tall seats, nicknamed tombstone by some because of their shape, really block vision from the rear seat. It is particularly uncomfortable for children who are riding low in the back seat. The driver must rely entirely on his mirrors for rear vision. The new seats do muffle out some of the engine noise, however, and they are extremely well engineered and comfortable. The buttons on the dash are all flat and padded to comply with regulations and the steering wheel is the collapsible type.

The three point safety harness is by far the most usable safety restraint we have seen in many a test. The belt, with diagonal shoulder harness attached, pulls out on the door side of the front seats and very simply stretches across the body to attach to a metal hook mounted between the seats. To release the harness you merely pull up on a small knobbed handle mounted just forward of the hook. The harness is easy to adjust for the most fumble-fingered among us, and it is also comfortable to wear. There are standard type seat belts for the rear seat passengers.

With the advent of 12 volt electrical systems, the dim lights on Volkswagens vanished into mythology. The headlights throw a good beam for highway driving. The dimmer switch is incorporated into the turn indicator stalk on the left of the steering wheel.

The big husky bumpers look almost too large for the Volks. They are well attached and should afford protection for the body in parking lots. The gas tank now has an external filler cap on the right side just forward of the windshield with a release handle under the dash that forms an effective lock.

Despite the hue and cry raised recently by the publicity given to the fact that Volks lost out to a two-ton Ford sedan in a crash test, the car is no doubt as safe as any on the road provided the driver is performing safely. Even a Sherman tank is apt to be crushed by another tank that is twice its size and weight. Due to the actual configuration of the Bug, it does have its quirks including the need to watch tire pressures. Every owner who is truly interested in safety will watch details and check his car at regular intervals. The driver is the real clue to safety on the road.

Comfort and convenience

The Volkswagen has many conveniences and the new front seats are certainly comfortable. Still the overall feeling is one of confinement and there just isn't much room inside. Everything is within easy reach of the driver, except for the heater vent covers on the front footwell. The heater temperature and rear seat heater controls are between the front seats just forward of the safety harness hook. We didn't really try the heater during the summer test period, but past experience probably holds true with a fair amount of heat provided, but with heat distribution generally poor.

The speedometer reads to an optimistic 90 mph, and a gas gauge and total mileage counter are included in the center of the circular speedometer. That is it for instrumentation except for the usual warning lights which are spotted around the bottom of the speedometer. In the center of the dash, over the radio there are switches for windshield wipers, brake warning light and headlights. The windshield washer switch is on the floor. The rather small ashtray in the center of the dash has a dandy feature in a small deflector on the top of the tray. This keeps one from burning the dash material while groping around for the ashtray in the dark. There is a handy grab handle over the medium sized glove box. Inside the glove box is the handle to release the trunk lid. The familiar sounding horn is actuated by a half ring on the large diameter steering wheel.

It is awkward to check water level on the battery since that object rides under the rear seat. Some effort is required to undo things and gain access to the battery.

With two good sized men in the front

The trunk will carry very little other than carefully chosen soft pieces. The interior trunk release handle forms an effective lock for valuables stashed in the nose.

The famous Volks engine scarcely needs description. Engine access is somewhat hampered by the Meir-Line air conditioning unit, but the cool air is dispensed in an efficient manner and is well worth the inconvenience in the engine bay.

seats, elbows and shoulders are very close together. The rear seats are impossible for adults with the larger front seat backs. Leg and foot room is negligible even for tots, and climbing into the back seat is quite a chore. Once you get close enough to reach it, the deep well under the rear window will hold quite a bit of soft luggage or any amount of oddiments.

The windshield is still flat glass, and the windshield wipers still park raggedly well up on the glass. With the gas tank taking up most of the space in the trunk, luggage has to be carefully planned or fitted in the nooks and crannies. The spare tire rides in the trunk as does the tool kit and jack. The tool kit is a nicety that has all but disappeared from cars. The Volks kit supplies a spare fan belt, pliers, a screwdriver with reversible head for straight or Phillips head, and open end and a socket wrench, and a plug wrench that does double duty on the fan pulley and the wheel bolts.

One of the biggest conveniences of the Volks is the really extensive dealer and service shop network all over the world. Anywhere you take your Beetle you will find courteous and quick service. Every dealer seems to have an unending supply of parts as well. Coupled with the fabled longevity of the car, the service network is largely responsible for the astounding success of the Volkswagen Beetle — a car that is no longer modern in appearance or concept.

Summary

Although there are many rumors that the days of the Beetle are numbered, the car carries on and on. Volkswagen has introduced several other models in the last ten years, but the Beetle is still the cornerstone of the company's continuing success in the market place. It has stiff competition from both domestic and imported cars, but the sales figures go right on rising yearly. The VW syndrome is a serious headache for Detroit auto men.

We enjoyed driving the Volks on the road and in town. The somewhat cramped quarters are the major complaint, but it is nice to be able to reach across a car to roll the opposite window down. The staff rated the Beetle as a most usable means of transport. The high level of quality control is quite impressive as is the high resale value of any year Beetle. It makes an ideal go-to-work car for the commuter offering long service, good fuel economy, and reasonable comfort. Even with the air conditioning the price of a new Beetle is within reach of every car shopper. Some mornings on the freeway it looks like everyone in town has one.

Regular updating has kept the Beetle in the ball park with the other imported cars, but it is still a very old basic design. Nonetheless, it is a good investment and a good performer for the driver who wants a car for daily use. ♠

Volkswagen 1500

Data in Brief

DIMENSIONS

Overall length (in.)	158.6
Wheelbase (in.)	94.5
Height (in.)	59.1
Width (in.)	61.0
Tread (front, in.)	51.6
Tread (rear, in.)	53.3
Fuel tank capacity (gal.)	10.6
Luggage capacity (cu. ft.)	7.1
Turning diameter (ft.)	36.0

ENGINE

Type	Horizontally opposed 4 cylinder, OHV, air-cooled
Displacement (cu. in.)	91.1
Horsepower (at 4200 rpm)	53
Torque (lb. ft. at 2600 rpm)	78.1

WEIGHT, TIRES, BRAKES

Weight (as tested, lb.)	1885
Tires	5.60x15
Brakes, front	drum
Brakes, rear	drum

SUSPENSION

Front	Independent, trailing arms, torsion bars, tube shocks anti-roll bar
Rear	Independent, swing axles, torsion bars, tube shocks

PERFORMANCE

Standing ¼ mile (sec.)	20.79
Speed at end of ¼ mile (mph)	61.98
Braking (from 60 mph, ft.)	159.4

Road Test

CAR AT A GLANCE: Four more horsepower... Higher power peak ... Cracks the 20-second barrier from zero to 60... Traditional beetle quality overall and in detail ... Traditional beetle wind bobble.

by Don MacDonald
photos by Lester Nehamkin

Except for the slim tires the beetle is just as much at home on bad roads as any dune buggy. Acceleration on washboard is free of hop.

1970 VW SEDAN...Stock Long Legs at Last!

The people in Englewood Cliffs who import Volkswagens enjoy making fun of their product, even to the extent of compiling anecdotes and distributing them to 3.5 million owners via the publication "Small World." Beneath the surface of this levity, though, lies the certainty that someday the bubble must burst.

The factory people in Wolfsburg do not indulge in or even understand this brand of humor but they, too, are aware that a 25-year idyl must someday end. Thus we see efforts at diversification such as the purchase of NSU and Audi and a renewal of component inter-change with Porsche. We see new models such as the 411 and the 181 utility, plus first official recognition that dune buggies exist. The fact being faced is that beetle sales seem to have reached a plateau in world markets and, if you can sort out extraneous factors such as uncertain currency, dock strikes and the like, there's even indication of a slump in the offing.

A styling department has been created but it's doubtful if they'll ever be called upon to bestow new sheet-metal on the beetle. They could create an all-new car, of course, but they can't restyle a syndrome. Thus, the beetle's survival has been left in the hands of the engineers and as a result, more basic changes have been made in the last four years than in the 21 others of its existence combined. This model season in particular sees a beetle that's good enough to break out of the cult and woo buyers who never considered the car seriously before.

I'm speaking specifically about performance as it pertains to U.S. driving conditions. The premise is that a certain modicum of acceleration is necessary both for your own safety and to facilitate the flow of traffic. Though zero to 60 mph figures are generally

Enlarged turn signal and parking light, the latter on with headlights, is a little too bright, reflecting on highway signs a 100 feet ahead.

The new slots in the engine lid are essentially the same as used on the convertible but may affect usage of luggage racks. No advice is available on this.

meaningless on the street, they are widely available for any car and they translate to the meaningful — yea, vital — 50 to 70 mph passing range. Just three years ago, the VW 1500 was the most sluggish of 10 popular imports in its general price range by factors ranging from 1.2 to 8.6 seconds in the zero to 60 department and 1.1 to nearly 10 seconds for passing. Those 10 or even 1.1 extra seconds of exposure to oncoming traffic while you pass a truck could prove rather meaningful to your welfare plus that of innocent others.

The 1967 stickshift beetle with 53 horsepower and weighing 1880 lbs. required 20.6 seconds to achieve 60 mph from a standing start and 18.1 seconds to move from 50 to 70 mph. The 1970 version with only four more horsepower and about the same weight accelerates from zero to 60 in 18.2 seconds and will perform the passing increment in 16.2 seconds. These improvements may not seem like much, but they move the beetle up from a solid last among imports to about midway in agility. The difference stems from both horsepower and torque peaking at significantly higher rpms.

On the way from Las Vegas to Los Angeles via Interstate 15 there's an import killer of a grade just before the town of Baker called Halloran Summit. It's not higher than some of the others on the route, just steeper. Our test VW 1600 climbed this in 4th gear and never dropped below 50 mph. I know of no earlier stock beetle that isn't forced to shift to 3rd at 40 mph, unless the driver is totally insensitive to a laboring engine. For clarification, this comparison of the two cars involves only a driver and a couple of suitcases.

Another desirable consequence of moving the power peak ahead is that the '70 beetle sounds a lot happier cruising at 70 mph than it does between 55 and 65 mph. The factory quotes 83 mph as the maximum for the new model, but we all know that any beetle of recent vintage will do that — at least according to the speedometer. The new one, though, will wind up to where the needle covers the oil warning light on a long straight. That should be an honest 90, shouldn't it?

The beetle syndrome consists partly of tolerating traits that would cause lesser imports to be rejected out of hand. And to be fair, these traits are undoubtedly tolerated in return for larger benefits such as unmatched durability and the little matter of getting almost as much for the car second-hand as you paid for it new.

Appearance changes for '70 include larger auxilliary lights plus some extra slots in the engine lid. Inside, those towering head rests have been slimmed a bit.

Vulnerable Porsche-like reflectors are a '70 addition, as are the tubes to drain water that might seep in from the slots in the engine lid.

Instrumentation and trim is carryover. Large ignition key which locks the wheel is still sometimes difficult to insert.

Optional sunroof is leak and dust proof, operates easily. When open it helps alleviate harmonic drumming experienced at highway speeds.

Those I speak of that peeve the most are wind wobble and that oppressive harmonic drumming somewhere in the headliner that occurs at varying highway speeds and window settings.

Nothing has been done about these for the new year. Despite its relatively new fully independent, semi-trailing arm rear suspension the '70 beetle *seems* to bob about as much as ever in gusty crosswinds or from the air blast of a passing truck. However accustomed one becomes to this, it is nevertheless tiring to driver and passengers on a long trip. We should emphasize, though, that our experience over the years invariably has

involved low mileage cars. VW experts note that the bobbling tends to diminish after the suspension "softens" at the 6000-mile mark or thereabouts.

The harmonic drumming is undoubtedly related to a lot of variables such as body shape and size, upholstery and deadening materials and also, of course, constantly shifting relative winds and the position of the windows. The fact remains, though, that there are other small cars that don't create this racket so there must be a way of getting rid of it. Perhaps if factory engineers and executives had their company Karmanns and 411E's taken away from them and

were forced to drive beetles for a spell, then they would come up with a solution.

Checks on fuel consumption resulted in figures that are familiar to most beetle owners. We recorded a low of 20.9 mpg which was a combination of heavy traffic and high-speed Interstate driving. Our best figure was 28.6 mpg on an Interstate run where speeds were kept to the legal 65 mph night limit. During miscellaneous driving with no attempt at achieving maximum economy, but not beating the car either, you can expect the usual 25 mpg. It should be remembered, though, that we re-

VOLKSWAGEN 1600 SEDAN
Specifications from the Manufacturer

ENGINE:
Type: Rear-mounted, overhead valve, horizontally opposed four, air-cooled.
Bore and stroke: 3.36 x 2.72 ins.
Displacement: 96.66 cu. ins. (1584 cc)
Horsepower: 57 @ 4400 rpm
Torque: 81.7 lbs. ft. @ 3000 rpm
Compression ratio: 7.5 to 1

TRANSMISSION:
Type: 4-speed fully synchronous manual, 3-speed semi-automatic optional.
Gear ratios: 1st-3.80, 2nd-2.06, 3rd-1.26, 4th-0.89
Rear axle ratio: 4.125

SUSPENSION:
Front: Independent torsion bar with stabilizer
Rear: Fully independent torsion bar, semi-trailing

STEERING: Roller, curb-to-curb 36 ft.

WHEELS AND TIRES: Bolt-on steel disc with 5.60 x 15 bias-ply tires

BRAKES: Dual-circuit hydraulic drum

CAPACITIES:
Fuel: 10.6 U.S. gals
Oil: 2.5 U.S. qts.
Transmission: 5.3 U.S. pints

BODY AND FRAME: Steel body, platform chassis

DIMENSIONS AND WEIGHTS: Wheelbase 94.5 ins., Overall length 158.7 ins., Width 61.0 ins., Height 59.1 ins., Weight 1808 lbs.

Spare fan belt is still standard equipment along with a tool kit. That padlock is installed on all company cars owned by Volkswagen Pacific.

The underside of the '70 model will be familiar to the owner of any recent beetle. Stone guards on shocks were added some time ago.

ceived the car with nine miles showing on the odometer and turned it in with 1065 miles. Economy naturally tended to climb as the motor wore in. When the car went in for its somewhat delayed "600-mile" check, the crankcase showed a consumption of one quart. Sometimes I wished oil were sold in pint containers, for these last 300 miles across the desert with the dipstick reading just above the "add" mark and a crankcase containing only perhaps 1.6 quarts of "break-in" oil was a little disconcerting. It's either pints or VW should install a metered oil reservoir.

Perhaps an owner would have drained and refilled at the proper time at a convenient gas station but VW frankly had me intimidated with the seriousness they attach to the first lubrication. It's not so much the engine oil but the requirement to drain and refill the transmission at the 600-mile point. The average nightime attendant at a desert station might not be adept at this, mainly because from thereon in, the SAE 90 hypoid oil is theoretically good for the life of the car.

Any discussion of beetle handling would not only be redundant but foolish. Vigorous pursuit of the point of no return in an unfamiliar curve all too often ends up with a toppled bug, wheels spinning futilely in the air. When a pound of tire pressure, one way or the other, can affect your insurance rates for years to come, I'll leave this

Continued on Page 121

BEETLE 1600

THE ubiquitous Beetle comes with a two-fisted punch for 1970: a 1600-cc. version has been born, joining the 1500 on the South African market, and with much more get-away ability than before.

Current joke from America, it is reported, is that the Beetle "has joined in the horse-power race".

There is more ·than a grain of truth in this — the steady growth in engine capacity from 1200 to 1300, to 1500 and now 1600, is symptomatic of modern car-manufacturing trends, though in fairness it should be remembered that even a 1600 Beetle develops little more power than the average 1200-cc. car.

NEW ENGINE

The 1600 engine is basically that used in earlier Volkswagen 1600 models, but with a single carburettor and modest 7·5 to 1 compression ratio.

The lower c.r. is intended to improve reliability, and both 1500 and 1600 engines this year have larger oil channels to improve cooling, for the same reason.

The new 1600 engine has a bigger bore than the 1500 (85·5 mm., against 83 mm.) and the same stroke, and develops an extra 4 b.h.p. S.A.E. This is 7·5 per cent increase in power, accompanied by a 5·2 per cent increase in torque and longer engine range (4,400 r.p.m., against the 4,200 r.p.m. of the 1500).

NEW FEATURES

Priced at R90 more than the 1500 Beetle, the new 1600 has some extra luxury features in addition to its bigger engine. It has full floor carpeting and extra seat padding, plus a cigar lighter, wooden gearlever knob and anti-dazzle rearview mirror.

Most important of the new features is that the rear side windows are now hinged to open outwards and improve ventilation.

Externally, it has an exterior rearview mirror on the driver door, wheel trim rings and "VW 1600" script on the bonnet to distinguish it from the 1500.

Both 1970 Beetle models have additional horizontal air louvres on the rear bonnet, which are as much an ornamental feature as to provide extra cooling in the engine compartment.

ANOTHER 20 YEARS

It is confidently predicted by Volkswagen that the Beetle will still be around in 20 years' time, looking much the same as it does today and has for the past 30 years.

This is possible, mainly on the basis that the Beetle price will remain fairly constant as the years go by.

Beetle owners may become unhappy about the lack of interior and trunk space, the noise and other features, but it will remain economical basic transport with a high standard of manufacture.

SWING AXLES

Three years ago, VW tacitly admitted that swing axles were unhealthy by changing over to a safer dual-universal-joint system for the rear axles of the Kombi models: an improvement which has since been extended to the VW 1600 Automatic models and the new VW 411.

The sooner this comes on the Beetle models, the better.

One small, but important, improvement in the 1970 Beetle 1600 is the introduction of a decimal counter on the odometer — just in time to become obsolete in 1971 when the Republic goes over to the metric system!

PERFORMANCE FACTORS

There is an insignificant increase in weight in the 1600, but with the new 57-b.h.p. engine the weight-power ratio improves from the 38·2 lb./b.h.p. of the 1500, to 35·6 lb./b.h.p. The extra torque of the 1600 engine is important, as well as the increased engine range — from 4,200 to 4,400 r.p.m.

Gearing remains at roughly 20 m.p.h./1,000 r.p.m. in top — a good measure of overgearing — but the 1600 goes higher in the gears. In particular, it will go to 65 m.p.h. true speed in 3rd without losing power — an improvement of about 5 m.p.h. over the 1500.

PERFORMANCE

The car gets away from rest with wheelspin, and with snap upshifts at 25, 42 and 65 m.p.h. it gives new dimensions to Beetle performance. A comparison with the 1500 (CAR Road Test, July, 1968):

			1500	**1600**
0–50	..	..	13·3	**11·7**
0–60	..	..	20·0	**18·4**
¼ Mile	..	..	20·9	**20·3**

The Test car — works-prepared — tailed off rather badly at the top end. Tapley pull at 70 was actually inferior to that recorded in 1968 with the 1500 Beetle, and the 1600 would

SPECIFICATIONS

ENGINE:
Cylinders . Four opposed, rear-mounted
Carburettors . Single Solex 30 PICT 2
Bore . . . . 3·37 in. (85·5 mm.)
Stroke . . . 2·72 in. (69·0 mm.)
Cubic capacity . 96·7 cu. in. (1,584 c.c.)
Compression ratio . . . . 7·5 to 1
Valve gear . . . . O.h.v., pushrods
Main bearings . . . . . . Three
Aircleaner . . . Oilbath, 0·7 pints
Fuel rating 91-octane
Cooling . . . Air jacket, blower fan
Electrics . . . . . . 12-volt DC

ENGINE OUTPUT:
Max. b.h.p. S.A.E. 57
Max. b.h.p. net . . . . . . 48·5
Peak r.p.m. 4,400
Max. torque/r.p.m. 82/3,000

TRANSMISSION:
Forward speeds . . . . . Four
Synchromesh . . . . . . All
Gearshift . . . . Floor
Low gear . . . . . . 3·80 to 1
2nd gear . . . . . . 2·06 to 1
3rd gear . . . . . . 1·26 to 1
Top gear . . . . . . 0·89 to 1
Reverse gear . . . . . 3·61 to 1
Final drive . . . . . 4·125 to 1
Drive wheels . . . . . . Rear
Tyre size . . . . . . 5·60 x 15

BRAKES:
Front . . . . Drums
Rear . . . . Drums

Total lining area . . . 96·1 sq. in.
Boosting . . . . Nil
Handbrake position . Between seats

STEERING:
Type . . . Worm and roller, damped
Lock to lock . . . . . . 2·7 turns
Turning circle . . . . . 36·0 ft.

MEASUREMENTS:
Length overall . . . . . .158·6 in.
Width overall . . . . . 61·0 in.
Height overall . . . . . 59·0 in.
Wheelbase . . . . . 94·5 in.
Front track . . . . . 51·4 in.
Rear track . . . . . 53·4 in.
Ground clearance . . . . 5·9 in.
Licensing weight . . . . 1,730 lb.

SUSPENSION:
Front . . . . Independent
Type . . . Trailing arms, torsion bars
Rear . . . . Independent
Type . . . Swing axles, torsion bars

CAPACITIES:
Seating . . . . Five
Fuel tank . . . . . . 8.8 gal.
Luggage trunk . . . . . 5·0 cu. ft.
Utility space . . . 4·9–17·6 cu. ft.

SERVICE DATA:
Sump capacity . . . . : 4·4 pints
Change interval . . . . 3,000 miles
Gearbox diff. capacity . . . 4·4 pints

Change interval . . . 30,000 miles
Air filter service . . . . . 6,000 miles
Greasing points . . . Front axles (4)
Greasing interval . . . . 3,000 miles
(These basic service recommendations are given for guidance only, and may vary according to operating conditions. Inquiries should be addressed to authorised dealerships.)

TYRE PRESSURES:
Crossply: Front . . . . 16 to 22 lb.
Rear . . . 24 to 30 lb.
Radial ply: Front . . . 22 to 26 lb.
Rear . . . . 26 to 32 lb.

WARRANTY:
Six months or 6,000 miles.

BASIC PRICES:
Coast and Reef R1,716

PROVIDED TEST CAR:
Volkswagen South Africa, Uitenhage.

STANDARD EQUIPMENT:
Semi-reclining front seats, door pockets, convertible rear seating/luggage space, heater, cigar lighter, semi-automatic windscreen washers, headlamp flasher, two coat hooks, two-speed wipers, two coat hooks, two assist straps, dash grab-handle, wheel trim rings, exterior rear-view mirror, wooden gearshift knob, anti-dazzle rear-view mirror.

MAKE AND MODEL:
Make . . . . Volkswagen
Model . . . . . . 1600 Super-Beetle

PERFORMANCE FACTORS:
Power/weight (lb./b.h.p.) . . . . 35·6
Frontal area (sq. ft.) . . . . . 25·0
Drag at 60 m.p.h. (lb.) . . . . 112·5
M.p.h./1,000 r.p.m. (top) . . . . 19·9
(Calculated on licensing weight, gross frontal area, gearing and net b.h.p.)

INTERIOR NOISE LEVELS:

	Min.	Wind	Road
Idling . . .	58·5	—	—
30 m.p.h. . .	70·0	72·0	78·0
45 m.p.h. . .	75·0	77·0	82·5
60 m.p.h. . .	83·0	85·0	87·0
Full throttle . .			See graph
Average dBA at 60 . .			85·0

(Measured in decibels, "A" weighting, averaging runs both ways on a level road; "Minimum" with car closed; "Wind" with one window fully open; "Road" on a coarse gravel surface.)

ACCELERATION FROM REST:
0–30 . . . . 4·4
0–40 . . . . 8·0
0–50 . . . . 11·7
0–60 . . . . 18·4
0–70 . . . . 36·3
¼ Mile . . . . 20·3

OVERTAKING ACCELERATION:

	3rd	Top
20–40	6·8	13·4
30–50	8·1	13·5
40–60	10·7	15·7
50–70	—	27·7

(Measured in seconds, to true speeds, averaging runs both ways on a level road, car carrying test crew of two and standard test equipment.)

MAXIMUM SPEED:
True speed . . . . . . 78·0*
Speedo reading 81-82
Calibration:
Indicated

20	30	40	50	60	70

True speed

18	28	38	48	57·5	67

(*Calculated to the nearest 0·5 m.p.h.)

FUEL CONSUMPTION:
30 m.p.h. . . . . 54·0
45 m.p.h. . . . . 45·6
60 m.p.h. . . . . 35·7
Full throttle . . . . . . See graph
(Measured in miles per Imp. gallon, averaging runs both ways on a level road.)

BRAKING TEST:
From 50 m.p.h.:
First stop . . . . 2·9
Tenth stop . . . . 2·7
Average . . . . 2·83
Handbrake stop . . . . . . 6·2
(Measured in sec., with stops from true speeds at 30-sec. intervals on a good bitumenised surface.)

RADIENTS IN GEARS:
Low gear . . . . . . 1 in 2·8
2nd gear . . . . . . 1 in 4·1
3rd gear . . . . . . 1 in 6·8
Top gear . . . . . . 1 in 11·5
(Tabulated from Tapley g. readings, car carrying test crew of two and standard test equipment.)

GEARED SPEEDS:
Low gear . . . . 20·5
2nd gear . . . . 37·8
3rd gear . . . . 61·8
Top gear . . . . 87·3
(Calculated to true speeds, at engine peak r.p.m. — 4,400.)

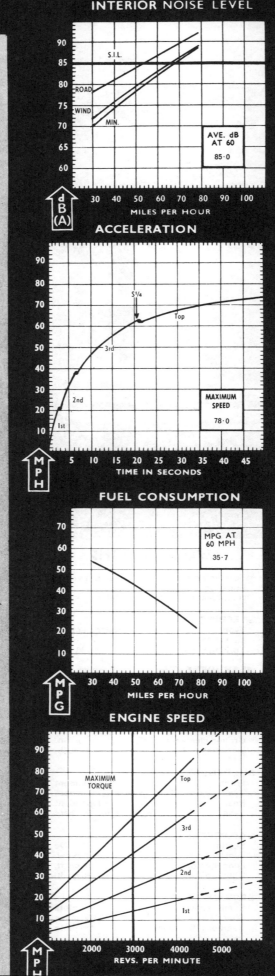

INTERIOR NOISE LEVEL

S.I.L.

ROAD

WIND

MIN.

AVE. dB
AT 60

85·0

dB(A)

MILES PER HOUR

ACCELERATION

S¼

Top

3rd

2nd

1st

MAXIMUM
SPEED

78·0

MPH

TIME IN SECONDS

FUEL CONSUMPTION

MPG AT
60 MPH

35·7

MPG

MILES PER HOUR

ENGINE SPEED

MAXIMUM
TORQUE

Top

3rd

2nd

1st

MPH

REVS. PER MINUTE

SILENCE LEVELS:
Mechanical . . . . Poor
Idling . . . . . Very Poor
Transmission . . . Very Good
Wind . . . . Good
Road . . . . Fair
Coachwork . . . . Very Good
Average . . . . Poor

ENGINE:
Starting . . . . . Very Good
Response . . . . Very Good
Smoothness . . . . Very Good
Accessibility . . . . . Good

STEERING:
Accuracy . . . . . Very Good
Stability at speed . . . . . Fair
Stability in wind . . . . Poor
Steering effort . . . . Very Good
Roughness . . . . . . Good
Road feel . . . . . Very Good
Centring action . . . Very Good
Turning circle . . . . Poor

BRAKING:
Pedal pressure . . . Very Good
Response . . . . Very Good
Fade resistance . . . Very Good
Directional stability . . . . Fair
Handbrake position . . Very Good
Handbrake action . . . Excellent

TRANSMISSION:
Clutch action . . . . . . Fair
Pedal pressure . . . . . Fair
Gearbox ratios . . . . . Good
Final drive ratio . . . . . Good
Gearshift position . . . . Good
Gearshift action . . . Excellent
Synchromesh . . . Excellent

SUSPENSION:
Firmness rating . . . Very Good
Progressive action . . . . Good
Roadholding . . . . . . Good
Roll control . . . . Very Good
Tracking control . . . . Poor
Pitching control . . . Very Good
Load ability . . . . . Good

DRIVER CONTROLS:
Hand control location . . . Good
Pedal location . . . . . Fair
Wiper action . . . . . Good
Washer action . . . Very Good
Instrumentation . . . . Poor

INTERIOR COMFORT:
Seat design . . . . . Good
Headroom front . . . Excellent
Legroom front . . . . Good
Headroom rear . . . . Poor
Legroom rear . . . . Poor
Door access . . . . . Good
Lighting . . . . . . Good
Accessories fitted . . . . Fair
Accessories potential . . . Fair

DRIVING COMFORT:
Steering wheel position . . Very Good
Steering wheel reach . . . Good
Visibility . . . . . . Good
Directional feel . . . . Poor
Ventilation . . . . . Poor
Heating . . . . Very Good

COACHWORK:
Appearance . . . . . Good
Finish . . . . Very Good
Space utilization . . Very Good
Luggage capacity . . Very Good
Luggage access . . . . Fair

TEST CONDITIONS:
Altitude . . . . At sea level
Weather . . . . Fine, windy
Barometric reading . . 29·99
Fuel used . . . 93-octane
Test car's mileage . . . 820

not quite match the maximum speed of the 1500.

This may be due to the altered torque and power curves, as in other respects the 1600 proved very much stronger than the 1500. In second and third gears, in particular, the new model showed up very well and proved capable of enthusiastic motoring.

FUEL ECONOMY

The fuel economy pattern also alters considerably: the 1600 engine is more economical at low speed, while at higher speeds it uses more fuel than the 1500. A comparison:

	1500	1600
M.p.g. at 30 ..	.. 51·0	**54·0**
M.p.g. at 45 ..	.. 43·4	**45·6**
M.p.g. at 60 ..	.. 36·2	**35·7**
M.p.g. at 70 ..	.. 30·4	**28·9**

This increase at higher speeds is consistent with an increase in engine capacity by boring, but is little enough to make the 1600 Beetle very economical to run.

STOPPING ABILITY

Brakes are the well-founded drums used on the 1500, giving thoroughly-sound stopping ability from medium speeds, and good stopping from cruising speed.

The Test car was pulling to the right in hard stops, but nevertheless managed a clean stop from 70 in 4·3 sec. These drum brakes are exceptionally good, and stand up well to punishing use.

VENTILATION AND NOISE

In spite of the hinged rear windows, which improve ventilation in the rear of the car, the ventilation system is indifferent, with a low and inflexible inlet capacity.

The demisting flow at the windscreen is good, however.

Noise levels are much the same as with the 1500: too high for comfort, but not objectionable inside the car, except during acceleration using maximum revs.

HANDLING AND RIDE

Two sterling Beetle features are the strong and resilient torsion-bar suspension with big 15-inch wheels, and the light and responsive steering. The car has a capable ride under bad conditions, including corrugations.

The wider rear track introduced with the 1500 was an improvement, but the Beetle still is directionally unstable, particularly in windy wea-

ther. During this Test we had a fresh south-easterly wind, which reacted with the tracking action of the swing axles to produce wandering tendencies which needed determined correction at speeds over 50 m.p.h.

The car will take loads well, but at the cost of severe variations in rear-wheel camber.

DRIVER CONTROLS

We had not noticed it in previous Beetle Tests, but possibly because a stronger clutch is used with the 1600 engine, the clutch pedal seemed rather hard, and its long travel was highlighted. Or possibly it is just that so many cars today have light diaphragm-spring clutches, that a contrast is created.

A woman test driver commented on this, as well.

In other respects the controls are functional and useful. The wooden gearlever knob is attractive and comfortable, and the new seats are fatigue-resistant without being too plushy.

The windscreen wipers leave a blind spot on the driver side at right on the windscreen, and the indicator switch is on the wrong side of the steering column for right-hand drive.

It's disconcerting when lights have to be dipped, or a change of direction indicated, just when the left hand is occupied in changing gear!

SUMMARY

The VW 1600 Beetle is sure to go down at least as well in South Africa as its stable-mate, the 1500 Beetle — in fact, it should overtake the 1500 model in sales before long.

It is a new and exciting mixture of Beetle virtues, characteristics and faults; notably quick off the mark and much stronger up the hills.

Like the 1500, it is impressive value for money, both in its quality construction and economical performance. Easily the most exciting Beetle yet! ●

DATA AT 70	
Min. noise level . . .	85·5 dBA
0–70 through gears . .	36·3 sec.
M.p.g. at 70 . .	28·9
Braking from 70 . . .	4·3 sec.
Reserve power at 70 .	0·019 g.
Max. gradient at 70 (top) .	1 in 52·7
Speedo error at 70 . .	4·3% over
Speedo at true 70 . .	73
R.p.m. at 70 (top) . . .	3,510

The 1600 engine looks not much different, but has 7·5 per cent more power.

Controls are improved by decimals in the odometer, and a wooden gearshift knob.

Still with swing-axles, but with the wider track of the 1500, the 1600 Beetle can be cornered better than earlier models.

Close-up of the hinged rear side window, which aids ventilation.

Volkswagen is the biggest motor manufacturer in Europe, their Beetle—coming up to 13,000,000 strong—the world's most popular car. But how much longer can this giant German company rely on a design conceived over 30 years ago? Charles Bulmer and Anthony Curtis have been to Wolfsburg to investigate VW's fortunes and plans

Beetles forever

This magazine should first hit the bookstalls (all being well) during the afternoon of Tuesday April 7, by which time a total of 12,806,843 Volkswagen Beetles will have been produced. Give or take a few hundred that is, for more than three of them come off the lines every minute, 16 hours a day, five days a week; a considerable production achievement even by American standards where annual production of one model rarely exceeds 750,000. So by the time you have read thus far, yet another of the species *Coleoptera Wolfsburgae* will have passed through its larval stage. Will nothing rid us of this plague of Beetles?

Nothing will, it seems, or at least that's the way it looks from the 11th floor of the 13-storey Volkswagenwerk admin. block in

the executive suite of Dr Carl Hahn, protegé of the great Heinz Nordhoff in his lifetime and currently director in charge of marketing on the executive board now headed by Dr Kurt Lotz. For so far the Beetle, with its extraordinary evolutionary adaptability, has proved a strain highly resistant to the most powerful competition produced by any other manufacturer. A few years ago, Dr Hahn told us, home-market sales of the Beetle slumped badly because Germans were bored with living in a one-model country. Top management got quite nervous about it, but the crisis soon passed and the car began to sell more vigorously than ever before. "The Beetle is not an automobile," said Dr Hahn, "It is like a tool, a spoon . . . its shape has such a wide acceptance . . . it is divorced from styling trends." Volkswagen's present share of the home market, he pointed out, is close to 50 per cent—just what it has been for the past 20 years, but maintained in the face of far fiercer opposition. Similarly their sales in America continued to be as excellent as ever and they were happy with the progress they had made in Britain.

Here we interrupted saying that VW sales in Britain had fallen off since 1967.

Dr Hahn conceded this but said they had been putting through an extensive reorganization of the British dealer network during the past four years (to raise the already high standard of servicing and spares availability) which was just beginning to bear fruit. Preliminary sales figures for this year showed a great improvement, he said.

Did they not fear the introduction of sub-compacts like the Gremlin? "We've seen the Gremlin," replied Dr Hahn, "and we're delighted by it." It is too closely related to the standard American car to be much threat to the Beetle market he went on to say. In basic form the Gremlin has only two seats while the optional rear ones are very small, and its low price applies only as a difficult-to-obtain "loss leader". Though the Americans could compete in price—there had been times when they

Dr. Carl Hahn, marketing director.

Then as now the surroundings of the huge Wolfsburg plant are rural by factory standards. Wheat was grown in the grounds, at first from absolute necessity, and then as a symbolic reminder of hard times, but the practice has now been abandoned. No prizes are offered for knowing when this photograph was taken.

had sold their very large "standard"-sized cars for the same price as a Beetle—Dr Hahn thought that no one had really exploited the market for small European-style cars in America. He believes it to be potentially vast and to be increasing in importance due to the very real recession that the Americans are currently suffering.

Certainly there is much in the sales statistics for North America to support Dr Hahn's argument. It is true that Volkswagen sales were 551,366 in 1969, 5.2 per cent of the whole, whereas in 1968 they were 569,292, 5.4 per cent of a similar total. It is also true that Toyota sales have shot up from 16,000 in 1966 to 110,000 in 1969, during which time VW's share of the imported car market has dropped from around 65 per cent to under 50 per cent. Nevertheless Volkswagen seem to be selling

The boss—Dr. Kurt Lotz.

Anthony Curtis (left), the Editor (centre) and Dr. Carl Hahn, marketing director, discuss Volkswagen sales policy.

a comfortable ½ million cars annually in a market that is expanding to other manufacturers whose sales do not seem to be gained much at the expense of the Beetle or other Wolfsburg products.

Not quite convinced we continued to cast doubts on the everlasting qualities of the Beetle. The customers' standards change we said: it must eventually fall out of favour. Could Volkswagen not find themselves in a position analogous to that of Ford at the end of the Model T era?

It was perhaps Dr Hahn's great enthusiasm for the Beetle that caused him to reply with a trace of impatience. The position was not, nor could it be, analogous, he said. For one thing the Beetle was subject to continuous development. For another they were far from being a one-model company as were Ford, who virtually abandoned production for 18 months while preparing the Model A. Last year, for example, the Volkswagen group sold around 2.1 million vehicles of which 1.2 million were Beetles. Of the other million over 250,000 were 1600s, and more than 250,000 were light commercial vehicles. Then there was their Auto Union Audi NSU group, the fastest growing in the medium-car class, which last year produced 120,000 Audis alone.

Was this the reason why VW had bought Audi NSU? Partly, yes and partly for their additional research and development facilities, for the increased model range they offered, and for their dealer network. It was also an advantage to be represented by more than one marketing organization.

While on the subject of the Audi NSU group, we asked about the present British Audi-Mercedes-NSU marketing muddle. Dr Hahn told us that VW were working to untangle the situation and that there was nothing he could tell us at the moment that would not add further confusion to the affair.

Volkswagen's gradual move away from one-model reliance is exemplified by the production of the Porsche-Volks 914 sports car. In most countries this is to be added to the ranges of existing Volkswagen dealers most of whom have already been selling the pure Porsche models. But marketing—of all Porsches as well as the hybrid 914—is to be done by a new company shared equally between Porsche and Volkswagen, called Volkswagen-Porsche Vertriebgesellschaft. Dr Ferry Porsche is president and Dr Hahn vice-president. (Porsche (GB) Ltd will sell the 914 in Britain for at least the next year.)

This joint company represents the only direct links between the two firms, Volkswagen owning no stock in Porsche. But by tradition the two companies have always worked closely together, with Porsche building prototypes and carrying our research and development work for Volkswagen on a contract basis.

"They have been doing this for some time, and you have already seen one of their prototypes—it's the Beetle," said Dr Hahn with a smile.

Naturally Volkswagen do plenty of research and development of new models themselves: Dr Hahn pointed out to us from his window their new research centre, a mile or so away across the railway track, which is still under construction. Set about with tower cranes it looked in the distance as big as a small town; it already houses 2000 people who have been responsible for such projects as the development of electronic fuel-injection in conjunction with Bosch; the evolution of their automatic transmission systems; and the introduction of the "Type II" commercial vehicle. Nevertheless, such forward thinking on advanced models is a relatively new element in VW policy. The building of the new centre was started as recently as 1964 and their wind tunnel was opened in 1966.

But the existence of such a research centre means that Volkswagen are not likely to be caught out technically if the time ever comes for the Beetle to be replaced. Nor, as we have seen, is the company likely to be caught out commercially since their range of other cars is wide enough and extensive enough for their sales to cushion any such loss. Moreover, they own NSU, a completely separate company which is also in the small-car field—and whose Prinz 4 model incidentally, sells better in some countries, such as Italy, than the Beetle. Volkswagen can use NSU as Fiat use Autobianchi: to try out advanced designs in production runs which by VW standards are effectively of pilot size. So when the Beetle finally runs out of mutations to cope with the pesticide of change it will probably die with a whimper rather than a bang.

Small beginnings—a few of the first civilian VWs produced for the allied forces just after the war.

You and your car

6 Volkswagen 1300/1500 Beetle

We included the Beetle 1300/1500 in this series of owner surveys to find out whether the car really does justify its reputation for reliability—and VW agents their reputation for good service. And if so, whether these important points outweighed the car's shortcomings of mediocre roadholding, performance, accommodation and anachronistic styling. The answer, overwhelmingly, is that they do. Our respondents' cars, though by no means faultless, have been very nearly 100 per cent dependable. And customer satisfaction is high. On these points, the VW Beetle fares significantly better than any of the British cars in this present series of surveys.

The analysis is based on questionnaires completed by 90 VW owners.

1 WHO BOUGHT IT?

Sample size	90
Respondents' age	%
25 and under	18
26 — 35	29
36 — 45	19
46 — 55	19
56 and over	14
No answer	1
Average age	39

Area of residence	
London, Home Counties, S. East & S. West	39
Midlands, Wales & Anglia	25
North, N. East & N. West	23
Scotland	7
Others	6

Comment: although an inexpensive car the Beetle is clearly not a youngster's car when you consider that 42 per cent of our Imp respondents were under 25, compared with only 18 per cent here.

2 BACKGROUND INFORMATION

Sample size	90
Car's age	%
6 months or less	11
7 — 12 months	15
13 — 18 months	11
19 — 24 months	20
25 — 36 months	32
over 3 to 3½ years	11
Average age (months)	22
Car's mileage	
10,000 miles or less	20
11 — 20,000	26
21 — 30,000	28
31 — 40,000	13
over 40,000 miles	13
Average mileage × 1000	23
Bought new or used	
New	87
Used	13
Ownership	
Private	94
Company	6
Gearchange	
Manual	92
Automatic	5
No answer	3
Where garaged	
Inside	62
Outside	33
Both 50/50	2
No answer	3

Comment: surprising really that the VW isn't used more extensively by fleet managers as a company car because of its reliability and low maintenance costs. But, as you see, only 6 per cent of our respondents had company VWs. Perhaps at this level the "buy British" factor outweighs other considerations.

The average age and mileage of the VWs here is similar to that of other cars in the series of surveys—an observation that will have some relevance later on in the "faults" and "reliability" sections.

3 HOW IT WAS SERVICED

Sample size	90
Minor/routine jobs	%
Respondent/unpaid friend	53
Local garage	5
Manufacturer's agent	42
Maint./medium repairs	
Respondent/unpaid friend	20
Local garage	10
Manufacturer's agent	70
Major Overhauls	
Respondent/unpaid friend	2
Local garage	5
Manufacturer's agent	63
No overhaul needed yet	30*

*Not a fair indication of those not needing an overhaul as some answered in terms of where they would take their car if/when such was required.

Comment: only about 45 per cent of our Cortina, 1100/1300 and Imp respondents went to the manufacturer's agent for maintenance and medium repairs. Note that 70 per cent of the VW owners do so—a reflection, no doubt, on the very high standard of service that is demanded by the Volkswagen concessionaires of their agents. The situation may be confused, though, by the reluctance of some local garages to service foreign cars, because they don't have the right tools and equipment.

4 WHAT WENT WRONG?

Sample size	90

Total faults mentioned	230
To do with:	%
Engine	18
Transmission	9
Steering, suspension	9
Brakes	9
Electrical	23
Body, paint, chrome	13
Fittings, trim	12
Instruments	7

Average number of faults mentioned per respondent	2.6

Comment: until this VW analysis the lowest number of faults mentioned by each respondent was 4.9 for the Cortina 1600; 5.1 for the Cortina 1600E; and 5.2 for the Cortina 1300 and BLMC 1100. The VW has 2.6—roughly half as many. To complete the picture, we should add that Viva 90 respondents mentioned an average of 8.9 faults per car and those with a Lotus Plus 2, 9 faults per car. Except for the 1600E all the cars, on average, had done just over 20,000 miles in a little under two years, so the comparisons are strictly valid on an age and mileage basis.

Though it is much less troublesome than any other car we have yet surveyed the VW is not yet perfect. Here is a summary of the faults mentioned by our respondents.

Engine: as for practically all the other cars we have so far covered, the exhaust system/ silencer gets the most number of gripes. Until manufacturers start using expensive stainless steel, or some better form of protection for the exhaust

system, failures of the original unit seem inevitable—often sooner than many owners expect. Trouble with the automatic choke was mentioned by 5 per cent.

Transmission: 10 per cent mentioned clutch trouble (less than half the percentage for most other saloons we've covered); another 10 per cent mentioned the gearbox.

Steering/suspension: the only item here showing any regular fault pattern is the hydraulic steering damper mentioned by 9 per cent. We should add, though, that 16 per cent mentioned other individual faults under this section.

Brakes: brake faults (binding/ grabbing/pulling to one side/ need skimming) were mentioned by 10 per cent of our respondents.

Electrical: this seems to be the VWs single most troublesome department. 44 per cent of all respondents had at least one electrical fault; 11 per cent mentioned the indicator/flasher unit; 10 per cent the switch/light/connections; 7 per cent the wiper motor; 7 per cent the coil/ dynamo; 4 per cent the battery; 4 per cent the horn. Another 17 per cent had individual electrical faults.

Body/paint/chrome: rust, bubbles or cracks somewhere in the paintwork were mentioned by 11 per cent; rusting bumpers by 7 per cent.

Fittings, trim: knobs and switches, 7 per cent; window winders, 6 per cent. 19 per cent mentioned other individual faults.

Instruments: as usual, the speedometer is the least reliable instrument: 12 per cent gave trouble.

followed by 3.7 days (18 months, 20,000 miles) for the BLMC 1100. The VW's off-the-road time averages 0.8 days over a similar period and mileage. Between 70 and 80 per cent of all those cars up to 30,000 miles spent, on average, less than a day off the road for repairs

6 WARRANTY CLAIMS

Sample size	90

	%
No faults put right under manufacturer's warranty	58
At least one fault put right under warranty	42

Sample—those with experience	38

	%
Satisfied with scheme	68
Not wholly/at all satisfied	32
It not, why not?	
Still faulty	16
Others	21

Comment: just to rub the point home: 58 per cent for "no faults put right under warranty" is by far the highest we've yet had in these surveys. Respondents satisfied with the scheme—68 per cent—is also above average, though not the highest score we've had here: the Cortina 1300 scored 70 per cent.

7 SPARES

	Total VW
Sample size	90

	%
Availability of parts	
Good	78
Fair	10
Bad	1
Don't know yet	11
Trouble getting parts?	
No parts been difficult	91
At least one part has been difficult	9

Comment: no particular part was mentioned by more than one respondent. On the whole, the spares situation looks good.

8 ASSESSMENT OF QUALITIES

Owners were asked to rate the items shown on the list below. An excellent got 10 points, good 7, average 4, poor 2, bad nil.

	1500	1300
Sample sizes based on	60	30

	Score out of 10.	
Roadholding	5.6	6.0
Steering	7.7	7.5
Braking	7.7	6.4
Acceleration	5.6	4.5
Ride comfort	6.5	6.6
Seat comfort	7.4	6.4
Gearchange	8.3	8.4
Gear ratios	6.8	6.5
Overall reliability	9.8	9.3
Fuel consumption	5.9	6.5
Visibility	4.0	3.5

Noise	5.1	4.1
Heating	5.7	4.6
Ventilation	3.1	3.0
Instruments	5.4	4.6
Wear on tyres	9.1	9.0

Comment: the table tells its own story. To get 9.8 out of 10 for reliability (1500), practically every respondent marked it down as excellent on this score. Other attributes with good (or `better') ratings for the 1500 are steering, braking, gearchange and tyre wear. It gets pass marks on most other counts except visibility and ventilation. Perhaps if we'd included luggage accommodation in our list (as we should have done), there'd have been a third low score. Predictably the 1500 gets better marks than the 1300 for acceleration, poorer ones for economy. Roadholding was rated similar to that of the Cortina 1300/1600 (a little flattering to the VW we'd have thought—except in snow when its better traction makes it superior). All other cars in our survey have scored better marks here.

9 WOULD YOU BUY ANOTHER?

Sample size	90

	%
Yes would buy another car of this model	66
No definitely not/not sure	34
If not/not sure, why not?	
Interested in others/like a change/ depends what's available	10
Need larger car/larger boot	9
But with 1500/1600 engine	8
Depends on money available	4
Not powerful enough	3
Prefer 4 doors	3
Others	11

Comment: we still regard this table the best one for reflecting customer satisfaction. As you see VW owners are generally more satisfied with their lot than owners of other cars we've surveyed. The percentage of "yeses" is the highest yet (the next best here is the Cortina 1600E with 60 per cent). Three cars in our survey—the Lotus Elan Plus 2, Vauxhall Viva 90 and 1600—got more "noes" than the VW got "ayes", which seems to put the whole thing in perspective.

5 TIME OFF THE ROAD
(excluding routine servicing)

	Total	10,000 or less	11,000–20,000	21,000–30,000	31,000–or more
*Sample sizes**	78	18	22	18	20
	%	%	%	%	%
Nil days	69	72	77	78	50
½/1 day	15	17	14	17	15
2–4 days	12	6	5	—	35
5–8 days	3	5	4	—	—
9–14 days	1	—	—	5	—
Average number of days	0.8	0.6	0.6	0.8	1.2

* Based on those having car from new.

Comment: many faults were put right during routine servicing and so have not been included here. Although the sample sizes are small within the mileage groups, percentages have been shown to illustrate the approximate

point at which the days off the road starts to build up. The table is further evidence of the VW's dependability. The previous best "average days off the road" was three days (in 19 months and 24,000 miles) for the Cortina 1600,

Road Test

Most of the '70 changes show in this shot including ventilating slots in the engine lid, larger tail and running lights and bumper-mounted reflectors.

1970 VW SEMI-AUTOMATIC SEDAN...

What's that beetle doing in the middle of the intersection with its engine churning madly and going nowhere?
The stupid jerk driving it has his hand on the automatic stickshift lever, that's what.

Even though we knew all about this trait, it happened to us during the first hour of our test and at least once a day thereafter. And equally hard to cure was stepping on the brake at the wrong time with our left foot, a natural habit born of manipulating the controls that come with a proper stickshift. Of course, the owner of one of these machines would never admit it happens to him. Only parking lot attendants, magazine test drivers and their wives are that dense.

When the owner's manual clearly spells this out for anyone to read, you can't fault the car, and certainly the Ferodo mechanism was designed mainly for Europeans who are giving up shifting for themselves at a much slower rate than the rest of the world. Even here, it's no ball of fire saleswise with only 1.7 out of every 10 beetles being sold so-equipped Chevrolet and Ford, incidentally,

CAR AT A GLANCE: 4-5 second penalty in zero to 60 acceleration ...3 mph penalty in top ... About equal economy . . . Reverse difficult to select . . . Overall and detail quality remains superior.

by Don MacDonald

photos by Lester Nehamkin

Only about two out of ten of the newly arrived beetles in the background are of the automatic variety, a ratio disproportionate to the usual American preference for automatics.

are experiencing even a poorer ratio than this with their semi-automatic Novas and Mavericks.

The device does, however, have very definite advantages to offer. The main one is predicated on the premise that a stock beetle is hardly a contender in traffic light drags so why even bother. Just leave the thing in drive or "2" as it's called on the ashtray squibble and you can potter off at a fairly brisk pace. Or in actual city traffic "1" serves up a rather nice ratio. The purpose of "L" or low is obscure except perhaps for going down Pikes Peak with no brakes. The idea of using it to rock out of snow or mud is simply not feasible, as if ordinary VW's are conceded to be difficult to get into reverse, this one is all but impossible in one simple motion. It's a maneuver best attempted in the privacy of your garage.

The mechanism doesn't seem to slip too much except in "2" on full throttle starts. Loss in acceleration, especially on the timed runs we do for these tests, stems mostly from the necessity of lifting your foot off the gas between shifts. Maybe there was a way of speed-shifting it but

Wrongly separated (by modern usage) wording "stick shift" will be permanently recorded if you use the window defroster before you scrape off the sticker.

we weren't about to try in a borrowed car. The result was 23-24 second times between zero and 60 mph rather than the 18.5 seconds that the clutch model can achieve with its new power. Then, too, the same problem occurs while passing. Let's say you're doing 50 in "2" and want to pass a truck. If you

drop down to "1" you'll lose time even though "1" is useable up to 55 mph

Fortunately VW has one of the better parking brakes in the business for there is no parking pawl provided in the transmission. The brake would also be useful should the 8-amp fuse that protects the control

valve blow while you're in gear. When that happens you're stuck in the gear of the moment and if you shut the engine off, you'd not get it started again until the malfunction was corrected and the fuse replaced.

Lastly, though it should be noted that this might be peculiar to our test car alone, the

Cornering with vigor produces little lean but will invariably raise the inside front wheel off the pavement. Note absence of rear-wheel tuck-under in latest suspension design.

Ferodo mechanism emits a definite but not annoying rumble in "2" at speeds below 60 mph. Above that speed there are enough other noises to render an isolated one unnoticeable. The addition of an automatic doesn't cure buffeting in the headliner or the sounds wafted back from the busy engine the first being a nuisance and the latter, comforting.

When the beetle is in perfect tune, as was our test car, one can understand the reason for incorporating an ignition switch that has to be turned most of the way back before you make a second try at starting. The engine started instantly but sort of took its time to get to idle speed and was almost dead

Instrumentation for the semi automatic is identical except for an extra warning light for transmission temperature and the shift-point markings on the speedo.

silent during that second or so. Without this protection, you could easily assume it hadn't started and cause that nasty ratcheting noise characteristic of Cadillacs with female drivers in supermarket parking lots.

Other handling traits, of course, are not changed by Ferodo's contribution. Steering is pleasant and precise although if you're a left foot braker, you tend to move the seat up closer to the wheel than you would in the clutch model. This, in turn, gets your nose close enough to the windshield that one wonders why some enterprising optometrist doesn't start grinding this glass to prescription.

A note about the rear window is in order here, too Unless you want your new automatic stickshift beetle to go through its life with the fact that it is a stickshift permanently stuck to the glass, don't turn on the rear window defroster until you've scraped off the decal.

At least, though, that's better than "Fiat Breaking In" or some such lasting the car's lifetime.

(Continued on Page 87)

What can be seen of the semi-automatic's mechanics are familiar although underneath, the driving units and particularly the shift linkage are quite different.

THE WORLD'S LARGEST MANUFACTURER OF DUNE BUGGY INNARDS IS MAKING THEM BETTER THAN EVER

VOLKSWAGEN A.S.S.

Having established itself as the world's largest manufacturer of dune buggy innards, Volkswagen is not going to let up now. It's been a tough climb, but thanks to single-minded attention to detail and unswerving progress toward the long-ago selected goal, Wolfsburg has made it to the top. Now VWs make better dune buggies than any other brand, leading or otherwise.

Of course, VW's current renown in the field wouldn't have been possible had not lip service been paid to the multitudes who were looking for some uncomplicated surface-to-surface transport device. But it was only lip service. The product planners wisely diverted a small portion of their atten-

tion to the beetle-shaped coachwork which is bolted to the marvelous dunebuggy chassis at the factory. Not too much attention, mind you. But enough to learn how to squeeze a few extra BTUs out of the heater as the years went by and to keep the passengers sitting on recent developments in the world of vinyl. Consequently, you have to be a trained member of the Beetle Spotters Corps to distinguish today's product from one which has reached its majority. And all the while brilliant German engineers and technicians were making devastating progress with the dune buggy underneath. The engine has been completely redesigned, made larger and almost doubled in horsepower. It has gone from 32 horsepower in 1949 to 57 for 1970—a fantastic

improvement. Four of these horsepower are new in the 1970 model, along with an increase in displacement from 1493 to 1584 ccs. And all of the engineering talent hasn't been confined just to the engine. Over the years the transmission has gained a full complement of synchronizers and the moody and irresponsible swing axles were replaced with an honest, fully independent rear suspension. There is no doubt that the internal workings of today's Beetle are better suited to their real task than were those of their predecessors.

VW has appeared, all along, to be candid about the disparity in the number of improvements between the body and the buggy underneath. Spokesmen for the factory have always denounced planned obsolescence as a trick of capitalistic devils and have explained that time not wasted on new fenders could be put to good use in the vital power plant and chassis within. But experienced observers could see some muddying of the waters. In reality, time spent on new fenders was time taken away from the dune buggy. But a logical and appealing party line to the contrary was necessary because of a quirk in the habits of dune buggy buyers. They almost never buy new parts. You can see then the necessity of fostering the image of the VW as an automobile so that it might obtain a first owner. The result of this indoctrination has been so successful that the vast majority of Beetle owners are totally unaware of their "car's" greater possibilities.

This being the situation, we yield to the public and our road test has concerned itself with both aspects of the VW. Both have been improved for 1970 but we are most enthusiastic about the dune buggy. As mentioned earlier, the engine has been enlarged, the entire displacement increase resulting from an increase in the cylinder bore. The acceleration tests were disappointing, in that we couldn't feel the punch of the additional 4 horsepower and 3.6 lb-ft of torque. It's entirely possible that you won't be able to feel it either, but you can read it on the specification page. For reasons best known, and perhaps only known, to Wolfsburg the test car was slightly slower than an identically equipped 1968 model previously tested (September, '68)—21.2 seconds at 61.5 mph in the

(Text continued on page 87
Specifications overleaf)

PHOTOGRAPHY: HUMPHREY SUTTON

ACCELERATION standing ¼ mile, seconds

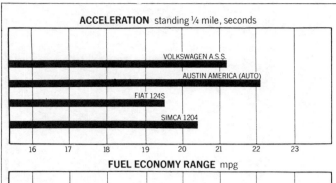

VOLKSWAGEN A.S.S.	
AUSTIN AMERICA (AUTO)	
FIAT 124S	
SIMCA 1204	

16 17 18 19 20 21 22 23

BRAKING 70-0 mph panic stop, feet

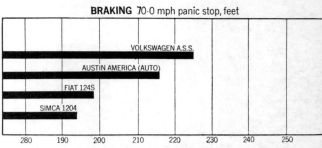

VOLKSWAGEN A.S.S.	
AUSTIN AMERICA (AUTO)	
FIAT 124S	
SIMCA 1204	

280 190 200 210 220 230 240 250

FUEL ECONOMY RANGE mpg

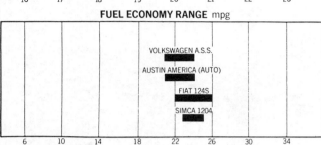

VOLKSWAGEN A.S.S.	
AUSTIN AMERICA (AUTO)	
FIAT 124S	
SIMCA 1204	

6 10 14 18 22 26 30 34

PRICE AS TESTED dollars x 1000

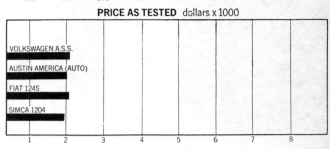

VOLKSWAGEN A.S.S.	
AUSTIN AMERICA (AUTO)	
FIAT 124S	
SIMCA 1204	

1 2 3 4 5 6 7 8

VW TYPE 1 SEDAN

Importer: Volkswagen of America
Sylvan Avenue
Englewood Cliffs, New Jersey

Vehicle type: Rear engine, rear-wheel-drive, 4-passenger sedan

Price as tested: $2083.95
(Manufacturer's suggested retail price, including all options listed below, Federal excise tax, dealer preparation and delivery charges, does not include state and local taxes, license or freight charges)

Options on test car: Type 1 Sedan with A.S.S., $1978.00 ($2063.00 West Coast); dealer preparation, $35.00; radio, $70.95

ENGINE
Type: 4-opposed, air-cooled, light alloy block and heads, cast iron cylinders, 4 main bearings
Bore x stroke . . 3.36 x 2.72 in, 85.4 x 69.0 mm
Displacement . . . . 96.6 cu in, 1584 cc
Compression ratio . . . . 7.5 to one
Carburetion . . . . 1 x 1-bbl Solex
Valve gear . . pushrod operated overhead valves
Power (SAE) . . . . 57 bhp @ 4400 rpm

Torque (SAE) . . . . 82 lbs/ft @ 3000 rpm
Specific power output . . . . 0.59 bhp/cu in, 36 bhp/liter

DRIVE TRAIN
Transmission . . . . 3-speed, all-synchro, automatic clutch
Max. torque converter . . . . 2.1 to one
Final drive ratio . . . . 4.38 to one

Gear	Ratio	Mph/1000 rpm	Max test speed
I	2.06	8.5	42 mph (4900 rpm)
II	1.26	14.0	68 mph (4900 rpm)
III	0.89	19.7	76 mph (3860 rpm)

DIMENSIONS AND CAPACITIES
Wheelbase . . . . 94.5 in
Track, F/R . . . . 51.6/53.1 in
Length . . . . 158.7 in
Width . . . . 61.0 in
Height . . . . 59.0 in
Ground clearance . . . . 5.9 in
Curb weight . . . . 1865 lbs
Weight distribution, F/R 38.9/61.1%
Battery capacity . . . . 12 volts, 45 amp/hr
Alternator capacity . . . . 360 watts
Fuel capacity . . . . 10.6 gal
Oil capacity . . . . 2.7 qts

SUSPENSION
F: Ind., trailing arms, torsion bars, anti-sway bar
R: Ind., semi-trailing arms, torsion bars

STEERING
Type . . . . Worm and roller
Turns lock-to-lock 2.9
Turning circle curb-to-curb . . . . 35.8 ft

BRAKES
F: . . . . 1.57 x 9.05-in drum
R: . . . . 1.57 x 9.05-in drum

WHEELS AND TIRES
Wheel size . . . . 15 x 4.0-in
Wheel type . . . . stamped steel, 4-bolt
Tire make and size . . . . Continental 560-15
Tire type . . . . bias ply, tubeless
Test inflation pressures, F/R . . . . 16/24 psi
Tire load rating . . . . . . 970 lbs per tire @ 32 psi

PERFORMANCE
Zero to	Seconds
30 mph	4.6
40 mph	7.4
50 mph	12.3
60 mph	19.8
70 mph	32.4

Standing ¼-mile . . . . 21.2 sec @ 61.5 mph
Top speed (observed) . . . . 76 mph
70–0 mph . . . . 225 ft (0.73 G)
Fuel mileage . . . . 21–24 mpg on regular fuel
Cruising range . . . . 223–254 mi

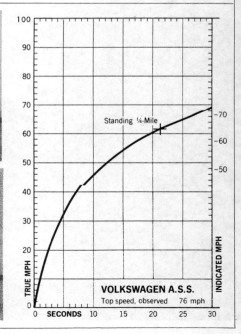

Standing ¼-Mile

VOLKSWAGEN A.S.S.
Top speed, observed   76 mph

quarter for the new Beetle compared to 21.1 seconds at 63.0 mph for the old one. Both cars were equipped with the A.S.S. (the internationally recognized abbreviation for Automatic Stick Shift). The A.S.S. has almost no application for dune buggies and is no more than a concession toward those who wish to use the VW as a car. It is essentially straightforward, being the top three gears of the standard 4-speed transmission which you still have to shift manually. To improve acceleration it comes with a higher numerical axle ratio—4.38 for the A.S.S. compared to 4.13 with the 4-speed. The "Automatic" refers to a power-operated clutch that disengages whenever you apply pressure to the shift lever, and to a torque converter that allows you to stop in gear without clutching. Considering that it's only half automatic, its price, as an option, of $139 is a bit unfriendly. Just under 15% of the Beetles sold in the U.S. are so equipped—"all we can get," according to the importer. Since its introduction in 1968 there has been one particularly useful improvement in the A.S.S. Now when someone inadvertently leans his knee on the lever the clutch doesn't turn the engine loose.

Clearly the most significant of buggy advances is the independent rear suspension, first used on A.S.S. cars in 1968 and then across the board in 1969. The new system uses a single trailing arm for each rear wheel with double-jointed halfshafts, and effectively eliminates the wild camber changes characteristic of VW. Now your buggy can roll on the full width of its Can-Am or Indy tires rather than mostly on the corners of the tread like before. There are some advantages for the car too. Where old Beetles liked to tuck a wheel under and go belly up in the ditch, the new ones slew around corners in an almost predictable fashion. We pronounce the suspension an unqualified improvement.

Since VW improvements are normally bolted on somewhere underneath they almost always go undetected to the home-to-work oriented first owner. This year there is something even for him, the seats. In the VW tradition they don't look any different at all, but highly placed officials report that the head restraints "have been reshaped and made somewhat smaller." Because of subtle improvements in the contour of the buckets, even we could tell that they were more comfortable than the visually similar ones introduced in 1968. And we are definitely impressed with some of the hardware associated with the seats—by turning a lever the backrest angle adjusts to four different positions and the backrest release button is located high and facing the door so that you don't have to bend over and fumble around in a tangle of belts whenever you want access to the rear seat. But some of the other safety-inspired equipment is not so pleasing. More accurately, it's hardly bearable. VW finally got around to installing some kind of key-in-the-ignition warning system, but instead of using a conventional, moderately infuriating buzzer the Beetle has a lilliputian air raid siren. It's not a warning not to leave your key, it's punishment if you do.

If, after the seats, you give up looking just for improvements in the interior and broaden your search to include "changes" you can score a new glovebox door—black rather than body color like before. The exterior offers very little more. Turn signals and marker lights are larger and a couple of columns of air slots have been added to the engine cover. That's it. That's the new VW and hopefully it will be attractive enough so that there will be an abundance of used 1584cc engines and IRS chassis a few years from now.

There is possibly no need for buggy builders to panic just yet but the VW's popularity isn't what it used to be. Volkswagen is still the largest selling import by a four-to-one margin over its closest competitor, Toyota, but its share of the business has dropped considerably. In 1965 VW enjoyed 67% of the import market but last year it dropped below 50%. We wouldn't want to be accused of crying wolf or anything like that, but if this continues, along about 1987 Bruce Meyers and everybody following in his footsteps will have to start looking somewhere else for parts. ●

VW SEDAN

Continued from Page 83

In our road test of the clutch beetle a few months back, we recorded that fuel consumption ranged from a low of 20.9 mpg to a high 28.6 with an average of 25 to be expected under average conditions. This is indeed heresy, what with owners regularly getting 35 mpg or more at cocktail parties, but surprisingly, no reader challenged us. Now we'll try once more with the figure for the automatic stickshift. It isn't good either but at least, you don't pay much of a penalty for shiftless driving. We got 241.9 miles on an even 10.0 gallons of regular which works out, natch, to 24.2 miles to the gallon. Since the tank only holds 10.6 gallons, we'll vouch for the unusual accuracy of Volkswagen's single instrument. The needle was nearly to the edge of the little pickaxe that marks reserve, and until the station loomed into view, we were wishing that the old "switch to reserve" system had been retained.

This particular test car was the first VW we've driven in a long while that was troubled with gas fumes on a full tank. Yet that's only five or so beetles in the last couple of years and if one in five gives trouble, maybe it's a complaint that the service people might look into. Lord knows, it was years before Wolfsburg got around to supplying a pressure-sealed cap.

One of the newer accessories with which the test car was equipped was a casette-type monaural tape player in combination with the radio, and with it comes a reel of Herb Alpert, one number on each side. It was like sitting within a foot of an old-fashioned juke box with only the tweeter working. Let's face it. The radio alone is a better bet as it would be easier to search out preferred music on it than be changing casettes every few minutes.

Now, the *64 pfennig* question arises. Is the $139.95 increment for the semi-automatic over the base $1,839 (Gulf and East Coast) price of the beetle worth it? We are inclined to say no and apparently 8.3 out of every 10 beetle buyers agree with us. The semi-automatic doesn't add all that much to the simplicity of beetle driving. In fact, some might say that it detracts from the simplicity.

AUTOTEST

VOLKSWAGEN SUPER BEETLE 1600 (1,584 c.c.)

AT-A-GLANCE: Larger-engined Beetle with revised front and rear suspension. Same top speed as before but quicker acceleration at the expense of heavier fuel consumption. Safer handling, larger front boot and better ventilation. Good brakes.

MANUFACTURER
Volkswagen AG, Wolfsburg-Nedersachen, Germany.

UK CONCESSIONAIRES
Volkswagen Motors Ltd, Volkswagen House, Brighton Road, Purley, Surrey.

PRICES
Basic	£668 10s 0d
Purchase Tax	£206 11s 0d
Total (in G.B.)	£875 1s 0d

PRICE AS TESTED	£875 1s 0d

PERFORMANCE SUMMARY
Mean maximum speed	80 mph
Standing start ¼-mile	20.7 sec
0-60 mph	18.3 sec
30-70 mph through gears	31.1 sec
Typical fuel consumption	27 mpg
Miles per tankful	250

Above: As well as being more bulbous, the nose of the Super Beetle is now a few inches longer. Note the new extractor vents on the rear quarters

Left: There is nothing external to give away that the engine is 91 c.c. larger than before, although the porting in the heads has been improved

SALES of the Volkswagen Beetle are something of a latter-day marvel. To date about 13.5m have been built and over 300,000 have been imported here. The reputation of the make and particularly this model for quality and reliability is tremendous and the main reason, as far as we can establish, for the popularity worldwide. It seems that you buy a VW because you want an efficient machine that will always work; appearance, performance and comfort are of very minor importance.

This *resumé* of the VW philosophy sets the mood for our latest test. Just before the motor show season some important revisions to the Beetle were announced unexpectedly. From a single basic model in the beginning, the range had extended to give the customer a choice from three engine sizes on the Beetle plus two more in the 1600 and 411. Rationalization was obvious and now the Super Beetle 1600 (called the 1302S on the engine cover and elsewhere in the world) replaces the 1500. The 1200 is still the same old favourite with 1,192 c.c. engine and original front and rear suspension. The new 1300 (called the 1302) and 1600 have been given MacPherson struts at the front and "proper" semi-trailing arms at the rear.

Extra capacity compared with the 1500 is obtained by larger cylinder bores. Swept volume goes up by 6 per cent and peak power by nearly 14 per cent without any increase in the compression ratio or rev range; volumetric efficiency has been given an additional boost by new head porting. Maximum torque is now 78

lb.ft., which is only 5½ per cent more than before.

Even with 14 per cent more power, the total output of 50 bhp DIN is very modest for the size of engine. There can hardly be another engine left in production which turns out only 31 bhp per litre. However, aided by what is a smooth and low-drag body shape, even 50 bhp is enough to give the Beetle a top speed of 80 mph. Even at the maximum, engine revs are only 4,050 rpm so this speed can be held for cruising all day long.

Scrutiny of our previous test (25 November 1966) shows that there is virtually no difference in top speed between the 1500 and 1600 which is explained by the fact that there has been no change in gearing. Acceleration times in each gear are marginally better, as would be expected from the small increase in torque, and the standing starts showed marked improvements.

Two factors detracted from what might otherwise have been greater gains. The test car had covered only a small mileage (2,100) at the time the figures were measured and there was quite a blustery wind on the day in question, compared with a dead calm in 1966. Even so, the 1600 was over 3½sec quicker from rest to 60 mph than the 1500 and actually managed to reach its top speed downwind from rest in only 45sec.

Not only the performance is affected by wind however and, in spite of the considerable suspension improvements, the Beetle still gets badly blown about by side gusts. Battling up

the M1 motorway at 70 mph called for quite a lot of courage and often more road than the width of one lane.

Fuel consumption has always been a keen arguing point among VW owners, so during this test we kept more detailed records than usual and tried hard on occasions to behave like typical owners. The best figure was for a gentle run in wet weather to the West Country and back at 26.8 mpg for 481 miles. Our worst figure in very heavy rush-hour traffic was just over 20 mpg, and overall our average was 24.0 mpg.

All these results are appreciably worse than those measured on the 1500 Beetle (27.4 mpg overall), as were the steady-speed measurements which completely eliminate driving technique. At a steady 70 mph, for example, the 1600 covers only 24.2 mpg compared with 29 for the 1500 and this difference is even greater at slower speeds. It will be a very careful VW driver indeed who gets 30 mpg from his Super Beetle, 27 mpg being a much more honest claim. An advantage often overlooked is that the Beetle will run happily on the cheapest 91 octane fuel available. The mileage recorder, incidentally, was dead accurate on the test car.

The real reason for the change to MacPherson strut front suspension is to make way for more luggage room, although at the same time it has been possible to increase the front track by 3in. As far as the driver notices, the front end behaves much the same as before, although there does seem to be a little

Left, upper: There have been very few changes to the over-all Beetle shape since it was introduced. Below: Stout bumpers front and rear are free-standing

Below: The chrome strip has gone from the facia and the pedals are farther apart than they used to be. A straight gearlever is new

Above: Capacity of the front boot has been increased by 85 per cent. The bottle on the left is for the screen washer

Right: The spare wheel now lies flat between the new front struts

more bump thump and road noise on some surfaces. At the rear the double-jointed drive shafts and semi-trailing arms first used on the semi-automatic Beetle (to accommodate its longer fluid clutch) have been standardized, with all the accompanying improvements in wheel camber changes.

As far as handling is concerned now, the Beetle is an understeerer. At the limit on a wet road it is the front end which lets go first and it is only by deliberate and clumsy misuse of power or brakes that the tail can be made to flick out of line. Throwing the car hard at a tight turn in the dry causes a kind of oscillating conflict between front and rear ends with the rear weight bias winning in the end, as it always has. The test car was shod with Semperit Favorit cross-ply tyres made in Yugoslavia, which can hardly have done much for its handling at the limit.

Under braking tests on a dry track we recorded over 1g for 100 lb effort, with the left-hand rear wheel locking early but not affecting stability. The non-servo disc-drum braking system is unchanged and has the same response characteristics as before. The handbrake held the car easily on the 1-in-3 hill and recorded 0.43g on its own from 30 mph. Fade resistance was excellent.

Steering effort is heavier than before and we suspect that there is now more front wheel offset to give strut clearance. Ride is reasonable without being great and the whole car feels very taut and robust, like it always has.

There is nothing very different either about the interior and the way the driver sits up to the wheel and the facia. A steering lock is now combined with the ignition and there is a new fresh air ventilation system with extractor vents in the rear quarters. Despite this pressure bleed, it is just as hard as ever to shut the doors, so one wonders whether the vents are effective enough. The performance of the heater is hardly any better and it still suffers from the same fundamental faults. The worst of these is that it depends upon engine speed for its air flow which is not enough to counter misting up in heavy traffic. There is also no temperature control as such and the only regulator is for hot air volume.

The new fresh air system has been skimped to get it in behind the existing facia and it passes only a gentle ram breeze, never a real cooling blast. Whereas two levers and a switch do all that is required on most other cars, the VW system is operated by a total of eight controls, scattered all round the car. They are simple to understand and easy to operate, except for the two front footwell flaps which are out of reach of a properly belted-in driver.

Pedals still sprout from floor-mounted pivots but they are farther apart than they used to be. The clutch is so far over to the left, in fact, that there is now no room beyond it for resting the left foot. It requires an effort of 40 lb over a travel of 6in. which is too much by today's standards.

On the 1500 version of the Beetle there was a rearwards crank in the gearlever to bring it nearer to hand. This has now been removed

and the lever shortened, so that although the movement is improved as a result, it is more of a stretch for a driver who likes to sit well back.

A single circular dial houses the speedometer, mileage recorder and fuel gauge, there being no other instruments. Wipers now have two speeds and there is a four-way hazard warning flasher as standard.

The release for the front luggage locker lid has been moved to a position inside the glove box and the safety catch is worked by a push button in the outside handle. Capacity inside the boot is 85 per cent more than previously, partly because the spare wheel now lies flat on the floor and partly because the lid has a more bulbous shape. Quite a large suitcase will now fit in here and it is amazing what can be packed in and not foul the lid when it shuts down. There is still a deep well behind the back seat as well, but that is much more difficult to get at.

Despite all the engineering improvements a lot of the faults in the Beetle still go on. Things like the new ventilation system are a step in the right direction and the extra acceleration and better cornering are well worth having. Like the 1500 Beetle before it, it is the best Beetle yet, but it still comes a long way behind its competitors in qualities like styling, comfort and prestige. Even at the latest price of £875, though, it represents good value for money especially if one takes into account the all-important resale value and long-term running costs. □

ACCELERATION

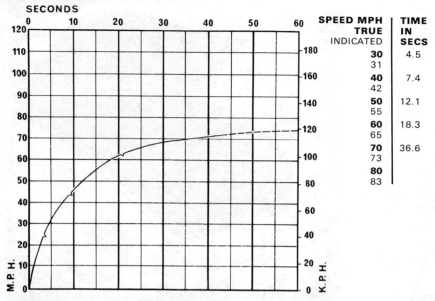

SECONDS

SPEED MPH TRUE INDICATED	TIME IN SECS
30	4.5
31	
40	7.4
42	
50	12.1
55	
60	18.3
65	
70	36.6
73	
80	
83	

SPEED RANGE, GEAR RATIOS AND TIME IN SECONDS

mph	Top (3.38)	3rd (5.20)	2nd (8.50)	1st (15.68)
10-30	—	8.6	4.9	—
20-40	13.4	7.9	5.2	—
30-50	14.5	9.2	10.0	—
40-60	19.3	12.1	—	—
50-70	30.6	—	—	—

Standing ¼-mile
20.7 sec 62 mph

Standing kilometre
40.0 sec 72 mph
Test distance
1,075 miles
Mileage recorder
accurate

PERFORMANCE
MAXIMUM SPEEDS

Gear	mph	kph	rpm
Top (mean)	80	129	4,050
(best)	82	132	4,160
3rd	71	114	5,530
2nd	51	82	6,500
1st	28	45	6,500

BRAKES
(from 70 mph in neutral)
Pedal load for 0.5g stops in lb

1	50		6	55-50
2	55		7	55-50
3	55		8	55-50
4	55-50		9	55-50
5	55		10	55-50

RESPONSE (from 30 mph in neutral)

Load	g	Distance
20lb	0.08	376ft
40lb	0.43	70ft
60lb	0.61	49ft
80lb	0.92	33ft
100lb	1.05	28.7ft
Handbrake	0.43	70ft

Max. Gradient 1 in 3

CLUTCH
Pedal 40lb and 6in.

MOTORWAY CRUISING

Indicated speed at 70 mph	73mph
Engine (rpm at 70 mph)	3,550 rpm
(mean piston speed)	1,630ft/min.
Fuel (mpg at 70 mph)	24.2 mpg
Passing (50-70 mph)	30.6 sec

COMPARISONS

MAXIMUM SPEED MPH

Austin-Morris 1300 Super 2-door	(£855)	91
Datsun 1200 de luxe	(£865)	89
Fiat 128 2-door	(£834)	86
Triumph Toledo	(£889)	83
Volkswagen Super Beetle	**(£875)**	**80**

0-60 MPH, SEC

Datsun 1200	15.3
Fiat 128	16.3
Austin-Morris 1300	16.4
Triumph Toledo	17.6
Volkswagen Super Beetle	**18.3**

STANDING ¼-MILE, SEC

Fiat 128	19.8
Datsun 1200	19.9
Austin-Morris 1300	20.6
Volkswagen Super Beetle	**20.7**
Triumph Toledo	21.1

OVERALL MPG

Datsun 1200	31.2
Triumph Toledo	30.3
Austin-Morris 1300	30.2
Fiat 128	29.2
Volkswagen Super Beetle	**24.0**

GEARING (with 5.60-15in. tyres)

Top	19.74 mph per 1,000 rpm
3rd	12.83 mph per 1,000 rpm
2nd	7.85 mph per 1,000 rpm
1st	4.26 mph per 1,000 rpm

TEST CONDITIONS:
Weather: Fine. Wind: 10-50 mph. Temperature: 12 deg. C. (54 deg. F). Barometer: 29.7 in. hg. Humidity: 54 per cent. Surfaces: dry concrete and asphalt.

WEIGHT:
Kerb weight 16.5 cwt (1,850lb—838kg) (with oil, water and half full fuel tank). Distribution, per cent F, 40.7; R. 59.3. Laden as tested: 19.8 cwt (2,210lb—1,002kg).

TURNING CIRCLES:
Between kerbs L, 34ft 5in.; R, 33ft 10in. Between walls L, 35ft 7in.; R, 35ft 1in. Steering wheel turns, lock to lock 3.0

Figures taken at 2,000 miles by our own staff at the Motor Industry Research Association proving ground at Nuneaton.

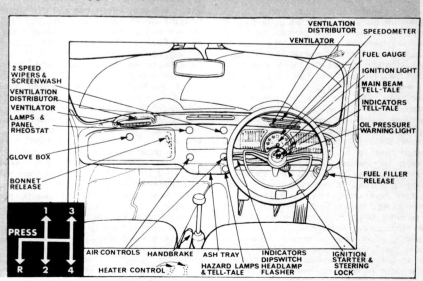

CONSUMPTION

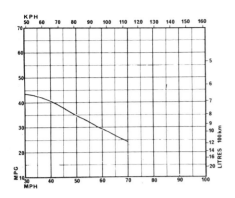

FUEL
(At constant speeds—mpg)

30 mph	43.5
40 mph	40.8
50 mph	34.9
60 mph	29.4
70 mph	24.2

Typical mpg	27 (10.5 litres/100km)
Calculated (DIN) mpg	26.8 (10.6 litres/100km)
Overall mpg	24.0 (11.8 litres/100km)
Grade of fuel	Regular, 2-star (min. 91 RM)

OIL
Miles per pint . . . . . (SAE 30/30W) 1,000

SPECIFICATION REAR ENGINE, REAR-WHEEL DRIVE

ENGINE
Cylinders	4, horizontally opposed
Main bearings	4
Cooling system	Air, ducted fan
Bore	85.5mm (3.36 in.)
Stroke	69.0mm (2.72 in.)
Displacement	1,584 c.c. (96.6 cu.in.)
Valve gear	Overhead, pushrods and rockers
Compression ratio	7.5-to-1 Min. octane rating: 91RM
Carburettor	Solex 34 PICT
Fuel pump	Pierburg mechanical
Oil filter	Gauze strainer in sump
Max. power	50 bhp (DIN) at 4,000 rpm
Max. torque	78 lb.ft. (DIN) at 2,800 rpm

TRANSMISSION
Clutch	Fichtel & Sachs diaphragm spring 7.9in. dia.
Gearbox	4-speed, all-synchromesh
Gear ratios	Top 0.88
	Third 1.26
	Second 2.06
	First 3.80
	Reverse 3.62
Final drive	Spiral bevel, 4.125-to-1

CHASSIS and BODY
Construction	Separate platform chassis, steel body

SUSPENSION
Front	Independent, MacPherson struts, lower links, coil springs, telescopic dampers, anti-roll bar
Rear	Independent, semi-trailing arms, transverse torsion bars, telescopic dampers

STEERING
Type	Worm and roller
Wheel dia.	15.0 in.

BRAKES
Make and type	ATE, disc front, drum rear
Dimensions	F 10.9 in. dia. R 9.0 in. dia. 1.57 in. wide shoes.
Swept area	F 165 sq.in., R 89 sq.in. Total 254 sq.in. (257 sq.in./ton laden)

WHEELS
Type	Pressed steel disc, 4-stud fixing 4.5 in. wide rim.
Tyres—make	Semperit (on test car)
—type	Favorit cross-ply tubeless
—size	5.60-15 in.

EQUIPMENT
Battery	12 Volt 36 Ah
Generator	Bosch, 30 amp d.c.
Headlamps	Hella 90/80 watt (total)
Reversing lamp	Extra
Electric fuses	12
Screen wipers	2-speed
Screen washer	Standard, air-pressure
Interior heater	Standard, hot air
Heated backlight	Extra
Safety belts	Standard for front seats
Interior trim	Pvc seats and headlining
Floor covering	Moulded rubber/carpet
Jack	Friction pillar
Jacking points	1 each side under body
Windscreen	Toughened
Underbody protection	Phosphor treatment prior to painting

MAINTENANCE
Fuel tank	9.2 Imp. gallons (42 litres)
Engine sump	4.4 pints (2.5 litres) SAE 30/30W Change oil every 3,000 miles. Clean strainer element every 3,000 miles.
Gearbox and final drive	5.5 pints SAE 90EP Change oil every 30,000 miles.
Grease	No points
Tyre pressures	F 16; R 24 psi (normal driving) F 19; R 27 psi (fast driving) F 17; R 26 psi (full load)
Max payload	837 lb (380 kg)

PERFORMANCE DATA
Top gear mph per 1,000 rpm	19.74
Mean piston speed at max power	1,838 ft/min
Bhp per ton laden	50.5 (DIN)

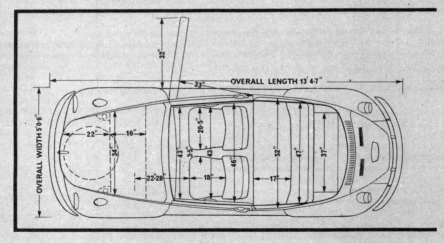

STANDARD GARAGE 16ft x 8ft 6in.

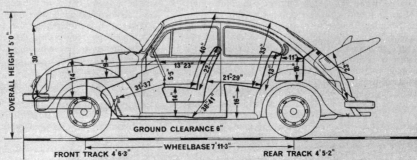

SCALE 0.3in. to 1ft
Cushions uncompressed

91

Tuning Topics

"A 2-LITRE VW BEETLE? —COMING UP RIGHT AWAY, SIR!"

EMPI'S RIVERSIDE LINE-UP.—A modified Volkswagen rests in company with two of the Company's Imp dune buggies and another Beetle with radically restyled bodywork.

ONE OF THE biggest Volkswagen strongholds in the World is America, and within America there is one area, Southern California, where they just cannot get enough of the Bug and its big brother Microbus derivative. Around Los Angeles the humble Beetle succeeded in outselling the Ford Mustang, even when the latter was at the height of its favour with the young: at present when you look around there is little doubt the Beetle is outselling all other forms of transport for the under-30-year-old group. However, the point is that many of these VWs are completely different from the ones you see for the most part in Britain: US-owned Beetles have style and performance in many cases. Even if the owner has been restricted by economics his Beetle will not be standard: a generally accepted "Stage 1" tune seems to be the adoption of 8-in.-rimmed rear wheels and a rowdy exhaust.

In general, the average American VW owner is well content with his steed in production form except for two things—straightline performance and the standard of interior appointment. If he is at all "switched on" he may have also heard that the handling of the older VWs was interesting when provoked. Allow a short period for this to ferment in his mind and the chances are that he will either buy his next VW ready modified, or convert the existing one.

In this area there are more speedshops and engine-conversion specialists than anywhere else in the World. However, all but three or four of these establishments will deal with the homegrown V8s as well, and only one of the VW specialists is really geared to catch the eye of a potential customer. The name is Engineered Motor Products Incorporated (EMPI) and they are by far the biggest in the Volkswagen accessory and tuning business, both in the USA and abroad.

The company is one interest of a local Riverside tycoon called Joe Vittone, who operates Econo Motors selling VWs, Fiats, Hondas. Datsuns and Subarus on a scale that would shatter an English dealer, For example it is a gloomy month when Vittone does not manage to sell more of the Wolfsburg products than the local GM dealer can shift Chevrolets! Since Chevrolet is the most popular car brand in America, one gets the impression that this middle-aged former Bonneville salt flats speed record holder, riding various motorcycles, has an above-average amount of drive and business sense.

Vittone started his Volkswagen agency in 1955: in those days the Beetle used to burn out valve guides under the hot local operating conditions. When a guide had burned, the VW owner was obliged to buy a new aluminium cylinder head, because the factory maintained that the head would be damaged by taking out the old guides and inserting new ones. Vittone found a way of doing just this reliably, and by 1956 EMPI was founded to develop various other ideas Vittone had for improving the VW. The most famous item was undoubtedly the EMPI Compensator Bar which, when installed on the Beetle's swing-axle rear suspension, eliminated the dreaded wheel tuck up which was a problem even in the USA. Having tried turning off a four-lane freeway into a 25-m.p.h. limited "Ramp" semi-hairpin we can report that the art of negotiating bends is still necessary!

Nowadays EMPI offer over 500 items from stock, still specialising in the Beetle, though in the future they expect to offer an increasing number of accessories for the ever-growing numbers of Japanese cars which Vittone and others are selling. Apart from an administration office with full showroom and demonstration facilities (there's a supply of Empi's Imp Volkswagen-based dune buggies for those who would like a quick run into the desert close to smoggy Riverside).

there is also a racing workshop looked after by Vittone's 27-year-old son Darrell. In this latter department we found their 2-litre "Inch Pincher" Beetle dragster which covers a standing quarter-mile in 11.8 sec. with a terminal speed of 114 m.p.h. The Weber downdraught carburated engine gives around 210 b.h.p. (SAE), and this straight-line activity, plus another 2-litre Beetle set-up for the Baja over the rough events, makes sure that they do not lag behind on development.

As an example of the engine development work they do we had a look at the Baja machine's engine, which has been prepared to give a wide spread of power. The exact capacity is 1,994 c.c., obtained by using the 88-mm. bore cylinder barrel and piston kit plus an SPG of Germany roller-bearing crankshaft/connecting-rod assembly, as retailed by Empi over the counter. They quote DIN-measured b.h.p. figures for a new 1500 VW at 27 b.h.p., while this single Weber-carburated engine with its long individual tube intake manifolding gives a peak of 74 b.h.p. at 4,000 r.p.m., with 71 brake horsepower available for 500 r.p.m. above and below that peak.

Leaving aside the wide variety of individual non-functional, functional and mechanical accessories that the Company sells, Vittone also had a very clever idea: its name is the GTV and it consists of four stages to dress up the VW, improve its suspension and add some useful accessories, such as twin oil-coolers and improved instrumentation in the more expensive GTV bolt-on kits. The idea is so bright because car salesmen make much more money on a car with accessories than a production car, thus the volume of Vittone VW sales is kept healthy. In fact when we were there things were not too good as they had no cars left to sell!

The Company offers all the parts that a Beetle owner would be likely to ask for in the engine line. One can choose from Solex, Zenith or Weber twin-choke carburetters, fully-modified twin-port cylinder heads with 39-mm. intake valves and 32-mm. exhausts, pistons suitable for 1,700 and 1,994-c.c. engines and their "normal" compression ratio of 10 to 1, high-lift rocker arms (in short supply at present; they are made in Japan and I was surprised how many other parts come from, or will be coming from, that source), double valve springs for racing use, eight millimetre shorter push-rods to use with the high-lift rocker arms, and a range of camshafts to fit most early and late model units in varieties from vigorous to very vigorous.

The bolt-on kits to increase the displacement of the 1,300, 1,500 and 1,600-c.c. engines consist of the 82-mm. roller-bearing crankshaft, balanced and complete with connecting-rods and bearings (£126), or the 82-mm. big-bore cylinder barrels which give 160 c.c. increase on their own and come with four pistons and pins for £37. Finally, fo: a charge (all our prices are for the USA) of approximately £128, the 88-mm. super big-bore cylinder barrels which give 2-litres when used with the roller-bearing crankshaft.

There are two firms in Britain I know of which can get EMPI parts, but if you seriously want some of their parts I would suggest contacting EMPI direct at PO Box 1120, Riverside, California, 92502: their full scale catalogue costs $2 and I would allow at least a further dollar for posting that mammoth work across the ocean! The two companies in England which have successfully procured parts are Speedwell at Chesham (who did a marketing deal with EMPI some years ago) and Skyspeed, who have a couple of shops in the Feltham area of West London. The respective telephone numbers for the British firms are— Chesham 6961 and 01-890 1180.

We were lucky to drive Mr. Vittone Senior's personal car, which illustrates the amount of equipment that can be supplied and represents around £1,870 of best Beetle: at least I think that's what the Public Relations man said, but even his normal efficiency may have been obliterated by the healthy racket of the 160-b.h.p. power unit! Incidentally, that much power in the tail of a Beetle, loaded down with accessories and the 1,994-c.c. kit, is enough to propel it from a standing start through the quarter-mile in a claimed 14 seconds dead. This means a terminal speed in the region of 100 m.p.h., and enough acceleration to put all but the best American Super Cars (e.g., 7-litres plus of a bulky Chrysler, or similar full-sized machine) fractionally behind one. We could not check this fully for ourselves, but independent magazine tests show times of 15.1 seconds for the quarter-mile and speeds in the 86-m.p.h. area, or under 15 seconds without a fan belt—which is NOT a good idea for everyday use!

To obtain this sort of power two Weber 48 IDA carburetters were used together with the equipment we described for the engine earlier on, and some other parts as well. The gearbox featured closer-ratio 3rd and 4th gears and the overall final drive ratio was calculated for American conditions, providing a top speed in the region of 110 m.p.h. The suspension is as is featured in the most expensive GTVs (Hmmm . . . I wonder what Alfa Romeo will say about that label!), with new 19-mm. anti-roll bars front and rear, Koni or Bilstein adjustable shock-absorbers, and 14 × 5⅜ in. wheels with 185-section radial ply tyres. The interior had some very useful features indeed, with tachometer and auxiliary instruments mounted in front of the driver: in fact, our car had a prototype three-dial layout, but production cars have three different sizes of instruments, which are not all that easy to see.

Bucket seats, even for the rear, also form part of the inside story with the traditionally sombre matt black so hallowed by some enthusiasts and those who strive for the "GT" look. We were always told that it was the English who demanded planks of wood strewn around their car interiors for decoration, but now it appears that EMPI's young customers have gone overboard on simulated wood to complete the decor of dashboard and doors. Naturally the same material was used to finish off the expensive Nardi steering-wheel: apart from that the steering is one of the few parts of the car to remain as the German designer intended.

To the average American enthusiast I should imagine a different looking and better performing Beetle is really rather like possessing a properly executed model car is to an Englishman. It is a toy, and

STRIPEY BEETLE.—The GTV we tried had installed on it just about every accessory sold by EMPI. The engine had been enlarged to 2-litres and gave it tremendous performance. Twin oil-coolers are mounted above the engine lid, this position being dictated by style and airflow considerations.

the regular driver sadly commented to the author that he was unable to get the quicker Camaros and Mustangs to play at drag racing on the road! However, he was presumably rewarded by the looks we received from the owners of six, seven and even eight-litre battle-cruisers who were accelerating on their air-conditioned way up into the popular desert hideouts.

In fact "our" immaculate orange VW would appeal very strongly in this country (the pin-striping effect is strictly an optional stick-on item) as it handles in a very flat and sportsmanlike fashion, with reserves of road-holding that are quite extraordinary considering the saloon's unfashionably high roofline. Accelerating hard from a standstill will leave black marks on the tarmac, while the engine howls

delight as one approaches the 6,000-r.p.m. mark, where it is best to change gear in the interests of engine life. The car we drove had covered 35,000 carefully serviced miles, the only sign of the distance it had covered being a howl from the gearbox on releasing the throttle.

The gear-change was among the car's best features because the company's EZR control lever was fitted. The latter component does not affect the standard linkage back to the gearbox, but acts by offering increased leverage via a revised fulcrum point, so the movement between gear positions is nearly halved, whilst a collar on the lever makes it much easier to select reverse. On the West Coast of America this improved gear-change device costs a little over £5, so even with import taxes and cut for the British importer, it's certainly the most practical idea for a VW.

The brakes were up to coping with an attempted 80 m.p.h. suicide dive from a Freeway turnoff. When we had recovered our composure we asked the Public Relations gentleman what had been done to make the car stop in Porsche style. His reply was that the 1970 Microbus models have power-assisted front disc brakes and these had been installed. This modification certainly worked, but I believe late model Volkswagens have disc brakes that work well anyway.

Altogether an enjoyable, if surprisingly raucous, machine. However, that wasn't quite the end of the story, for we followed "Mr. PR" out to the hills up above the smog of Riverside: this time he was driving his own 1,700-c.c. version, while we had a cooking 5-litre 1969 Mustang. The surprises were that the VW made the Mustang breathe very hard to keep up in a straight line, whilst the Mustang astonished local hill residents by staying on the road and definitely within contact of the agile Volkswagen around the hairpins. All the same, we came to prefer European/Japanese cars for the twisty bits of the USA, though pleasantly surprised at the improvement American manufacturers have made throughout their sporting-car ranges.—J. W.

CONTINUED FROM PAGE 39
very loud horn. The instrument lighting is rheostat controlled. There is also a steering column lock with the column in which the key must be returned if the engine doesn't fire first time, map pockets in both doors and excellent armrests.

One of the real features of the car is the ventilation system. Two dashboard knobs control a flow of fresh air through three vents at the base of the screen. The air intake is on the outside just below the screen. The old and ridiculous vague turn-knob near the gearlever has been replaced with two lift-up levers from the VW1500 which control air flow and heat to front and rear. The front foot-level vents have sliding covers which help direct demisting air to the screen. Everything works well with only two faults — the warm air hits the driver on the ankle and there is still (the age-old complaint) a smell when the heater is being used because the system draws its warm air from over the engine.

So that's the 1500-engined beetle, a mixture of some of the old faults but with enough overall performance now to make it competitive with the later 1.5 litre sedans — which it never was before. We repeat — it's the best Volkswagen yet, and we wish it long life.

It'll probably have that, anyway.   #

VW SUPER BEETLE

The best Beetle yet, but still not as good as the competition

VOLKSWAGENWERK of West Germany is in the unique position of having one of the most successful products of all time, the VW Beetle. No matter how successful in its time, though, in the world of technological goods a product is eventually outdated by progress. The problem is, how does VW replace the Beetle? Fortunately for VW, the Beetle has built up such a following, has established such a legend, that there's still time to find the answer. To that end VW is expanding its product line and decreasing its dependence upon the Beetle. The Type 3 line, known to Americans as Fastback and Squareback, was the first attempt to branch out and continues to be popular. Last month we tested the 411, VW's new "large" car embodying the classic rear-engine layout. After taking over NSU and Audi, VW latched onto the excellent new NSU K70, a front-drive sedan one price class above the 411, and gave it the VW name. Next step will be the introduction of a radical mid-engine sedan in the 1200-cc class just below the Beetle. Finally, it is entirely possible that NSU's luxurious Wankel-powered Ro80 will take the VW name too, to give the marque a range from very small to large and expensive.

Meanwhile, new capital has been pumped into the Beetle to keep it alive a few more years. The result is a Super Beetle, with its wheelbase stretched 0.8 in., 3.2 in. more length in its front end, new front suspension, a flow-through ventilation system and a less austere interior. The old Beetle continues, and for the American market it is now offered in a version plainer than the Deluxe sold before so that VW can continue to have a price leader. Both models got the 1584-cc engine for 1971: this is the same unit as in the Type 3 but with carburetors instead of fuel injection. It produces 60 bhp, up from the 57-bhp output of last year's 1493-cc unit. The Super Beetle, at $1985 POE after the latest round of increases, is $140 more than the new "stripped" model.

In performance Volkswagens have grown steadily better over the years, but other economy cars have been getting faster too so that VW's performance remains leisurely by comparison with most of them. Fuel economy, however, remains exceptionally good and with only a 7.5:1 compression ratio the Beetle will run on any gasoline available in America. Too, it is as true as ever that all the Beetle's performance can be extracted habitually, including cruising at its 79-mph top speed, without risking premature engine failure. But using the VW's potential entails a lot of noise; the air-cooled engine makes a big racket going up through the gears,

GORDON CHITTENDEN PHOTOS

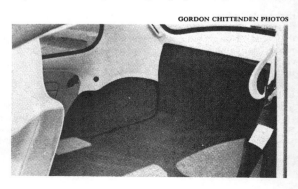

and only in 4th gear does it settle down to a reasonable noise level. As always, 4th is relatively "tall," giving great economy and a feeling of a relaxed, though not really quiet, engine. On our test car the engine did not idle consistently, but otherwise it ran smoothly and cleanly.

Shifting is a perennial problem in rear-engine cars and the Super Beetle breaks no new ground here. Perhaps further break-in use will improve it (the test car had just over 1000 miles on its odometer) but the shift lever was stiff and sticky in action. First gear is a stump-puller—that's why VWs seem to always race off from stoplights—but the other three are generally useful ratios.

Having redone the rear suspension two years ago to get rid of the notorious swing axles, and now having gone to MacPherson-strut front suspension on the Super Beetle, VW people have done about everything possible to make the car a good handler. (A cynic might say all that remains to be done now is to design an all-new body and get rid of the rear engine.) The tall body and big rearward weight bias mean that the Beetle, Super or not, is sensitive to sidewinds and still quite prone to oversteer at highway speeds. Could this be why one finds *Seitenwind* (sidewind) signs on super-highways in Germany?

In around-town driving, though, the Beetle still can boast maneuverability, simply because it's light and small. Its steering is quick, which makes it slightly heavy, and while redesigning the front end for the Super the engineers have reduced the car's turning circle to a handy 31.5 ft. And up to about 50 mph the Super Beetle's handling characteristics are quite decent. It's above that speed that the problems become evident and each increase in the VW's performance capability accentuates them.

The ride is not good either. It's bouncy and harsh, and despite the car's great height there appears to be a dearth of suspension travel; even gentle freeway undulations sometimes seem to bottom out the rear suspension with only the driver aboard. The body is as staunch as ever, which helps on rough roads, but at speed there are wind leaks around the doors and with the generous supply of road noise (and the aforementioned engine) highway driving becomes a veritable cacophony.

For the American market VW sticks with drum brakes all around. They're fairly big and have good fade resistance, but they take a bundle of pedal effort and are not capable of stopping the car in short distances from highway speeds. We also found in the test car a trace of the lumpiness that has been characteristic of VW brakes for so many years.

The Super Beetle configuration adds 3 cu ft of luggage space, all of it up front despite the smaller turning circle, and in addition this model comes with a fold-down rear seat that turns the rear passenger compartment into a large luggage area for the traveling couple. It's just as well, because there is next to no space for people in the rear seat: despite the tall body headroom is extremely limited there, and legroom is nothing to brag about either. The Super Beetle is jazzed up with carpeting (the stark but durable Teutonic kind) and adjustable seatbacks, the 3-point seatbelts go into place with one simple operation, and the materials are of good quality and well fitted. After that there's little else to say about the Super Beetle's interior; it's minimum, it's narrow and it's old-fashioned. Getting into it and out of it is awkward, again in spite of an expected advantage from a tall car. The new ventilation system—previous VWs really didn't have a ventilation system—is appreciated, but one has to open a windwing to get a fair flow of air through it and even at that it isn't up to today's standards of ventilation.

The Beetle, whether in standard or Super form, has three main points to recommend it: fuel economy, workmanship and its reputation for long life and good service. If you value those three virtues above all others, then the Beetle is for you. Otherwise it is hopelessly outdated and outdone by both Japanese and American economy cars.

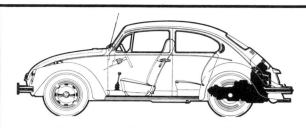

ROAD TEST RESULTS

PRICE

List price	$1985
Price as tested	$2349

ENGINE & DRIVE TRAIN

Engine	ohv H4
Bore x stroke, mm	85.5 x 69.0
Displacement, cc/cu in	1584/96.7
Compression ratio	7.5:1
Bhp @ rpm	60 @ 4400
Equivalent mph	88
Torque @ rpm, lb-ft	82 @ 3000
Equivalent mph	59
Transmission	4-speed manual
Gear ratios: 4th (0.89)	3.67:1
3rd (1.26)	5.19:1
2nd (2.06)	8.49:1
1st (3.80)	15.65:1
Final drive ratio	4.12:1

GENERAL

Curb weight, lb	1970
Weight distribution (with driver), front/rear, %	44/56
Wheelbase, in	95.3
Track, front/rear	54.3/53.3
Overall length	161.8
Width	62.4
Height	59.1
Steering	worm & roller
Turns, lock to lock	2.7
Brakes	9.6 x 1.7-in. drum front, 9.09 x 1.7-in. drum rear

ACCOMMODATION

Seating capacity, persons	4
Seat width, front/rear 2 x 20.0/52.0
Head room, front/rear	38.5/34.0

HANDLING

Speed on 100-ft radius, mph	30.4
Lateral acceleration, % g	0.617

PERFORMANCE

Top speed, 4th gear, mph	79
Acceleration, time to distance, sec:	
0–100 ft	3.6
0–250 ft	6.9
0–500 ft	11.0
0–750 ft	14.5
0–1000 ft	17.5
0–1320 ft (¼ mile)	21.1
Speed at end, mph	63
Time to speed, sec:	
0–30 mph	5.6
0–40 mph	8.1
0–50 mph	12.2
0–60 mph	18.4
0–70 mph	31.0
0–80 mph	47.5

BRAKE TESTS

Panic stop from 80 mph (projected):	
Max deceleration rate, % g	75
Stopping distance, ft	353
Control	very good
Fade test: percent increase in pedal effort to maintain 50% g deceleration rate in six stops from 60 mph	12
Overall brake rating	good

SPEEDOMETER ERROR

30 mph indicated is actually	27.0
40 mph	36.5
60 mph	55.0

CALCULATED DATA

Lb/hp (test weight)	39.5
Mph/1000 rpm (high gear)	19.6
Engine revs/mi	3050
Piston travel, ft/mi	1381
R&T steering index	0.85
Brake swept area, sq in/ton	173

FUEL

Type fuel required	regular
Fuel tank capacity, U.S. gal	11.1
Normal consumption, mpg	28.7

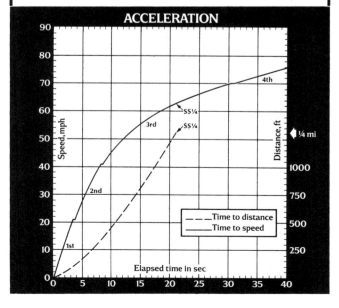

1300 BEETLE

SOUTH Africa has a changed range of VW Beetles for 1971: more power and other improvements for both models, but neither yet has the revised styling and new suspension introduced in Germany at the end of 1970.

As they've been saying in the advertisements, it's "the same old story" with this ageless car, though there is a considerable measure of improvement in the changes made for 1971.

It is remarkable that the production Beetle is 33 years old this year, and going stronger than ever. In South Africa, for instance, it has notched its third successive year as top-selling car, having regained this position after an interval of several years, and achieved record sales of over 20 000 in 1970.

ECONOMY MODEL

The smaller-engined 1300 Beetle is the economy model, yet it should not be looked down on — it is streets ahead of the earlier 1300 in performance and, amazingly, it actually rivals the earlier 1500 Beetle from a standing start!

The 1300 virtually takes the place of the 1500, and at its competitive price of R1 598 it is intended primarily for the second-car market and fleet requirements.

It does not have the luxury equipment of the new 1600, but it has all the essentials, plus sound road performance and outstanding operating economy.

HANDLING FACTOR

We have said it before, and must repeat that the abolition of the swing-axle rear suspension on the Beetle models is overdue. Volkswagen started introducing dual-jointed rear axles several years ago, and both the VW 411 range and the Kombi-Microbus-Transporter models have long had this vastly-improved rear-end configuration.

The modern, wider-tracked Beetles are much more stable than those of a decade ago, but the 1971 South African models remain wander-prone at speed, and can be quite a handful when a gusty wind is blowing.

The 1971 Beetle range announced overseas at the motor shows has completely-revised suspension, front and rear, and we hope that this important development will not be long in coming to the Republic.

NEW FEATURES

Both of the 1971 Beetle models recently announced in the Republic have a considerable number of detail changes. Styling is slightly revised, with body side mouldings mounted higher to raise the "waist-line," and a small change in bonnet outline to set the rear number plate nearly vertical.

Windscreen washer capacity has been raised to 1 litre — still powered by spare-wheel pressure — the steering column locks, and headlamps are wired through the ignition switch.

A very welcome new feature is the through-flow ventilation system, though owners are probably going to be disappointed at its capacity. We found that, set at full capacity, it hardly produced enough fresh air to be felt at the inlet louvres, let alone cool the interior, even at cruising speeds and with a headwind.

INCREASED POWER

The 1300 engine (same stroke as the 1600, but with smaller cylinder bore diameter) gets a 10 per cent increase in power output on the new model.

This is achieved by a rise of two points in compression ratio and a bigger carburettor with 31-mm choke tube. The specifications are not given in detail, but doubled inlet ports, improved distributor and a new fuel pump all play a part.

This new 1300 engine achieves full value, giving the car better 0–60 acceleration, and much the same maximum speed potential, as the earlier 1500 engine of the 1968-69 "Super-Beetle".

PERFORMANCE FACTORS

The new 1300 retains the 4·375 to 1 final drive of the 1200/1300 models (1500/1600 take 4·125) yet in the Beetle tradition, it is still over-geared with its indirect top gear, to be a fine cruising car.

The third gear ratio has been changed from the 1·32 to 1 of the earlier 1300 to a much closer 1·26 to 1. This gives more third-gear range and is a key ingredient in the improved performance.

The extra equipment added from year to year brings with it small increases in mass, and the 1971 model is listed at 820 kg, compared with the 780 kg of the earlier 1300 model.

PERFORMANCE

With much more getaway punch, we found that a quick snatch of wheelspin could be induced with the 1971 model by dropping the clutch smartly, and the easy snap-changing of the gear lever is a traditional Volkswagen advantage in getting moving.

The 0–100 km/h time of 21·5 seconds is a highly-meritorious achievement by Beetle standards, and we were even able to record a respectable 0–120 time. Overtaking ability is good up to about 110 km/h, then tapers off with the overgeared top.

A comparison with the earlier 1300 and 1500 models (using the Imperial measures of the earlier Tests) is a good illustration of the capabilities of the new model (previous Tests were: Beetle 1300, March 1966, and Beetle 1500, July 1968):

		1300	1500	New 1300
0–40	..	9·7	8·0	**8·2**
0–60	..	24·5	20·0	**19·5**
¼ Mile	..	22·3	20·9	**21·3**
Speed	..	74·9	78·5	**78·2**

We pushed the 1300 pretty hard in performance tests, and it stood up

SPECIFICATIONS

ENGINE:

Cylinders .	Four, horizontally opposed, rear-mounted
Carburettor	Solex PICT 31
Bore	77 mm (3·04 in.)
Stroke	69 mm (2·72 in.)
Cubic capacity .	1 285 cm³ (78·4 in.³)
Compression ratio . . .	7·5 to 1
Valve gear . . .	Ohv, pushrods
Main bearings	Three
Aircleaner . .	Oil Bath, 0·4 litres
Fuel rating	91-octane
Cooling . . .	Air, blower-driven
Electrics	12-volt DC

ENGINE OUTPUT:

Max. power SAE .	38·8 kW (54 bhp)
Max. power net . .	34·3 kW (46 bhp)
Peak rpm	4 600 (see text)
Max. torque/rpm . .	92·2 N.m/ 2 600 (68·3 lb. ft.)

TRANSMISSION:

Forward speeds	Four
Synchromesh	All
Gearshift	Floor
Low gear	3·80 to 1
2nd gear	2·06 to 1
3rd gear	1·26 to 1
Top gear	0·89 to 1
Reverse gear	3·88 to 1
Final drive	4·375 to 1
Drive wheels	Rear
Tyre size	5·60 x 15

BRAKES:

Front	TLS drums
Rear	SLS drums
Total lining area	N/S
Boosting	Nil
Handbrake position .	Between seats

STEERING:

Type	Worm and roller
Lock to lock . . .	2·6 turns
Turning circle . . .	11·0 m (36 ft.)

MEASUREMENTS:

Length overall . .	4·03 m (160 in.)
Width overall . .	1·55 m (60·5 in.)
Height overall . .	1·50 m (59·0 in.)
Wheelbase . .	2·40 m (94·5 in.)
Front track . . .	1·3 m (51·4 in.)
Rear track . . .	1·36 m (53·4 in.)
Ground clearance . .	0·15 m (6·0 in.)
Licensing mass . .	820 kg (1 800 lb)

SUSPENSION:

Front	Independent
Type . . .	Torsion bars, stabiliser
Rear	Independent
Type . . .	Torsion bars, swing axles

CAPACITIES:

Seating	4/5
Fuel tank . . .	40 litres (8·8 gal)
Luggage trunk . .	0·14 m³ (5 cu. ft.)
Utility space	0·14–0·5 m³ (4·9–17·6 cu. ft.)

SERVICE DATA:

Sump capacity . .	2·5 litres (4·4 pints)
Change interval .	5 000 km (3 000 miles)
Gearbox/diff capacity	2·5 litres (4·4 pints)
Change interval .	50 000 km (30 000 miles)
Air filter service .	10 000 km (6 000 miles)
Greasing points . .	Front axles (4)
Greasing interval	5 000 km (3 000 miles)

(These basic service recommendations are given for guidance only, and may vary according to operating conditions. Inquiries should be addressed to authorised dealerships.)

TYRE PRESSURES:

Crossply: Front . 1·7 to 1·8 bars (24/26 lb)
Rear . 1·9 to 2·2 bars (28/32 lb)
Radial ply: Front . 1·8 to 1·9 bars (26/28 lb)
Rear . 1·9 to 2·5 bars (28/36 lb)

WARRANTY:

Six months or 6 000 miles.

BASIC PRICE:

Coast and Reef R1 598

PROVIDED TEST CAR:

Volkswagen South Africa, Uitenhage, C.P.

STANDARD EQUIPMENT:

Cigar lighter, headlamp flasher, semi-reclining front seats, convertible rear seat/luggage space, pressurised windscreen washers, dash grabhandle, coat hooks, wheel trims, exterior rear-view mirror, assist straps, door pockets.

MAKE AND MODEL:

Make	Volkswagen
Model	1300 Beetle, 1971

PERFORMANCE FACTORS:

Power/mass (kg/kW)	22·4
Frontal area (m²)	2·33
km/h/1 000 (top)	30·4

(Calculated on licensing mass, gross frontal area, gearing and net power output.)

INTERIOR NOISE LEVELS:

	Min.
Idling	59·0
60 km/h	73·0
80 km/h	78·0
100 km/h	83·5
Full throttle	See graph

(Measured in decibels, "A" weighting, averaging runs both ways on a level road; "Minimum" with car closed.)

ACCELERATION FROM REST:

0–50	5·1
0–60	7·1
0–70	9·8
0–80	12·9
0–90	16·2
0–100	21·5
0–110	30·0
0–120	47·3
400 m	21·3

OVERTAKING ACCELERATION:

	3rd	Top
40–60	5·7	8·7
60–80	6·0	8·6
80–100	9·5	13·0
100–120	—	35·9

(Measured in seconds, to true speeds, averaging runs both ways on a level road, car carrying test crew of two and standard test equipment.)

MAXIMUM SPEED:

True speed	122·9
Speedo reading	129·0

Calibration:

Indicated	40	60	80	100	120
True speed	40	59	78	97	116

FUEL ECONOMY (litres/100 km in brackets):

60 km/h	17·7 (5·7)
80 km/h	15·4 (6·5)
100 km/h	12·7 (7·9)
Full throttle	9·0 (11·1)

(Measured in kilometres per litre averaging runs both ways on a level road.)

BRAKING TEST:

From 80 km/h:

First stop	2·6
Tenth stop	2·7
Average	2·66

(Measured in sec, with stops from true speeds at 30-sec intervals on a good bituminised surface.)

GRADIENTS IN GEARS:

Low gear	1 in 3·6
2nd gear	1 in 5·4
3rd gear	1 in 8·8
Top gear	1 in 15·7

(Tabulated from Tapley (x gravity) readings, car carrying test crew of two and standard test equipment.)

GEARED SPEEDS:

Low gear	33·1
2nd gear	61·2
3rd gear	100·0
Top gear	139·4

(Calculated to true speeds, at engine max. rpm — 4 600.)

TEST CONDITIONS:

Altitude	At sea level
Weather	Warm and windy
Fuel used	93-octane
Test car's odometer	2 200 km

INTERIOR NOISE LEVEL

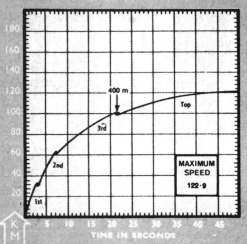

Min. dB AT 100 — 83·5

ACCELERATION

400 m

MAXIMUM SPEED — 122·9

FUEL CONSUMPTION

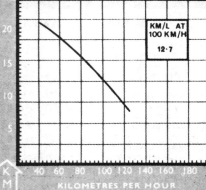

KM/L AT 100 KM/H — 12·7

ENGINE SPEED

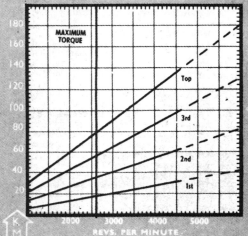

MAXIMUM TORQUE

SILENCE LEVELS:

Mechanical	Poor
Idling	Very Poor
Transmission	Good
Wind	Good
Road	Fair
Coachwork	Very Good
Average	Poor

ENGINE:

Starting	Very Good
Response	Good
Smoothness	Good
Accessibility	Fair

STEERING:

Accuracy	Very Good
Stability at speed	Fair
Stability in wind	Poor
Steering effort	Very Good
Roughness	Very Good
Road feel	Very Good
Centring action	Fair
Turning circle	Good

BRAKING:

Pedal pressure	Very Good
Response	Excellent
Fade resistance	Fair
Directional stability	Fair
Handbrake position	Excellent
Handbrake action	Very Good

TRANSMISSION:

Clutch action	Good
Pedal pressure	Fair
Gearbox ratios	Good
Final drive ratio	Fair
Gearshift position	Very Good
Gearshift action	Very Good
Synchromesh	Excellent

SUSPENSION:

Firmness rating	Very Good
Progressive action	Good
Roadholding	Good
Roll control	Excellent
Tracking control	Good
Pitching control	Very Good
Load ability	Very Good

DRIVER CONTROL:

Hand control location	Good
Pedal location	Poor
Wiper action	Good
Washer action	Very Good
Instrumentation	Poor

INTERIOR COMFORT:

Seat design	Good
Headroom front	Excellent
Legroom front	Good
Headroom rear	Good
Legroom rear	Fair
Door access	Fair
Lighting	Good
Accessories fitted	Fair
Accessories potential	Fair

DRIVING COMFORT:

Steering wheel position	Good
Steering wheel reach	Fair
Visibility	Fair
Directional feel	Poor
Ventilation	Poor
Heating	Excellent

COACHWORK:

Appearance	Good
Finish	Very Good
Space utilization	Very Good
Trunk capacity	Poor
Trunk access	Poor

well. The new third gear gives easy 100-km/h capability, where the earlier model started running out of revs before this key speed was reached.

FUEL ECONOMY

Except at the very top end, the new 1300 is also ahead of the old model in fuel economy — a factor of growing importance in today's world. A brief comparison (in mpg) tells the story:

		Old 1300	New 1300
30 mph	..	50·1	**53·9**
45 mph	..	41·4	**45·7**
60 mph	..	34·3	**37·4**
75 mph	..	26·8	**25·2**

The new model goes on to a much lower full throttle figure, which is understandable with greater breathing capacity and speed capability, but should be more economical overall — and a top contender among 1300-cm³ models.

STOPPING ABILITY

Local content requirement is given as the reason for the Beetle's reversion to drum brakes all round, after a brief essay into the field of front discs (on the 1500 model) four years ago.

These are exceptionally good drum brakes for normal purposes and about-town speeds, but in stops from high speeds it is a different story: a 120 km/h stop took 4·8 seconds on this test car, showing inadequate heat dissipation in the high-speed stop. Rear wheels lock at lower speeds, but were doing this evenly on the test car, so that directional stability was not seriously affected.

ROAD ABILITY

The torsion-bar suspension of the Beetle is capable of soaking up punishment, and teamed with the big 15-inch wheels, makes this a most capable car over bad surfaces and gravel. There is almost total absence of pitch and body roll, and loadability is outstanding by light car standards.

Weight distribution is poor, with too much on the rear wheels, and the oversteer tendency is easily provoked. This makes the car very sensitive to tyre pressures, and we have found it advisable never to let rear-tyre pressures drop below 1·9 bars (28 lb psi).

The throbbing note of the rear engine is always present, and mechanical noise becomes quite severe at cruising speeds.

DATA AT 120

Min. noise level . . .	87·5 dBA
0–120 through gears . .	47·3 sec
Economy at 120 . .	9·0 km/l
	(11·1 litres/100 km)
Braking from 120 . . .	4·8 sec
Reserve power . .	0·013 x gravity
Max. gradient (top) . . .	1 in 77·1
Speedo error . . .	3·3% over
Speedo at true 120	116
Rpm (top)	3 950

DRIVER CONTROLS

Instrumentation is unchanged on the Beetle models, the 1300 having the usual speedometer and odometer without decimals (fully metricated on 1971 models) plus fuel gauge.

The high-parking windscreen wipers are a dated feature, and the indicator/dip-switch/flasher lever on the steering column should be on the right (the left hand is busy enough with gearshifting).

SUMMARY

An amazing car, this Beetle. There is very little that is inspiring about it, yet it has so many undoubted virtues: that useful utility space behind the rear seat, the rear seat folding capability, the solid and weatherproof coachwork, fine paintwork, attention to detail in finish, and spares/service facilities which are a model for others to follow.

It is a plain, good-value serviceable car — and the sales statistics prove that this is what South Africans want! ●

IMPERIAL DATA

Major performance features of this Road Test are summarised below in Imperial measures:

PERFORMANCE FACTORS:

Power/mass (lb/bhp) . .	39·2
Frontal area (sq. ft.) . . .	25·0
Mph/1 000 rpm (top) . . .	18·9

ACCELERATION FROM REST (in seconds):

0–30	4·9
0–40	8·2
0–50	13·7
0–60	19·5
0–70	37·8
¼ Mile	21·3

MAXIMUM SPEED:

True speed	78·2

FUEL CONSUMPTION (mpg):

30	53·9
45	45·7
60	37·4
75	25·2
Full throttle	21·4

GEARED SPEEDS (mph):

1st gear	20·6
2nd gear	38·0
3rd gear	62·1
Top gear	86·7

The engine looks the same, but has bigger carburettor and improved breathing to give 10 per cent more power . . .

Good body angle in a hard turn, but the tail was starting to break.

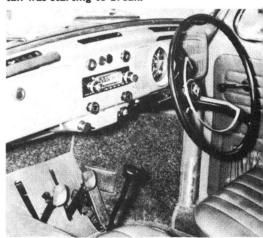

Instrumentation and controls are unchanged, except that speedometer and odometer are metric.

The front trunk is very shallow, and needs a waist-high lift for loading.

VOLKWAGEN '71

■ Volkswagen's "bug" comes in two versions for 1971: the Beetle and the Super Beetle.

While the Beetle features added power, a flow-through ventilation system and a number of other improvements for 1971, the new three-inch-longer Super Beetle incorporates more engineering changes than any VW since the first "bugs" came to America 21 years ago.

Despite the slightly larger size of the new model and its many special features, there is no mistaking the family relationship of the two cars. According to Stuart Perkins, president of Volkswagen of America, "The new Super Beetle shows what our engineers—men who have been designing small cars for 25 years—can do to put even larger mea-

sures of performance, economy, comfort and convenience into the type of 'package' that has made our car the best-selling small car in the world."

Both 1971 Beetles have a new 60-horsepower engine, up from last year's 57-hp. powerplant, which gives them a top and cruising speed of 81 miles per hour, the company states. VW's air-cooled engines have consistently set performance and economy standards in the past and this year's powerplant is expected to have even greater durability.

"That is due," Perkins said, "to use of a new light metal alloy in our crankcase and to new chromed exhaust valve stems as well as to a new valve guide material."

Engine modifications, a new carburetor and an evaporative control

fuel system keep both Beetle powerplants within the allowable emission levels in the company's continued campaign against smog. Perkins pointed out that Volkswagen's Wofsburg factory—the company's "home plant"—was the first European test center accredited as an official California smog-control laboratory back in 1965.

While both the Beetle and Super Beetle share in a number of improvements for 1971—including the flow-through ventilation system, added theft protection and an aluminum oil cooler—the Super Beetle has many more all to itself.

They include stronger bumpers on the 161.8-inch-long car which measures 3.2 inches longer than the Beetle. The new bumpers are

THERE ARE TWO BEETLES NOW—ONE TAGGED SUPER! BOTH HAVE 60 HP ENGINES AND THE SUPER HAS A NEW FRONT SUSPENSION.

LEFT: Super Beetle (in foreground) has new front end which about doubles front trunk space while reducing its turning circle by about four feet. ABOVE AND BELOW: Super is 3 inches longer than the standard VW. Standard equipment includes flow-through ventilation system with 2-speed blower.

6

VOLKSWAGEN '71

equipped with rubber inserts, especially useful in parking lot scrapes.

Among additional features in the Super Beetle are:

—A larger front trunk with more than nine cubic feet of luggage space, nearly twice as much as before.

—A relocated and slightly larger gasoline tank with an 11-gallon capacity.

—A front track of 54.3 inches—2.7 inches wider than the Beetle—and a tighter turning circle of 31.5 feet.

—A fresh-air blower to keep air moving through the passenger compartment during those slow-moving traffic jams on rainy days.

—Larger front brakes.

—Easier steering.

Standard equipment includes a smooth-shifting, four-on-the-floor manual transmission. The Super Beetle is optionally available with VW's torque-converter Automatic Stick Shift transmission which gives the driver the ease of an automatic but still lets him shift for himself if he wants to run through the gears.

The Super Beetle's enlarged front trunk, made possible by a MacPherson-type independent front suspension, permits stowage of the spare wheel in horizontal position at the bottom of the trunk. The easy-to-use jack also was given a new stowage position under the rear seat where it is protected from exposure to weather that causes corrosion.

Both 1971 Beetles share a major convenience feature, a fool-proof headlight switch that "remembers" to turn off the headlights if the driver forgets to do it when the ignition key is turned off. As the headlights automatically switch off, the parking lights turn on to reduce the drain on the battery.

Special convenience and comfort features found on the Super Beetle include a carpeted floor, a pocket on the passenger door, an electrically-operated rear window demister and defroster, a vanity mirror on the right-hand sun visor and an added ashtray in the rear compartment. Both Beetles can be equipped with

VW-built air conditioners.

All 1971 VWs are covered by a 24-month or 24,000-mile warranty and are delivered with coupons good for free VW Diagnosis at 6,000-mile intervals during the first 24,000 miles traveled.

Perkins said that "our Diagnosis program which we introduced at the start of the 1970 model year has proved to be an important service for VW owners."

He explained:

"With it, problems which might not become apparent until long after the warranty period has passed can be found and be corrected by us during the warranty period."

VW Diagnosis set an industry first when it was introduced at authorized VW dealerships throughout the U.S. at the start of the 1970 model year. •

7

SUPER BUG

ULTIMATE BEETLE

WE THOUGHT OF A COMPARISON WITH A 10 YEAR OLD PORSCHE BUT DIDN'T WANT TO EMBARRASS THE STUTTGART FIRM.

Under that incredibly old fashioned exterior there lies roadholding beyond the belief of pre-1971 VW owners. It is so good, we ask is this the best handling small car?

IT WAS ONE of those downhill, 170 degree, switchback corners that really proved it. The other car, a sporty European sedan, ploughed through in understeer at 30 mph and we worried about locking up a wheel under brakes during entry to the corner and getting the car on line for the next, even tighter, bend. □ In the Super Bug it was a dream. A dab of the brakes, then full power, a tiny turn of the wheel, a touch of opposite lock and you were through at 40 mph and enjoying it. □ For owners of old Beetles all that sounds remote and impossible, but it is an almost everyday occurrence in the latest VW Beetle. Ever since the car received the MacPherson strut front suspension and the semi-trailing arm rear end (previously reserved for the semi-automatic model) the Bug has been a real Q-ship among small cars. □ And the new rear end was not fitted because of any design advances, which include not only the improved roadholding but a significant reduction in turning circle, but because it was cheaper to produce so it is almost an accident. □ With astonishing regularity owners of supposedly fine handling cars have been astonished to find the Bug can leave them behind in the twisty bits and at least keep up on the less windy areas. It is only on very steep hills or long straights that it has no chance. □ Somehow

Photography: Uwe Kuessner

SUPER BUG
ULTIMATE BEETLE

the car's fun character cancels out the acknowledged failings of a cramped interior, poor visibility and inadequate ventilation and gives the Beetle another stay of execution before time, at last, catches up.

There are those who believe it already has, but with sales now past the 15 million mark, and the record T-model Ford figure, the Beetle lives on.

And excuses have to be made for the inadequacies of the now close to 40-year-old body but the refreshing VW way of doing things gives the car an honest and strong appeal to customers searching for practical value.

Of course the VW has its limitations — even the most rabid fanatics admit that — but it is one of the few small cars we've driven recently which really attracts drivers (apart from Shamus, of course). And that, today, is often enough to ensure a wide market which is a complete addition to those who regard the Beetle as the best example of solid, reliable transportation.

You tend to think of the Super Bug as not being a 1600 in the sense that a Datsun 1600, or Toyota Corona or even a Cortina is and certainly its perform-

Top: Boot goes up in steps over MacPherson struts and petrol tank. It holds a surprising amount of room and can be supplemented by now covered area (middle) behind the rear seat. Additional engine vents (bottom) and bigger rear window are only styling changes over old car.

Super Bug in understeer. Note tyre distortion, test car ran radial ply tyres, treated corners with contempt and proved to be astonishingly quick in twisty sections.

ance is not as good although it is a vast improvement over the 1300 Bug we tested earlier this year.

VW's traditional low revving engine deliberately restricts the power output but the top speed is now close to a genuine 85 mph and, of course, that is also the maximum cruising speed. Fuel consumption is rather lower than we expected but it didn't drop to the low 20s as had been experienced in some of the early Super Bug tests. From the mid-20s to a best of 30 mpg can be regarded as normal.

By VW standards the engine is flexible — at least you can pull away from 30 mph in top gear without transmission snatch and engine vibration and by changing down to third there is almost a push in the back as the little car accelerates forward.

By pushing the engine to an hysterical limit it is possible to reach a genuine 26, 46 and 70 mph in the intermediate gears but far more sensible change-up points would be 20, 40 and 60 for acceleration which is almost as quick and far less noisy. Taking the engine right out we achieved a 0-60 mph time of 16.5 seconds and covered the standing quarter mile in 20.3 seconds.

wheels road test
technical details

MAKE	VOLKSWAGEN
MODEL	Super Bug
BODY TYPE	2-door sedan
PRICE	$2387
OPTIONS	Radio, radial ply tyres
COLOR	Mustard
MILEAGE START	1747
MILEAGE FINISH	2206
WEIGHT	1918 lb

FUEL CONSUMPTION:

| Overall | 25.6 mpg |
| Cruising | 24-28 mpg |

TEST CONDITIONS:

Weather	Fine, cool
Surface	Hot mix
Load	Two persons
Fuel	Premium

SPEEDOMETER ERROR:

Indicated mph	30	40	50	60	70
Actual mph	29	38	46	56	66

PERFORMANCE

Piston speed at max bhp	(6032 m/min) 1994.6 ft/min
Top gear mph per 1000 rpm	(31.4 kph) 196
Engine rpm at max speed	4300
Lbs (laden) per gross bhp (power-to-weight)	(14.5 kg) 31.9

MAXIMUM SPEEDS:

Fastest run	(138.3 kph) 86 mph
Average of all runs	(135 kph) 84 mph
Speedometer indication, fastest run	(146.4 mph) 91 mph

IN GEARS:

1st	(41.8 kph) 26 mph (5500 rpm)
2nd	(75.6 kph) 47 mph (5500 rpm)
3rd	(112.6 kph) 70 mph (5000 rpm)
4th	(135.1 kph) 84 mph (4300 rpm)

VOLKSWAGEN SUPER BUG

3rd 70mph
STANDING ¼ MILE 20.3
2nd 47mph
TOP SPEED 84mph
1st 26mph
ACCELERATION THROUGH GEARS WITH CHANGE POINTS

MPH ▶ ELAPSED TIME IN SECONDS

ACCELERATION (through gears):

0-30 mph	5.2 sec
0-40 mph	7.7 sec
0-50 mph	11.7 sec
0-60 mph	16.6 sec
0-70 mph	26.0 sec

	2nd gear	3rd gear	4th gear
30-40 mph	4.1 sec	6.5 sec	11.0 sec
30-50 mph	6.0 sec	6.6 sec	10.4 sec
40-60 mph	—	7.1 sec	11.1 sec
50-70 mph	—	9.5 sec	13.0 sec

STANDING QUARTER MILE:

| Fastest run | 20.2 sec |
| Average all runs | 20.3 sec |

BRAKING:

| From 30 mph to 0 | 1.3 sec |
| From 60 mph to 0 | 3.0 sec |

SPECIFICATIONS

ENGINE:

Cylinders	Four, opposed
Bore and stroke	(3.36 in. x 2.72 in.) 85.5 mm x 69 mm
Cubic capacity	(96.6 cu in.) 1584 cc
Compression ratio	7.5 to 1
Valves	Overhead pushrod
Carburettor	Downdraught, auto choke
Fuel pump	Mechanical
Oil filter	Full flow
Power at rpm	60 bhp at 4400 rpm
Torque at rpm	81.6 lb/ft at 3000 rpm

TRANSMISSION:

Type	Four speed, manual, all syncro
Clutch	SDP
Gear lever location	Floor

OVERALL RATIO:

	Direct	Overall	mph per 1000 rpm	(kph)
1st	3.80	15.675	4.6	(7.3)
2nd	2.06	8.498	8.5	(13.6)
3rd	1.26	5.198	13.9	(22.3)
4th	0.88	3.671	19.6	(31.4)
Final drive	4.125			

CHASSIS AND RUNNING GEAR:

Construction	Tubular centre section welded to floor pan
Suspension front	McPherson struts, anti-roll bar
Suspension rear	Semi-trailing arms, torsion bars
Shock absorbers	Telescopic
Steering type	Cam and roller
Turns lock to lock	26
Turning circle	(95 m) 31.5 ft
Steering wheel diameter	15.5 in.
Brakes type	Disc/drum
Dimensions	(27.7 cm) 11 in., (23 cm) 9 in.

DIMENSIONS:

Wheelbase	(240 cm) 95.3 in.
Track front	(138 cm) 54.3 in.
Track rear	(135 cm) 53.2 in.
Length	(406 cm) 13 ft 4.6 in.
Width	(158 cm) 5 ft 2.4 in.
Height	(149 cm) 4 ft 11 in.
Fuel tank capacity	(34.8 litres) 9.2 gallons

TYRES:

Size	155SR x 15
Pressures	(1.3/1.9 kg/cm²) 18/27 psi
Make on test car	Goodyear

GROUND CLEARANCE:

| Registered | (15 cm) 5.9 in. |

SUPER BUG: ULTIMATE BEETLE

VW gear change is still one of the best although in reducing the travel between ratios it is more notchy than we remember from 10 years ago but still precise and with unbeatable syncromesh. The clutch travel is long and a little sticky.

Pedal positions have been adjusted so there is room between the brake and the clutch for the driver's left foot but the angle of movement is awkward and it takes time getting from the accelerator to the brake.

With big front discs, actual braking is very good with a progressive, if heavy, pedal and it takes a crash stop to promote any wheel lock-up.

One peculiar trait we did notice was that under hard braking or after a spell of quick cornering a smell of petrol infiltrated the interior although there was no sign of liquid leaking out of the filler cap.

With fully independent suspension VWs have always had a good ride by small car standards and the Super Bug continues the tradition with a reduction in pitch although the car doesn't perhaps have the same indestructable feeling over very rough roads.

The seats are German so they are firm, flat and large without much support against sideways movement but with the driver firmly belted-in they proved surprisingly comfortable over a long mileage. A four position squab adjustment is provided by a crude cam at the base of the seat but the most reclined position is the only one we ever used and it is almost impossible to adjust positions without getting out of the car.

The driving position is good for most people with the exception of the poor pedal layout. The steering wheel, now with four spokes just like the Porsche 911, is beautifully placed for easy movements.

Where the Beetle really feels ancient is in the interior. The driver and front seat passenger almost rub shoulders with each other and the doors and anybody unlucky enough to occupy the rear seat had better be a legless midget.

It seems VW increases the size of the windows every other year and this time it has been the turn of the back window. It has gone up 11 percent, but even so visibility is poor by modern standards with very thick pillars. In wet conditions it is even worse — the wipers are positioned for left hand drive so there is a large blind triangle in the bottom right hand corner of the windscreen. Wiper/washer operation has been simplified, however — it is now worked by a steering column stalk.

While we are talking about changes the others incorporated in the latest model include larger disc pads, additional vents on the engine lid for better cooling, reduced exhaust emission, reversing lights are standard and a luggage lid has been fitted above the area behind the rear seat.

But the most significant change is completely hidden from view. Each 1972 VW comes with a computorised, plug-in service system called VW diagnosis. The system is claimed to reduce by 20 percent the cost of routine servicing.

The actual plug is in the engine compartment and easy to reach. VW's aim is to cut out blind servicing so the customer pays only for rectifying what is really necessary. More than 53 checks can be made in an hour covering anything from wheel alignment to ignition timing. Buyers of new VWs are entitled to five free "health checks", the first to be done at 600 miles, the remaining four at 6000 mile intervals up to 24,000 miles.

The vehicle maintenance record will be stored in a computor at VW's headquarters so that ultimately a complete rundown on a car's history will be available at the press of a button.

Owners of pre-1972 VWs will be able to have the checks done on their vehicles at a recommended charge or $5.25.

Otherwise the car is last year's Super Bug.

Ventilation has supposedly been improved with fresh air slits at the top of the dash panel but these give only a weak flow of air and they can't be assisted by a fan since there isn't one. Heating still depends very much on the engine's revs, the more revs the more hot air enters the cabin. Actual temperature is hard to control too.

Opening front quarter vents are retained and are a necessity during summer months as a supplement to normal ventilation. The rear side windows don't open and this, together with the tombstone front seats, gives back seat occupants a very closed-in feeling.

Under hard acceleration the noise level is high but it falls away, when cruising in top gear, to a reasonable level although it is never as quiet as equivalent water-cooled cars.

The dashboard is the same hard, flat panel containing one single instrument, a few rubber faced controls which have been moved around on the new car, the radio speaker and a passenger's grab handle.

Finish is superb by anybody else's standards but it seems to have fallen below the perfect level set a few years ago with a couple of rough edges visible in the interior.

But the Super Bug still registers in our collective minds as a marvellous little car with enormous potential as a quick point to point machine and within the limitations of its apparently immortal body it has achieved a high degree of efficiency.

According to VW the car will pass all the safety legislation on paper at the moment so there is no reason to think it will be killed off in the immediate future. But we can't help thinking how much better it would be with a very 1972 style body providing plenty of interior room and maximum visibility to go with the incredibly good road behaviour. *

Current Beetle shape poses problems if car is to pass 1975 US crash tests but VW claim it will without major restyling.

Engine is unchanged in power output but exhaust emissions have been reduced and computerised plug servicing is built-in.

The Baja Beetle

It's more for on-road show than for off-road g...

by W.R.C. Shedenhelm

Volkswagen's public relations problem these last few years has been that it is not alone in the economy car field anymore. As the Beetle's engine was enlarged from 1200cc to 1600, the earlier 30 miles per gallon figures disappeared, and could no longer be made a major sales issue. Even the under-$2000 price figure is being challenged from several fronts, and VW had to drop some of the standard accessories on the regular Beetle, and add the Super Beetle with them, but at $2229.

VW has apparently decided to place greater stress on the engine's excellent engineering, its durability, its reliability and its ease of servicing and repair. And where have these factors been better demonstrated than in the well-publicized races in Baja California: the "Mexican 1000" and the "Baja 500." The buggies raced in Baja, and in most

other off-road races, are almost always powered by VW engines, and in most cases use the front and rear suspension from a Beetle.

In last June's "Baja 500," for example, the overall winner was Bobby Ferro driving the 557 miles solo in his VW-powered Sandmaster buggy. Next overall were two pickup trucks, then a tandem-seated VW buggy. Eleventh overall, and first in the "Production Two-Wheel Drive Passenger Vehicles" category was a VW Beetle, as were second and third in this class.

A few months ago Volkswagen of America announced its new "Baja Champion SE" for $70 over the price of a new Super Beetle. The "SE" was for "special edition," or some such, and only a few thousand were made. They all had a metallic blue paint job, special wheels, and the Bosch halogen fog lights were $58.95 extra.

Now VW has come out with a dealer-installed kit for the Super Beetle, for $129.95, to make it into a "Baja Beetle." This kit includes the Baja side stripes, a Superior Speed Shifter, the Bosch fog lights, a leatherette steering wheel cover, mag-type wheel covers, a stick-on walnut dash kit, tapered exhaust tips and rubber-faced bumper over-riders all around. You can choose any color Super Beetle you wish.

While the kit itself is a lot cheaper than you could buy the individual items and have them installed, the one fly-in-the-bank-account is the cost of the Bosch fog lights. They're halogen bulbed, but are about the same intensity as a standard filament fog light. So why $58.95 the set, when you can buy a set of filament fog lights from Sears for less than $14 a set, or the real high-intensity quartz-iodine driving lights from Sears for less than $26, or a set of narrow and

broad beamed QI's from Dick Cepek for $29.95. Why? VW says it's because these are Bosch lights. We say "bosh!"

Although the factory insists that these Bosch fog lights are "halogen" lights, they are quite ordinary intensity, and therefore are legal in all States. Thinking them to be the super-brights one associates with Baja racing, we immediately got a set of padded covers from Cepek, in case we were stopped by the Highway Patrol. The covers looked jazzy, but were not really needed except to protect the amber lenses against stone damage.

The real trouble with the "Baja Beetle" kit, though, is that it's on the wrong model Beetle. The basic reason for VW's being so successful in Baja is not only the reliability of the engine and suspension, but their excellent ground clearance. The regular under-$2000 Beetle still has this. With the Super Beetle, however, the factory switched to the coil-spring, MacPherson-strut front

suspension used on the 411 models. These struts pivot from the center of the underpan to the lower part of the front wheel back plates. One good rock, that you didn't dead-center the Super Beetle over, and you'd bend or rip off a strut. So the snazzy-looking "Baja Champion SE" or "Baja Beetle" ends up being just that: snazzy looking — but not for any-place in Baja that isn't paved.

Our test Baja Beetle had the new dealer-installed air conditioner. It's a very neat unit that fits tightly under the normal dash, matching perfectly and becoming apparently an integral part of the dash. We didn't even know it was there until we opened the engine lid and saw the pump, running off an extra pulley on the end of the crankshaft.

There is no question that air condi-tioning is a very desirable asset in many parts of the country, both for tempera-ture control and, by its slightly pressur-izing the car's interior, keeping out dust. Turning that A/C pump is going to

"Baja Champion SE" is a "Special Edition" version, of which only a few thousand were made, comes with silver-blue metallic paint, special wheels, but with the fog lights extra. Cost is $70 over the Super Beetle price, lights are $58.95 and are legal.

subtract horsepower from the Beetle's already not-too-hot 60 bhp, so let's match a few figures against an earlier test we did of a non-A/C Super Beetle in the February 1971 issue of ROAD TEST. In all cases, with our A/C Baja Super Beetle, we have corrected for the 1-percent low speedometer-odometer reading. In the non-A/C Super Beetle we got 25.1 (country) mpg on regular grade gas; with the A/C pump turning, but the actual air conditioning not turned on, we got 23.99 mpg. We did not have a chance to make a long-enough run with the A/C on full blast, but as the acceleration figures show, it

Fancy wheel covers are part of the $129.95 "Baja Beetle" dealer-installed package, are not the same fancy wheels as on the harder-to-get "Baja Champion SE" version of the Super Beetle. Tires are standard.

VW's new "Baja Beetle" is actually a dealer-installed kit for the Super Beetle. Exterior items include Baja stripe, fancy wheel covers, bumper over-riders and Bosch halogen fog lights.

"Baja Beetle" kit includes leather-covered steering wheel, "walnut" dash trim, a Superior Industries' speed shifter (which this test car didn't have) and does not include the air conditioning under the dash panel, which our test car did have.

Remember back when the engine compartment of a Beetle looked so empty? It's full now, with emission controls and, on our test car, the air conditioner pump at left, belt driven off the end of the crankshaft pulley at lower center. The A/C does use up a fair amount of that 60 bhp.

Air conditioning is a dealer-installed package at $295.00, fits neatly under the dash. Right knob at bottom is A/C temperature, left knob is volume flow. Above standard emergency flasher knob and lighter are regular interior air controls.

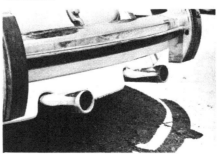

Tapered exhaust tips are included with the "Baja Beetle" package, as are the rubber-faced bumper over-riders. Only a true VW-freak could detect any difference in sound from this setup.

would probably knock the mileage down a good 2 mpg.

In the non-A/C Super Beetle, 0-30 mph took 5.4 seconds; with the A/C off it took 5.8 to 6.0, and with it full on 6.4 to 6.7. The non A/C did 0-45 in 10.2 seconds; with A/C off we got 10.8, with it on we got between 11.8 and 12.3. Our 0-60 mph figure for the non A/C Super Beetle was 17.3 seconds; with the A/C off 18.9, and with it full on

20.4. Quite a noticeable difference, so it's up to you what price you're willing to pay for comfort. The A/C's have been drastically lowered in price just recently, and the installation now costs $295.00. You'll have to decide how much of a bargain this is for your particular needs.

An overall opinion? The Baja Beetle was a ball to drive, it attracted both cheers and hoots, but it's strictly for show, not go. If we really wanted a "Baja Beetle" we'd buy the standard model, with its good road clearance, not the Super. I'd stick two of Cepek's quartz-iodine lights on the roof — not on the bumper! — put in the Superior or a Hurst shifter, get some Armstrong Norseman or similar on/off-road tires on the factory wheels and head for La Paz.

There's an old automotive adage, that "Wire wheels do not a sports car make." For obvious reasons you won't see many "Baja Beetles" in Baja once you get off the pavement. ●

VW 1500 BEETLE

OWNER REPORT

14 3 18 12 km

★ **Tops in value and quality of manufacture — and with improved reliability — the big-engined Beetle is unchallenged sales leader in South Africa . . .**

Successive Volkswagen Beetle models have featured in Owner Reports in CAR through the years — in fact, the original Beetle was reported on in July, 1961, in one of the first Owner Reports published.

The 1200 model had its turn in December, 1964, and the 1300 followed in July, 1969. This time it is the 1500 Beetle which undergoes owner scrutiny, and there is a growing folder of 1600 Beetle reports which should be ready for processing later this year.

As befits the car which has set a world record in sales, and remains unchallenged in top position in South Africa, it is also the only model which has featured so often in these reports — who knows, we may yet see a Beetle 1700 coming up for assessment in a few years' time!

OBJECTIVE VIEW

On going through the folder of reports on the 1500, we were struck by the objective view taken by owners: they praise the car for its virtues — yet are not blind to its faults and shortcomings. In total, the reports are fair and frank, and they show that while the Beetle undergoes annual revision and improvement, it has not changed that much in character in more than a decade.

The praises and criticisms heaped on the 1200 and 1300 models are still there, more often than not — though changes in percentage figures in some cases are significant.

It is clear that, broadly speaking, the Beetle is chosen for hard-headed economic reasons — its price, low running cost and good resale value — and that owners are prepared to put up with some unsatisfactory features inherent in a 40-year-old basic design, for the sake of its serviceability and good value.

GOOD ECONOMY

Average monthly use of the cars is

higher than most at nearly 2 000 km (1 200 miles), and this is spread broadly: only a handful of the cars reported on were business vehicles notching ultra-high mileages.

Economy gets both criticism and praise. It works out at 27,9 mpg about town, 33,7 on the open road — a consumption rate in metric terms of 10,1 litres per 100 km under urban conditions, and 8,4 when cruising. This is a small drop over the averages recorded with the smaller-engined models: the 1200 gave 28,5 and 34,4 mpg, respectively, and the 1300 gave 29,6 and 34,5 mpg.

It is clear that the bigger engine is more efficient, and is the reason why nearly half of owners listed "fuel economy" as one of the car's good features.

RELIABILITY

The Beetle went through some rough patches, mechanically, about 10 years ago, but VW has been improving engine cooling and reliability in the bigger-engined models. So while a few owners of 1500's report engine failures and overhaul work, it is heartening to see that "reliability" is back on top with the 1500 models, with a 60 per cent vote. (It got 43 per cent on the 1200, and 34 per cent on the 1300.)

This time, body finish drops to second place, though still with a strong vote, and is followed by "ease of driving" — something that hardly featured at all in earlier reports. Speaking from Road Test experience, we agree that the Beetle is very easy and pleasant to handle under normal conditions, and we are not surprised that half of owners give specific mention to this fact.

COMFORT FEATURES

Overall fuel economy gets a similarly high vote, and an important newcomer in the list of good features is "operating economy", which is a compound of low running costs, from original price to service charges.

Owners praise long-standing Beetle features: the car's fine ride (35 per cent — with specific mention for dirt-road comfort), smooth and well-rated gearbox (24 per cent), solid coachwork (17 per cent), and interior comfort (17 per cent). The good heating system, cruising ability and long tyre life are singled out for mention (see tables and graphs), though it is a bit disappointing to see "performance" rate a vote of only one-in-10 for a car which was originally billed as "the Super-Beetle".

SHALLOW TRUNK

The main criticisms have not chang-ed much in a decade — and there is not very much that can be done about them in most cases, without a radical alteration of basic design: the shallow front trunk, the inaccessibility of the rear luggage space, plus lack of rear seat space, together get criticised by the majority.

The rudimentary ventilation system — even though supplemented by hinged rear windows on later models — is a cause of irritation, particularly in family motoring, and while it was improved on the bigger-engined models, directional instability still features strongly, notably among owners in the more windy coastal areas.

The change to a 12-volt electrical system during the 1500 model run eliminated a major source of complaint: only a few owners of the earlier model complain of the hard starting and poor headlamp throw associated with the old 6-volt system.

BRAKES CRITICISED

Some hardy annuals which recur as criticisms of the Beetle models are the sparse instrumentation, and interior noise levels (both 25 per cent), as well as the left-hand-drive windscreen wipers (14 per cent).

Brakes come in for some criticism on the later models — on the early 1500, VW fitted disc front brakes, and owners of these cars are delighted with the high-speed braking capacity. But for local content reasons, the company had to revert to drum brakes, and their high-speed capacity gets some adverse comment.

Brakes also emerge as the major source of mechanical complaint with the 1500 model: one owner in four reports trouble of some kind, usually with the front brakes. The main problem appears to be ovality of brake drums (this can be caused by overheating in high-speed stops, and causes uneven stopping as a kick-back action on the brake pedal). Uneven pull in the brakes took second place in this department.

ENGINE OIL LEAKS

Nearly half of Beetle 1500 owners reported no trouble at all with their cars (this figure does not vary much from the 1200 and 1300 reports, though the faults tend to be less serious on the 1500).

Brakes take first place, followed by oil leaks — something comparatively new in the Beetle, unless it was merely overlooked in earlier reports because of more serious faults. One owner in six reports trouble with engine oil leaks, and a smaller number with axle oil seals.

Engine overhauls caused by cam-

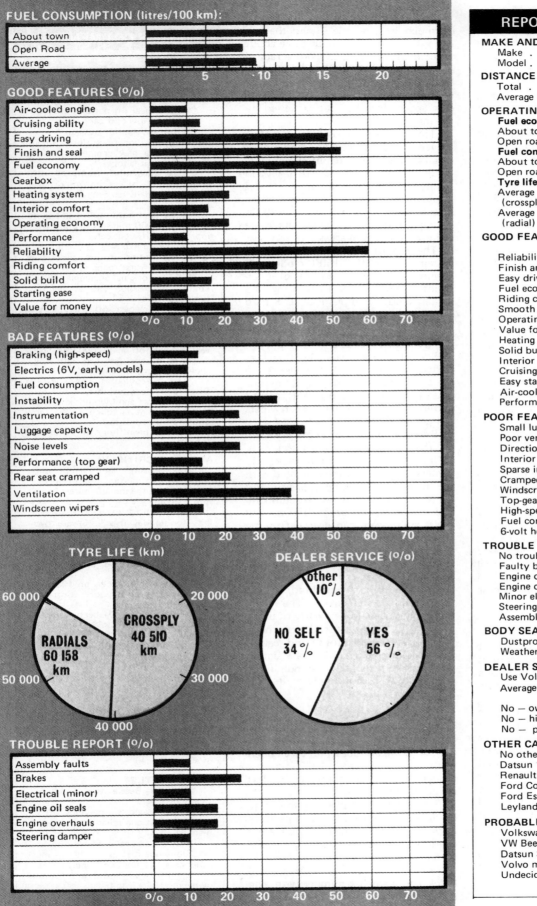

FUEL CONSUMPTION (litres/100 km):

About town	
Open Road	
Average	

Scale: 5, 10, 15, 20

GOOD FEATURES (%)

Air-cooled engine, Cruising ability, Easy driving, Finish and seal, Fuel economy, Gearbox, Heating system, Interior comfort, Operating economy, Performance, Reliability, Riding comfort, Solid build, Starting ease, Value for money

Scale: %, 10, 20, 30, 40, 50, 60, 70

BAD FEATURES (%)

Braking (high-speed), Electrics (6V, early models), Fuel consumption, Instability, Instrumentation, Luggage capacity, Noise levels, Performance (top gear), Rear seat cramped, Ventilation, Windscreen wipers

Scale: %, 10, 20, 30, 40, 50, 60, 70

TYRE LIFE (km)

RADIALS 60 158 km, CROSSPLY 40 510 km
60 000, 20 000, 50 000, 30 000, 40 000

DEALER SERVICE (%)

Other 10%, NO SELF 34%, YES 56%

TROUBLE REPORT (%)

Assembly faults, Brakes, Electrical (minor), Engine oil seals, Engine overhauls, Steering damper

Scale: %, 10, 20, 30, 40, 50, 60, 70

REPORT SUMMARY

MAKE AND MODEL:
Make . . . . . Volkswagen
Model . . 1500 Beetle, 1967-1970

DISTANCE COVERED:
Total . . . . . 1 431 812 km
Average monthly . . . 1 978 km

OPERATING ECONOMY:
Fuel economy:
About town 9,9 km/1
Open road 12,0 km/1
Fuel consumption:
About town . . 10,1 litres/100 km
Open road . . 8,4 litres/100 km
Tyre life:
Average per set
(crossply) . . . . 40 510 km
Average per set
(radial) . . . . 60 158 km

GOOD FEATURES:
	Per cent
Reliability	60
Finish and seal	52
Easy driving	49
Fuel economy	46
Riding comfort	35
Smooth gearbox	24
Operating economy	21
Value for money	21
Heating system	21
Solid build	17
Interior comfort	17
Cruising ability	14
Easy starting	10
Air-cooled engine	10
Performance	10

POOR FEATURES:
Small luggage capacity	42
Poor ventilation system	39
Directional instability	35
Interior noise levels	25
Sparse instrumentation	25
Cramped rear seat	21
Windscreen wipers	14
Top-gear performance	14
High-speed braking	14
Fuel consumption	10
6-volt headlamps (early models)	10

TROUBLE REPORT
No trouble encountered	45
Faulty brakes	25
Engine oil seals	18
Engine overhauls	18
Minor electrical	10
Steering damper	10
Assembly faults	10

BODY SEAL:
Dustproof	98
Weatherproof	95

DEALER SERVICE:
Use Volkswagen service	56
Average quality . . . . good, tending to excellent	
No — own service	34
No — high cost	7
No — poor service	3

OTHER CARS CONSIDERED:
No other	28
Datsun 1600 models	18
Renault models	18
Ford Cortina	10
Ford Escort GT	10
Leyland Mini models	10

PROBABLE NEXT CAR:
Volkswagen Type 4	32
VW Beetle 1600	21
Datsun SSS	10
Volvo models	10
Undecided	10

IMPERIAL DATA

A summary of main figures from this report are given below in Imperial measures, for comparative purposes:

DISTANCES COVERED:
Total . . . . . 889 876 miles
Average monthly . . 1 235 miles

OPERATING ECONOMY:
Fuel economy:
About town . . . . 27,9 mpg

Open road . . . . 33,7 mpg

Tyre life:
Average per set
(crossply) . . . 25 286 miles
Average per set
(radials) . . . . 37 500 miles

shaft, piston, valve or main bearing failure are isolated, and total 18 per cent.

Other operational complaints are in minor volume: 10 per cent of owners report minor electrical faults or steering damper trouble, usually attended to under warranty.

SEAL AND SERVICE

The quality of body seal gets the best vote ever recorded for a Beetle model: 98 per cent on dustproofing, and 95 per cent on weather seal. This has come to be a traditional Beetle feature, and the VWSA assembly plant deserves an accolade for this result.

Just under half of Beetle owners report making full use of VW dealership service facilities, and they rate it somewhere between "good" and "excellent", overall. The majority of dealerships get a "good" rating, and the overall standard is so high that it is almost unfair to single out particular areas. But we must report that owners from Durban, Pretoria, Uitenhage and Pietermaritzburg all gave "excellent" ratings to their dealerships — usually quite emphatically.

Only insignificant percentages of owners reported that they did not use dealership facilities, because of its quality or cost.

OWNER SERVICING

What is significant, though, is the large increase in the number of owners undertaking routine service work themselves in home workshops. With the 1200, this figure was 8 per cent; it rose to 10 per cent with the 1300; and has now rocketed to 34 per cent with the 1500 model.

It is confined primarily to minor servicing: oil changes and routine lubrication and adjustment, and is in keeping with a general tendency for owners to undertake minor work themselves on many makes of cars.

As one owner in a country town states: "I can do routine servicing as well as any mechanic — and afterwards, I know what has been done!" A Transvaal man said: "It saves on costs — and I trust my servicing more!" and his sentiments are echoed from a neighbouring town: "I can look after my car best — because it is my own!"

GOOD TYRE-LIFE

Though it may vary considerably with driving style, the average tyre life reported by 1 500 owners is most satisfactory: 40 500 km on crossply tyres, and a bit over 60 000 km with radials. There is not much difference in the life achieved on gravel or bitumenised roads, though on balance, people who use their cars exclusively on tarred surfaces seem to get a bit of extra distance from a set, with routine rotation.

Many owners report fitting radials (155 size) on replacement, and are very pleased with the results — both in terms of tyre life, and general handling. "Now that I have fitted radials, the car is more stable, and a real pleasure on the open road!" is a typical comment.

LITTLE COMPETITION

It would appear that Beetle ownership is loyal — few owners considered other makes when buying, and only the Datsun 1600 models and Renault models (both 18 per cent), the Ford Escort GT and Cortina range (10 per cent), and the Leyland Mini's (10 per cent), posed any temptation. In fact, 28 per cent of Beetle owners considered no other car, but went straight to the nearest VW showroom.

This follows through to their probable next purchase: more than half unequivocally want another Volkswagen, with the Type 4 models (32 per cent) featuring strongly. Ten per cent are undecided, and the only other models getting significant mention are Datsun SSS and Volvo (both 10 per cent).

SUMMARY

The Beetle has grown to become an institution, world-wide — and notably so in the Republic. It may not be the greatest car to drive — particularly as regards performance and stability — but it has made firm friends in their tens of thousands, for its undoubted value and quality of manufacture.

It is firmly-entrenched as South Africa's top-selling car, with no effective challenger in sight. ●

Interior comfort — characterised by the adjustable front seats and heating system — gets a "good feature" rating.

This cornering picture — showing rear-wheel tuck-under — illustrates one of the main complaints by owners: lack of directional stability.

The sparse instrumentation is always a source of dissatisfaction to owners — but they like the car's easy-driving characteristics.

The shallow front trunk causes grouses — even though it is supplemented by a rather inaccessible luggage space behind the rear seats.

Vere der Assistant Editor Wayne Cantell drives der Beetle vot vas first made in der liddle castle in der Black Forest by der liddle elves . . .

SUPERBUG—

THE new Superbug's big windscreen increases headroom and gives better all-round visibility. Pushed hard on a loose surface the Beetle will oversteer but can be controlled very easily with a little opposite lock and more power. Note the tyre distortion on the right rear wheel.

GONE is the old flat paint-finish dash. The new padded dash features through-flow ventilation, a proper glove box and of course there is the attractive Porsche-type steering wheel. The fuse-box (centre) is too low and can catch your left foot when using the clutch.

For a car which has been around the Australian Market for the past 20 years, the Volkswagen Beetle continues to occupy a small but steady sector of the buying market.

In fact in 1972 Volkswagen claimed a total overall share of about three percent — half of which was accounted for by the Beetle, the rest by everything else in the range, and that includes the Type Threes, Kombies, commercial vehicles and campervans.

But the Beetle is without a doubt the most popular car the VW markets in Australia.

And of the Beetle models, the Superbug is way out front.

Last year it accounted for 85 percent of all Beetle sales, and indications so far this year show that it will probably increase this share during the next 12 months.

The cars are assembled by the Motor Producers group in Melbourne, with a local content which varies slightly from time to time but generally stabilises around 60 percent.

The Beetles are rolling off the production line at the rate of between 40 and 70 units a day.

One of the most important and innovate ideas introduced by VW in the past five years was the vehicle diagnosis service which they introduced with the first of the Superbugs in 1970/71.

This allowed the cars to be *plugged* into a complete maintenance and diagnosis service which is connected to the appropriate equipment in the dealer's service department.

This diagnosis service has now been introduced throughout Australia and is a compulsory part of any dealer's workshop equipment.

Overseas, the diagnosis service has been improved already to utilise proper computer analysis of performance and engine conditions, and it's anticipated that this extension of the diagnosis will be introduced to Australia in about two years.

With a release date set for mid-April, we were able to grab the very first new model Superbug off the production line for a snap photography session — and later followed this up with a full test.

It's still a Beetle — but a Beetle with modern, civilised, up-to-date trimmings . . .

You're not going to believe it — but it's true!

Volkswagenwerk AG has finally designed a Beetle with a *curved* windscreen.

Amazing, you might say — but whatever your reaction is, this simple effective change has transformed the interior of the VW Superbug from a claustrophobic suitcase, to an open "spacious" small sedan!

In fact the new windscreen is 42 percent bigger than the old flat style.

The curved screen has in one simple move increased forward visibility, increased headroom in the passenger compartment, and removed that hangover from the 1930s, the flat windscreen.

The new curved windscreen — in the non-laminated form — will retail as a replacement part for $29.75, an increase in price over the slightly curved model on post-1971 models which sold for $18.00.

The early model flat screens could be replaced for about $12.00 — or even cheaper if you found a friendly glass shop which would cut one out of a piece of safety glass.

But VWA sees no problem in having small wayside garages stocking the new curved screens.

They claim the slightly curved version met with no resistance and there's little likelihood of this new model generating any.

But only time will tell! With stone damage a major problem in Australia, small wayside repair shops are not going to want to spend hours replacing the tricky curved screens, and may not bother to stock them.

If this turns out to be the case then VW may have to look at fitting laminated screens as standard fittings.

It's not because VW screens are more likely to break, or are more difficult to fit than other makes, but the car is a low volume seller and small-turnover/small-profit organisations don't like to have $30 worth of replacement screen sitting about just in case it is needed some day!

The 1973 Superbug — released about a fortnight ago — also has several other subtle interior changes aimed at civilising the somewhat

SUPERCOOL?

clinical, Teutonic interior finish of the Beetles of years past.

To complement the windscreen, there's a *real* dashboard with a proper steering wheel! Safety rocker switches replace the familiar old knob-types and there is a proper glovebox, which is even split in two levels with handy little compartments for the storage of small objects. The interior of the glovebox is padded, but lacks a courtesy light.

The dash even has through-flow ventilation outlets with tiny face-level outlets at either end of the dash, and a central panel of adjustable louvre outlets. The heater-demister unit features a two-speed fan and demister outlets which run the full width of the new windscreen.

The heater controls have not changed and heat is still supplied to the interior by adjusting the twin levers located on either side of the handbrake.

The circulation of air — through the various dash outlets is varied by twisting two small knobs on the dash.

Unfortunately these knobs have a very low profile and are a nightmare to the woman with long, immaculately kept fingernails.

In fact as nail-breakers they rate second only to the door handles on the TC Cortina!

Outwardly the new Beetle has few changes to set it apart from the early Superbugs.

The mudguards have been restyled slightly, the windscreen of course is an obvious change, the bumper bars have been lifted slightly to meet safety regulations, and at the rear, the bumper has been taken back further to give a little more protection to the twin tailpipes.

But the most obvious outward changes can be split clearly into two categories — to the front, the windscreen; to the rear, the tail-light cluster.

We've already dealt with the screen, but the tail-lights have to be seen to be believed!

And seen they are . . .

THE divided padded glovebox is a welcome addition to the Beetle dash. The lever in the top right corner opens the bonnet.

UNDER hard cornering conditions the Beetle's tail squats down over the wheels with pronounced body roll. It is not unstable.

MODERN MOTOR FIFTH WHEEL ROAD TEST

ROAD TEST DATE — SPECIFICATIONS

Manufacturer: Motor Producers Ltd., Centre Road, Clayton, Victoria
Make/Model: . . . . Volkswagen Superbug 1600L
Body Type: . . . . 2-door sedan
Pricing: as tested: $2808
     basic: $2629
Options/prices: Radial tyres ($52); Radio ($98); Carpets ($14); Stoneguards/mudflaps ($15).
Test car supplied by: Volkswagen Australia Pty. Ltd, 27 Waterloo Road, North Ryde, Sydney NSW.
Mileage start/finish: 639/1354

ENGINE

Cylinders: . . . . Four horizontally opposed
Bore x stroke: . . . . .3.37in (85mm) x 2.72in (69mm)
Capacity: . . . . 96.66 CID (1584cc)
Compression: . . . . 7.5 to 1
Aspiration: . . . . Single downdraft carburettor
Fuel pump: . . . . Mechanical
Fuel recommended: . . . . 91 Octane
Valve gear: . . . . OHV, pushrods
Max. power (gross): . . . . 60bhp @ 4400rpm
Max. torque: . . . . 78lbs/ft @ 3000rpm
Specific power output: 37.88bhp/litre

TRANSMISSION

Type/locations: 4-speed, all-syncro, floor mounted on central console
Clutch type: . . . . Sdp
Clutch pedal pressure: 20psi

Gear	Direct Ratio	Overall Ratio	MPH/1000	km/h
1st	3.78	14.65	4.92	(7.92)
2nd	2.06	7.98	9.04	(14.55)
3rd	1.26	4.88	14.78	(23.78)
4th	0.93	3.60	20.04	(32.24)

Final drive: 3.875

CHASSIS AND BODY

Type: Pressed steel unitary floor pan/all steel unitary body.
Weight as tested incl. fuel, oil, water
    (no occupants): 2078lbs (944.5kg)
Distribution front/rear: . . . . 41percent /59percent
Kerb weight: . . . . 1904lbs (865.45 kg)

SUSPENSION

Front: . . . . Independent with McPherson struts, coil springs and lateral control arms.
Rear: . . . . Independent trailing arms wi diagonal links and transverse torsion bars, swing ax
Shock absorbers: . . . . Telescopic all-rou
Wheels: . . . . Pressed steel discs, 4.
Tyres: . . . . Goodyear 155SR15 Radi
Pressures: Rear: 22psi (1.53kg/cm
     Front: 16psi (1.12kg/cm

STEERING

Type: . . . . Worm and roller with hydraulic damp
Ratio: . . . . 16.5 to
Turns lock to lock: . . . . 3.
Wheel diameter: 15.75in (40c
Turning circle, between kerbs: 31.5ft (9.6
     between walls: 33.75ft (10.3

BRAKES

Type: . . . . Disc front/Drum re
Dimensions: . . . . Front 10.9in (27.7cm)/Rear 9.1in (23c
Total swept area: 125.8sq.in. (876cm

DIMENSIONS:

Wheelbase: 95.3in (242cr
Track, front: 54.8in (139c
    rear: 53.6in (136c
Overall width: 5ft 2in (158.5c
    length: 13ft 7in (414c
    height: 4ft 11in (149.9c
Ground clearance: 5.9in (14.9c
Overhand, front: 27.25in (69.25c
Overhang, rear: 38.00in (96.00c

EQUIPMENT:

Battery: 12V 45A/
Headlamps: . . . . 40/45 wa
Jacking points: . . . . 2 side-poin

CAPACITIES:

Fuel tank: . . . . 9.2 gals (41.6 litre
Engine sump: . . . . 5.3 pints (3.0 litre
Final drive/Gearbox: . . . . 6.3 pints (3.6 litre

One of the most interesting exercises of this test was to zip in front of an obvious diehard VW-owner, then blip the stoplights and watch the rear vision mirror.

Behind you a remarkable change in scenery would take place.

STAGE ONE: A quick down-change, a few extra revs, on with the blinkers, pull out, change blinkers, pull back in, slow down, "blip" the brakes.

STAGE TWO: (in other Beetle) Sneer — so you've got a nice shiny new Beetle — well it's no different to mine! (Meanwhile dropping back slightly to a safe travelling distance.)

STAGE THREE: (As brake lights are flicked on) Shock, disbelief, wild pointing and gesticulating (if others are in the car), a mad burst of acceleration — bumpers almost touch, relief, acceptance and the now disheartened Beetle (old) driver moves back to his position in the traffic.

That's it — the whole scene, not just once but a hundred times over.

Even the new curved windscreen — which made a number of other Beetle owners stall at the lights after the shock of realising that alongside them was a Beetle of no ordinary standing — didn't create the same interest as the tail-lights.

They are huge!

They could double as billy-cans, soup plates, crash helmets or hatboxes.

But they do serve a very useful purpose. They can at least be seen easily in any kind of weather.

The one unit houses the indicator, tail, brake and backing lights and is fixed to the guard by four simple screws which seal the plastic cover on a rubber mounting strip.

They are high on the guard and well protected by the bumper (a good thing because the replacement assembly retails for around $21.00).

Mechanically the 1973 model does not vary much from the earlier models.

A more durable (?) clutch has been fitted, clutch pedal pressure has been reduced and softer gearbox mountings have been used to reduce the transfer of transmission noise.

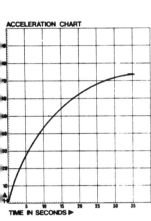

THE huge rear tail-lights are a distinctive feature of the new rear end treatment.

BOOTSPACE has been enlarged by a few inches,

THIS picture highlights the change in the windscreen shape. The pronounced curve and higher profile increases screen area by 42percent.

WARRANTY, INSURANCE, MAINTENANCE, RUNNING COSTS

Registration: $84.68

Insurance:
Quoted rates are for drivers over 25 with 60percent no-claim bonus and where the car is under hire-purchase. This is the minimum premium level, decreasing rates of experience and lower age groups may have varying excesses and possible premium loadings.
Non-tariff company $64.06
Tariff company $70.00
RMA $73.65

Warranty:
Six months or 6000 miles. Warranty covers all parts and labor charges for defective materials, components, or workmanship. Components from outside suppliers, such as batteries tyres etc., are covered by their own manufacturers.

Service:
Initial service .... free
This covers the first 600 miles and covers lubrication and maintenance. Materials (lubricants etc.) are chargeable.
Other service:
Lubrication and maintenance services every 3000 miles. Listed below are the manufacturer recommended labor charges.
3000 miles $2.75
6000 miles (includes full diagnosis
free of charge) $14.75

Spare parts — Recommended cost breakdown
Disc pads (set of 4) $11.52
Muffler $22.33
Windscreen $29.75
Shock absorbers front (strut unit new) $50.83
                        (exchange unit) $28.35
                rear $10.17
Headlamp assembly $22.78
Tail light assembly $20.66

Color Range
Grasshopper green, regatta blue, clipper blue, radar red, Kalahari tan, mustard, wattle, Antarctica white.

PERFORMANCE

Test conditions for performance figures; Weather: ...... Fine
Wind: .... 2/3 knots W

Humidity: 60percent
Max. Temperature .... 68 degrees
Top speed, average: .... 76mph (122.28 km/h)
        best run: .... 78.9 mph (126.95 km/h)
Standing Quarter Mile, average: .... 20.7 secs
        best run: .... 20.0 secs
Speed at end of Standing Quarter: ...... 65mph (104.6 km/h)
Acceleration, standing start:
0-30 mph: .... 5.1 secs
0-40mph: .... 7.9 secs
0-50mph: .... 12.8 secs
0-60mph: .... 18.2 secs
0-70mph: .... 28.7 secs

Speed in Gears:

Gear	Max. mph	(Kph)	rpm
1st	29mph	(46.7)	5900
2nd	53mph	(85.3)	5900
3rd	75mph	(120.7)	5100
4th	78.9mph	(126.9)	3940

Acceleration holding gears:

	2nd	3rd	4th
20-40	5.4 secs	7.9 secs	12.8 secs
30-50		8.9 secs	14.8 secs
40-60		10.5 secs	16.1 secs
50-70		14.8 secs	

Fuel consumption:
Average for test: 29.7mpg
Best recorded: ...... 30.5mpg (over 110 miles, all conditions)
City average: 28mpg
Country cruising: 27-30mpg

Braking: Five crash stops from 60mph

Stop		G	Pedal
1	3.6 secs	.8	60psi
2	3.8 secs	.7	65psi
3	4.05	.7	64psi
4	4.1 secs	.6	64psi
5	5.1 secs	.6	60psi

30-0mph: .... 4.2 secs in 42ft (12.8 metres) with an average g-force of .699 g
60-0mph: .... 3.6 secs in 156ft (47.8 metres) with an average g-force of .753 g

Calculated Data:
Bhp/ton: .... 70.59 bhp/ton (10.65 watts/kilo)
Piston speed at max rpm: .... 69.97ft/sec (21.34 metre/sec)

Speedo Corrections: IND:	20	30	40	50	60	70
ACT:	17 2	7	38	48	58	67

SUPERBUG

The new Superbug L is at the top of the three-model range and will sell for $2629 in the basic form.

The Superbug S ($2539) and the 1300 Beetle ($2409) also get the new dash layout but otherwise continue unchanged.

Even with this latest price increase, value-for-money the Volkswagen still comes out well ahead of many of its competitors.

This value doesn't necessarily relate to size or performance, but more particularly to honest-to-goodness quality.

And whether or not you'like the ride, looks, or performance of the car you cannot deny the quality of the workmanship.

Everything is finished off nicely, even to the smallest detail — such as a soft rubber cover on the flip-catch for the bonnet release.

The paintwork is superb, without blemishes or patches which have been missed in production, and without overspray on any unrelated parts.

The upholstery is strong and attractive, the seats are well finished (even though lacking a little in support), the seat belts are neat and easily adjustable and the interior is well planned and functional.

To the uninitiated, driving a Beetle for the first time can be a *frightening* experience.

Slipping onto the *extra*-firm seats with the steeply sloping nose tapering away very quickly in front of you, you feel very high off the ground and very vulnerable.

This feeling is heightened while driving.

The seats are flat and to an average-to-lightweight occupant provide very little support at all.

As a result, even with the seat belt done-up tight, you slip from side-to-side when cornering. The relatively high centre of gravity adds to this situation and gives a feeling that the whole car is about to tip over when cornering hard.

This in fact was a problem which plagued the early Beetles — hard cornering, a high centre of gravity and the swing-axles were a dangerous combination in the VW and many Beetles were found laying on their backs with their *"legs"* waving helplessly in the air.

Thankfully the development and introduction of the Porsche-type suspension and double-jointed swing axles has made the roll-factor in VW Beetles a thing of the past.

The ride is harsh, but not uncomfortable. Road and engine noise is reduced to a minimum and in the test car (with carpets fitted) was almost negligible.

The steering is still relatively heavy for a car with all the weight over the rear wheels. Weight distribution is 49percent front, 51percent rear.

At cruising speeds the steering is extremely precise, and direct and this

can result in rear-seat passengers being *flicked* violently if a sudden change is made while cornering.

At low to medium speeds the Beetle tends to understeer quite heavily but will breaking into tail-swinging oversteer with any over-exuberant pedal-pushing, or a sudden lifting of the foot.

But the breakaway is predictable (once you have become used to the rear-engine rear-wheel drive characteristics) and with the new double-jointed swing-axles gives little rise to terror.

The soft torsion bar/trailing arm combination at the rear gives a good hold on any surface, but the front coil/strut system misses out badly on adhesion when it comes to corrugated or pot-holed surfaces.

If it was not for the steering damper, road shock transfer through the steering wheel would be quite severe.

The low-reving, flat-four motor is definitely not a rubber-burning off-the-line power plant, but still ensures that the VW owner is no sluggard off the lights.

First runs to a noisey 29mph — but for optimum performance reaching for second at around 20-25mph gives you access to a long-legged second gear which runs rapidly to 53mph. Third gear is a normal drive ratio and once out of the traffic, top provides that easy-going overdrive ratio which allows the Beetle to cruise effortlessly at 70-75mph for literally days-on-end.

The gearchange still features that now familiar Volkswagen chunkiness which allows the selection of forward gears with absolutely no doubt as to where they are in the shift pattern.

The ratios are widely spaced and rely on the use of maximum revs in each gear to ensure that speed is maintained.

Despite what the experts claim — top gear in a Volkswagen is really nothing more than a cruising, or overdrive gear!

Fuel consumption runs right in line with performance, and under normal driving conditions there is no way the car could return less than 25mpg. Normal running is more likely to produce between 27 and 30mpg — with sustained periods of cruising at 60mph (in the open without stops and starts) producing startling consumption figures. For instance during one 100 mile run at an almost constant 60mph the 1600cc motor happily consumed fuel at the rate of 32.8mpg!

And with petrol costs and shortages the way they are at present, such economy is most welcome!

While economy and performance go hand-in-hand, the braking on the Superbug could be suited to a far more powerful car.

The disc/drum combination pulled the Beetle up from 60mph in times ranging between 3.6 and 4.3seconds.

The car pulled up in a perfectly straight line on every occassion with a minimum of tyre squeal and no sign of lock-up. The only indication of hard braking was a faint smell which became noticeable only after the eighth stop.

Inside the car the effects of the crash stops were negligible! The stops were all smooth and progressive, and easing off the pedal slightly just before reaching a standstill stopped the final lurch as a complete stop was reached.

This easing off had no affect on stopping times, and increased stopping distances by an average of only two to three inches.

The brakes did fade slightly over the eight stops, but this was reflected in the computer analysis figures as only a 0.7 seconds difference in stopping times and a g-force reduction of only 0.7percent.

Obviously during normal driving — even under peak-hour stop/start conditions — there would be no fade.

The interior of the Superbug is pleasant and intelligently set out.

The instruments are all housed in a single hooded binacle in front of the driver. The face of the speedo includes the fuel gauge and the mileage meter, and warning lights for the indicators, high beam, oil pressure and ignition.

But the *overall* appearance of the interior is greatly enhanced by the new dash treatment.

To the left of the steering wheel are the small central outlets for the through-flow ventilation fresh-air system. These are housed under the lower edge of the dash recess. Small face level outlets are housed at either end of the dash.

Immediately below them is the radio, and below that again a second recess which houses the ashtray, air-flow controls, two blank switch panels and the emergency flasher switch. (The blank switches are utilised on the European models for fittings not available in Australia.)

On the right of the steering wheel is the headlight switch and a rheostat control for the dash lights.

All the switch gear — or should I perhaps say both switches — are the new safety-rocker kind, and replace the push/pull switches which have been a feature of VW cars since their introduction to Australia.

The only other fitting to utilise the space on the right edge of the dash is the speaker for the radio. This is housed behind a neat perforated panel in the lower edge of the dash facia.

The steering wheel is also worthy of a mention.

It's the Porsche-type wheel with the wide central horn/safety panel which was introduced to the Type-3 range about two years ago, and first made its debut in the Beetle last year.

On the right of the steering column is a stalk controlling the two-speed wipers and the pressurised washer system.

On the left — a second stalk which operates the idicators/high-low beam and headlight flasher.

Believe me, to find the indicator at your left-hand fingertips is quite confusing to start with — but it's something which you adjust to very quickly and can't shake quite as easily.

In front of the passenger is the glovebox — Volkswagen's first real attempt at making provision for those

CONTINUED ON PAGE 121

SUPERBUG

CONTINUED FROM PAGE 120

little bits-and-pieces which everyone wants to put out of the way.

The lockable door flips down to reveal a spacious partitioned storage space.

The lower shelf is split in two sections, with the upper area providing a full-width shelf.

For the maps and larger items which won't fit in the glove box there are handy "map pockets" in the door trim panels.

As I remarked earlier, the seats are over-firm for the average person but this is not a problem restricted to Volkswagen.

Mercedes suffer from it (MM March), and so does the BMW (MM April).

The seat belts slip easily into the catch mechanism which is mounted on the centre tunnel between the two front seats. Adequate adjustment is provided — although the process can become quite messy at times because of the excessive amount of extra belt provided.

The front seat-backs fold forward to allow access to the rear and are released by a simple knob in the outside edge of each seat-back.

The rake can be adjusted by turning a small metal knob at the base of the seat squab. However, these do 'not provide enough adjustment to suit all drivers. The almost infinitely adjustable system as on Type 3 models would present a far better proposition.

With the front seats forward there is a good deal of legroom, but with the seat back to suit the long-legged driver or front seat passenger, legroom in the back is reduced to a bare minimum. The rear seat-back can be folded down to increase the rear luggage space in a "wagon" format.

Luggage space is quite remarkable for the size of the vehicle and accepts two medium-sized cases and a large quantity of soft luggage without problems.

It carries enough luggage for two people — and at a pinch would probably hold enough for two adults and two children.

The Superbug is reliable, it's strong, it's well finished it handles reasonably well and above all is economical.

In two words, it's *good value!*

VW SEDAN

Continued from Page 71

investigation to others. Let's just say that a beetle of any vintage driven sensibly is an eminently safe car, but those that aren't driven in this manner are from whence dune buggies stem.

It's also redundant to discuss standards of finish and other items of quality control. Only God can make a bug with fewer defects, and both He and Wolfsburg have had about the same amount of practice.

VW prices on all models have gone up about 2% to where the basic beetle now lists at $1924 exclusive of local taxes, freight and handling. Another hike is at least being discussed due to current fluctuation of the *Deutschmark*. Nevertheless, it represents a bargain because you've not being charged for the new electronic diagnostic centers now being operated by all VW dealerships. A no-charge trip through these is a part of each warranty inspection and, of course, the facilities are available to owners of older cars.

As a final note, I should point out that while the new 1600 engine peaks at higher rpms, this fact is not reflected in those little red marks on the speedometer that tell you when to shift. Theoretically it tells you to eschew 3rd for high at 55 mph, but our zero to 60 mph times were achieved by staying in 3rd and during the 50 to 70 exercise, the engine was completely happy in 3rd at 65. This information is proferred merely as our experience and not as a recommendation. Even though the speedometer is a carryover, you're technically abusing the car by exceeding the red marks in gear.

CONTINUED FROM PAGE 47

offers, plus a variety of engines, transmissions, suspensions, and brake systems. These features are shuffled around as the need arises, seemingly to keep the sales of a particular model from sagging. After all, it isn't as if Volkswagen has a new model every year to keep the public's interest up.

Therefore, peering simultaneously into the VW parts bin and our Hurst crystal shifter, we can see Volkswagen equipping the Beetle with the fully automatic automatic now sold on the 1600s outside the U.S., putting the new rear suspension on the manual-shift cars, fitting the front disc brakes now standard only on European models, redesigning the front suspension to give a lot more luggage room, squaring up the body a bit to make more people room (and better visibility), and adopting the electronic fuel injection system across the board.

Don't hold your breath. They also said Hitler was a flash in the pan.

The Beetle 1200, 1974 Style.
The Real Porsche?

Below:
Porsche FLA is 1974 version of the long life concept. Porsche design team responsible for FLA claims it has been engineered to run for 20 years without major mechanical repair work. It is not a prototype but is intended to prove that practicality and durability far beyond conventional standards is realistic. Trouble is the beetle proves the concept was just as valid four decades ago.

JERRY SLONIGER has been driving the cheapest, most basic of all the new VWs. One hundred thousand changes later it is still very much the same old beetle even to the lack of a fuel gauge.

Volkswagen apparently feels you don't need a badge to identify the beetle after — how many millions?

A CAR YOU design once and ignore for the next 10 years? A car which runs on almost any fuel except lemon extract, at the lowest of revs for the longest of lives, with a minimum of things to go wrong?

Porsche would like us to believe it just hit on that idea with its LFA (for Longlife Development Automobile) first shown late last year.

But even Porsche's own files show a Porsche-designed car four-times-10 years old which does all that already. It's called the basic VW beetle and every driver should try one of these painted-bumper wonders every decade or so, if only for perspective.

This fleet-car special is even more than plain to eliminate random worry points. I can see they don't need a badge on the tail — but no passenger sun visor?

To prove it is a modern machine VW naturally fits the pressurised windscreen washer and a plug for the diagnostic system. (I thought nothing could go wrong with a design refined over a quarter century.)

Maybe Wolfsburg has made too many running changes since the '49 launch. It now claims a cool 100,000 — everything but the strip which holds the engine lid seal in place. If general body shape hasn't changed any more than women's fashions since '49, why alter something that works well?

Drive a 1184 cm³ 1974 beetle and you discover why such owners hardly notice speed limits. Once the upgrade exceeds a couple of degrees

Is It...
Long Life

1949

1974

A dial for speed and a lever on the floor to look after the reserve fuel tank. Old Professor Porsche might have designed that steering wheel. There are just three dashboard controls and one of them is required by law.

Beetle styling (?) parallels women's fashions — full circle in 25 years of production.

they can't use the 80 km/h (50 mph) outside lane anyway.

The problem of beetling along is less those side winds of yore than the way your trip stretches into infinity whenever a head wind crops up. It isn't so much a question of whether this really is a long-life car as it is the fact that life just seems so long.

Subjectively the VW 1200 (or any "economy-engined future machine") isn't going to seem like a dragster either. Objectively — honest now — when was the last time it took you

37 seconds to reach 100 km/h (60 mph) from a standstill?

One ploy might be offering them free to the Arabs. Never mind 17.4 km/l (32 mpg) which should be better with so little action anyway — it is more the certainty that the Arabs would instantly release enough oil for better cars after one day in this machine, whose best ventilation trick is obtained by opening the glove box for stray drafts. You don't go fast enough for anything else to work.

Better yet, let's make such

machines standard wear for bureaucrats who parrot the long-life idea without considering what technology achieves in each yearly update. VW boasts of 4000 running changes a year within that beetle body.

We were pleased to note, however, that it eschewed the fuel gauge in favor of mental arithmetic as you cope with dawdling speed limits. Knowing when you might have to move that half-hidden lever from main tank to reserve saves frantic freeway fumbles.

Not that this basic beetle is a bad '49 model. Merely that 800 km (500 miles) in one is the best answer to letting non-designers freeze our transport at some governmental level as an easy substitute for tackling real traffic problems. Making cars run slower/longer doesn't reduce your road exposure.

As VW says, its machines run and run and run: they have to if you want to get anywhere. Is that forward thinking?   *

Comparative road test
MINI DE LUXE and BEETLE 1300

BROWSE IN THE bargain basement of the South African car market and you can hardly ignore those veterans of our motoring folklore, the Leyland Mini and the Volkswagen Beetle. If only because they have been around so much longer than their competitors, have sold in such greater numbers and possess such striking, contrasting personalities. And when you consider the enduring qualities which have endeared them to so many for so long, and the bouts of recurring modification which have refined them over the years, then both cars still make sound economic sense; which is why they are still available — and selling strongly.

When we approached this comparison, we planned to set the Mini Clubman (R3 070) alongside the 1300 Beetle (R3 180). The price gap would have been only R110 and we reasoned that trim and appointment levels would probably be evenly matched, while the 187 cm³ difference in engine displacement seemed insignificant, in view of the Beetle's heavier bodywork. But when Leyland were unable to supply a Clubman in test trim, we settled for the Mini De Luxe — which has lower equipment levels but uses a slightly detuned version of the same engine/transmission package. It also has the cheekier, short Mini nose instead of the stubby

Clubman front; and although its price (R2 855) stretched the differential to R325, we did not consider this excessive, in view of the classic nature of the resultant confrontation: basic Beetle against cheapest Mini!

Contrasting concepts

To put them into quick perspective, the Beetle is of course the older car; and since it was designed 40 years ago, 19 million examples have rolled from production lines world-wide. But although its key concept of rear-mounted, air-cooled, flat-four engine fathered a string of related vehicles to expand the fantastic VW success story, it was not adopted by

other manufacturers. And Volkswagen itself was to swing, eventually, to the use of a water-cooled, front mounted engine and front-wheel-drive for most vehicles in its current range.

The 18-year-old Mini saga presents about as strong a contrast as you could get. For this model not only pioneered the use of a transversely-mounted water-cooled "four" to drive the front wheels: it blazed a trail to optimised roominess and fail-safe handling which inspired such manufacturers as Fiat, Peugeot and Renault to develop comparable designs. Over four million cars have been sold since 1959 and, as VW did with the Beetle, Ley-

A classic confrontation: can 23 million motorists be wrong?

An alternator is now used on both Mini (above) and Beetle (below). Both engine bays are cluttered but DIY men easily cope.

Character galore comes across in the cars' rear end view (below). Contestants in the ring, seconds out . . .

land followed through with a run of related models, none of which has enjoyed a comparable success.

So although both Beetle and Mini were designed to provide budget transportation, to sell on initial value, operating economy and sheer practicality, they are poles apart in character. And when you drive them in rapid succession, their strengths and weaknesses do not lie dormant and hard to spot: they leap out and bite you!

The sturdy, elliptical, crescent-shaped Beetle is a larger, heavier car than the chunky Mini — over a metre longer, 140 mm wider and with 166 kg more mass. It is also

160 mm taller from the tarmac and uses axles 370 mm further apart. But so effective is Issigonis' radical formula for a compact city car that the Mini gives the more spacious impression, once you are inside it. In the Beetle, you sit in the tradition of a previous automobile age, with head and shoulders surrounded by glasswork and your legs thrust forwards under the scuttle: in the Mini, you unwind into a squat, flat-wide box which is weirdly larger than it looked from the outside. To anyone raised in the era of the upright motor car, the Volksie seems an old fashioned but "proper car": the Mini, a clever alternative.

And from the moment you

twist the key and bring the cars to life, the contrast develops. The Beetle bursts into that slightly remote, pulsing rumble that you know would propel you to Timbuctoo without problems; the Mini, into a burbling, vibratory din that says "I'm eager to go, it'll be fun to explore." There's nothing remotely like either of them, and you already sense some clues to why these cars have inspired such affection in their owners, it seems slightly potty to the uninitiated.

They both warm up smoothly — the Beetle with an efficient automatic choke, the Mini with that twist-to-set SU richening device — and both accelerate with reasonable

vigour, though performance is not a strong point. The Mini's rod-shift gear linkage and remotely mounted lever makes a tremendous improvement over the old wobbly-wire system of the earlier cars but a firm, thrusting technique has to be learned to get the best results and it's still necessary to prod second before selecting first, if you want to be sure of easy engagement. Once you know the car, the change is precise and fun, though not in the same class as the Beetle — whose gearbox set new standards many years ago.

Running on 15-inch wheels with masses of ground clearance and good cross-country capabilities, the Beetle gives a

Features	TESTER'S COMMENTS	Points awarded out of ten	
		Mini De Luxe	Beetle 1300
Body styling	Highly individual on both cars. Neither aerodynamic nor visually attractive; but capable of inspiring great affection because the character of both vehicles comes across strongly.	5	5
Scratch protection and bumpers	As both cars are priced at the bottom end of the market, it's not surprising that the owner wanting car-park scrimmage protection would have to fit side trims himself. Mini bumpers look flimsy with no crumple space. Beetle's are massive, spaced well away from body.	4	6
Boot design and size	Mini's boot is an 18-year-old joke but the car provides loads of stowage space, including deep rear side pockets. Beetle has secure front boot of limited size and useful stowage space behind rear seat which folds forwards for carrying bulky loads when two-up.	4	6
Exterior finish	Beetle's finish and paintwork virtually impossible to fault — there are now even metal kick pads inside the footwell of this basic model. While the Mini's paint was very good, both boot and bonnet were "fouling" in places and the bright trim was rippled and insecure.	6	9
Seating and upholstery etc	On the De Luxe Mini tested, the seating is absolutely basic with pivoting short-backed non-adjustable front seats. But carpets are fitted and the Clubman (still R110 cheaper than the Beetle) provides much better seats. Beetle has rubber floor mats and reasonably comfortable seats with restricted adjustment range.	5	7
Dashboard	Mini retains central combination speedo which is difficult to read and includes one "dummy" warning light but nothing to warn of overheating (though a sender is in the head!) Beetle's instruments are basic but readable and adequate. (Clubman Mini has proper dashboard with good instrumentation).	5	7
Heating and ventilation	Beetle now has through-flow but weak ventilation, allied to powerful heating with good distribution controls. Mini has simple but powerful heater and demisting and good eyeball vents (which increase the noise level when used).	7	5
Under-bonnet accessibility and appearance	Both cars have crowded engine bays but all components requiring regular attention are reasonably accessible and generations of D-I-Y owners have learned to cope with few problems.	7	5
Main controls	Beetle has the better driving position with less deflection and more space for pedal operation and adjustable seating. Mini takes getting used to but is then immensely controllable. All controls light on both cars.	5	6
Ancillary controls	Use of second stalk for two-speed wiper and electrical washer have improved Mini significantly. Mini heater control crude but effective. Beetle controls functional and sound.	6	6
Throttle response	More immediate and urgeful on the Mini which uses much lower gearing. But the acceleration times show that the Beetle, which seems less direct, more docile, is almost as fast from 0 to 100 km/h, though much more sluggish in its overdrive top gear.	8	6
Steering	Mini's rack and pinion gives sensitive, immediate response with exceptional feel. Beetle's worm and roller is rather vague and the car is apt to wander at high speeds, which calls for constant correction.	8	5
Gearchange	Latest rod linkage and remote control have transformed Mini gearchange: stiff into first but direct and precise, provided you use thrustful technique. Beetle's gear-change is legendary.	7	9
Handling and cornering	Mini extraordinarily agile, clinging to the road and able to turn on a 5c piece without loss of stability. But its tiny wheels don't suit potholes and ground clearance is limited. VW now much more stable than ten years ago — but still prone to oversteer and a handful in strong winds.	9	6
Ride quality	Beetle ride good for character and price but noisy when engine working hard, until cruising in top — when din is left behind. Mini noise levels too high for long distance use and ride uncomfortably hard.	4	6
Braking	Both cars use drums without boosting and their braking improves when radials are used. As tested, both cars were stable in repeated crash stops but VW braking was significantly more powerful.	6	8
Fuel tank	Although the Beetle's tank (40 litres) is six litres larger than the Mini's the difference in range is insignificant — about 15 km (see text).	7	7
Fuel cap	Mini now equipped with lockable cap — an object lesson to one or two cars costing more than twice as much. VW has locking cap behind flap.	8	8
Horns	Rudimentary on both cars with press-stalk operating buttons.	6	6
Lights/signals	Adequate for current conditions in both cars.	6	6

The De Luxe (left) retains the original cheeky Mini nose, looks nimble and alert. The latest Beetle 1300 (right) sports Rostyle wheels, through-flow extractors and heavy steel bumpers which look as if they are meant to be used.

comparatively good ride, its wider track and subtle suspension changes making it a vastly more stable car than it was during its first 30 years of life. But it still becomes a handful in gusty crosswinds and it's still prone to wander and oversteer once proceeding at a gallop. These problems could have been dealt with by a switch to the dual-jointed rear end and strut front suspension used in the Super Beetle in the USA and elsewhere — which economic reasons have presumably prevented from introduction to this market. At current speeds, and for average purposes, it provides safe and comfortable (if somewhat confined) motoring of the "upright" era and its simplicity and trustworthiness have given it strong appeal to women. Many motorists who learned to drive in a Beetle have never found good reason to make a change, particularly since each new model has introduced practical improvements without loss of the quality of manufacture and finish which has always distinguished the car among its budget competitors.

Docile city car

Gearing mods have been made but the Beetle still has an overdrive top gear giving 30,2 km/h/1 000 r/min overall, and besides being a docile, adequately manoeuvreable city car, it will cruise effortlessly on the open road, tending to leave its noise behind it but requiring third for any sizable hill.

A good ride was never among the Mini's claims to fame and although the return to rubber cone suspension got rid of the lurching which afflicted the

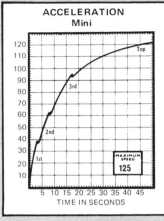
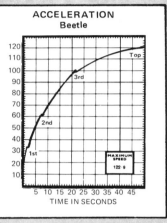

application of Hydrolastics to such a short wheelbase, it did nothing for the comfort. Current springs and dampers have somewhat softer settings but the car has a hard, uncomfortable ride and high noise levels which can become tiring on a long drive. But allied to the ride are the phenomenal roadholding, torquey motor and rapid, accurate steering response which Minimotorists have valued for nearly two decades. When a Peugeot 504 charged blindly past a parked truck and city stop street, we could spin the wheel (and curse the other driver) without ever really getting ruffled; with most other cars, it would at least have been disturbing.

The Mini scoots along, close to the ground and alert; conferring tremendous confidence which has helped many a racing driver acquire his first skills. While its brakes are not in the Beetle's class (see tables), you can use them strongly in a corner, if need be, without problems: with the VW, that's definitely best avoided.

Although the Mini's smaller mass and lower gearing work to its advantage in acceleration, there's surprisingly little in it, against the stop watch. While the Mini claws from 0 to 100 km/h in 20,4 seconds, the Beetle 1300 takes just over a second longer; and for those who still care, their top speeds are virtually identical at 123/125 km/h.

When it comes to fuel consumption, however, the 1100 Mini uses half a litre less per 100 km at a steady 80 on a level road. With the hurly burly of stop-starting, overtaking and bend-swinging, the gap increases and in our 100 km fuel consumption run, the Mini used 6,3 litres and the Beetle, 7,2. When you divide these overall figures into the tank capacities, the Mini's 34 litres gives a town-and-country range a shade under 540 km, while the Beetle's 40 litres yields only 15 more.

On hill climbing the Mini excells with the ability to mount a 9,5:1 gradient in top: while anything steeper than 15,7:1 forces the Beetle owner to change down to third, if it's prolonged.

Some of our criticisms of the Mini De Luxe fall away if

ACCELERATION Mini — MAXIMUM SPEED 125 — TIME IN SECONDS

ACCELERATION Beetle — MAXIMUM SPEED 122·9 — TIME IN SECONDS

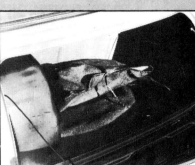

A contrast in boots (see "Tester's Comments" page 49). Above: Mini; Below: Beetle.

Tip-up seats are used for both Mini (above) and Beetle (below).

you pay the extra cash and buy the Clubman which is closer to the Beetle's price. The crude, short-backed seats, the central hard to read instrumentation (which should have been placed in front of the driver long ago!) are then exchanged for satisfactory equipment. However, even the basic Mini now has long-life drive-shafts, wind-up windows, eyeball vents, electric washers and two-speed wipers (on stalk controls) and a locking petrol cap: the only changes we feel could be expected, at this lowest-of-all prices, is a switch to a larger, dipping interior mirror (which must cover the width and depth of the rear screen!) an overheating warning light and better finish on the assembly line.

Similarly, the Beetle's improvements include weak but through-flow ventilation, (supplemented by large quarter vents) more performance and economy, enhanced vision and more powerful lighting; but it still suffers from a bad blind spot when the wipers operate and this should be dealt with in future production. Its quality of finish and assembly remain superb.

The driving position is not good with either car, though it's more awkward and deflected in the Mini: when you buy these models, you have other things more in mind. Both cars provide ample room for four people with five acceptable at a squeeze, but the Beetle scores with its rear storage space to augment the front boot, and when the rear seat is folded forwards, its capacity for bulky loads becomes surprising.

Both cars now have alternators to strengthen their electrical systems and although their mechanics require knowing and are not the easiest to work on, their basic ruggedness and lack of sophistication has endeared them to generations of D-I-Y owners.

If it's basic, honest cut-price motoring you're after, the proven record of both these cars demands a long hard look. Can 23 million motorists be wrong?

●

Performance and Specifications

Mini De Luxe R2 855
Beetle 1300 R3 180

MAKE AND MODEL:

	Mini De Luxe	Beetle 1300
Make	Leyland	Volkswagen
Model	Mini De Luxe	Beetle 1300

INTERIOR NOISE LEVELS:

	Mini De Luxe	Beetle 1300
Idling	51	59
60 km/h	75	73
80	80	78
100	84	83

(Measured in decibels, "A" weighting, averaging runs both ways on a level road with car closed.)

ACCELERATION FROM REST:

	Mini De Luxe	Beetle 1300
0-60	7,2	7,1
0-80	12,2	12,9
0-100	20,4	21,5

OVERTAKING ACCELERATION:

	3rd	Top	3rd	Top
40-60	4,6	6,5	5,7	8,7
60-80	4,8	7,1	6,0	8,6
80-100	7,6	10,6	9,5	13,0

(Measured in seconds, to true speeds, averaging runs both ways on a level road, car carrying test crew of two and standard test equipment).

MAXIMUM SPEED:

	Mini De Luxe	Beetle 1300
Top Speed (km/h)	125 (estimate)	123 (true)

Speedo calibration:

Indicated:	60	80	100		60	80	100
True speed:	56	76	96		59	78	97

FUEL CONSUMPTION (litres/100 km):

	Mini De Luxe	Beetle 1300
60	5,2	5,7
80	6,0	6,5
100	7,4	7,9

(Stated in litres per 100 kilometres, based on fuel economy figures recorded at true speeds.)

FUEL CONSUMPTION (Overall)

6,3 litres/100 km . . . . 7,2 litres/100 km

(Recorded over two laps of a 48 km varied road circuit with the cars travelling in close company and with one mid-point driver change).

BRAKING TEST:
From 100 km/h:

	Mini De Luxe	Beetle 1300
First stop	4,3	2,6
Tenth stop	4,4	2,7
Average	4,3	2,66

(Measured in sec with stops from true speeds at 30-second intervals on a good bituminised surface).

GRADIENTS IN GEARS:

	Mini De Luxe	Beetle 1300
Low gear	1 in 3,3	1 in 3,6
2nd gear	1 in 4,3	1 in 5,4
3rd gear	1 in 6,2	1 in 8,8
Top gear	1 in 9,5	1 in 15,7

(Tabulated from Tapley (x gravity) readings, car carrying test crew of two and standard test equipment).

GEARED SPEEDS: (km/h)

	Mini De Luxe	Beetle 1300
Low gear	39	33
2nd gear	61	61
3rd gear	94	100
Top gear	135	139

(Calculated at peak power engine speeds — 5 400 for the Mini and 4 600 for the Beetle).

ENGINE:

	Mini De Luxe	Beetle 1300
Cylinders	4 in line, transverse	4, horizontally opposed
Carburettors	SU	Solex PICT 31
Bore	70,6 mm	77 mm
Stroke	69,8 mm	69 mm
Cubic capacity (cm³)	1 098	1 285
Compression ratio	8,0 to 1	7,5 to 1
Valve gear	ohv, pushrods	ohv, pushrods
Main bearings	three	four
Aircleaner	dry element	dry element
Fuel requirement	93-octane (Coast) 88-octane (Reef)	91-octane (Coast) 88-octane (Reef)
Electrics	12-volt AC	12 volt AC

ENGINE OUTPUT:

	Mini De Luxe	Beetle 1300
Max power SAE (kW)	30	39
Max power net (kW)	27	34
Peak r/min	5 400	4 600
Max torque (N.m) at r/min	74 at 2 300	92,2 at 2 600

TRANSMISSION:

	Mini De Luxe	Beetle 1300
Forward speeds	four	four
Synchromesh	all	all
Gearshift	floor	floor
Low gear	3,525 to 1	3,8 to 1
2nd gear	2,214 to 1	2,06 to 1
3rd gear	1,435 to 1	1,26 to 1
Top gear	Direct	0,89 to 1
Reverse gear	3,5 to 1	3,88 to 1
Final drive	3,76 to 1	4,375 to 1
Drive wheels	front	rear
km/h/1 000 r/min (top)	25,1	30,2

WHEELS AND TYRES:

	Mini De Luxe	Beetle 1300
Road wheels	10 inch pressed steel	15 inch pressed steel
Tyres	520 x 10 crossply	5,60 x 15 crossply
Tyre pressures (front)	170/200 kPa	110/130 kPa
Tyre pressures (rear)	170/200 kPa	195/220 kPa

BRAKES:

	Mini De Luxe	Beetle 1300
Front	178 mm drums	TLS drums
Rear	178 mm drums	SLS drums
Boosting	none	none
Handbrake position	between seats	between seats

STEERING:

	Mini De Luxe	Beetle 1300
Type	rack and pinion	worm and roller
Lock to lock	2,7 turns	2,6 turns
Turning circle	8,7 metres	11,0 metres

MEASUREMENTS:

	Mini De Luxe	Beetle 1300
Length overall	3 000 mm	4 030 mm
Width overall	1 410 mm	1 550 mm
Height overall	1 340 mm	1 500 mm
Wheelbase	2 030 mm	2 400 mm
Front track	1 220 mm	1 300 mm
Rear track	1 180 mm	1 360 mm
Ground clearance	160 mm	150 mm
Licensing mass	594 kg	760 kg

SUSPENSION:

	Mini De Luxe	Beetle 1300
Front	independent	independent
Type	rubber cones, dual-jointed half axles	torsion bars, stabiliser
Rear	independent	independent
Type	rubber cones	Torsion bars, swing axles

CAPACITIES:

	Mini De Luxe	Beetle 1300
Seating	4/5	4/5
Fuel tank	34 litres	40 litres
Luggage trunk	150 dm³	140 dm³
Utility	none	140-500 dm³

VOLKSWAGEN 1600 'FUN BUG' MODEL

1974 ROAD TEST

CRUISING AT 80

Mech. noise level	75,5 dBA
0-80 through gears	9,8 seconds
km/litre at 80	13,7
litres/100 km	7,3
Braking from 80	2,9 seconds
Maximum gradient (top)	1 in 12,0
Speedometer error	4% over
Speedo at true 80	83 km/h
Engine r/min (top)	2 450

★ Produced as a celebratory gesture, this special model has many useful features . . . .

Argued purely on the basis of its sales success over a period of nearly 30 years, the Volkswagen Beetle is the greatest car the world has known.

And even though many more glamorous models have joined the VW stable, the Beetle is going to be with us for a long time yet, and may become the first vehicle to achieve total sales of 20 million.

This has been a big year for VW South Africa, and to focus attention on the enduring success of the Beetle, the company has produced a limited

KEY FIGURES

100 metres sprint	8,1 seconds
Terminal speed	70,0 km/h
litres/100 km at 80	7,3
Fuel tank capacity	40 litres
Fuel range at 80	292 km
Engine revs per km	1 840
National list price	R2 495

series (about 1 600 units) called the "Fun Bug", with special trim and equipment.

EFFECT OF RADIALS

This Test of the Fun Bug has also given us a chance to update on South Africa's top Beetle model, which now has radial-ply tyres as standard equipment, and has undergone some small revision of gearing.

In comparison with our last Beetle Test in May, 1972, the final drive ratio on the current model has changed from 4,125 to 1, to 3,875 to 1. At the same time, the top gear ratio has been altered from 0,89 to 1, to 0,93 to 1. This gives overall ratios in top of 3,68 to 1 for the 1972 model, and 3,604 on the current model, so that km/h/1 000 r/min. in top goes up slightly from 32,0, to 32,6 — all to the good at a time when economy is vital.

But as we expected, it is the radials that are the most vital factor: the radial-shod Fun Bug gains dramatically in handling, performance and economy over the earlier models with cross-ply tyres. The economy gain is mainly at low speeds and high speeds, but would give an overall gain in everyday use.

SPECIAL EQUIPMENT

The Fun Bug — at a price R100 above the 1600-L — comes in one of three vivid colours: red, yellow or gold. It is given a striking appearance by the matt-black external treatment of bumpers, windscreen wipers, door handles, and even badges. Sporty side stripes and "Fun Bug" crests add a touch of dash.

It is a jaunty, youthful-looking model, and with some attractive extra features inside: 60-mm rev-counter, oil pressure gauge, voltmeter, and adjustable integral headrests on the front bucket seats are things that any Beetle owner would want. Then there is a smaller, sports-style and leather-bound steering wheel which gives tight — but slightly heavier — steering control, and leather-bound gearshift knob.

Radials on Rostyle wheels are standard, and mechanically, it is no different from the other 1600 Beetle models.

TOTAL REFINEMENT

It is sheer quality which has led to the Beetle's unrivalled popularity in recent years. There are more than 5 000 individual parts, and every one has undergone refinement and improvement at some time in the annual revisions of the car. Many components have been improved repeatedly, so that the car has a rare degree of refinement and finish.

This is evident as soon as one drives a Beetle — it comes near to perfection in many aspects of its construction: something which has taken three decades to achieve, and which no car —

Special instrumentation includes medium-sized rev-counter at right.

ENGINE:
Cylinders . 4 opposed, rear-mounted
Carburettor . . . .Solex 34 PICT
Bore . . . . . . 85,5 mm
Stroke . . . . . . 69,0 mm
Cubic capacity . . . 1 584 cm³
Compression ratio . . .7,5 to 1
Valve gear. . . . ohv, pushrods
Main bearings. . . . . .four
Aircleaner. . . . . .oil bath
Fuel requirement. 93-octane Coast,
88-octane Reef
Cooling . . . air, blower-driven
Electrics . . . . .12-volt DC

ENGINE OUTPUT:
Max. power SAE (kW) . . 44
(58 b.h.p.)
Max. power net (kW) . . 37
Peak r/min 4 000
Max. torque (N.m.) at r/min . 106
at 2 800

TRANSMISSION:
Forward speeds . . . . .four
Synchromesh . . . . . .all
Gearshift . . . . . . floor
Low gear . . . . . 3,80 to 1
2nd gear . . . . . 2,06 to 1
3rd gear . . . . . 1,26 to 1
Top gear . . . . . 0,93 to 1
Reverse gear . . . . 3,61 to 1
Final drive . . . . 3,875 to 1
Drive wheels . . . . . rear

WHEELS AND TYRES:
Road wheels . . 15 inch Rostyle,
5-stud
Rim width 4½J
Tyres . . . 155 x 15 SR radials
(SP 49 Dunlops)
Tyre pressures (front) .160 to 180
kPa (24 to 26 lb)
Tyre pressures (rear) .180 to 210
kPa (26 to 30 lb)

BRAKES:
Front . . . . . .TLS drums
Rear . . . . . SLS drums
Pressure regulation . single circuit
Boosting . . . . . . nil
Handbrake position . between seats

STEERING:
Type . . . . worm and roller
Lock to lock . . . 2,6 turns
Turning circle . . 11,2 metres

MEASUREMENTS:
Length overall . . . 4,03 m
Width overall . . . . 1,55 m
Height overall . . . . 1,50 m
Wheelbase . . . . . 2,40 m
Front track . . . . 1,30 m
Rear track . . . . 1,36 m
Ground clearance . . . 0,16 m
Licensing mass . . . 730 kg

SUSPENSION:
Front . . . . . independent
Type . . torsion bars, stabiliser
Rear . . . . . independent
Type . . torsion bars, swing axles

CAPACITIES:
Seating 4-5
Fuel tank . . . . .40 litres
Luggage trunk . . . 130 dm³
Utility space . . . 110-500 dm³

WARRANTY:
Six months or 10 000 km.

TEST CAR FROM:
Volkswagen South Africa, Uitenhage, in conjunction with Motors W.P. Services, Paarden Eiland, Cape.

---

no matter how expensive — can gain overnight.

And in spite of its old-fashioned running boards and those big tail-lights (which would look ridiculous on any other car) it has a neat and functional look.

PERFORMANCE

The test car's SP-49's gave it fine traction in a standing start, with just a touch of wheelspin to smooth things. The rev-counter showed 5 000 r/min. as permissible maximum, and using all of this the car showed the smooth accelerative ability for which the Beetle is renowned — and which often surprises owners of more powerful cars at robots!

The car is overgeared and does not have much pull below 60 km/h, nor is there much top-gear punch for hill-climbing. But it cruises effortlessly and is easy-driving.

The uprated clutch introduced in recent years is fairly heavy-acting and takes sharply, but a driver becomes accustomed to this. The gearbox is famous for its slick action — this is one of the few cars that almost any driver can snap-change.

ECONOMY AND BRAKING

The economy pattern has changed a bit since our last test, coming up as more of a curve, with big gains at top and bottom. At middle speeds, there is not much change, and the car's 7,3 litres/100 km (nearly 40 mpg) at 80 km/h gives it sound economy and range.

The test car had the fairly common failing of a slightly-oval front brake drum, which made light-pressure stops a bit jerky. In full-scale brake tests, however, this was less apparent, and the car showed very good stopping ability and balance on a good bitumen surface.

The radials should make the Beetle faster than before, by a small margin — we reckon it would reach a genuine 136 km/h on a level road at sea level, compared with the 132,2 we recorded in the 1972 Test.

SUMMARY

By car model standards, the Beetle is just about immortal, and VW reports that it plans to keep it that way. Right up to the first half of this year it has remained an easy top-seller on a world-wide basis, and production is running at something close to 5 000 units a day — in spite of the new models introduced by VW recently.

The South African-developed Fun Bug is a happy gesture by the Uitenhage plant — and another milestone in a motoring epic without parallel. ∎

PERFORMANCE FACTORS:
Power/mass (W/kg) net . . .44,9
Frontal area (m²) 2,33
km/h/1 000 r/min (top) . .32,6
(Calculated on licensing mass, gross frontal area, gearing and net power output).

SERVICE REQUIREMENTS:
Sump capacity . . . 2,5 litres
Change interval . . . 5 000 km
Gearbox/diff capacity . 2,5 litres
Change interval . . .50 000 km
Air filter service . Up to 10 000 km
Greasing points . front axles — 4
Greasing interval . . . 5 000 km
(These basic service recommendations are given for guidance only, and may vary according to operating conditions. Inquiries should be addressed to authorised dealerships).

STANDARD EQUIPMENT:
Cigar lighter; headlamp flasher; semi-reclining front seats; pressurised windscreen washers; dash grabhandles; coat hooks; full wheel trims; exterior rearview mirror; assist straps; door pockets; through-flow ventilation; heater; steering lock; parcel shelf; leather-bound sports steering wheel; rev-counter; oil pressure gauge; voltmeter; sports gearlever; Rostyle wheels; radial-ply tyres.

TEST CONDITIONS:
Altitude . . . . At sea level
Weather . . . . fine and mild
Fuel used . . . . . 93 octane
Test car's odometer . . 1 804 km

Engine is the standard 1600 unit, but there are some small gearing changes.

The radials, on Rostyle wheels, have a major effect on both handling and performance.

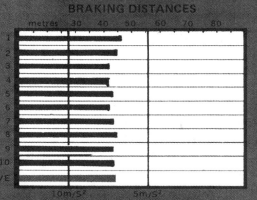

MAXIMUM SPEED
136

Time in seconds

km/h

BRAKING DISTANCES

metres 30 40 50 60 70 80

1
2
3
4
5
6
7
8
9
10
AVE.

10m/S²   5m/S²
(10 stops from 100 km/h)

ENGINE SPEED

Top
3rd
2nd
1st

km/h

2000   3000   4000   5000
Revs per minute

GRADIENT ABILITY

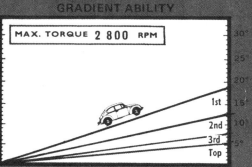

MAX. TORQUE 2 800 RPM

30°
25°
20°
15°
10°
5°

1st
2nd
3rd
Top

(Degrees inclination)

PERFORMANCE

MAKE AND MODEL:
Make . . . . . Volkswagen
Model . . . . . . Fun Bug

INTERIOR NOISE LEVELS:

	Mech.	Wind	Road
Idling	57,0	—	—
60	71,0	—	—
80	75,5	77,5	78,0
100	80,0	82,0	82,0
Full throttle			See graph
Average dBA at 100			81,3

ACCELERATION FROM REST:
0-60 5,5
0-80 9,8
0-100 15,8
100 m sprint 8,1

OVERTAKING ACCELERATION:

	3rd		Top
40-60	4,4		6,8
60-80	4,8		8,0
80-100	5,9		9,3

(Measured in seconds to true speeds, averaging runs both ways on a level road, car carrying test crew of two and standard test equipment).

IMPERIAL DATA

Major performance features of this Road Test are summarised below in Imperial measures, for comparative purposes:

ACCELERATION FROM REST (seconds):
0-50 10,0
0-60 15,0

MAXIMUM SPEED (mph):
Road estimate 85

FUEL ECONOMY (mpg):
30 mph 54,0
40 mph 46,0
50 mph 38,4
60 mph 32,5

MAXIMUM SPEED:
Road estimate 136
Calibration

Indicated:	40	60	80	100
True speed:	37	57	77	97

FUEL CONSUMPTION (litres/100 km):
40 4,8
60 5,9
80 7,3
100 9,0

(Stated in litres per 100 kilometres, based on fuel economy figures recorded at true speeds).

BRAKING TEST:
From 100 km/h:
First stop 3,7
Tenth stop 3,4
Average 3,43

(Measured in sec. with stops from true speeds at 30-second intervals on a good bituminised surface).

GRADIENTS IN GEARS:
Low gear . . . . . 1 in 2,9
2nd gear . . . . . 1 in 4,5
3rd gear . . . . . 1 in 7,3
Top gear . . . . . 1 in 10,6

(Tabulated from Tapley (x gravity) readings, car carrying test crew of two and standard test equipment.

GEARED SPEEDS: (km/h)
Low gear 31,9
2nd gear 59,0
3rd gear 96,5
Top gear 130,4

(Calculated at engine peak r/min — 4 000.)

NOISE VALUES

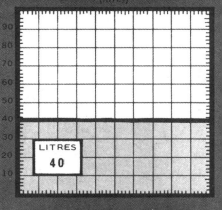

dBA

MECH.   WIND   ROAD   AVE.
(at 100 km/h)

FUEL TANK CAPACITY
(litres)

LITRES
40

FUEL CONSUMPTION
(litres/100 km)

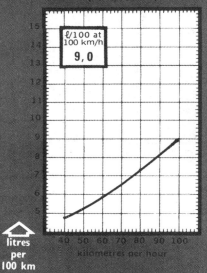

ℓ/100 at 100 km/h
9,0

litres per 100 km

40 50 60 70 80 90 100
kilometres per hour

FUEL CONSUMPTION
(litres/100 km)

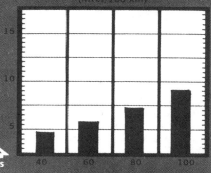

litres per 100 km

40   60   80   100
kilometres per hour

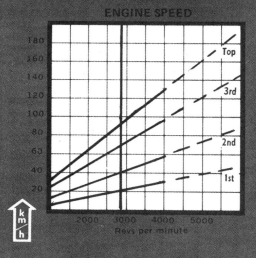

ROAD TEST

Ubiquitous (yoo-bik-wi-tis): Being or seeming to be everywhere at the same time—American Heritage Dictionary Of The English Language.

You've got to give the Volkswagen Beetle this much: it may not be what you call your thoroughly modern design, but it certainly seems to be just about everywhere. And why not? There have been, after all, more than a few of the things built—something like 18.75 million, worldwide. U.S. import totals once reached as high as 423,008 per year (1968), but for 1977 the import figure is down a goodly amount; there'll be a mere 30,000 Beetles imported this year. The figure was slightly larger last year, and almost certainly will be slightly smaller next year. So, finally, the Beetle is on the downward part of its cycle. The last time VW imported about 30,000 Beetles? That was when the Beetle was in the upwards part of its cycle, in 1955, when 32,662 Beetles were imported.

What's important here is not the sheer numbers involved; rather, it's that the Beetle almost surely is the most recognizable automobile in the U.S. today. That's due as much to the fact of the car's sheer numerical strength as it is to the fact that while detail changes have been many, the car's overall design, its outward shape, its visual personality, has not changed very much at all.

And therein lies the problem with the 1977 Beetle. It's an automotive zoot suit: no matter how well-tailored it may be (and indeed, fit and finish are up to the usual high Volkswagen standards), no matter how much you loved your first, second, third, and in some cases fourth example, serious consideration of a Beetle today (or of a real, live zoot suit, for that matter) better be approached with a good deal of caution. Simply put, there are much, *much* better ways of getting from point A to point B, and one of them is Volkswagen's Hope For The Future, the Rabbit— the base version of which costs a full $100 less than what the base

132

Volkswagen Beetle

An old friend revisited.

Beetle costs. Granted, the base Beetle has more standard features on it than the base Rabbit, but that's nickle-and-dime stuff. What's important is that we're comparing a near state-of-the-art piece of equipment with a design that has been around for more than 40 years.

Old Dr. Porsche laid down the basic design for the People's Car in 1933. Prototype Beetles were trundling around Germany in 1937, the car was into production by 1938—and by the following year had temporarily been phased out of production and replaced by jeeps and trucks.

This latest, 1977 honing of the old concept really isn't too far removed from that original car: rear, air-cooled engine, drum brakes all around, independent suspension (indeed, much the same front suspension now as then) and the same basic shape.

Ah, the shape. Who, among those of us with all five senses, could fail to recognize a Volkswagen Beetle? Very few of us, that's who, and therefore somehow it comes as no great surprise that

nowhere on the '77 Beetle's exterior does it say "Volkswagen." Try as you might, you'll find nothing but "Fuel Injection" lettered in chrome italics on the engine cover. The only marks of identification are stamped into the wheel hubs: each one wears a tiny VW logo. And why not? Everybody knows what the car is, though probably they'll never know—or care—that this particular one is a '77 model.

Take our word for it—in a lot of ways, the Beetle is like an old friend. It's a car nearly anybody can feel comfortable in right away, because by our best reckoning, nearly everybody has driven a Beetle at one time or another. The latest version feels pretty much the same as the older versions, and it pretty much sounds the same. That's good, because if you're a true Beetle driver, you know exactly when to shift gears—you haven't had to look at the gear selector markers on the speedometer dial in a long, long while. Those shift marks are gone now, leaving the shifting points to guesswork and/or a well-trained ear.

What a spirited run up through the gears nets you is 63.9 mph in the quarter-mile, with the long, hard climb to 60 mph taking 17.2 seconds. For while the car will cruise easily at 75 mph over flat ground, its fuel-injected, 1584cc engine develops but 48 bhp at 4200 rpm, down from the 60 bhp available in 1971.

But never mind that; the Beetle's reputation was made on reliability and economy, not performance. And while there have been one or two lean years when neither of those characteristics were present in the Beetle to any great degree, this latest edition has the same, run-forever feel of most of the earlier examples.

While engine performance is something less than earth-shaking, the performance of the car's chassis was quite a surprise. To begin with, it's basically the standard old VW chassis, virtually unchanged in concept for many years, with one important exception. That exception concerns the rear suspension. It's still independent and torsion bar sprung as always, but now uses double-articulated half-shafts and a trailing arm for each wheel instead of the old swing-axle. The current system, which has been in production on U.S.-bound cars since 1969, presents the driver with considerably better controllability and somewhat higher cornering limits. Front suspension is the standard twin torsion bar, twin trailing arm arrangement that the Beetle has used (with the exception of the now defunct MacPherson Strut-equipped Super Beetle) since Year One. The front end is equipped with a very slender anti-roll bar.

For the most part, it all works quite well, though really fast running doesn't feel all that secure, especially on the bias-ply tires our test car wore. High corner entry speeds are just a little worrysome, because with semi-trailing arm rear suspension, takes it very little to bring the car's rear-end around in a bit of oversteer with the brakes on and some steering lock cranked in. Once you have learned your lesson about *that*, however, and have modified your driving technique to suit the Beetle's character, some pretty respectable speeds can be generated through the curvy parts, as reflected by the .70 lateral acceleration figure the car turned in on the *RT* skidpad.

Likewise the brakes: an unremarkable system with drums front and rear—disc-braked Beetles died with the Super Beetle/LeGrand Bug in 1975. But drum brakes or no, the Beetle stopped from 60 mph in an impressive 151 feet, generating an average deceleration rate of .80 in the process. The car is light, has a relatively low center of gravity, and has its weight mass (read engine and transmission) at the rear of the car, an ideal layout for superior braking performance. We were unable to make them fade, at least one reason being that it took a good, long while to get back up to 60 mph for another stop, and by the time we did, the brakes had cooled. It can be anticipated, however, that in a spirited drive down a mountain road repeated hard brake applications could bring about more fade than might be suitable.

Just because the Beetle remains largely unchanged doesn't mean that Volkswagen's engineers have been sitting on their hands. Their most apparent activities have included drawing stunners like the Rabbit and Scirocco, but they've been busy upgrading the Beetle as well. The seats in the car are new this year and provide ample room and comfort in front, minimal room and comfort in back; the heating and vent system has been vastly upgraded and a fresh-air blower is now part of the package, as is fuel injection, a catalytic converter and one tailpipe.

But while VW engineers have quietly massaged the Beetle, it is still a 40-year-old design. That makes it an old friend to many of us. But getting into a 1977 Beetle after sampling the smart performance and inventive space utilization of some other designs makes you feel as though you've just discovered that your old friend has a solid case of necrophilia. Somehow this old Beetle just seems rather less acceptable than it once did. Shows you how your perspective can change.

If you should find that yours hasn't, and that the Beetle sounds like just the car for you, that's fine, because it has some solid strong points going for it: fine workmanship and finish, it's easily as reliable as just about anything else available today, it'll go more than 300 miles on 10 gallons of gas, and the way things look, it'll probably never go out of style. ∎

SPECIFICATIONS

ENGINE

Type	OHV opp4
Displacement, cu in	97
Displacement, cc	1584
Bore x stroke, in	3.36 x 2.72
Bore x stroke, mm	85.5 x 69.0
Compression ratio	7.3:1
Hp at rpm, net	48@4200
Torque at rpm, lb/ft, net	75@2200
Carburetion	fuel inj.

DRIVELINE

Transmission	4-spd manual
Gear ratios:	
1st	3.78:1
2nd	2.06:1
3rd	1.26:1
4th	0.93:1
Final drive ratio	3.88:1
Driving wheels	rear

GENERAL

Wheelbase, ins	94.5
Overall length, ins	163.4
Width, ins	61.0
Height, ins	59.1
Front track, ins	51.5
Rear track, ins	53.1
Trunk capacity, cu ft	9.8
Curb weight, lbs	1890
Distribution, % front/rear	40/60
Power-to-weight ratio, lbs/hp	39.4

BODY AND CHASSIS

Body/frame construction	separate
Brakes, front/rear	drum/drum
Swept area, sq in	125.2
Swept area, sq in/1000 lb	66.2
Steering	recirc. ball
Ratio	14.34:1
Turns, lock-to-lock	2.8
Turning circle, ft	34.4

Front suspension: Independent, twin trailing arms, torsion bars, tubular shocks, anti-roll bar

Rear suspension: Independent, semi-trailing arms, torsion bars, tubular shocks

WHEELS AND TIRES

Wheels	15 x 4.5
Tires	6.00-15 Continental

INSTRUMENTATION

Instruments: 5-100 mph speedo, fuel level
Warning lights: directionals, high beam

PRICE

Factory list, as tested: $3959.00
Options included in price: AM/FM—$150; leatherette upholstery—$50; sunroof—$115; Calif emiss test—$45.

TEST RESULTS

ACCELERATION, SEC.

0-30 mph	4.9
0-40 mph	7.3
0-50 mph	11.9
0-60 mph	17.2
0-70 mph	27.6
Standing start, ¼ mile	20.7
Speed at end ¼ mile, mph	63.9
Avg accel over ¼ mile, g	0.14

SPEEDS IN GEARS, MPH

1st (5000 rpm)	24
2nd (5000 rpm)	45
3rd (4600 rpm)	68
4th (3900 rpm) (calc.)	80
Engine revs at 70 mph	3400

SPEEDOMETER ERROR

Indicated speed	True speed
40 mph	40 mph
50 mph	50 mph
60 mph	60 mph
70 mph	70 mph
80 mph	80 mph

INTERIOR NOISE, dBA

Idle	62
Max 1st gear	81
Steady 40 mph	74
50 mph	75
60 mph	78
70 mph	79

BRAKES

Avg stopping distance from 60 mph, ft	151
Avg deceleration rate, g	0.80

FUEL ECONOMY

Overall avg range	22-29 mpg
Range on 10.6 gal tank	307 miles
Fuel required	unleaded

HANDLING

Avg speed on 100-ft rad, mph	32.3
Lateral acceleration, g	0.70
Transient response, avg spd, mph	22.8

RATING

PERFORMANCE/ECONOMY

*Acceleration	1
*Fuel Economy	4

RIDE/HANDLING

*Lateral Acceleration	3
Subjective handling	2
Predictability	2
Ride	3
Steering	3

ENGINE/DRIVETRAIN

Starting	4
Throttle Response	4
Noise/Vibration	2
Shifting Action	4

*Denotes recorded data

BRAKES

*Stopping Distance	4
Fade Resistance	3
Subjective Feel	2

COMFORT/ERGONOMICS

*Interior Noise	2
Controls/Instruments	4
Visibility	3
Entry/Exit	3
Front Seat Comfort	3
Rear Seat Comfort	2
Space Utilization	1
Interior Environment	3

QUALITY

Assembly	5
Finish	4
Hardware/Trim	4
TOTAL	**74**
Percentile rating	**59**

5=Excellent, 4=Above Average, 3=Average, 2=Below Average, 1=Poor, 0=Unacceptable.

Test Equipment Used: Testron Fifth Wheel and Pulse Totalizer, Lamar Data Recording System, Esterline-Angus Recorder, Sun Tachometer, EDL Pocket-Probe Pyrometer, General Radio Sound Level Meter

VOLKSWAGEN BEETLE CONVERTIBLE

Our last test of the little charmer

BY HENRY N. MANNEY III

VOLKSWAGEN NEEDS NO introduction from me and especially the Beetle, as enduring a cult object as the teddy bear. Over the years the marketing people at Wolfsburg have seen fit to offer dressier alternatives such as the Ghia, a quasi Afrika-Korps Kübelwagen (the Thing) and the subject of this test, the Convertible, in a quite successful effort to keep loyal customers happy who wanted something just a trifle different. But all cults fade, sooner or later, and faced with the new New NEW advertising barrage from other companies, sales of the Beetle have commenced to fall off. To be truthful, the package is a bit dated but it is a moot point whether the imbalance of the Deutsche Mark vs the dollar (thus making a $2500 car into a $4500 one) or simple fashion has the most to do with its decline in sales. If the VW had never existed and were introduced fresh today, I think sales would take off like a rocket as fundamentally the Beetle is an honest automobile.

The Convertible has always been a bit special, built as it is by Karmann of Osnabrück, and frankly I don't see why they sold at all. The car is downright ugly except to kitsch fanciers, until recently it housed the gutless 1300 engine, and the price was alarming to say the least. However, in recent years it has become one of the few 4-seat convertibles available and thus recherché, as what is nicer on a summer evening than taking yr sweetie for a ride with the top down? According to VW, the Convertible has become the "in" thing in Europe for gilded youth; that may well be a crafty sales dodge (1977 is the last year for the Beetle sedan in the U.S. but the convertible continues in 1978) but it is nice to see, after VW's humble beginnings, the Convertible going down with Erté, Louis·Vuitton, Yvette Horner, Biba, Bobiejaan Schoepen and the Casino at Monte Carlo as milestones of funny culture. Out here, of course, the young carry surfboards in them.

The Convertible looks more or less like the one in which H*tl*r was photographed in 1938 approx, aside from the attractive red paint job, but there have been a few changes mechanically since then. Chassiswise it owes a lot to the Super Beetle with its

MacPherson front suspension while in the back, the smog-gear-ridden carburetor engine has given way to a more tractable 1584-cc fuel-injection unit. Theoretically fuel injection should do away with a multitude of ills and so it has on three cars I have owned, but this particular unit wasn't happy at all. Most of our staff complained that it was bog slow while I thought that the tappets were all up too tight, the rate of progress and exhaust sound being more appropriate to a Lion-Peugeot vertical twin rather than a flat-4. A trip to our local VW dealer produced a slight improvement and dark mutterings about a vacuum leak at the air intake sensor (?) but what it all boils down to is that a VW is a VW and goes like one. Perhaps we have all been driving too many sports cars.

Several of the R&T people commented that one had to have

owned an earlier VW to appreciate the Convertible properly. Certainly there have been refinements over the years but Beetle people are as specialized as those gourmets who put HP sauce on everything. I would like to point out again that there is nothing wrong with owning a series of cars with a strong family resemblance as you always know what that funny noise really is and the nice collection of specially bent wrenches in the garage means that you can do your own maintenance. The VW is one of the great tools of our time and a tremendous value before the politicians commenced larking about with the currency. At any

CONTINUED ON PAGE 169

PRICE

List price	$4799
Price as tested	$4944

GENERAL

Curb weight, lb	2120
Weight distribution (with driver), front/rear, %	42/58
Wheelbase, in.	95.3
Track, front/rear	54.9/53.1
Length	164.8
Width	62.4
Height	59.1
Fuel capacity, U.S. gal.	11.1

CHASSIS & BODY

Body/frame	platform frame with separate steel body
Brake system	9.6 x 1.7-in. drums front, 9.1 x 1.7-in. drums rear
Wheels	steel disc, 15 x 4½J
Tires	Dunlop B-7, 6.00 x 15
Steering type	rack & pinion
Turns, lock-to-lock	3.5
Suspension, front/rear: MacPherson struts, lower lateral links, coil springs, tube shocks, anti-roll bar/semi-trailing arms, diagonal links, torsion bars	

ENGINE & DRIVETRAIN

Type	ohv flat 4
Bore x stroke, mm	85.5 x 69.0
Displacement, cc/cu in.	1584/96.7
Compression ratio	7.3:1
Bhp @ rpm, net	48 @ 4200
Torque @ rpm, lb-ft	73 @ 2800
Fuel requirement .. unleaded, 91-oct	
Transmission	4-sp manual
Gear ratios: 4th (0.93)	3.61:1
3rd (1.26)	4.89:1
2nd (2.06)	7.99:1
1st (3.78)	14.67:1
Final drive ratio	3.88:1

CALCULATED DATA

Lb/bhp (test weight)	47.3
Mph/1000 rpm (4th gear)	20.9
Engine revs/mi (60 mph)	2870
R&T steering index	1.10
Brake swept area, sq in./ton	188

ROAD TEST RESULTS

ACCELERATION

Time to distance, sec:

0-100 ft	3.7
0-500 ft	10.7
0-1320 ft (¼ mi)	20.4
Speed at end of ¼ mi, mph	64.5

Time to speed, sec:

0-30 mph	4.3
0-40 mph	7.0
0-50 mph	11.3
0-60 mph	17.0
0-70 mph	26.2

SPEEDS IN GEARS

4th gear (4000 rpm)	83
3rd (4600)	74
2nd (5000)	50
1st (5000)	28

FUEL ECONOMY

Normal driving, mpg	23.0

BRAKES

Minimum stopping distances, ft:

From 60 mph	163
From 80 mph	na
Control in panic stop	very good
Pedal effort for 0.5g stop, lb	38
Fade: percent increase in pedal effort to maintain 0.5g deceleration in 6 stops from 60 mph	nil
Overall brake rating	very good

HANDLING

Speed on 100-ft radius, mph	32.5
Lateral acceleration, g	0.704
Speed thru 700-ft slalom, mph	51.0

INTERIOR NOISE

All noise readings in dBA:

Constant 30 mph	71
50 mph	77
70 mph	82

SPEEDOMETER ERROR

30 mph indicated is actually	31.0
60 mph	60.0
70 mph	71.0

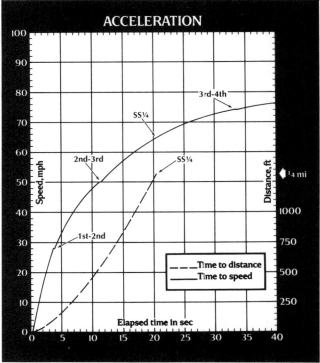

OWNER REPORT
1340702
km

74

Beetle,1970 onwards

A car which has become a legend to generations of South African motorists, still shows a loyal following for its quality and value...

The axiom about there being safety in numbers emerges as an influencing factor in the popularity of that motoring veteran, the Volkswagen Beetle.

An East London man reports that in deciding to buy a Beetle 1600 a few years back, he relied on the fact that millions of motorists — about 16 million at that time, and now more than 18 million — could not all be wrong!

In summarising this report from South African owners, we found that many depended on word-of-mouth recommendations from colleagues and friends when choosing their cars, and list the good reputation of the Beetle in the fields of value, quality and reliability as a major deciding factor. And as the reports show, they seldom had cause for any serious regret.

SUCCESSIVE MODELS

This is our fifth Owner Report on the VW Beetle, setting a record for any one car which will not easily be broken. The first was published in July, 1961, and featured the original Beetle models of fond memory. It was, in fact, one of the first Owner Reports done by CAR.

Then came the well-loved 1200 model in the December, 1964, issue, followed by the 1300 in July, 1969. The Beetle 1500 was reported on in April, 1973, and this time it is the turn of the modern 1600 model, from 1970 onwards — but excluding the "L" and "Superbug" models and their derivatives, such as the "Lux Bug", "Jeans Bug" and other special versions.

This report is on the basic 1600 as it existed in the first half of this decade and up to 1976, with cross-ply tyres and no frills in either appearance or equipment.

COUNTING THE COST

Beetle owners would not lay claim to being bold and adventurous in their car-buying — they are more the pragmatic type of car-owner, concerned with getting dependable motoring at reasonable cost. They tend to do below-average distances — working out to just over 1500 km monthly, which is less than was recorded in earlier Beetle reports, and may well be influenced by today's restrictive motoring conditions.

Nevertheless, their aggregate is 1 340 702 km, representing about 72 years of individual motoring experience — so that the figures and comments given are authoritative and representative.

As with earlier Beetle reports, it is notable that owners are objective in their assessment of the car: while they may praise it for its virtues, they are also prepared to criticise it impartially for its failings.

STANDARD OF FINISH

This time it is the standard of manufacture and finish (69 per cent) which takes top placing among the car's good features, followed by mechanical reliability with 55 per cent of votes.

Next comes the excellent torsion-bar suspension, which provides a smooth and comfortable ride under bad conditions — yet is tough enough to take loads well and to withstand any amount of punishment. Nearly half of owners single the suspension out for specific praise.

The car's cruising ability, ease of handling and general operating economy are praised by one owner in three. In particular, they are complimentary about low maintenance and service costs. This is reinforced by a 21 per cent vote for the car's solid construction, and the widespread and efficient service and parts facilities provided by the dealership network.

ECONOMY FEATURES

One owner in six is pleased with the tyre life and fuel economy of his Beetle 1600, as well as its acceleration, smooth gearbox and efficient interior heater.

Seating comfort, resale value, mechanical simplicity (for D-I-Y purposes) and roadholding under dirt-road conditions are praised by one owner in seven, and there is a ten per cent vote for engine willingness, and the convertibility of the rear seat space by folding down the backrest to accommodate either young children or bulky luggage. This last is in contrast to a considerable volume of criticism of rear seat comfort and luggage carrying capacity by more than half of owners when it comes to listing the features they do not like about the car.

DIRECTIONAL INSTABILITY

Even more than in previous reports, owners of the 1600 are critical of its directional instability and wander in crosswinds. This is their most serious criticism, totalling 62 per cent in volume, and it is followed by a 52 per cent indictment of high-speed braking capacity — many owners claim that the car is difficult to stop from cruising speeds in emergency stituations.

The capacity of the ventilation system (24 per cent) and the engine noise levels (21 per cent) are features which adversely affect interior comfort, owners report,

and there is criticism in smaller volume of the sparse instrumentation, the top-gear performance (particularly in climbing and overtaking) and the underseat placement of the battery.

The car's well-known oversteer tendency, its two-door configuration and the tyre-wear rate come in for low-volume criticism, as well as a new feature — body rattles, apparently arising mainly from the folding backrest of the rear seat.

TROUBLE IS MINIMAL

While only 62 per cent of owners report that their Beetle 1600's gave trouble-free service, complaints are usually directed at comparatively minor failures. There were only isolated engine failures reported on this occasion, for instance — though a few instances of burnt valves or piston slap are listed.

Carburettor tuning ("flat spots") and oval brake drums were the principal source of trouble, reported by one owner in five in each case.

This is a considerably better record than with previous reports on the bigger-engined models, and suggests that VW's programme of improvements has borne fruit in producing greater mechanical reliability.

FUEL ECONOMY

The fuel economy figures listed in this report are on the conservative side in terms of present-day conditions, as they include some figures from pre-petrol-restrictions motoring conditions.

This would not affect the 10,6 litres/100 km (26,6 m-p-g) average obtained under about-town conditions — which should be a very realistic figure — as much as the 8,9 litres/100 km (31,8 m-p-g) obtained on the open road. This cruising economy level might be even better with speed restricted to 90 km/h.

Tyre life averages out to a reasonable 33 750 km on a set of cross-plies, with most owners reporting that they travel on both tarred and dirt roads.

FITTING RADIALS

Several owners reported fitting radials on replacement, and their comments deserve some attention. They report getting an average of 56 000 km with radials — an improvement of just over 60 per cent.

"I fitted 165 UniRoyals and VW Ro-style rims," a Transvaal man states, "and the result was a big improvement in handling, roadholding and fuel economy."

A similar comment comes from a Pretoria family: "Dunlop SP 49's in 165 size were fitted and made a vast improvement — both my wife and I enjoy driving our radial-shod Beetle." A Paarl owner said he found both roadholding and handling better on a friend's car fitted

FUEL CONSUMPTION (litres/100 km):

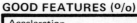

About town	
Open Road	
Average	

20   15   10   5

GOOD FEATURES (º/o)

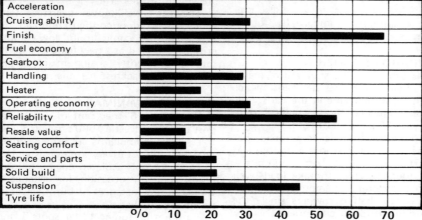

Acceleration	
Cruising ability	
Finish	
Fuel economy	
Gearbox	
Handling	
Heater	
Operating economy	
Reliability	
Resale value	
Seating comfort	
Service and parts	
Solid build	
Suspension	
Tyre life	

º/o   10   20   30   40   50   60   70

BAD FEATURES (º/o)

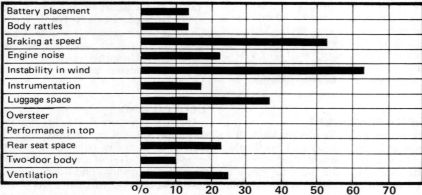

Battery placement	
Body rattles	
Braking at speed	
Engine noise	
Instability in wind	
Instrumentation	
Luggage space	
Oversteer	
Performance in top	
Rear seat space	
Two-door body	
Ventilation	

º/o   10   20   30   40   50   60   70

TYRE LIFE (km)

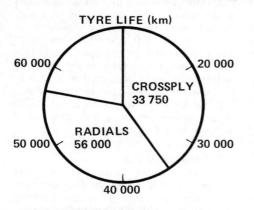

60 000   20 000

CROSSPLY
33 750

RADIALS
56 000

50 000   30 000

40 000

DEALER SERVICE (º/o)

Self
17%

Poor 3%

Yes
80%

TROUBLE REPORT (º/o)

Brakes (drum ovality)	
Carburettor tuning	
Minor engine trouble	
Minor troubles	
No trouble encountered	
Rear axle oil seals	

º/o   10   20   30   40   50   60   70

REPORT SUMMARY

MAKE AND MODEL:
Make . . . . .Volkswagen
Model . . . . .1600 Beetle
Model years . . . . . 1970 onwards

DISTANCE COVERED:
Total . . . . 1 340 702 km
Average monthly . . . . . . 1 554 km

OPERATING ECONOMY:
Fuel consumption:
About town . . . . .10,6 litres/100 km
Open road . . . . . 8,9 litres/100 km
Tyre life:
Crossply . . . . 33 750 km
Radial ply . . . . 56 000 km

GOOD FEATURES: %
Finish. 69
Reliability 55
Suspension 45
Cruising ability 31
Economy of operation 31
Handling 28
Solid build 21
Service and parts 21
Tyre life 17
Fuel economy 17
Heater 17
Acceleration 17
Gearbox 17
Seating comfort. 14
Resale value 14
Mechanical simplicity. 14
Roadholding on dirt 14
Engine willingness. 10
Convertable load space 10

BAD FEATURES: %
Instability in wind 62
Braking at speed. 52
Luggage space 38
Ventilation. 24
Rear seat space 24
Engine noise. 21
Instrumentation. 17
Performance in top 17
Battery placement 14
Oversteer. 14
Body rattles 14
Two-door configuration 10
Tyre wear rate. 10

TROUBLE REPORT: %
No trouble encountered 62
Carburettor tuning 24
Brakes (drum ovality) 21
Minor engine trouble 17
Rear axle oil seals 10
Minor troubles. 10

BODY SEAL: %
Dust-proof. 76
Rain-proof. 87

DEALER SERVICE: %
Use VW service 80
Average quality . . . . .fair to good
No — do own servicing 17
No — poor service. 3

OTHER CARS CONSIDERED: %
No other 41
Fiat 124 14
Leyland Mini 10
Chrysler Colt 10
Datsun 1200. 10
Ford Escort 10
Toyota Corona 10

REASON FOR CHOOSING BEETLE: %
Reliability 24
Good value. 21
Good reputation 17
Owned one before 14
Low running costs 10
Best trade-in 10

PROBABLE NEXT CAR: %.
Undecided 28
VW Audi 100 17
VW Passat/Audi 80 17
Beetle again 14
Citroën GS. 10

with radials — as well as more stable in windy conditions.

SERVICE IS GOOD

The body seal report (76 per cent dust-proof and 87 per cent rain-proof) is way below the usual Beetle standards, and suggests there has been a drop in the standard of Beetle finishing-off on the production lines. The 1973 report on the 1500 model gave 98 and 95 per cent, respectively.

The introduction of the VW electronic diagnostic service appears to have countered a trend towards do-it-yourself maintenance among Beetle owners: only 17 per cent of 1600 owners say they do their own minor servicing — and most report that they go to dealerships for diagnostic and major servicing at intervals of a year or so.

Dealerships get a very even "fair-to-good" rating, with insignificant volume of real criticism.

LOYAL — BUT . . .

The fact that nearly half of 1600 owners considered no other car is a strong indication of that owner loyalty which has always characterised the breed. A handful of other popular light cars came into the running, but not in significant volume. Owners said they chose the Beetle for its reliability, good value and

sound reputation, among other things — and a fair number had owned one before.

But it is the probable choice of car next time which shows that the immortal Beetle is starting to lose ground — mostly to its own cousins, the new front-wheel-drive Volkswagen models. Only one owner in seven plans to buy another Beetle, while one in three intends getting an Audi or Passat model.

The only outside competitor to emerge at this stage is the Citroën GS with a 10 per cent listing, and 28 per cent of owners are undecided.

SUMMARY

There is lots of life in the Beetle yet. It remains in volume production in several parts of the world — including South Africa — and the chances are good that it will eventually notch up a phenomenal 20 million sales total.

The owner loyalty is still there — particularly among younger motorists — and several owners gave total-cost breakdowns which showed remarkably-low overall running costs, to illustrate why Beetle ownership makes good sense.

The Beetle has become a legend to generations of South African motorists. Like the Wellington, Cape, man who said he chose the 1600 "because I wanted a Beetle from my childhood . . ."

Instrumentation and controls have always been rather rudimentary on the Beetle.

Owners like the reliability of the 1,6-litre engine — but not its noise output.

Luggage capacity — including the shallow frontal trunk — is a point of criticism.

OWNER'S COMMENTS

SOME PRAISE . . .

"Has not missed a beat in more than 60 000 km."

"After heavy rains made roads impassable for 22 days, only my Beetle and I got through." (A Natal owner).

"Fantastic reliability."

"Wonderful service in long-distance motoring all over the Republic."

"Best car in its class." (Several owners).

"Good for both town driving and long-distance runs."

"After enduring six years of wind and weather, coachwork condition remains spotless."

"Bodywork is solid and well-finished." (Many owners).

"Re-sale value is good."

"Diagnostic service system is excellent."

"Better than my previous Beetles."

"No teething troubles, and it just goes on and on."

"The Beetle is among the best small cars ever made."

"Takes rough roads well."

"Handles well on dirt."

"I love the way it seems to be eager to go!"

"The convertable rear space is a boon with children."

"No trouble on an 8 000 km tour of SWA."

"Wonderful overall economy because o little goes wrong."

"Most efficient handbrake I have come across."

"With the fold-down back seat and easily-removeable passenger seat, it is amazing what large objects can be carried."

"Quality of materials and finish are outstanding."

. . . AND SOME CRITICISM

"Lacks pulling power in top gear." (Several owners).

"Ventilation poor — needs a bigger air intake area." (Several owners).

"The fuel tank position in front of the windscreen is unsatisfactory, because of the fire danger in a head-on accident, and overflow leaks when the car stands in hot sun."

"Beetle concept is becoming outdated."

"Should have disc brakes at front." (Two or three owners).

"Very unstable in cross-winds." (Many owners).

"A few annoying rattles . . ."

"Both engine and wind noise levels are high."

"Luggage compartment is too small." (Several owners).

"Driving rain can wet the engine and cause hard starting."

"Access to the rear seat is poor."

"Instrumentation is sparse."

"The battery position under the seat is irritating."

"The car's tail tends to whip suddenly in hard cornering."

WHY A BEETLE?

"It has proved its reliability through the years."

"The best value for money." (Several owners).

"I need a dependable car for long-distance work."

"Price!"

"High trade-in offered on old car."

"Suits my pocket and saves me money."

"Had excellent service from previous Beetle." (Several owners).

"I like the shape!"

"There is something about Beetles . . ."

"A good car!"

"Its quality is unexcelled in its price range."

IMPERIAL DATA

A summary of the main figures from this report is given below in Imperial measures, for comparative purposes:

DISTANCES COVERED:

Total. . . . . 835 126 miles

Average monthly. . . 9 496 miles

OPERATING ECONOMY:

Fuel economy:

About town . . . . . . 26,6 m-p-g

Open road . . . . 31,8 m-p-g

Tyre life:

Cross-ply . . . . . . 21 000 miles

Radial-ply . . . . . . 35 000 miles

The Beetle That Tips Its Hat

In the 47 years since it was designed, and the 33 that it has been in civilian production, the VW Beetle has come half circle.

That is to say, the one that is still being sold in the U.S. has traveled those 180 degrees; the rest have spun the full 360 several times, twirling in some celestial dance to the place where Great Artifacts go when they die.

What we have left is the Beetle convertible; what the Beetle convertible has left is a great deal more than it started with. A third of the way through the 20th Century, the Beetle was conceived by Dr. Ferdinand Porsche as a European car that could do for the Continent what the Model T did for the U.S.—put its average working citizen on wheels. No customer car was produced until after the Second World War, but even those coming off the Wolfsburg production lines from 1945 until the mid-Sixties were faithful to Dr. Porsche's dream. They were utilitarian, they were efficient, they were cheap, they were durable—they were, in sum, exactly what their name said they were: people's cars.

And there is no question but that they worked a social revolution. The success

It is not long for this world, and when the VW Convertible is gone, we will have lost a friend—to say nothing of America's newest automotive status symbol

by Leon Mandel

of that revolution—the introduction of true mobility to Europe—was exactly correlated to VW's success in offering an alternative to contemporary European cars. Prior to the war, Europeans clung to the notion that cars should be expensive objects; perhaps not playthings for the rich, but certainly not utilitarian appliances for the proles. In the face of bitter opposition from the German auto industry, VW changed all that. The car for the common man had arrived—but only after its designers and builders fought a series of bitter battles on behalf of simple and

cheap transportation and the concept of providing everyone with an automobile.

That simple, straightforward car has joined the Scarab (an automotive beetle of another kind) in an Entymological Heaven. And a very strange transformation has overtaken its last living relative, the convertible.

It would not be fair to say that, with the convertible, the Beetle has gone soft in the head; but it *has* taken on a new role, it has rejected its humble origins, forgotten its simple forbears and become, yes, the darling of the DiscoSuedes.

USC cheerleaders in tassled Nikes troop in from Beverly Hills to buy white-on-white convertibles. Westchester matrons in Amalfis order them black-on-black. In Fort Worth, orange is big, a nice Southwestern contrast to $100 layered jeans. In Fairfield County, the Saks and Bonwit shoppers are not particular about color; the VW convertible is simply another outer garment to go with the current multi-skin look favored by suburban matrons. For at $7000, out the door, the once diffident bug has taken on a new aristocratic mein; it is the status car of the rank-conscious; the new-

The Beetle Convertible, one of the least likely candidates to have become an auto status symbol in the U.S., strikes a haughty pose in front of the stately governor's mansion in Carson City, Nevada.

Beetle Convertible

wave image of the born again profligate; the adorable ornament of the Highway Culture.

So if the Beetle convertible is trendy—on the cutting edge of trendy, as a matter of fact—it's only fair to ask why; asking at the same time whether fashion in this case is accompanied by value. How much car is it?

More than it looks to be. First off, it is perhaps the most highly developed appli-

ance of our times. During that near half-century in which first Dr. Ferdinand Porsche and then Heinz Nordhoff defined and then refined the Beetle, the car has undergone more running changes than a Las Vegas chorus girl. Nordhoff, the man who put VW back on its feet after the Second World War, might have a shot at recognizing the '78 Beetle convertible, but Dr. Professor Porsche would have to look long and hard at the plush and docile bauble built by Karmann for VW before he would recognize the outlines of his *kleinauto* in its silhouette.

In the grim Porsche days and after, the VW had a crash box, a split rear window and windshield, an engine that made barely enough power to propel the pre-cambrian VW downhill—so long as the hill was steep—virtually no amenities and doors that opened from the front.

The current convertible is an Eldo by comparison. It lacks a velour steering wheel, and there is neither simulated imitation wood-grained ashtray nor cathode ray tube readout miles-to-go and under-trunk temperature module. But it's got everything else a body could ask: engine, transmission, seats, top and—brace yourselves—running boards. Furthermore, all these automotive frivolities have been developed to a high degree. The once

vague shifter is now crisp and sure of itself; the engine, although encumbered with emissions equipment that would do a copper smelter proud, makes enough horsepower to get the driver into trouble if he's so inclined; the seats are typically German, that is to say, supportive if not compliant; and the top is what German tops have always been: plush, weatherproof and manual.

Nor, if Dr. Porsche could rise from the grave and be replanted behind the wheel of the VW, would he find much resem-

blance in feel and performance between his child of the '30s and this bright ornament of the last quarter of the century.

Early VWs—in fact VWs right up until the late '60s—had a penchant for treachery. That is to say, their drivers had to watch them every mile of the way, else they might find themselves looking at the engine cover through the windshield. Simply, VWs, no matter how compensat-

ed for weight bias, were almost as inclined to shuffle down the highway backwards as forwards. They were loud: The air-cooled engine seemed to do everything in its power to let the car's occupants know how hard it was working. They were 2000-pound weaklings. VW owners could get out of the way of your average spavined cow, they could avoid speed-observing wheelchairs, but in stock form they weren't exactly street racers. They were stingy. An unidentified miser in Australia once got 58 mpg on a VW, and 40 mpg was common. They were visible. In the '50s, VW jokes were Bob Hope staples. "...and how about the Texan who admitted his VW wasn't air conditioned but said he always kept a couple of cold ones in the refrigerator?" That kind of thing.

They are still loud and they are still stingy (test mileage over 1250 miles was just over 30 mpg). But in this 55-mph world, suddenly the Beetle's anemic performance doesn't seem objectionable. It is an honest 80-mph car and, as has always been true, 80 mph is also its cruising speed. It will get there gently but ineluctably.

It is in the handling, however, that great changes have been wrought. What was once a veritable cossack twirler of a car has become so intent on pursuing a safe, sane forward course that it is almost difficult to bend around a corner. As David Pearson might put it, the sumbitch pushes something awful. "Understeer," is what the technoids would call it. And that is part of VW's 180-degree turnaround. For a car that once wanted to pirouette down the interstate, the VW has become a model of single-minded pursuit of a straightline path of rectitude. You almost feel as though you're driving a '65 Dodge, it's so disinclined to help you help it around a bend in the road. That may not endear the convertible to embryonic Niki Laudas, but it sure makes life a lot easier for new VW

CONTINUED ON PAGE 172

Then and now: Back in 1939 motoring journalist Gordon Wilkins was invited to drive the first Volkswagen. Gordon, who at the time was on the staff of The Autocar, is seen (left) with the late Laurence Pomeroy, who was technical editor of the rival journal The Motor, during their test run of the first VW in Berlin, in February 1939. And 42 years later Gordon (below) was again invited to see a new Beetle – the 20,000,000th to be built – at Volkswagen Mexico's Puebla plant

Second time around

Another milestone for the VW Beetle

By Gordon Wilkins

IT IS ODD that the two best-selling cars in the history of the automobile have been "freaks," which had no lasting influence on car design in general. Henry Ford's Model T, having scored a world production record of 15,007,033, with its hand throttle, flywheel magneto and foot-operated gear change, was replaced by models which fell into line with contemporary practice, using conventional electrics, a synchromesh gearbox and manual gearchange. The VW Beetle, which broke the Model T's record in 1972, has failed to convert the rest of the world to rear engines, air cooling or swing axle rear suspension and was overtaken by water-cooled, front-wheel-drive models.

Both cars were promoted by superb organisers who employed the latest techniques of mass production (in Ford's case he invented mass production) to cut costs, who maintained strict quality control and made sure that spare parts were readily available. In the case of the Volkswagen, Heinrich Nordhoff promoted the rear engine and air cooling with such conviction that he persuaded other manufacturers that this was the only way to build a car The

Russians and the Japanese fell for it, driving themselves up the same blind alley. Even General Motors bought it, inflicting upon themselves one of the most expensive disasters in motoring history when they tried to translate the VW formula into

Bienvenidos a la producción del Volkswagen Sedán 20 millones.

Willkommen zur Produktion des 20 millionsten Käfers.

Welcome to the production of the 20 millionth Volkswagen Sedan:

American dimensions with the Corvair. It was more than an engineering and commercial failure; it unleashed Ralph Nader and the whole burgeoning consumer lobby to scourge the American industry.

Yet through it all the Beetle continues its incredible career. To say it has been replaced is not strictly true. Production ceased in Germany in January 1978, but continued in other parts of the world. We are unlikely to see another year like 1971 when 1,292,000 Beetles were built, but even in 1980 there was a respectable total of 245,208, of which 12,626 were exported to Europe for sale in Germany, Belgium, Italy, Austria and Switzerland. At present the car is being built in seven countries – Mexico, Brazil, Peru, Venezuela, Uruguay, Nigeria and the Philippines – and production is soon to start in Egypt. Current global production is about 1,000 a day. Not bad for a car which has been in production for 36 years.

As the last-known survivor of the journalists who were in Berlin in February 1939 to see the car launched and to try one of the 30 pre-production models built by Daimler-Benz, I was the guest of Volkswagen of Mexico on 15 May to see the 20 millionth Beetle roll off the assembly line at the Puebla factory.

After an ugly aberration with a

Old and new: Beetles and Golf (known in Mexico as Caribe) share the body line above the welcome sign at the Puebla factory

impressed me most was the VW's ability to cruise flat out at the maximum speed of 62 mph without the risk of breaking the engine. This was something unique in small-car design when the new *autobahnen* were littered with the smoking bits of engines that had failed during sustained fast driving. Even Rolls-Royce were advising their owners not to keep the throttle wide open for long periods.

There was just one instrument on that first VW, a speedometer. No fuel gauge was used. Instead a bit of bent wire worked the reserve tap on the fuel tank in the scuttle. Upholstery was in cheap cloth and general interior finish

The Mexican plant is one of several still producing large numbers of Beetles. There is less automation in the Mexican factory; there is no body drop, the chassis being jacked up to meet the body

curved windscreen, wide snout, MacPherson strut front suspension and double-jointed rear suspension, the Beetle is its old self once more, with flat windscreen, torsion bar front suspension and swing axles at the rear. Apart from a single-piece rear window, some exterior bright work, ventilation grilles behind the rear quarter windows and a nice metallic silver paint finish instead of the regulation blue-grey, the 20 millionth Beetle looked very like the car I drove in 1939 but in reality it is very different. Of 5,115 parts that go to make it, only one is the same as on the original — the rubber seal around the front bonnet over spare wheel, fuel tank and luggage space.

Seeing lines of them standing ready for delivery in the Mexican sunshine, it struck me more than ever that this is quite a beautiful shape which has resisted the passage of time since it was finalised in 1938 astonishingly well.

In 1939 the feature that

was very austere. The gearbox had no synchromesh; you had to learn how to double de-clutch in those days. And the brakes were cable-operated because the Nazis would not pay royalties to the Americans for a hydraulic system. The heater was feeble and output varied with engine speed, but as very few cars had any heaters at all, this was progress.

Nearly 200,000 Germans were buying savings stamps each week and when they had a book full, worth 990 Reichmarks — about 800 hours' pay for a skilled workman — they could exchange it for a car. None ever did, of course, but the claims haunted the new VW management after the War. A long legal battle resulted in the survivors being sold cars at a discount. The rest of the German motor industry never believed it could be done anyway, maintaining that the price of 990 Reichmarks would not even cover the cost of labour and materials, which was why Hitler had decided the State must do it.

During the War the factory at Wolfsburg was bombed and

All VW mechanics on experimental work were enrolled into the SS. Here they demonstrate the lightness of the car

when it was over, it had no legal owner. Neither the British nor the American industries wanted either the car or the factory. Henry Ford's remark that it was "Not worth a damn" has become a classic, and there it would have ended but for the British Army.

Lt-Col Michael McEvoy, who had worked with Arnold Zoller on superchargers for racing cars before the war, took over the ruined plant at Wolfsburg (then called Fallersleben, from the name of a nearby village) and used it as a repair workshop for tanks and trucks. Major Ivan Hirst was put in charge and as early as 1945 began building a few cars for the British Army.

Having got production running, Hirst was encouraged by Col. Radclyffe, the British military governor for the area, to sell some cars to German civilians, and then start an export campaign to raise funds to lessen the burden on the British

taxpayer. His experience with fleets of trucks held up during the War for lack of spare parts, led Major Hirst to insist that no cars were to be exported until stocks of spare parts had been established. He even went so far as to hold up the first consignment of export cars, destined for the Dutch importer Ben Pon, because the stipulated spare parts had not been ordered. So while the British Government was driving our own manufacturers to export every possible car whether spares and service were available or not, the British Army was establishing the policies which ensured the long-term success of the Volkswagen.

But the Army could not continue as a car manufacture for ever. One day a former manager of the General Motors truck plant at Brandenburg arrived on a

bicycle looking for a job. He seemed the right man to run the place, so Major Hirst handed the factory over to him as a going concern. That man was Heinrich Nordhoff.

He looked at the product and said "We are not selling a car; we are selling transportation." And 34 years later 1,000 buyers a day are still finding it the right transportation for their needs.

There are 1.95 million of them still running in West Germany, or about 8.5 per cent of the total cars in operation. Last year, with 146,000 sales they took 18.5 per cent of the Brazilian market and in Mexico 33,000 Beetles represented 11.6 per cent of the market.

The car may incorporate design principles now discredited, but it has been continuously developed and improved. Strict quality audit ensures that it maintains the same high standard of fit and finish wherever it is produced. There are local differences. In Mexico there is less automation and more hand work in the body; it simply would not be economic to install the fully automated body production with which Wolfsburg shook visitors from Detroit. And for sunny climes like Mexico and Brazil, the number of coats of paint is perhaps not as high as is required for the salt-laden winter roads of northern Europe.

As the Beetle soldiers on towards its 21st million, it proves once again that a great number of motorists are more interested in proven quality, reliability and economy than in the technical features of the design. ☐

Left: Austere interior of first VW. Top: The last survivor of the 30 pre-production VWs built by Daimler-Benz in 1938. It has done more than 300,000 miles. Above: The 24 hp engine of the first VW. The current model delivers more than twice as much power—

Gordon Wilkins (left) with Major Ivan Hirst, the man who started up production of the VW after World War II

COST CALCULATIONS FOR THE VOLKSWAGEN

A Contemporary View in 1939

Year of Proclamation of VW Project	19
	37
Foundation stone laid at VW Works	26
	5
	19
	38
Speed in km/h	100
Horsepower	24
Fuel consumption (lit/100 km.)	7
Length of car in cm.	420
Width of car in cm.	150
Height of car in cm.	145
Reichmarks	**990**

Figures for car dimensions were slightly adapted to get the right answer but the tabulation reflects the industry's view of the impracticality of making a car at the price fixed by the Nazis at that time.

La Cucaracha

by Jim Hall

PHOTOGRAPHY BY RANDY LEFFINGWELL

How often have you said, "These new cars are junk! I'd really like a brand-new car just like my '68 VW." Well, fret no more. A gang of California maniacs has just the car for you—a 1983 Beetle.

Yes, the famed Beetle was indeed dropped from German production lines, but it has since continued to be the mainstay of VW's Brazilian and Mexican factories. In fact, after it was unceremoniously dumped from the market in Germany, VW decided to import the Bug from Mexico to help satiate the diehard Kafervolks.

A group of astute Beetle lovers recently formed—brace yourselves—The Peoples Car Company (Solana Beach, California, 619/481-3505). Their plan is to import and certify Mexican Beetles. Taking advantage of the comical exchange rates of the peso in recent months, The Peoples Car Company can provide you with a brand-new 1983 Beetle for as little as $6995.

Your seven grand will buy you the only replicar built by the same company that manufactured the original. The Peoples Car Company Beetle is everything the 1968 Beetle was, for more. Remember the vague, heavy steering of the Beetle? It's

still there, as is the oceanliner-like throttle response. When driving the Peoples Car Beetle on the freeway, the engine merrily buzzes away begging you to shift into 5th. Depress the clutch, move the lever, and you realize there's no gear to shift into. Suddenly it's 1968. On the other hand, the potential for economical operation and (with proper maintenance) bulletproof reliability that made the original Bug such a phenomenon are still present. The air-cooled flat four is still a viable concept, at least in countries where it hasn't been regulated to death.

A few things have been improved since the last Beetle sedans were sold here back in 1976. The most noticeable of the improvements are the infinitely adjustable backrests on the front buckets. The ventilation system is loads better, too, though almost anything, even a broken windshield, would have been an improvement.

The less-than-contemporary road manners of the '83 Beetle will deter few of the car's potential buyers. Neither will the rather limited list of standard equipment; the long-time Beetlephile isn't really cognizant of the exact use of an instrument light rheostat anyway. And the option list with only air conditioning, Yugoslavian 165R15 "tires," and stylish sport wheels finished in genuine Chromette (fitted to the car in the photos) doesn't offer the kinds of features that swing sales. No, the Peoples Car Beetle is just the thing hundreds, maybe even thousands of Beetle owners have been waiting for. This car created a special kind of love affair, and love, as we all know, can occasionally transcend practical considerations. Which is why these folks would rather shell out seven grand on a bug than on a new Toyota Corolla SR-5. The Peoples Car Company is gonna sell as many as it can run across the border. (MT)

PHOTOGRAPHY: RON LIEBERSON

Sun Country VW Beetle

Interesting insect life from exotic Mexico.

• You can't kill the Beetle. It keeps coming back, just like some kind of tin cockroach. Even now, Beetles are scuttling across the border from Mexico, and a new infestation north of the Rio Grande is in the making.

The whole business began two years ago when the peso suffered radical devaluation. Boomers and hustlers on this side of the border realized that the disparity in value between dollar and peso made it potentially profitable to smuggle $2500 Beetles into the U.S. When the customs boys caught on to this act, most of these shady gringos went out of business. As a result of renewed interest in the Beetle, though, a number of legitimate entrepreneurs went into the business of purchasing Beetles made in Mexico and certifying them for the U.S. market.

The most serious of Beetle brokers appears to be Sun Country Leasing, 205 North Country Club Drive, Phoenix, Arizona (602–833–1872). Not only has Sun Country found a way to purchase Mexican Beetles by the boatload, but it's developed a country-wide distribution network and arranged a warranty program. Barry Mitchell, Sun Country's general manager, believes that the inquiries he's already received from enthusiasts, average citizens, rental-car companies, and more than a few car dealers (including Volkswagen dealers) indicate that Americans are ready to scoop up more than 20,000 Sun Country Beetles in the next eighteen months.

It doesn't take much more than a trip around the block to figure out why Americans like the Bug. It looks like one of those friction-motor toy cars you had when you

were a kid, and you get the same exhilaration from driving it as you did the first time you launched one of your toy cars across the living-room rug. The Sun Country Beetle is alert and willing, as friendly as the grin on its face.

A day of motoring around Phoenix brought out the made-in-Mexico Beetle's resemblance to the last Bugs seen within these shores. It's so utterly plain that it makes such commuter cars as the Chevette look downright pretentious, and its fit and finish are excellent. A slam of the door confirms that this Beetle is just as watertight as Volkswagen advertised it as in the mid-Sixties, making it the appropriate vehicle for those encounters with the *vados* of Baja. Even the price is still reasonable, at $6995

Vehicle type: rear-engine, rear-wheel-drive, 4-passenger, 2-door sedan	
Base price: $6995	
Engine type: air-cooled flat-4, magnesium crankcase, iron cylinders and aluminum heads, 1x2-bbl Solex carburetor	
Displacement	97 cu in, 1585cc
Power (C/D estimate)	48 bhp @ 4200 rpm
Transmission	4-speed automatic
Wheelbase	95.3 in
Length	163.4 in
Curb weight	2100 lbs
EPA fuel economy, city driving	26 mpg

(the last Beetle in the U.S., the convertible in 1977, cost $4919). The biggest difference is that this bug actually rides and handles better than ever before, thanks to the Goodyear Arrivas that Sun Country retrofits in place of the Mexican rubber.

Still, this is not exactly a brand-new replica of the German Beetle. As with the Brazilian Bug, the Mexican version is a hodgepodge of parts built with tooling shipped to the third world by the Volkswagen parent company. According to those who claim to be able to tell one Beetle from another, the body with the flat windshield and small rear window dates from the pre-1971 model, while the front fenders come from the Super Beetle and the rear taillights from the '73 German edition. Many of the interior controls and materials resemble those of the Rabbit. Drum brakes can be found at each wheel, and underneath the 1585cc, dual-port engine can be found a swing axle similar to the one that can be found in Dr. Porsche's original drawings for the car in the Thirties.

To bring the Mexican Beetle into compliance with DOT regulations, Sun Country fits the appropriate buzzers and lights, DOT-approved glass, new seatbelts and seat fabric, and door beams. Mechanical modifications include the Goodyear tires and a dual-circuit master cylinder. Finally, and most important, Sun Country doesn't skimp on the engineering of the Beetle's EPA-certified engine. Fairway Engineering gives the car an air-injection pump, twin three-way catalysts, and the feedback carburetor from the base '83 Rabbit. The result is a car that has the crisp throttle response and taut feel of a Beetle that could have been made in Germany only yesterday. And whereas maintenance can be a problem for the typical exoticar brought into the U.S. by gray-market boomers, you need look no further than your local circular of free advertising for a source of parts and service.

All the bad stuff about Beetles has been built in as well, of course. The body is about as aerodynamic as a paper cup, the front tires tuck under in the corners, and you have to open the door to fasten the seatbelt. These flaws remind you of how good the Volkswagen Rabbit really is. Even so, the Beetle is still wonderful to drive, a true participatory sport.

But why go on? We all know what the Beetle is about. It's almost as if it had been imprinted on our minds at birth. We can't help overlooking its anachronistic design and admiring its frank purposefulness. This is still a good car, and Sun Country has done a service by bringing it to us in spirit as well as in body. If, as Mitchell claims, the '85 EPA and DOT regulations will ensure that this is the last waltz for the Beetle, let it be known that it belongs on your dance card. You'll never know what driving is all about until you've been behind the wheel of a Bug. —*Michael Jordan*

Golden Beetle

The once and future Beetle.

BY TONY ASSENZA

• You already know all about this car. What hasn't been written about the Volkswagen Beetle you could put on the back of a postage stamp, and you'd still have lots of white space to play with. You don't need *Car and Driver* to tell you what the Beetle is all about. But 1988 is the 50th anniversary of the *Käfer* (German for "Beetle"), so we figured we'd take a look at how it came to be—and take a test drive

in the Golden Beetle, a real, remade-in-America Bug that you can buy today.

Of course, we're not dealing with just another car here. We're entering that weird universe where a car transcends being just a car and becomes an icon. Like the Coca-Cola bottle, the Xerox machine, the hammer and sickle, and even the swastika—to which it is historically related— the VW Beetle is a permanent cultural ar-

tifact, a feature of everyone's mental landscape. Anything that achieves such status requires little explanation. Send somebody to the fridge for beer and he knows just where to go, even if there is no Frigidaire in sight. Ask somebody to Xerox something and, no matter how much the Xerox Corporation resents the bastardization of its trade name, he knows just what to do, even if the nearest copier is an

IBM. Tell somebody that a Timex is the VW Beetle of wristwatches and the message is delivered in shorthand: it's cheap, durable, and accessible to anybody. And you can fix it with a pocketknife or a well-placed knuckle.

There is some confusion about the Beetle's origins, however. Contrary to what many believe, the Beetle did not spring fully formed from the mind of Ferdinand Porsche in 1934. Although Porsche's contributions should not be minimized, the concept of a lightweight people's car powered by a rear-mounted, air-cooled engine had been around for decades. Such automotive pioneers as Hans Ledwinka, Edmund Rumpler, Karl Rabe, and Josef Ganz all participated in projects that directly influenced the development of the Beetle.

Rumpler, for instance, patented a swing-axle design in 1903. The first manufacturer to use his design was the Blood Brothers Manufacturing Company, of Kalamazoo, Michigan, which introduced the Cornelian auto in 1913—and withdrew it from the market soon thereafter. In 1912, Ferry Porsche himself designed an air-cooled opposed four-cylinder aircraft engine for Austro-Daimler. But even Porsche's engine was not entirely original: De Dion–Bouton had patented a similar

design in 1895.

Rumpler unveiled his Tropfen-Auto (water-drop car) at the Berlin Auto Show in 1921. An aerodynamic and packaging triumph, the car was shaped roughly like a vertical airfoil and incorporated swing axles and a midships-mounted engine. The following year, the Czech maker Tatra introduced the Type 11, designed by Ledwinka An extremely influential car, it

featured a central tube backbone, swing axles, and a front-mounted, air-cooled opposed two-cylinder. Its tube backbone derived from the British Rover, built in 1904, and the French Simplicia, built in 1909. The Tatra's central backbone and the Tropfen-Auto's aerodynamics and packaging ultimately influenced the design of the Beetle.

Similarly, years before Adolf Hitler,

Ferdinand Porsche, and Daimler-Benz executive Jakob Werlin sat down at the Kaiserhof Hotel in Berlin to sketch out the *Führer*'s plans for a people's car, the German auto industry, together with the auto press and the government, was convinced of the country's need for an everyman's car—a practical vehicle that the average factory worker could afford to buy and maintain. When Hitler embarked on his mission to build such an automobile, he was merely echoing the voice of *das Volk*.

Even the name "Volkswagen" wasn't Hitler's. In 1932, the German company Standard Fahrzeugfabrik had built the Standard Superior, designed by Ganz, with remarkably Beetle-like looks and a rear-mounted, air-cooled engine. The sales brochures billed it as a *Deutschen Volkswagen*.

What Ledwinka, Rumpler, Tatra, Daimler-Benz, Porsche and his designer Karl Rabe, and a host of other engineers and smaller companies had in common was an abiding interest in a small, lightweight car that they could produce easily and cheaply. It's no surprise, given the state of the technology available to them, that they all found similar answers to the same question.

The rest is a history known to all. Over four decades of production, Volkswagen sold more than twenty million Beetles. The Bug drove a huge wedge into the U.S. market, exposing generations of Americans to the novel experience of buying foreign. For many of us who grew up in the postwar years, the Bug—usually a model with 100,000 miles on its clock and a rusted-through floorpan—was our first car. We went off to school in Bugs, froze in them in the winter, found out how many people we could cram inside the things before the tires started to rub the fenders, and even learned the basics of engine mechanics when their air-cooled four-cylinders up and quit. Of course, some of us just abandoned our Bugs where they died, salvaged their plates, and went looking for something a little newer.

For others, the love affair has never ended. Today, 50 years after the assembly of the first batch of 30 pre-production *Kraft durch Freude* (Strength through Joy) VWs, you can order a remanufactured Beetle—and one that's probably better than most of the Beetles we remember. When not probing his patients' urological systems, Dr. Joseph V. DiTrolio presides over Golden B Motor Cars, in Wayne, New Jersey, and for about $7000 he'll put you into a completely rebuilt Bug.

The Golden B factory, in Missoula, Montana, starts with a clean body, strips it down to nothing, and installs new or remanufactured parts, a process that takes 100 hours. The standard motor is a 1.6-

COUNTERPOINT

• What a treat! I owned a '63 Bug in high school, but it had been ages since I'd even sat in one. Over the past few years, I'd driven everything from Hyundais and Yugos to Testarossas and Countaches. How would the venerable VW hold up against today's machines?

Pretty well, it turns out. The Golden Beetle's air-cooled engine springs to life and revs energetically, though on the highway its drone will convince you that you're at the helm of a Beechcraft twin. The shifter works just fine: it snicks into place as easily as my '63's did, back when I was practicing clutch work in my parents' driveway. The driving position is pretty darn good, too. My only serious complaint is that the Bug can be a white-knuckles Interstate ride: in a strong wind, you have to fight for your lane the whole way.

But as nostalgia that you can actually use, the Golden Beetle is good fun. It's almost good enough to generate fond memories of my high-school days.
—*Arthur St. Antoine*

As I drink of our frosty Bug for the first time, I realize it's been eons since I've sampled one. The sun, working winter hours, long ago headed south, Old Man Winter is bitter as hell, and I've already heard that the Golden Beetle's heater is less than golden. Lighting off the raspy old four-banger brings it all back in a rush of *déjà VuW*. I do not look forward to being scuttled along before the wind or maybe rolled like dice by the ice.

I find my distrust seconded by perma-fog windows, toy wipers that sound like Glenn Ford's saddle (*grich-grich . . . grich-grich . . .*), and a tangled web of de

Sadish restraint straps. But the heater does produce detectable heat. And except when the wind blows the Bug's nose, the thing proves capable of beetling cleanly across Mother Nature's midwinter mucus.

Still, you *must* soft-pedal the touchy chassis. This *may* allow you to keep your heading when all about you are losing theirs. This golden oldie might be a giggle in good weather, but its delicate balance is too sly to be trusted when facing winter head-on. —*Larry Griffin*

Let me say right off that I think the Golden Beetle is an absurd automobile in this day and age. This resurrected Bug has all the shortcomings of the original, including—to mention just a few—no power, no roadholding, no room, and no heat. And since Beetles aren't nearly rare enough to be worth collecting, I can't imagine why any reasonable person would buy one.

Having said that, honesty compels me to admit that the Beetle is not without its charms. It's one of the few cars around that can be driven flat out all the time. It even seems to enjoy the hard life. The engine loves to be flogged mercilessly between shifts. The transmission responds precisely to a light and easy touch, as does the direct, unassisted steering. The chassis doesn't provide much grip, but a late-model Beetle like our test car isn't exactly treacherous, either.

I still wouldn't want to own a Bug, but after a short drive in the Golden Beetle, I understand a little better why the original people's car remains the best-selling automobile of all time. —*Csaba Csere*

liter flat four, producing 52 hp. Two stages of tuning are available, yielding 68 and 75 hp. If you hunger for more, Missoula will substitute a 1.8-liter four, which produces a healthy 92 hp.

DiTrolio is in the business for all the right reasons. He likes the cars, which he calls Golden Beetles, and he's having fun running the company. He shipped us one of his standard models, and from the first turn of the wheel we felt as if we had booked passage on Mr. Peabody's Wayback Machine. Everything was there, just the way we remembered it. The goofy floor-mounted pedals, which Porsche never has shaken out of its genetic programming. The straight-backed seats. That thing with the round holes that passed for a dashboard and instrument panel. The clatter from the engine. The cardboard headliner. The claustrophobic cabin, like an upholstered phone booth. It was terrific.

When you're talking about Beetles, such terms as "handling" and "performance" are strictly theoretical. Like the Bugs of old, the Golden Beetle goes more or less where you point it and won't slide off the road without undue provocation. Its heating system is as hypothetical as its performance envelope. If you need a little warmth, press the cigarette lighter and wave it around the cabin. If you need a little more, buy a German shepherd and make him sit on your lap. DiTrolio and company have modified VW's heating system as best they could, but there is only so much one can do with Bug heaters.

Mechanically, the Golden Beetle is surprisingly well assembled. Most people would have a hard time duplicating the rebuild process in their back yards for the kind of money GB Motor Cars charges. In fact, you'd probably spend a lot more if you tried to match the build quality of the little ingot.

If you long to relive your golden youth in a Golden Beetle, call 201–890–0533. And then wait. Golden B Motor Cars produces only 100 Bugs a year, 25 of which are convertibles, and the line wraps around the block. You might have to content yourself with a Justy until your name rises to the top of the list. And if you live in California, you're out of luck: at this point in the Golden Beetle's development, it's available only as a 49-state car. The Bug may be immortal, but it can't pass California's tough emissions tests.

In the age of future shock, it's comforting that the people's car is still with us. It's not making as many friends as it used to, but we've got a hunch that it will be around for eternity. You can bet that someday soon, some kid going off to his first day at the University of Southern Mars will probably get there in a Beetle.●

Vehicle type: rear-engine, rear-wheel-drive, 2+2-passenger, 2-door coupe

Price as tested: $7500

Options on test car: base Golden Beetle, $6250; Empi wheels and all-season tires, $400; sound system, $200; sport stripes, $100; sport exhaust system and steering wheel, $50; freight, $500

Sound system: Unic RV-908 AM/FM-stereo radio/cassette, 2 speakers

ENGINE
Type	flat 4, magnesium crankcase, iron cylinders, and aluminum heads
Bore x stroke	3.37 x 2.72 in, 85.5 x 69.0mm
Displacement	97 cu in, 1585cc
Compression ratio	7.5:1
Carburetion	1x1-bbl Solex 30 PICT-3
Emissions controls	none
Valve gear	pushrods
Power (SAE net)	52 bhp @ 4400 rpm
Torque (SAE net)	82 lb-ft @ 3000 rpm

DRIVETRAIN
Transmission	4-speed
Final-drive ratio	4.13:1

Gear	Ratio	Mph/1000 rpm	Max. test speed
I	3.80	4.7	21 mph (4500 rpm)
II	2.06	8.6	39 mph (4500 rpm)
III	1.26	14.1	63 mph (4500 rpm)
IV	0.89	19.9	82 mph (4100 rpm)

DIMENSIONS AND CAPACITIES
Wheelbase	94.5 in
Track, F/R	51.6/53.3 in
Length	158.6 in
Width	61.0 in
Height	59.1 in
Ground clearance	5.9 in
Curb weight	1807 lb
Weight distribution, F/R	40.8/59.2%
Fuel capacity	10.6 gal
Oil capacity	2.7 qt

CHASSIS/BODY
Type	unit construction
Body material	welded steel stampings

INTERIOR
SAE volume, front seat	46 cu ft
rear seat	31 cu ft
trunk space	5 cu ft
Front seats	bucket
Seat adjustments	fore and aft, seatback angle
General comfort	poor **fair** good excellent
Fore-and-aft support	poor **fair** good excellent
Lateral support	**poor** fair good excellent

SUSPENSION
F:	ind, 2 trailing arms per side, torsion bars, anti-roll bar
R:	ind, semi-trailing arm, torsion bars

STEERING
Type	worm-and-roller
Turns lock-to-lock	2.9
Turning circle curb-to-curb	35.8 ft

BRAKES
F:	9.1 x 1.6-in cast-iron drum
R:	9.1 x 1.6-in cast-iron drum
Power assist	none

WHEELS AND TIRES
Wheel size	5.5 x 15 in
Wheel type	cast aluminum
Tires	B.F. Goodrich Lifesaver GT4 M+S, 165SR-15
Test inflation pressures, F/R	26/26 psi

CAR AND DRIVER TEST RESULTS

ACCELERATION — Seconds

Zero to 30 mph	4.2
40 mph	7.0
50 mph	10.8
60 mph	17.0
70 mph	26.7
Top-gear passing time, 30–50 mph	10.5
50–70 mph	17.0
Standing ¼-mile	20.2 sec @ 65 mph
Top speed	82 mph

BRAKING
70–0 mph @ impending lockup	245 ft
Modulation	poor fair good **excellent**
Fade	none **moderate** heavy
Front-rear balance	poor fair **good**

HANDLING
Roadholding, 300-ft-dia skidpad	0.62 g
Understeer	**minimal** moderate excessive

COAST-DOWN MEASUREMENTS
Road horsepower @ 30 mph	4 hp
50 mph	11 hp
70 mph	27 hp

FUEL ECONOMY
C/D observed fuel economy	**21 mpg**

INTERIOR SOUND LEVEL
Idle	64 dBA
Full-throttle acceleration	85 dBA
70-mph cruising	72 dBA
70-mph coasting	71 dBA

BUG PLUG

Wilson McComb goes on a Beetle hunt — and finds it a
fascinating pursuit

Subtle changes were made throughout the Beetle's life. This is a 'flat screen' car as opposed to later curved screen versions

THE car that almost nobody wanted after the Second World War — rejected by Sir William Rootes as having "not much future" when Britain had the chance of taking over the factory, and by Henry Ford II as "not worth a damn" when it was offered to America — is fast becoming one of the most sought-after of affordable collectors' vehicles. "The Volkswagen Beetle," one enthusiast said to me recently, "is really the only *different* car you can buy that's both reliable and available at a reasonable price."

If that sounds like an overstatement, that's how Beetle enthusiasts are. They have formed more than 80 clubs in the UK alone — heaven knows how many worldwide — and made the car an essential part of their lifestyle, with a special vocabulary (Split, Oval, Kübel, Cabrio, Hebbmüller, Baby Moon, Pope's Nose) that has to be learned before conversation can proceed. But I found them the most relaxed, friendly and helpful people I've met in a long time, their love for the Beetle so warm and infectious that I wanted to rush out and buy one.

For it is truly the most extraordinary vehicle. Well over half-a-century since Adolf Hitler instructed Dr Porsche to design an inexpensive car for the German people, it is still possible to buy a brand-new one in Mexico, where some 90 a day roll off the assembly lines together with CKD kits for such third-world markets as Nigeria. It's almost as if our own Series E Morris Eight had become such a success that, when production restarted after the War, it continued right through to today instead of being discontinued 40 years ago — not to mention the fact that the successor to the Series E, the Morris Minor, *also* went out of production 17 years ago! The VW Beetle is the best-selling motor car of all time, with a grand total of more than 20 million built, far outstripping the 15 million of that other famous People's Car, the Model T Ford. And since the basic design is now 55 years old it must be thoroughly outdated, so why do otherwise sane individuals go dotty about them?

Robin Wager, editor of the monthly *VW Motoring*, says the three main attractions of the Beetle are simplicity, reliability and character.

Simplicity was designed into the Beetle

from the start. A ribbed steel platform incorporates a tubular 'backbone' carrying the front suspension at one end and the air-cooled, flat-four engine and transaxle at the other. The body is fixed on top, and sealed up in such a way that, as the American ads used to say, "It definitely floats — but not indefinitely." The front or boot lid, the rear lid or bonnet, the four wings and two doors are all bolted on, but so well fitted that it's no easy task to close the second door unless you leave a window open. Accessibility is remarkable, on the whole, for the entire front 'axle' assembly is held by four bolts and a capable chap can whip out the engine in half-an-hour, but the main controls run inside the backbone. This keeps them well protected from the weather but is bad news if they ever do need attention; changing a clutch cable, for instance, is a three-hour job involving four-letter words.

There are few frills on a Beetle, and this ultra-simple specification forms the basis of the car's reliability, with its uncomplicated torsion-bar suspension and unstressed low-compression engine allied to an overdrive top gear that allows the (admittedly modest) maximum speed to be maintained indefinitely. A friend of mine owned his Beetle for 14 years, in which time 104,000 miles without needing more than routine servicing, one replacement clutch and three exhaust systems. In all that time he never had to take the heads off. There is in this country another Beetle which has now covered more than 800,000 miles in the hands of its original owner, who bought it new in Germany in 1951 (for £325). But this one, it must be admitted, went through three engines in its first 744,000 miles and needed a new gearbox after only 727,000.

Character? This, I suspect (and I should get danger money for saying it), owes much to the Beetle's designed-in idiosyncrasies. The combination of swing-axle rear suspension and a 41/59 per cent weight distribution makes for handling characteristics that are . . . well, *unusual*. Even Mick Martineau of the VW Cabriolet Owners' Club, who's owned half-a-dozen Beetles of various types, says: "In windy weather the front end sways around if you don't keep the fuel-tank full. Newcomers find it a bit terrifying at first, but you get used to it." Elderly Beetles have been known to burn out when a neglected petrol-pipe union drips fuel on to a hot engine: "As the engine's at the back, you don't smell the petrol and you may not smell the burning until it's too late." Less dramatically but still expensively, they may also overheat: "If there's any lack of power — slogging up a hill, say — you must stop at once and investigate. Water-cooled cars will plod on until they're boiling, and you see the steam. Beetles give no warning because they're air-cooled, so they will run until they sieze solid. The Cabrio is very inclined to overheat because it has fewer air intakes, and also the air-flow changes when you put the top down. Doesn't get sucked in so well."

Because it's at the back, you scarcely notice that the engine is noisier; air-cooled engines run on wider clearances than water-cooled units, and lack the sound-deadening effects of a water-jacket. Wider clearances probably contribute to the Beetle's well-known thirst. "Engine efficiency is terrible, really," says Peter Lambourne, who runs the 'Herbie Heritage' Beetle establishment near Chichester, "but that's where you get the reliability. Some of my customers' cars I don't see from one year to the next. I had one woman in here who said there was always a queue of cars behind hers — it wouldn't do more than 30mph. Turned out that the timing was almost 30 degrees out, but the damned thing was still going, still starting every morning and getting her to work. I fixed the timing and off she went!" On the subject of fuel consumption, Mick Martineau says: "By today's standards it's appalling, but it's very largely a matter of which way the wind's blowing. Beetles may look a slippery shape but they aren't — especially the flat-screen cars. The Cabrio is thirsty, top up or down, because it's so much heavier than the saloons."

There are other little foibles, like having almost no luggage space unless you use

Above, the well-presented interior of Peter Lambourne's 1956 split-window sedan, UPX 139 which is completely original except for a respray a couple of years ago

Mick Martineau's 1978 Cabriolet is well-known within the VW Cabriolet Owners Club. It's his eighth Beetle, counting the ordinary sedan that he uses as everday transport

the back seat; there's more in what Americans call the Superbug with its pregnant-looking front and MacPherson ifs, which allows the spare wheel to lie flat, but this suspension can be troublesome compared to the transverse torsion-bar and trailing link set-up. Some ardent Veedub types deny the very name of Beetle to these models, or even to 12-volt (post-1967) cars — but have you tried living with 6-volt electrics in modern traffic? It is possible to buy 6-volt halogen bulbs, but they take some finding. Otherwise the Bosch equipment is as good as you'd expect, and if the wiper motor burns out (which does happen) it's probably due to a build-up of rust on the wiper spindles. Talking of rust, you will soon regret it if you Waxoyl the sills on a Beetle. They're called 'heater channels', not sills, because they carry the hot air from the heat-exchangers, and a rust-proofing effort like this will fill the whole car with a horrible oily pong.

For would-be buyers, the long production life ensures an enormous price-range, the more sought-after models now in the five-figure bracket because collectors have snapped them up in the last five years or so. You will never see a split-window Beetle on the road in Britain nowadays, and even the oval-window cars are getting scarce. The 'good runner' of a year or two ago is now twice the £300-£400 it used to cost, and you have to shop around for anything decent at less than £1,000.

But that's fair enough for a Classic car, so which is the Beetle to look for? "Depends what you want to do with the car," says Peter Lambourne. "For practical mucking-about, Splits and Ovals are out. Young people go for the Superbug because it's sporty, the colours catch the eye, it goes well with the 1600 engine and it handles quite well, too (for a Beetle!). Me, I don't like them. I don't like the big windscreen, the seats are terrible, and the build quality isn't good. Neither is the metal. Work on a Sixties Beetle and you can get a nice-quality weld because it's good steel; weld a Seventies Beetle and it spits back at you, like a Fiat or an Alfa. For somebody who wants something a bit better, I'd say look for a really good Sixties Beetle — and a 1500 is the one to get."

Mick Martineau also feels the later Beetles were not so well made, while protesting that he hates to be quoted: "Everyone is entitled to his own opinion. You must buy what suits *you* — and be very wary of condition. I know a chap in Brighton who will buy a Beetle in any condition. Inside two days he'll have resprayed it over the rust, sent it to the Shoreham auction and doubled his money; he does that twice a week. People buy them because they look beautiful, they seem cheap, and in six months they're falling apart. I wouldn't even touch a car that's been undersealed; I like to see what's happening to the metal. I prefer ordinary body paint sprayed with Waxoyl.

"Beetles have this tremendous reputation for being solid, sturdy cars that don't rust and keep going for ever. Maybe it was like that when they were new, or say five years old. Now most of them are

15 years old or more and there's going to be things wrong with them; there's going to be some rust. Buying a car of that age, you've got to take a good look at it. There are a few specialist dealers but their prices are high; better to buy a well-maintained car through one of the VW clubs."

Peter and Mick both stress the need for reasonable maintenance, so many Beetles having been run on a shoestring with unfortunate results. "I had one guy," says Peter, "who complained that his engine had gone bang. I asked him when he'd changed the oil and found out he'd *never* changed it — and he'd had the car for seven years! People don't realise the oil is an intrinsic part of the cooling system on a Beetle. You must change it every 3,000 miles." Mick agrees: "Every 3,000 miles, religiously — and use a good-quality oil, not El Cheapo. Use a leaded petrol but not four-star, or it'll overheat in summer. *And leave well alone!* Beetles are not for the Sunday tweaker, forever fiddling about. Far better to spend your time washing the car underneath, where it matters. It only takes a minute or two with a hose. Then spray it once a year with Waxoyl." Peter says a Beetle will always give good service if it's looked after, but adds a warning: "The plug leads, the rotor arm, the distributor cap — they're only as good as on any other car, and they don't last for ever. I get panic calls for some silly little ignition fault; the engine's fine, really, but the car's broken down."

"You can buy cheaper panels but what you save in price you can lose on fitting time"

Modern garages are not much help with any Classic car, and the mechanics in your local VW-Audi establishment probably haven't a clue about Beetles, so you can either go to a specialist or look after the car yourself. The spares situation is marvellous, though, because the sheer volume of cars made ensures that the supply won't suddenly dry up. There are good pickings in the scrapyards, and sometimes you can strike lucky when a dealer is clearing out his old stock — though spares from dealers tend to be expensive. Indeed, most genuine German-made components are pricey and you may have to wait a long time for them, but the Beetle owner is fortunate because he has an alternative — he can buy parts made in Brazil, Mexico or elsewhere. "I would only use German clutches, brake shoes, stuff like that," says Peter Lambourne. "But it isn't everyone who wants to pay £20 for a German-made shocker when he can buy a Brazilian one for £12. Beetles are not performance cars, so you don't need top-rate stuff all the way. A proper VAG chrome headlamp rim for an early car is £27, but you can get a plastic one from Brazil for £6, and it looks just fine. Most of my body panels come from Veng in Denmark. There's a good range at the

right price, they're decent metal and they fit well. You can buy cheaper panels from Italy, for instance, but they're really terrible; whatever you save on price, you lose on fitting-time." Mick Martineau has found that windscreen specialists can supply almost any of the many different Beetle screens, toughened or laminated, and even with a top tint. "But don't expect you local Kwik-Fit to come up with an exhaust for you — they won't look at Beetles!"

Despite its apparent simplicity, a Beetle is complicated enough when it comes to doing a restoration. "There are a lot of little box-sections to play about with," says Mick, "and parts for the Cabrio have a way of being quite different from the equivalent saloon bits. Before spending the money involved in a proper restoration, I'd say you must *know* the Beetle and you must *love* the Beetle. You really have to study it — read as much as you can about it."

Although there are so many VW clubs in Britain, only one is listed as being RAC-recognised because members are for the most part not interested in speed events, rallies or other serious competitions. The VWOC of Great Britain is split into regional centres, of which the most active are in London and Hertfordshire, and their doings include visits to the VW factories in Germany *and* Mexico, plus get-togethers with Continental clubs. There is, I think, a tendency for Beetle clubs to shift around somewhat, appearing and disappearing or changing their names, but they seem to co-operate pretty well when it comes to organising their major affairs such as "VW Action" at Stoneleigh (usually in late August or early September, with an attendance of 30,000 or more).

On such occasions you can see examples of rare and much-cherished Beetles, hear heated arguments between Concours entrants about the correct wiper-arms or tail-lamps, or watch well-rehearsed teams drive a Beetle into the arena, remove and replace the engine in around two minutes (they bleed a lot, but they do it!), then drive it away again.

Know your Beetle

(This can only be a rough guide to Beetle models because there were so many. Changes were made at different times for Standard and De Luxe, saloon and convertible models, and for markets such as North America. Up to mid-1955, Beetles were designated by calendar year, but afterwards VW adopted the US Model Year system.)

Although the original design of the Beetle was finalised by the end of 1938, production was delayed until August 1940 and the first saloons were reserved for Nazi Party officials. Production restarted at the newly-renamed Wolfsburg plant in 1945, mainly for the British Army during the occupation of Germany. These were very simple cars with 1131cc (25bhp) engines, non-synchro gearboxes, mechanical brakes and no brightwork, All had the split rear window of 1938 (1937 prototypes had no rear window at all!).

Export versions with hydraulic brakes, softer suspension and a part-synchro

Above, don't let a tree fall on your Beetle, otherwise it may end up looking like this!

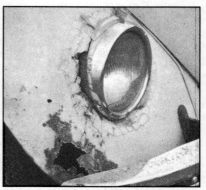

Mixed Beetles outside Peter Lambourn's business which is whimsically known as 'Herbie's Heritage' after the Disney film about the Beetle with a mind of its own

So Beetles don't rust, eh? This is an L-reg example showing its age

gearbox were an alternative in the early Fifties, and in March 1953 the distinctive split window was replaced by a small, one-piece oval rear window. In December 1953 the 1131cc engine gave way to an 1192cc unit rated at 30bhp in Europe (36bhp in the USA). Semaphore-arm trafficators were replaced by flashers in 1955 for the American market, but not until 1960 in Europe. 1958 Model Year cars had a larger windscreen and rear window.

A major redesign of the 1200 engine for 1961 included a new crankshaft and a higher compression ratio, but the gearing was made lower although there was more power and more torque — giving better acceleration but poorer fuel economy. Luggage space was increased, and an all-synchromesh gearbox fitted.

An optional 1300 (1285cc) engine was made available for 1966 and a 1500 (1493cc) engine for 1967, both in addition to the 1200 unit. In 1967 the original 6-volt electrical system gave way to 12-volt, with an alternator instead of a dynamo. New sealed-beam headlamps, placed vertically, replaced the earlier sloping lamps with separate bulbs. Automatic transmission was another option in the 1968 Model Year, with semi-trailing-arm rear suspension instead of swing-axle.

Mainly for America, VW produced the optional Series 1302 or Superbug in 1970. It had not only the trailing-arm rear suspension but MacPherson-strut front suspension, allowing the spare wheel to lie flat; the whole front end was reshaped, with a bigger front lid, to provide more luggage space. The optional 1500 engine gave way to an optional 1600 (1584cc),

this and the 1300 gaining twin outlet ports to improve their breathing. So there were now a minimum of four Beetle models: the 1200 with its torsion-bar front suspension; the same car with optional 1300 engine; the MacPherson-strut 1302 with 1300 engine; and the same car with 1600 engine. But for 1973 the 1302 Series was dropped in favour of the 1303 Series. This was mechanically similar but the flat screen was replaced by a large wraparound windscreen with a bigger rear window and large round tail-lamps. By 1974 the US-market cars had energy-absorbing bumpers and fuel-injection engines which offered a very poor performance.

In July 1974 the last Beetle was built at Wolfsburg but production continued at Emden, Brussels, Brazil and Mexico. The 1600-engined Superbug saloon was dropped in 1975 and the 1300-engined car in 1976, but both continued to be built in cabriolet form by Karmann until January 1980. Thereafter only the 1200-engined torsion-bar saloon remained in production. The last German-made Beetle saloon left the Emden plant on January 19 1978. Cars assembled in Brazil or Mexico were still marketed in Europe until the end of 1986. Volkswagen Beetles with 1200 engines and torsion-bar suspension are still built in Mexico today.

Among the first Volkswagen Beetles brought into Britain was this 1948 example bought by Mr A J Colbourne-Baber who went on to become the UK's first VW dealer in 1953

First job was to drain engine oil while it was warm and replenish the sump. Beetle doesn't have conventional filter but sludge-trap.

Be brave and save £80 a year with a ...

BEETLE SERVICE

VW created a legend in reliability with the Beetle. But open the boot-lid (or is it bonnet) and you will begin to wonder how such an abortion of pulleys, wires and pipes could ever slog on for mile after mile.

We decided to service a Beetle to see just how hard it is. And the job was an absolute pig.

But an explanation is required before all you Beetle owners rush off to your nearest VW dealer and lash out £40 plus parts for a major service.

The service would have been a relatively simple task, apart from needing a mammoth torque wrench, and magic mechanic Graham Auger was confident of knocking the job off in a few hours.

But our Beetle turned out to be the most cantankerous Kraut he'd ever had the pleasure of laying spanners on. We'll tell the story. Hopefully, you'll learn more than a little, not only about VWs but also the virtues of care and regular servicing.

The car had a slightly blurred history. It once belonged to the German post office and had been imported to England, given an X-registration plate and flogged to a colleague as a 1972 1,200 cc model.

However, none of the 1972-type parts we bought fitted and the old components had to be taken to a motor factors for matching up. The car was obviously older than the owner thought.

Lots of parts were seized (some beyond belief) despite the owner having it "regularly serviced".

The star ratings show how easy or hard we reckon the job — from ★★★★★ for incredibly simple down to ★ for leave it to the experts!

part one

Anyway, back to the biz and the first job was to loosen the wheelnuts (for later

removal), jack up the car and firmly support it with axle stands all round. It must be on an even keel for checking oil levels.

The sump plug was undone and the warm engine oil drained out into a suitable container. Our Beetle didn't have the usual throwaway filter but a metal sludge-trap which was unbolted from the sump and cleaned in solvent. The trap and plug were replaced and 4.4 pints of fresh oil poured into the engine.

We removed the Allen bolt in the side of the transaxle assembly to check that level. It was O.K.

The clutch pedal should have free movement of $\frac{1}{2}$ inch. Ours had none so Graham adjusted the cable by unscrewing the butterfly on the threaded clutch-housing end. Dead fiddly but not difficult.

While underneath, all metal brake pipes were inspected for rusting and flexible hoses for cracks or splits. Shock absorbers were examined for leaks and Graham had a good look at the floor-pan.

Unfortunately, the tail-end of the exhaust was holed with rust — an MoT failure point. The Beetle owner's certificate runs out soon but he was relieved to find out the section can be bought fairly cheaply and is easily fitted.

Brakes ★ ★ ★

Graham next turned his talented talons to the front end. He waggled and rocked the wheels to check for play in the bearings and swivel joints.

There was slight movement and he pinpointed it to the steering box. Another possible MoT failure point which will be dealt with shortly.

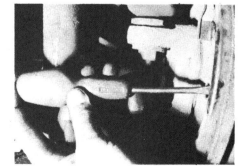

Brake shoes must be released to take off hub. A screwdriver is poked through a hole in the brake backplate to turn knurled nut.

Transaxle oil level was checked by removing this Allen screw. In our case it was O.K. Don't forget to keep car on even keel.

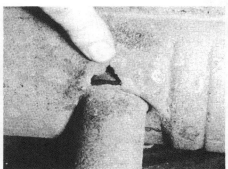

First bit of bad news. Exhuast tail-box was rotten which is an MoT failure point. Luckily it can be replaced fairly easily and cheaply.

Nearside front wheel cannot be removed until speedo cable retaining Allen screw is taken out. Big hub nut is left-hand thread on this side.

The wheels were removed and tyres examined. The front offside was worn on its outside edges due to under-inflation. More expense for the owner. The brake drums were taken off. The nearside drum is held by a left-handed thread nut. First, a small bolt was taken out from the speedo cable which drives through the hub. It's dead easy to lose so it was placed where we could find it again.

Rubber bungs in the brake backplates were prised out with a screwdriver. The two outside holes let you have a sneak look at the shoes to check for wear. The middle hole gives access to a knurled adjuster. The brakes were slackened with a screwdriver and drums gently tapped off.

What a sight. The shoes were down to their rivets and the drums so badly scored they needed replacing. Graham reckoned the drums hadn't been off for many thousands of miles (so much for "regular services") and clouds of dust billowed out. This stuff is dangerous with a capital D — don't inhale it.

The wheel cylinders weren't leaking or seized and new shoes were fitted which was a simple job. Just take off the spring-loaded retaining washers with pliers and prise off the shoes with a brake tool or stout pliers. Replacement is reverse of dismantling.

Fitting new drums meant new wheel bearings as a matter of policy.

The bearings were packed with grease and drums replaced. Retaining nuts were tightened to 15 lbs. ft. and then slackened so there was the tiniest hint of sideways play.

The brake pedal was depressed to centralise the shoes and then they were adjusted by turning the knurled nut through the hole in the backplate. Turn until the drum locks and slacken until it just turns freely.

Now for the back brakes . . . and we hope that Graham doesn't read this article and remind himself of the misery he suffered.

Rear drums ★★

Each drum is held by a big nut which is a trifle tight, shall we say. Graham selected the right socket and puffed and heaved for all he was worth. Large extension bars and foul language were also employed to no avail.

Finally, he got his biggest and most-treasured torque wrench, attached it to the socket and jumped on it. CRACK. Nut undone? No. Graham's wrench sheared its square-headed drive.

Luckily, he knows somebody who works on lorries and has an almighty pneumatic wrench. This only just did the job.

We appreciate that the nut is tight — 253 lbs. ft. — but it should have come off much easier. Had the car been regularly serviced etc. etc. . . . . you get the point.

The shoes were slackened in the same manner as the front sets and drum tapped off. Bare rivets, scored drums . . . exactly the same story. That added up to new shoes all round and four new drums. The wheel cylinders were O.K. (big deal).

Sometimes the handbrake cable needs adjusting after fitting new shoes. That's achieved by undoing or doing up the two

nuts underneath the rubber shroud on the lever. Luckily, ours didn't.

part two
Tappets ★★★

With all this misery behind him, Graham turned his attention to the tappets. Be thankful Mini and Cortina owners etc. Beetle tappets hang down the sides of the engine (flat-four, remember?). The easiest way to reach them is with the wheels removed which they still were, in our case. The two tappet covers are held by spring clips which are prised off with a screwdriver.

Plugs were removed, using a socket and extension, to make it easy to turn over the engine. All the tappets are set at six thou (cold) unless a sticker in the engine compartment states otherwise.

The procedure is involved but not complicated so take careful note. Number one cylinder is on the right of the engine (viewed from the rear) at the flywheel (gearbox) end. Number two is the same side at the rear of the engine (the bit nearest you). Number three is on the left at the flywheel end ' and number four immediately in front of it.

Turn the engine with a spanner until the rotor arm matches up with a notch on the distributor rim. This is number one firing stroke. Confirm this by looking at the timing mark on the crankshaft pulley which lines up with the join in the crankcase.

Both valves are now closed on number one and the tappets ready for adjustment.

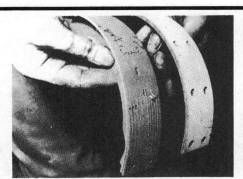

Just look at those shoes. The poor old Beetle obviously hadn't been properly serviced for ages. New shoes needed both sides.

Even worse were both front drums. They were too bad to save and needed replacing . . . an extremely expensive business.

Another MoT failure point. This tyre was well worn on the front offside. Wear was on edges indicating under-inflation.

Rear brake drums were absolute pigs to remove. Same story as the front. Worn linings had taken their toll with rivets scoring deeply.

Tappets hang down the side of the engine and are best reached with rear wheels removed. Setting them is involved but not difficult.

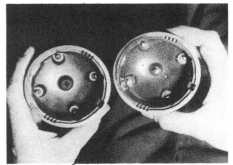

No wonder the Beetle had been running rough. Carbon brush in old distributor cap (right) had virtually disintegrated.

Simply slacken the locknut and adjust the screw, re-tightening the locknut.

Turn the engine anti-clockwise so the rotor arm rotates 90 degrees and repeat the procedure for number two cylinder. By progressively turning the rotor through 90 degrees, you can work your way round all the four pots.

Distributor ★ ★ ★

Graham examined the sparking plugs and two were as black as a coal-miner's hobnail boots. That was sorted out later. Anyway, a new set of plugs were gapped to 23 thou. and fitted.

The carbon brush in the distributor cap had virtually disintegrated and the rotor arm also needed replacing. We bought new ones together with a set of points.

Graham then turned to the ignition timing. And this is where things get a bit confused. All the engines are strobe timed at 7½ degrees b.t.d.c. Automatics with a torque converter are set at t.d.c. But throughout the years, the crankshaft pulleys had a varying number of notches denoting varying settings. Ours had one notch denoting t.d.c. and the 7½ degrees mark must be worked out with a protractor. There are so many variations it is easiest to get in touch with your local VW dealer and quote the engine and chassis number for an accurate reference.

Define the two reference points with white paint or, preferably, typists' correcting fluid. The engine should be timed at idling speed with the vacuum advance disconnected and plugged.

Static timing, however, is a lot easier although not so accurate on the 1,200 cc engine. You simply line up the notch and crankshaft join turning the engine clockwise.

Carburettor ★ ★ ★

The air cleaner was removed. It's an oil-bath type and was thoroughly washed and replenished with 0.25 litres of oil.

The carb obviously needed tuning judging by the sooty plugs. The engine was warmed up and set to a fast tickover. Screw in the volume screw until the motor starts to falter, out until it has the same effect and then to the midway point which should make it run evenly. It didn't and Graham discovered the inlet manifold was loose on one side of the engine. That explained why only two plugs were sooty. The last man to touch it had obviously over-enriched the mixture to compensate for the air leak.

Fan belt tension should be ½ inch. The pulley splits in two and has shims in the middle. Remove shims to tighten the belt.

Topping up ★ ★ ★ ★ ★

It was then a case of carrying out the simple nevertheless important jobs of topping up the battery and cleaning and lubricating its terminals with petroleum jelly, topping up the brake fluid and windscreen washer bottle, checking all lights and instruments, checking tyre pressures and lubricating all locks and hinges.

Don't be frightened to tackle your own. Graham just picked a bad one. Incidentally, we've just started a collection to buy him a new torque wrench.

TED CONNOLLY

CHECKLIST

Part one
● Change engine oil
● Check transaxle oil
● Check brakes
● Check suspension
● Adjust clutch
● Check tyres for wear
● Check wheel bearing adjustment

Part two
● Adjust tappets
● Change sparking plugs
● Change contact breakers
● Check/adjust ignition timing
● Clean air cleaner
● Tune carburettor
● Clean fuel pump filter
● Check fan belt
● Top up all levels
● Check lights and instruments

Data

Valve clearance (cold)	.006in (see text)
Sparking plugs	.023in.
Contact breaker points	.016in.
Dwell angle	44 to 50 degrees
Ignition timing	(see text)
Firing order	1-4-3-2
Transaxle	EP SAE 80
Tyre pressures (radials)	Front 18psi, rear 27psi

Air cleaner is oil bath type. It was washed in solvent and replenished with clean engine oil. Cleanliness is important.

Spark plugs from either side of engine showed contrast. One was normal, the other sooty. It was caused by inlet manifold leak.

Timing a Beetle is simple for static setting. Line up pulley notch and crankcase join. Strobe timing is more difficult (see text).

REACH FO

The chop-top business is looking up, reports Michael Stahl. There are plenty of conversions to help you reach for the sky. Just remember to keep your feet on the ground

n a country like ours, the lack of convertibles has always been lamentable. Short of a Mercedes SL or a BMW cabrio, about the only options open to drop-top desirers have been more specialised sporty machines like the Triumph Stag, MGB and Fiat X1/9. Since the '60s there has existed a ready-made market among the hep-hairdo set for a convertible that's inexpensive, reliable and fun. Ford hopes to cash in on exactly that need when it releases its sleek SA30 sportster in 1988.

For the past three years, however,

R THE SKY

open-air aspirants have been well-served by the humble Beetle. Being a four-seater, the Beetle is doubly suited to the drop-top treatment — a fact Volkswagen didn't miss when it farmed out 300,000 Beetles to the Karmann coachworks for conversion. Production of the Karmann cabrios ended in 1980.

On the other hand, with about 200,000 hardtop Beetles having been sold here, the scene was set.

"Women really led the movement into Beetle conversions," says Bernie Nichols, whose Sunbug Conversions concern has been lopping off lids since '83. "We sell probably 80 percent of our conversions to women; either unmarried professional types, or housewives after a second family car. Oh, and a lot of air hostesses."

Nichols has recently noticed a spread in his market. "It started almost exclusively in the 20-30s age bracket, but it's swollen now to 18-50 year-olds. We're getting a lot of older people, a lot of finance types, stock brokers and the like. Most are buying Sunbugs as a second car behind the Volvo or the Merc."

David Whitford, who started Convert-a-Bug six years ago as a "backyard summer business" before going full-time in '83, points out another

A TOPLESS SUMMER

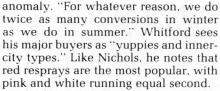

anomaly. "For whatever reason, we do twice as many conversions in winter as we do in summer." Whitford sees his major buyers as "yuppies and inner-city types." Like Nichols, he notes that red resprays are the most popular, with pink and white running equal second.

The boom has had a corresponding effect on the market for used Beetles. Nichols says the 1973-'74 L model Beetles are the most popular choice for conversion, although their availability has now become limited. "People who already drive VWs are not the sort of people to get them converted," Nichols says, "and the sort of people who are driving conversions wouldn't normally drive a VW."

Sunbug and Convert-a-Bug take markedly different approaches to their business. Convert-a-Bug's chief freely acknowledges that his motor industry experience is limited. "I get panel beat-

ers coming in for conversion plans," says Whitford, "but all any conversion takes is common sense."

Where Whitford supplies an engineer's certificate with each conversion, Sunbug has secured DMT Type Approval. Nichols says this avoids any worries about reregistration. Whitford argues that Beetles will eventually run out, and the expensive Type Approval will have been wasted.

Convert-a-Bug just chops off roofs — "we try not to get too far away from the point" — while Sunbug prefers to respray, retrim and fit new wheels and tyres. Spare Sunbugs, and there aren't many, are sold on Sunbug yards in Sydney and Wollongong. "For a completed car, we'd be pushing the very upper end of the market at $12,000," says Nichols.

That's not news to Charlie Gurgen, proprietor of Sydney's Paramount

Smash Repairs and arguably the first man in Australia to spend any time over a Beetle conversion. Charlie earned his panelbeater's stripes many years ago in Germany, and maintains a proper conversion costs a lot of money. "A lot of people have bought these cars and found they can't reregister them," he says. "I can't believe some of the cars I've seen."

These days Gurgen steers clear of the regular cabrio market, despite his widely-acclaimed Karmann copies of '83. Charlie has designed a neat 'dicky-seat' cabrio conversion, one that looks different enough for buyers to justify the additional cost of Gurgen's handiwork. "People who have bought my cars are sending me Christmas presents," Gurgen burbles.

Bob Rowland's Solaire Car Conversions flipped a few lids when it unveiled the Solaire Honda Prelude cabrio

ROOM AT THE TOP

THERE ARE upwards of half-a-dozen Beetle converters in Sydney alone, but the prices charged by those to whom we spoke are indicative of those commanded nationally.

● **Convert-a-Bug**, of 55 Jones Street, Ultimo, NSW 2007 (phone 02-692 8982), asks $725 for its basic roll-back roof conversion. This conversion leaves all side windows and pillars in place, cutting out only the roof between the side

gutters. Convert-a-Bug says this 'sardine lid' provides almost the enjoyment of a complete cabrio conversion, for which one must part with $2300. For this cabrio, Convert-a-Bug will only retouch the original paintwork, with full resprays costing extra. The company works only on customer-owned cars.

● **Sunbug Conversions** usually buys Beetles, converts them with full cabrio and retrimming and sells them on the yard for about $10,000. Customer con-

versions start at $850 for the roll-back roof. A full cabrio (conversion only) costs $3100, although Sunbug says that 70 percent of its customers go the whole hog with a two-pack paint respray and tinerior retrimming for $1200 and $900 respectively. Sunbug Conversions, 251 Anzac Parade, Kingsford, NSW 2032, phone 02-663 2367.

● **Chop-Top Conversions** (15 Marsden Street, Camperdown, NSW 2050, phone 02-519 5380) started two years ago converting Valiants "as a joke". These days, Chop-Top still specialises in big American-style pillarless iron, but Beetles make up about a quarter of its business. A Beetle cabrio, with roll-over bar, starts at $2500, but with considerable under-body strengthening

When is a Beetle no longer a Beetle?
– just as soon as you chop the top.
Structural strength is regained
by under-floor bracing and
addition of a roll-over hoop.
Be careful that the new top does
actually keep out the rain and wind,
and that the converted car is
still solid and twist-free

a couple of years ago (WHEELS July '84). Despite impressive workmanship and design and a full Honda new-car warranty, only 18 Preludes had been coverted when Rowland bailed out. Having lost nine months' design and research and $100,000, Rowland is well qualified to comment that "people don't want to buy the standard of work that I want to do".

Like Gurgen, Rowland built what were virtually new cars, using new components imported from Brazil where the Beetle is only now going out of production. His conversions cost about $6000 on a customer car, nearly triple the price of a Convert-a-Bug conversion. Rowland points out that chop-top shoppers tend to see a cabrio and lose their heads, forgetting that the cars must also be built to last.

Chopping a Beetle requires the addition of a rigid steel underframe.

Convert-a-Bug uses a fairly simple ladder-frame design underneath the floorpan, combined with a tube 'roll-over bar'. Convert-a-Bug concedes that this bar functions more as an anchoring point for the front seat belts while also providing some additional body rigidity. Sunbug has seen one of its conversions survive a rollover — its roof bar is of a T-top design, joining at the top of the windscreen.

The New South Wales Department of Motor Transport currently has no specific schedule covering cabrio conversions. The rule is that no alteration should cause a reduction in the level of safety or strength of the car. To this end, converters without Type Approval must contact recognised DMT engineering signatories and subject each car to a series of jacking tests.

Unfortunately, the standards set for structural rigidity are not always

matched by the quality of work and materials. Roof material can be anything between cheap vinyl that hardens in cold weather to the rubberised cloth used by Mercedes-Benz that sells for $97 a metre. Similarly, hood frames may be clumsily-bent aluminium 'boat bows', or heat-formed aluminium.

Potential buyers should check out the handiwork of the converter by talking to existing owners. How does it look with the roof up? Which materials are used? How well is it sealed across the top of the windscreen? Check down the rear edges of the side windows. Is there some sort of weather stripping, or a two-centimetre gap?

With the DMT keen to introduce some form of industry standard for conversions the future is looking a lot brighter. In the meantime, however, remember that there's more than one way to get burned going topless. □

Chop-Top can also do a complete cabrio, minus rollover bar, for "quite a bit more." When asked about the additional weight penalty of this conversion, Chop-Top's Rick Nock knew only that it "adds about 20 cents a year to the cost of the rego."
● Charlie Gurgen's **Paramount Smash Repairs**, at 2 Emily Street, Mortlake, NSW 2137 (phone 02-73 4011) is steering clear of normal cabrio conversions. Charlie built about 35 complete Karmann cabrio copies a few years ago and found that, at $14,000 apiece, the market wasn't prepared for them.

Thus came Charlie's 'dicky seat' conversion, which he says is "too hard for the bastards to copy". It's a complex conversion, combining judicious use of

under-body strengthening with inner-body plating. A fibreglass tail section is blended almost invisibly with the rear side panels. Six have so far been made.

Charlie runs right through each car, replacing rubbers and bushes, reconditioning or replacing engines and gearboxes. He says the conversion, with all bar a new engine and gearbox, would cost about $6000. Being German, he also has a soft spot for BMWs, and is currently designing a Baur-style cabrio for older Three Series models. He is seeking Type Approval for both of his conversions.
● **Solaire Car Conversions'** Bob Rowland at 20 O'Riordan Street, Alexandria, NSW 2015 (phone 02-699 4421), has built six Beetles but is now calling it a

day. He estimates that his cars cost $6000 to convert, including having rust cut out, rubbers replaced and engines reconditioned. His cars — a few still incomplete — have sat in a back workshop for a few months, and he's now prepared to sell them off for between $8500 and $9500.

"It's a shame we don't have the market to support an industry that wants to do the job properly," he says. □

Buying a VW Beetle

Some versions of the ever-popular Beetle have now attained classic car status — Chris Graham investigates the buyers' market.

The Beetle Cabriolet is the ideal Beetle to many people, and it is certainly fun to drive.

This general shot of the interior of Tony Levey's 1951 car illustrates well the carpets that were available at the time, and the unusual wheel type accelerator pedal.

For many millions of people throughout the world the term 'Beetle mania' not only conjures up images of over-crowded airports, screaming teenagers and yellow submarines, it also brings to mind a certain little car from Germany that was almost as popular as the Fab Four themselves. The VW Beetle, in its many forms, has been phenomenally successful by any standards. The initial concept and the inventive design were immediately jumped upon by the public who soon made the Beetle a best seller. The production figures are impressive enough on their own but when you consider also the effects of the war, they are amazing. Despite the war damage, production increased at a tremendous rate during the early post war years, and by 1950 the 100,000th Beetle had rolled from the factory gate. A mere five years later the total had topped the one million mark, and the car was truly established.

is simply impossible to cover them all in the limited space that I have available here. Instead, I shall endeavour to outline the salient points and models from the Beetle story, to create a general picture.

After the war production began again with the Type 1 Beetle powered by a 1131cc 4-cylinder horizontally opposed air cooled engine that developed 25bhp. To look at, this early Beetle was not so very different from the examples we see on the roads today. Its most noticeable feature however, was the split rear window — a feature that was to continue until 1953. Those early cars in their standard form were very basic inside and out. There were sparse instrument panels and rubber mats on the floor. The windscreen was completely flat, as was the rest of the glass and there was a complete absence of chrome trim for the body (this was first introduced for the export models in 1949). The hub caps and bumpers were all painted the same colour as the rest of the car (who says that colour coding is a new craze?!), and pillar mounted semaphores were the only form of directional indicators available. However, chrome trim was a feature of the Deluxe

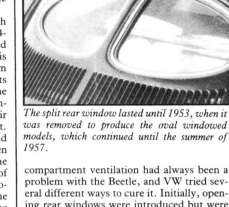

The split rear window lasted until 1953, when it was removed to produce the oval windowed models, which continued until the summer of 1957.

compartment ventilation had always been a problem with the Beetle, and VW tried several different ways to cure it. Initially, opening rear windows were introduced but were withdrawn again after just a year as they proved ineffective. Next they tried adding opening flaps in the front quarter panels, just behind the front wings to duct the fresh air in that way, but this too proved rather fruitless. Finally they hit upon the idea of adding opening quarterlights to the front windows, and this provided the long awaited answer and full flow ventilation arrived in 1971.

The running gear adopted by these early examples consisted of king and link pin front suspension with torsion bars and trailing arms, and a swinging axle, radius arms and single transverse torsion bars at the rear. This kingpin system was used in conjunction with this arrangement until the mid-1960s, when ball joints were preferred. However, one major snag with this set-up was the space that it took up, especially at the front. Because the Beetle is a rear engined car, the area under the 'bonnet' is used for luggage storage. This situation would appear encouraging until you open the lid to discover a bulky petrol tank and a spare wheel occupying most of the space. This space problem was not alleviated until the early 1970s when the MacPherson strut front suspension was adopted, which allowed the tank to be moved, and the spare wheel to be laid flat under a covering panel.

It seems that right from the start, great emphasis had been placed on the export

A glance at the rear of a Beetle usually gives the game away as to its approximate age, especially if it is an early model. The shape of the rear window changed several times during production, the rear brake lights remained as they are here until 1962, the twin exhaust pipes (as on the late fifties model on the left) became standard in 1956 and the whole engine cover was redesigned in 1967 to a much smoother finish without the moulding.

The story behind the production of the VW Beetle is most involved due to the fact that there were so many changes made to the original design as time passed. Not only were there a significant number of models and variations on those models, but also about 20,000 minor changes to the mechanical specifications and trim details. Therefore, it

Colour pictures:
We gathered together a representative selection of Beetles for this feature. The black split rear screen model in the background has been owned from new by its present owner, Tony Levy, who bought it in Germany in 1951. The car has been made famous by its astonishingly high documented total mileage of 795,473 miles. The overall Beetle design has proved to be remarkably resistant to change through the years. These three cars cover a time span of about 20 years and yet they all look virtually identical.

models.

The next major development came in 1954 when an increased engine capacity became available. The size was increased to 1192cc which initially produced 30 bhp, but subsequent alterations including a compression ratio increase, were to boost the power output to 34 bhp — and so the 1200 Beetle was born. This model was to prove one of the most enduring, with its production life continuing (in many forms), right through until 1978. The split rear window was dropped for this model, and replaced with an oval version to give better visibility. The 1200 'Oval' Beetle was also available in two forms: Standard or Deluxe. Hydraulic brakes were fitted on the Deluxe models.

In 1958 the rear window was again altered, and it was made bigger and more rectangular — presumably for the same reasons as before. From the start adequate passenger

Semaphore indicators are another clue to the age of a Beetle.

	1200	1200	1300	1500	1302S	1303S
Engine	1,131cc 4 cyl	1,192cc 4 cyl	1,285cc 4 cyl	1,493cc 4 cyl	1,584cc 4 cyl	1,584cc 4 cyl
Bore (mm)	75	77	77	83	85	85
Stroke (mm)	64	64	69	69	69	69
Comp. ratio	5.8:1	6.6:1 (7.1:1)	7.3:1 (7.5:1)	7.5:1	7.5:1	7.5:1
BHP at rpm	25 at 3300	30 at 3400 (34 at 3600)	40 at 4000 (44 at 4100)	44 at 4000	50 at 4000	50 at 4000
0-60mph (secs)	—	32.1	23.0	21.9	18.3	17.1
Top speed (mph)	62	72	75	81	80	82.4
Overall mpg	37.7	31.6	28.8	27.4	27	27
Prod. period	45-53	54-78	65-75	66-70	70-72	72-75

Note: *The figures in brackets represent changes that occured between models.*

The early Beetles suffered from a chronic lack of luggage space under the bonnet . . .

. . . and from this photograph, you can see the reason why. The petrol tank and the spare wheel were positioned in this manner because of the confines created by the torsion bar front suspension . . .

. . . but by the early 1970s Beetles were being fitted with MacPherson strut front suspension which liberated a great deal more space. The bonnet became much wider at the front, and more bulbous generally.

potential of the Beetle, and to this end the versions that were to be sold abroad were often better appointed than those offered to the home market. The success of this campaign became apparent when, during 1961, Volkswagen produced over ¾-million vehicles, and more than half of these were exported. Subsidiaries flourished in the United States, Australia, Mexico and Brazil — the success of the Beetle appeared to know no bounds. The magic million cars in one year target was to be broken no fewer than five times in the middle to late sixties, and the early seventies.

theme was the Karmann Cabriolet. It began life in the late forties and was an instant success. Export sales were to play a large part in it's popularity but the home market too found it thoroughly likeable. The first model, was the 1200 and this was followed by the 1300cc which was current until in 1967 a 1500cc version was brought out. This reigned for another four years when it was replaced by the 1302S Cabriolet, followed shortly by the 1303S model. Although the Cabriolets look similar to the standard cars, in terms of body shape, there are in fact considerable differences between the two. The

The Beetle Cabriolet was available from the late forties onwards in all model forms.

With the 1966 model came the 1,285cc engine that was to create the 1300 Beetle, and this was followed in 1967, by the long awaited 1500 version. Also in this year there was an important electrical change, and all cars were upgraded from 6 to 12 volt systems. Semi-automatic versions were also made available for the 1300, and the 1500, and later for the 1600. These came with I.R.S. and disc brakes at the front. The early 1970s was the age of the Super Beetle, namely the 1302 and 1303 models. These were noticeably more luxurious and featured a covered dashbaord (replacing the standard painted metal finish that had run before) with an improved instrument layout, and on the 1303 a curved windscreen to give a greater impression of space forward of the driving seat, a bonnet that was about 9" shorter from front to back and disc brake front suspension. Both the 1302 and the 1303 which followed after two years, were fitted with the 1300cc engine unless they were the 'S' models, in which case they had the 1,584cc unit.

The other famous variation on the Beetle

The Cabriolet models were not actually made by VW themselves, but by Karmann, and this is their official badge which is mounted low down on the front quarter panel.

panel sizes differ on the Cabriolet, with only the bonnet (not on early cars with the louvred engine cover), the engine cover and the wings being the same as those on the standard models. The doors are deeper and the windscreen differs also. One interesting illustration of the strength of the original design is that the only extra requirements needed to compensate for the removal of the roof, were two strengthening members that ran fore and aft beaneath the sills.

Beetle bug-bears

It makes a pleasant change to find a car that does not require a three and a half hour examination to determine whether or not it is worth taking further, and the VW Beetle appears to be one such example. As always, it is best to be methodical with your checking, so start with the outside and begin at the front. If the car in question is pre-1964 then it will have the king pin front suspension, and this needs to be checked for wear. Do this in the time honoured way with a jack to raise the wheel off the ground, and then check for vertical play by hand. If there is wear present it is not the end of the world as the replacement parts are no problem, but the fitting can be a struggle, so bear this in mind. Check as well for worn wheel bearings. While you are in the vicinity of the front wheels, check the inner wing panel. This does have a tendency to rust, but it is usually confined to the lower half, and so is relatively simple to put right. Check the chassis cross member at the front, as this rusts due to a water trap. Next check the outer face of the driver's footwell, where the master cylinder is attached — corrosion can be a problem here too. Check also the front axle beams at each end for rust. If you are looking at a 1302/3 model, check the steering for any play (replacement steering components are expensive) and check the struts for leaks.

The hood on the Cabriolet is one of the easiest and most efficient to operate that I have come across, and when erected it compliments the car rather than appearing loose and ill-fitting like so many other soft tops. Parts for older cabriolets especially can be scarce.

the body and collect water so corrosion often gains a hold here.

The almost legendary reliability of the Beetle engine has been one of it's major selling points over the years but of course, as with all engines, it does have it's own particular weaknesses which you should look out for when buying. There are probably only five main categories of trouble that can be expected from this engine and they are: a blowing head, burnt or broken valves, a blown piston, seizure due to lack of oil, big end wear and crankshaft end float.

Because the engine is air cooled its oil plays a vital role in its successful running. Some of the troubles already mentioned can be directly attributed to oil related problems. A lack of oil pressure is the first condition you should check for, but as there is no oil gauge to read from, try this simple test instead. Remove the ignition lead from the coil, thus enabling the engine to be spun without starting. Then sit in the car, turn the engine and note how quickly the oil pressure light is

The Beetle engine has always been a tight fit in its compartment. This is a detail of the late fifties version.

The spare wheel well is another area worth inspecting as the drain holes become blocked and a water trap is created. Moving down the car, the sills and the running board should be the next area of interest. The Beetle has two part sills that are welded together to form a box section, and it is the bottom edge of this that can give problems. The running board is bolted directly to the sill and replacements are cheap and easy to fit if necessary. The rear quarter panel (between the door and the rear wing) is another area to watch, with the bottom edge again being the most affected. There is not too much to check for at the rear of the car, but do take a look at the rear body mounts (behind the rear wheel on the inner wing panel — a bolt head should be visible) and the surrounding panel, and check the rear bumper iron supports. These bolt on to

The Beetle interior has always been a sparse aggair even on the 'luxury' models like this Cabriolet. Note the cut-down gearlever. This is a non-standard modification that makes a considerable difference to the gearchange action.

Spares availability

Generally speaking the spares scene for the Beetle is encouraging, especially for the cars dating from the very late fifties onwards. Pre-1957 cars though present more of a problem, and a lot will depend upon how much money you have at your disposal, and who you know. It is worth remembering that owing to the fact that the outward design of the Beetle has changed only slightly during its long life, that in the case some panels like wings for instance, modern ones can be fitted to the older car. It is true that some adjustments will be required, but these are only minor and so probably worth the trouble. The quality of the authentic parts now available from VAG or other sources, is excellent, but of course, they do cost a little more than their competitors. These are produced primarily in Brazil and Mexico and are in the main, of a lower standard all round. If in doubt about the German manufacture of a part look for the authentic VAG production stamp for proof.

Typical prices

Front wings (1200) £22 each
Front wings (1302/3) £28 each
Rear wings (early) £18 each
Rear wings (late) £20 each
Running board £7
Door skin £30
Door (new) £120
Door (s/h) £45 complete with glass
King pin assembly £16 a side
Ball joints £6.50 each
Engine cover (s/h) £23, new £65
Bonnet (s/h) £40, new £90
Piston kit £55 (1600cc)
Recon. engine £400
Exhaust £22 complete
Cyl. heads £65 each
Brake shoes £8
Wheel cyl. £10
Seats (s/h) driver's £20, Pass £15
Steering wheel £10
Gearbox 1302 (s/h) £65
Swinging axle £50 s/h

extinguished. If this happens straight away then the oil pressure is fine, but if the light flickers and takes a few seconds to go out completely, then this should give you cause for concern.

There were never any head gaskets fitted to the Beetle engines, and so a perfect fit between the aluminium head and the block is relied upon to produce an adequate seal. However, the arrangement can cause problems if for any reason, the engine begins to overheat — the soft head easily becomes warped due to heat distortion, thus allowing the engine to blow. However, another alternative cause is loose head bolts. Such a condition can usually be heard during the oil pressure test, and is recognisable by a characteristic huffing noise that sounds a bit like a blowing exhaust. Next start the engine, and with it running at tick-over, remove the oil breather pipe from the filler cap assembly to check for excessive sump pressure. This should be obvious if it is there as you will be able to hear and see it. This can be one of the symptoms of a tired engine suffering from for example, badly worn piston rings. Also listen for any excessive tappet noise, as the cam followers on some engines do wear. This is not a disastrous state of affairs (some engines run for several years with badly worn cam followers), but you should bear in mind that it will require work eventually.

A faulty lubrication system (or infrequent oil changes) can often promote valve guide wear which then leads to broken valve shafts. A simple lack of oil can be enough to initiate this process, so your attention should be drawn to any visible oil leaks. The engine only contains 4½ pints of oil so a moderate leak can very quickly wreak havoc. Favourite places for leaks are: around the rocker cover which is only held in place with clips, the sump, the flywheel oil seal the push rod tubes and seals and the oil cooler. Such leaks can often make the situation appear far more serious than it really is, although, if the flywheel oil seal is the problem it can be costly to get the replacement fitted as the engine has to be removed.

Oil leaks have another annoying side effect and that is that they pollute the heating system. The supply of hot air for the heater is ducted directly from the engine compartment, and so any oil vapour that may result from a leak is carried with it. The heater controls themselves are notorious for breaking in which case, it has to be operated manually — this usually means that it is switched on for the winter, and off again in the summer.

When you actually drive the car keep your ears open for any whining from the differential, and if you are driving an early car, pay particular attention to the gearchange. One of the first signs of any trouble with these boxes is a crunch as you drop from 3rd to 2nd as well as a general difficulty in selecting the gears. On the later cars (the 1302s and 1303s) try reversing the car — if it jumps out of gear and goes into neutral, you have problems. Post 1968 cars have a tendency to chip the 1st and reverse cogs. Any of these symptoms

Traditionally, the Beetle has always been equipped with just one dial, the speedometer. Within this is contained the fuel gauge and the warning lights.

This is yet another indication of how little things have changed — it is the control centre from a late fifties model. In those days however, you did not even enjoy the luxury of a fuel gauge.

A bud vase was an optional extra on the early cars. Today these fetch quite high prices.

provide an indication that major gearbox work will shortly be required, which is a complicated business and requires special tools. Often the simplest solution is to opt for a replacement unit to be fitted straight away, thus saving on some of the labour charges that may be involved in trying to repair the original.

One other problem area with the engine is No. 3 cylinder, which is tucked away in the left hand corner of the engine compartment and obscured by the oil cooler. This cylinder suffers from over-heating brought about by

its claustrophobic location. Cool air for ventilation is very scarce here and so the cylinder, its valves and the piston are always running hotter than the rest, which makes a burnt or dropped exhaust valve or a holed piston a possibility.

The interior trim on a car is not much of a problem in terms of spares availability; however, this does not mean that you can afford to simply buy a car without regard for it's interior. Common sense should tell you to get the best possible, and I would advise you to pay particular attention to the condition of the headlining — replacements are a real struggle to fit.

What to pay

The prices that are charged for Beetles seem to vary enormously according to both the model, and its condition. Obviously, some of the many versions are more desirable than others, and for these you are going to pay dearly. The very early Split screen examples (pre-53) are now fetching in the region of £2,000 for rough but restorable cars, and up to £7,000 for a car in mint condition. These high prices are simply due to the fact that the Split screens are now rare.

A rough Oval screen model can be bought for about £250 and for a top class example you will need to pay upwards of £4,000. The early Square screen models are much cheaper, ranging from £50 to £500. Thirteen hundred models from 1967 to 1971 can get as high as £1,200, and for a good 1500 from the same period you should expect to pay about £1,500. The 1302 and 1303 Beetles will range from £300 to £3,000 depending on condition.

Finally, the Cabriolet models range considerably in price and this is again governed by age and condition. The really early cars are fetching 'silly' prices these days. Cars from the 1960s sell for anything between £1,300 and £2,000, and late cars can be picked up in a rough state for £800-£900, or in reasonable condition for £2,500 upwards to £10,000 for a mint example.

To sum up

I have to admit that compiling this feature has changed my opinion of the Beetle. I think that I now understand a little more about how so many people became so very attached to these cars. They say that beauty is in the eye of the beholder and this I would guess is the maxim with which many owners regard their cars. For me the Beetle's design has few redeeming features and it is neither elegant nor attractive, but it does have something. It possesses some indefinable qualities which sew seeds of recognition in the brain at first sight. These remain firmly embedded until triggered by some association with the car, when they then blossom into a fully fledged affection, and before you know it, you love it!

For the purposes of this article I was kindly allowed to test drive Tony Bird's fine Cabriolet. This model is perhaps the one out of the range with the greatest visual appeal, and it has proved a favourite for years. Many Beetle enthusiasts make it their ambition (like Tony) to work up the range to finish eventually with a desirable Cabrio. Tony's example is left hand drive and is finished in a most attractive dark silver grey that is, strangely, officially classed as a blue. It was originally orange. The first thing which struck me on sitting in the car, was its size – it appeared surprisingly large. The driving position, although being comfortable, is low in relation to the top of the dashboard, and it is this which I think plays a significant part in the large-car-feeling that is created. The familiar VW engine noise is not as apparent as you might think when driving the car so this is obviously a treat saved especially for the pedestrians.

Tony had been having some problems with the steering on his car, and there was a noticeable degree of play evident, but disregarding this, the control was good and reasonably precise. In my ignorance I had imagined that the car might perhaps be inclined to wallow around the corners but this was not the case, and although no great speeds were achieved, the feelings were good. Tony has shortened the gearlever to about half of its original length, and this produces a very clean and quick action, though I did find it a little notchy. From the driving seat the folded hood provides quite an obstruction to rearward vision, and although the rear view mirror is adjustable to cope with this, I can quite believe that reversing and parking could

The rear windows on the Cabriolet are wound back just like those on a Sunbeam Rapier, to leave pillarless sides.

cause a few problems.

I did not have time to drive the car with the hood up but Tony assures me that it provides excellent insulation, there is very little wind noise and that it leaks only slightly just aft of the doors. Obviously the Beetle Cabriolet is not built for speed, or even for fast touring, but nevertheless a great deal of pleasure can be gained from driving it. With the hood down it is a complete convertible and there are no other roll bars, pillars or rear windows to impede the sense of freedom that it creates.

In comparison I find the saloon Beetles much more ordinary, and were I in the market I have to admit that the Cabriolet would be my personal choice. It gives the car extra appeal which added to the other benefits of superb reliability and tremendous practicality, produces a vehicle of considerable merit.

My thanks go to Tony Bird, and Tony Levy for the use of their cars, to Lord and Lady Camoys for the use of their home, Stonor Park, and to Terrys Beetle Services of Hanwell, W7 (telephone 01-567 3165) for all the tips and helpful information.

The Clubs

Volkswagen Owners Club GB
Membership Secretary, Miss S. Selkirk, The Chimneys, Frith Common, Tenbury Wells. Worcs. WR15 8JX.

VW Split Window Club
Membership Secretaries, Mike and Sue Mundy, 142 Junction Road, Burgess Hill, West Sussex, RH15 0PZ.

VW Cabriolet Owners Club of Great Britain
Secretariat, Mark and Wendy Ritchie, 58 Bronwydd, Larksbrook, Birchgrove, Swansea SA7 9QJ.

Historic Volkswagen Club
Membership Secretary, Mr S. Parkinson, 15 Linnet Close, Bournville, Birmingham B30 1XB.

CONTINUED FROM PAGE 137

rate, several of the progressive modifications have not been an unqualified success and for a company that knows as much about marketing as VW, there are some peculiar aspects to this particular car.

We brought a Beetle back from France with us in 1959 and after visiting Sebring, I drove it across the country. No tremendous thrill but a good workmanlike operation. My wife couldn't stand it and couldn't stand this one either, muttering about dodgy handling, funny brakes, tinny doors and a built-in side wind. We all know about VW's built-in headwind but she actually stopped the car and got out to see where the gale was coming from. No gale. The Convertible does weave about a bit at speed, in fact you can fantasize about yourself in one of those big 2-stage blown Auto Unions at the Ring, as belting along at 60 does require undivided attention. Cornering is a trifle sloppy as well and heavy braking produced a lot of tire squeal although the technical bods passed the brakes with flying colors. Well. The consensus is that (1) the suspension has been softened up for comfort although you wouldn't notice it, (2) VW should have kept their worm-and-roller steering, (3) the tires are junk. Radials are fitted as standard in Europe; why not here? Come to that, disc brakes are also fitted in Europe but not here, perhaps the reason that one gets the impression that the rear binders aren't working. How come VW is trying to palm off the old stuff on us?

With all that in mind, I will confound the skeptics by saying that the Convertible was rather fun. The inside is a bit narrow across the shoulders (like too small a bra, my daughter said) and the sills are a bit high to put the elbow on but the seats are nice, driving position good, controls fall readily to hand, etc. There does seem to be a lot of flimsy plastic about and the locks are stiff, chintzy and tend to stick but a gallon of WD40 helped. For once VW has done something about ventilation to the feet via a couple

of nonelectric rheostats on the dash; more air gets to the ankles than in our Merc which should prove something but, of course, there is nothing actually hot in front of the driver. In-house ventilation is pretty good as is demisting, aided by electrickery in the rear window, but the wipers are nothing to rave about even on a simple flat screen.

Of course, the Convertible is "supposed" to be driven with the top down and just as well too, as you b****y well can't see out with it up. The top is a model of its kind with no rattles, easy operation, and not much in the way of wind whistles; do you remember those contraptions on English sports cars? Furthermore it lends a graceful line, when down, to the rather stubby lines of the Beetle and cries out for a picture hat, yards of veil and floaty chiffon on your lady of the moment. A tour up over Ortega Highway on a nice day is reason enough to buy one of these little perishers as all nature is spread before you, most of the agricultural row of the VW engine is muted, and even at 55 or so the passenger compartment is reasonably protected. I remember one car that would empty its own ashtray and form a twister with the contents, not to mention instantly extracting every road map in sight. Progressing up the mountain, it became apparent after a while that the Convertible *does* go well enough for all practical purposes and, even as the Harley-Davidson Electraglide, is built for touring and not racing. Much of the apparent sluggishness comes from the placement of 1st and 2nd gears; 3rd and top are the touring gears and in them it performs very well, waffling along restfully without having to weld your foot to the floor. Ah yes . . . fresh air! Vintage motoring! The real justification for buying a Convertible, aside from pleasing the kids who think it is Neat, lies in pretending to ignore the envious looks from stylish ladies buttoned up in their modern tin boxes.

Perhaps they remember how it was in the rumble seat.

If you thought the VW Beetle was dead, think again. But is the Mexican-built import, complete with right-hand-drive conversion, 1.6-litre engine, two-speed wipers and lockable fuel cap, an authentic Beetle? Nikki Carvey investigates, photography by David Burgess

BEETLE-MANIA the Mexican way

I'VE NEVER BEEN AN A-TO-B aficionado, someone who just wants four wheels to get from one place to another. For me, a car reflects something about its owner (Datsun — prospective mini cabbie, Lotus — probably insecure about his height, BMW — more money than sense) and should have its own character. The VW Beetle is such a car — with a rounded body and bug headlamps, it's 100 per cent cute. So it's no surprise that it has wangled it way into motorists' hearts.

Most drivers will have encountered a wrinkly in an immaculately kept 1963 Beetle. But, more recently, this car's charm has endeared it to a new generation, who don't harp on about the old days, still appreciate the car's reliability and welcome the camaraderie among fellow drivers, who wave at each other.

Tapping into the new wave of enthusiasm for the 'car of the people' is Bournemouth-based Hughes Motor Company, which, aside from dealing in exotica such as Lamborghini and

Porsche, has taken to importing new Beetles from Mexico. "I didn't even know they were still making them," explains managing director Peter Bennett, "but my wife had a Mexican girl working for her who mentioned that her brother had just bought a new one."

"Basically the Beetle is for people who've got rid of their boy racer desires and want something reliable and economical to run," says Howard Cheese, secretary of the newly formed Mexican/Brazilian Beetle Register.

Interior of the Mexican-built Beetle is solid and smells good — a bit out of character. Engine is a 'powerful' 1600 unit and good for up to 70mph on the motorway

Available in white, yellow, light blue, dark blue and red, the Beetles are bought on a personal import basis. Customers place orders, the cars are shipped from Mexico to Europe, and the prospective owners pick them up. While the cars don't comply with Type Approval "because they're built in Mexico and the design is too old", Bennett is confident that neither this, nor the long wait (about three months) will put people off. "There's a huge market in secondhand Beetles and people are more than happy to pay large sums of money for a vehicle that's 12 years old, so it doesn't make sense for them to question buying a new one."

What they might question, however, is the price — £6995 for a left-hand-drive model and an extra £1250 (+VAT) for it to be converted to right-hand drive. Who's going to pay that for a Beetle? "We've had all sorts of people interested," says Bennett, "from parents buying them as presents, to a quite elderly guy who's had a Beetle for 20 years and is thinking of passing it on to his son if he can replace it with a new one. Beetles appeal to a following of all ages."

I have my doubts but I'm not going to let them get in the way of driving the first converted right-hand-drive H-reg Beetle in the country. In fact, in my green eagerness to get behind the wheel, I make the first *faux pas*. "Yes, Beetles are great. Mine had just been restored when I crashed it," I confide to Peter Bennett. Whoops. His face drops and his

fingers linger on the keys before opening the door on a gleaming white Beetle.

Settling myself into the untorn driver's seat (unusual for a Beetle!), the first thing that strikes me is that the car smells new. It is a peculiar experience: Beetles should smell of petrol, cats, dogs and chips but never that distinct aroma of fresh plastic. I eye the moulded-plastic dashboard and the fine-checked upholstered seats with mistrust — I could be sitting in a Fiat Tipo. Somehow, being new, the Beetle has lost its quaint charm and become just another production-line vehicle.

Stopping for a quick petrol fill (it runs on lead-free) before hitting the motorway, I learn the second rule of test-driving. Know all about the car before you get in. Along with its new, improved wipers that offer two speeds — as opposed to just off/on — this Beetle also has a lock on the petrol tank. After fiddling with the petrol cap for 10 minutes, and then watching a burly truck driver fiddle with it for another 10 minutes, I begin to despair until I spot a friendly AA man lurking beneath someone else's car. In no time at all the cap is off and I'm looking forward to some trouble-free motoring.

As with any car that's not capable of much more than 70mph, motorway driving in the H-reg is as boring as ever. But, in town, the Beetle is a joy. Used to a humble 1200cc engine, its 1600cc capacity means extra power, so that when leaving the lights I can sustain the illusion

of being in a fast car. In fact, with its smooth gear changes and responsive handling, at times I forget I am driving a Beetle — until the familiar engine buzz behind me serves as a reminder.

Despite the plastic, I enjoy the car. It is strange to be in a Beetle that feels so solid — nothing rattles and there is no niggling worry that something might snap at any moment. Reliable as my old Beetle is, turning on the ignition is always accompanied by the reassurance that I'm a member of the AA.

H-reg is definitely fun, but ultimately you're still paying a lot of dosh for a car that remains very basic compared with other new cars in the same price range. And while they offer a radio, heated rear window, central locking and electric windows as standard, in the new Beetles they're extras. For added convenience and comfort, you could be paying nearer £9000. Loveable as they may be, these Beetles are not for the new-car brigade but the enthusiast. "People don't buy them because they're good value for money," agrees Bennett. "They buy them because they want a Beetle."

Call me old fashioned but I feel a Beetle is like a leather jacket: it should be worn and worldly but still hanging on in there. Much as I enjoyed driving H-reg, if I had nine grand to spare, I'd rather spend £5000 on a restored Beetle and squander the rest on living it up. Thankfully for Bennett, not everyone is like me. ■
Hughes Motor Company — (0202) 744743

CONTINUED FROM PAGE 143

customers—those delicate and proper ladies who seem to be buying the things by the gross and who would certainly faint dead away if the rear end ever got loose.

And, of course, it is still visible. That is the secret of its current success. The convertible always was something of a showoff. In his book "Small Wonder," Walter Henry Nelson quotes a Chicago society columnist in the early '60s: "The snappiest auto we've seen of late was not a Rolls-Royce or a Mercedes-Benz or a Jaguar, but a Volkswagen convertible Mrs. Otis Hubbard drove to lunch the other day in Lake Forest." Likely Mrs. Otis Hubbard, whoever she is or was, is still driving to her lunches of destiny in a VW convertible. But it's sure nice to know that, at a time when we were consuming as conspicuously as we ever had in our history, someone in Chicago was keeping down with the Joneses. It's nicer to know we still are, and not just in Lake Forest.

But perhaps not for long. Karmann, an independent coachbuilder in Osnabrück, builds the convertible (as well as the Scirocco) on contract to VW. As a matter of fact, Karmann can be said to have invented the thing. In 1947 (and for two years thereafter) it built a drophead version of the Beetle called a Hebmueller—a project that was strictly Karmann's. Then, in 1949, the company went to Heinz Nordhoff, VW's chief, and suggested it build a convertible with his blessing. Nordhoff agreed to an initial run of 1000; Karmann has been hard at work on convertibles ever since. This year they will build about 13,000 cars, of which just over half will come into the U.S. They are so in demand that some dealers are paying $1000 over retail sticker to other dealers to get them. But the convertible's days are numbered. VW of America "hopes to have a convertible to sell in '79," but the factory has not made a decision on the matter. The trouble is in the engine. It was a remarkable power-plant in its day, but its day is almost over. When it was designed, the engine's greatest virtue was its room for development. In 47 years all that room has been occupied. And so, with U.S. emissions standards getting tougher, there is simply no place to go with the air-cooled engine. The more smog control devices VW uses on the engine, the hotter it runs and the less power it makes. VW, always a stickler for longevity and maintainability, simply doesn't want an engine that is poised on the brink of suicide.

It may be months, it may be as long as a year, but the days of the VW convertible are numbered. Pity.

Whatever else the Beetle convertible represents in 1978—and it represents a very great deal indeed—it has made one great technological stride. It is, without peer or parallel, the finest, the most accurate, the most clearly authentic replica ever built. MT

CONTINUED FROM PAGE 25

The disc/drum brakes require a fair prod but are decently powerful and progressive, once the rather badly-placed wide pedal has been mastered. The old characteristics of some steering shake and a too-lively ride have not been eliminated but then neither have the excellent finish, good interior trim and the very comfortable seats. The fuel filler is now external, covered by a flap at the front o/s of the body, and so it is no longer tamper-proof or replenishable from a normal can.

There are still reflections in the screen and rear window, the interior lamp remains on the n/s on r.h.d. models, and you either like the compact interior, simple instrumentation, and the luggage-carrying arrangement of the Beetle or you don't. The headlamps-flasher is on that well-contrived l.h. stalk and the entire car is rugged and implies reliability, which is why this make goes on selling and selling and selling. Just as the Model-A Fords, and before that Model-T, used to do.

In this form the VW isn't fast, being all-out at about 80 m.p.h. But this is of no moment to this Island's law-abiding drivers and it does out-accelerate most of the small semi-automatics. The test car was apt to stall from cold as a gear was selected and automation engaged it, which was annoying, and in 375 miles the engine had consumed a quart of oil. Personally, I was happy to be in an up-to-date Beetle. If you are in the market for one, the £83 extra which semi-automatic transmission costs can be offset by the feeling that you are being nice to the wife, while gaining the benefit of that under-steer handling for yourself! I won't argue with those who think the Beetle has dated. But at just over £841 in this country I still think it is good value and the only car which meets fully a number of specific requirements.

* * *